An example of art by a 13-year-old boy diagnosed with Asperger's disorder who at various times helped my research group with our investigations into the disorder.

DEVELOPMENTAL DISORDERS OF THE FRONTOSTRIATAL SYSTEM

Brain Damage, Behaviour and Cognition:
Developments in Clinical Neuropsychology
Titles in Series

Developmental disorders of the frontostriatal system

Neuropsychological, neuropsychiatric, and evolutionary perspectives

John L. Bradshaw
Department of Psychology, Monash University, Australia

Psychology Press
Taylor & Francis Group

HOVE AND NEW YORK

First published 2001 by Psychology Press Ltd
27 Church Road, Hove, East Sussex BN3 2FA

www.psypress.co.uk

Simultaneously published in the USA and Canada
by Psychology Press
270 Madison Avenue, New York NY 10016

Reprinted 2006

Psychology Press is part of the Taylor & Francis Group, an informa business

British Library Cataloguing in Publication Data
A catalogue record for this book is available from the British Library

Library of Congress Cataloguing in Publication Data
Bradshaw, John L., 1940–
    Developmental disorders of the frontostriatal system : neuropyschological,
neuropsychiatric, and evolutionary perspectives / John L. Bradshaw.
        p. cm. — (Brain damage, behaviour, and cognition)
    Includes bibliographical references and index.
    ISBN 1-84169-226-3
    1. Developmental disabilities. 2. Pediatric neuropsychology. 3. Pediatric
neuropsychiatry. 4. Developmental neurobiology. I. Title. II. Series.

    RJ506.D47 B73 2000
    618.92′89—dc21   00-040284

    ISBN 13: 978-1-84169-227-2 (pbk)
    ISBN 10: 1-84169-227-1 (pbk)
    ISSN 0967-9944

Cover design by Joyce Chester
Typeset in Times by Mayhew Typesetting, Rhayader, Powys
Printed and bound in Great Britain by Biddles Ltd, King's Lynn, Norfolk

Contents

Series preface

From being an area primarily on the periphery of mainstream behavioural and cognitive science, neuropsychology has developed in recent years into an area of central concern for a range of displines. We are witnessing not only a revolution in the way in which brain–behaviour–cognition relationships are viewed, but a widening of interest concerning developments in neuropsychology on the part of a range of workers in a variety of fields. Major advances in brain-imaging techniques and the cognitive modelling of the impairments following brain damage promise a wider understanding of the nature of the representation of cognition and behaviour in the damaged and undamaged brain.

Neuropsychology is now centrally important for those working with brain-damaged people, but the very rate of expansion in the area makes it difficult to keep up with findings from current research. The aim of the *Brain Damage, Behaviour and Cognition* series is to publish a wide range of books that present comprehensive and up-to-date overviews of current developments in specific areas of interest.

These books will be of particular interest to those working with the brain-damaged. It is the editors' intention that undergraduates, post-graduates, clinicians and researchers in psychology, speech pathology and medicine will find this series a useful source of information on important current developments. The authors and editors of the books in this series are experts in their respective fields, working at the forefront of contemporary research. They have produced texts that are accessible and scholarly. We thank them for their contribution and their hard work in fulfilling the aims of the series.

CC and GH
Exeter and Birmingham, UK
Series Editors

Preface

For many years my students and I researched lateral asymmetries in human and (vicariously) animal behaviour, as an entry point into the study of language and face recognition processes, and the organisation of skilled manual responding. We developed a range of novel visual, auditory, and tactual input devices, and techniques for measuring fine, serial movement sequences. It was a natural extension for us to study clinical cases of unilateral neglect following stroke. We then had the opportunity to work with another clinical group, patients with Parkinson's and Huntington's diseases, both disorders of the basal ganglia. By then the growing popularity of this kind of research among aspiring graduate students meant that we could extend from the *neurodegenerative* disorders (stroke, Parkinson's and Huntington's diseases, and eventually also Alzheimer's disease) to the closely related *neurodevelopmental* disorders of the basal ganglia and the wider frontostriatal system (Tourette's syndrome, obsessive compulsive disorder, attention deficit hyperactivity disorder, schizophrenia, autism, and depression). It would of course be a mistake to argue that these disorders exclusively involve frontostriatal structures; however, they do have sufficient clinical and neuropathological aspects in common to warrant careful comparison.

Our work has generally involved perceptual, attentional, and motor processes, and it has been my pleasure and privilege to work with some extremely gifted graduate students. Between us we have learnt how to apply a range of sophisticated new technologies, including movement kinematics, electrophysiology, transcranial magnetic stimulation, and neuroimaging. It has been an extraordinarily exciting and, I hope, profitable period for all concerned, and a period of study leave has enabled me to put together a wealth of material that has recently been accumulating in the literature.

The underlying theme to the book, apart from the commonalities and dissociations between these disorders, is unashamedly biological, in an attempt, within a wider and more general descriptive context, to review the contribution of the frontostriatal system. In the Decade of the Brain, we have seen increasing attempts to move away from the traditional localisationist approach, to address brain function more in terms of the operation of circuits or systems, which include integrative processes at both structural and neurochemical levels. This development parallels, but is largely independent of, the comparatively recent tradition in cognitive science of addressing function in information-processing terms at the level of discrete, independent, encapsulated modules. While from my own preferred biological viewpoint of hardware (or wetware) versus software, I find the modular approach rather unsatisfying and sterile, as it is essentially abstract, it has, to my mind, the added drawback of retaining (in the modules) old localisationist tendencies. Nevertheless it must be admitted that the new "systems" emphasis (though we have had the limbic system and language and memory circuits with us for quite some time) necessarily involves both localisation and some degree of arbitrariness in defining a "system". Of course we see the same in ecology and medicine—systems, like diseases, are arbitrary, artificial constructs that we impose upon nature in our attempts to "carve her at her joints". No system should be treated totally independently of the wider context—the central nervous system as a whole—within which it lies. Nor, indeed, should the *latter* be viewed as entirely independent of, for example, the *immune* system, as neuro-immunoendocrinologists (as the accreted title suggests) recognise.

Any book is a product of its times, its *Zeitgeist*. It is always an intriguing but fruitless speculation to wonder how another, independent but technologically just as sophisticated civilisation (Meso-America, maybe, had it remained ever isolated from the rest of the world) might have come to describe the same issues. Indeed, I argue in the book that the very disorders themselves should not be viewed independently of adaptive processes and the society within which they occur. Systems, syndromes, symptoms, disorders are all accidents of language, conveniences in trying to "get a handle" on things. In our own scientific society, we see one hundred years ago the separation of neurology and psychiatry, the growth of biological psychology, and a new synthesis, a hydra with many heads or a Gorgon with many names, like neuropsychiatry, cognitive neuroscience, neuropsychology, biological psychology, biological psychiatry—all trying to do much the same thing, but from slightly or sometimes considerably different starting positions and traditions.

I have tried to include all the latest findings that bear upon the six "disorders" that I believe have enough in common (frontostriatal dysfunction of a neurodevelopmental nature) to be compared and contrasted. Although I have written from a biological viewpoint, I have addressed a wider range of issues—evolutionary, sociocultural, epidemiological—so that the book might be useful to as many workers and students as possible. Each chapter (except the last, which is an overview, synthesis, and interpretation) contains a brief introduction to the topics addressed, and a final Summary and Conclusion section. The latter is deliberately fairly lengthy, and written as far as possible in simple, nontechnical language, to make the material accessible to people at all levels of expertise. Thus each final Summary and Conclusion section can stand alone, as can also the final chapter. A list of Further Reading at the end of each chapter documents very recent key review works that can be profitably read by those who wish to go further with the contents of that chapter. I believe the book to be as up to date and comprehensive as possible, within the confines I set myself in writing it.

The subject matter is one which one way or another is likely to have impacted fairly directly on many of us, as several of the disorders are far from uncommon. The book is likely to be of use to senior undergraduates in psychology, medicine, and possibly social work, and to graduate students, researchers, teachers, and practitioners in psychology, neuropsychology, neuroscience, psychiatry, neuropsychiatry, child and adolescent psychiatry, adult psychiatry, and possibly paediatrics. Because of the multilevel approach I have adopted, the book should be equally accessible to the expert and the beginner. I hope it is equally useful.

I would like to acknowledge the very considerable contributions made by my recent (1990s) graduate students to the development of the ideas presented herein: Mark Bellgrove, Louise Corben, Ross Cunnington, Nellie Georgiou-Karistianis, Aileen Ho, Debbie Howells, Katherine Johnson, Dean Jones, Ester Klimkeit, Jason Mattingley, Nicole Rinehart, Mark Rogers, Dianne Sheppard, and Melissa Slavin, many of whom have also become my valued colleagues, and all of whom remain among my greatest friends. Above all, I want to thank my wife, friend, and colleague of so many years, Judy, without whom, in *every* sense, this book would not have been written. She is the glue that keeps our laboratory together, the manager and the IT expert who helped me write it at every stage. Lastly, I must thank Monash University for affording me the time to do the writing, and Merton College (Oxford) and the University of Wales (Bangor) for giving Judy and me shelter at a critical phase.

CHAPTER ONE

Neuropsychiatry, neuropsychology, behavioural neurology, and other preliminary issues

"Begin at the beginning", the King said gravely, "and then go on till you come to the end; then stop."
—*Alice's Adventures in Wonderland*, Lewis Carroll, 1832–1898

INTRODUCTION

Before we consider the frontostriatal system as a region developmentally vulnerable to a group of related neuropsychiatric disorders, it is profitable to address the proliferation of disciplines, clinical and basic, which are concerned with the functions of the brain and mind in health and disease. In this chapter we shall review the historical division between neurology and psychiatry, and the newly emerging disciplines, often with considerable mutual overlap, of cognitive psychology, neuropsychology, (cognitive) neuropsychiatry, biological psychiatry, and cognitive neuroscience. We shall also touch upon the questions of comorbidity, genetic vulnerability, the possibly adaptive aspects of certain disorders, and the definition and utility of the concept of a disease or disorder.

A PROLIFERATION OF DISCIPLINES

In *A Project for Scientific Psychology* Freud proposed in 1895 that the cognitive mechanisms of normal and abnormal mental phenomena can be explained by a rigorous study of brain systems (Andreasen, 1997)—what nowadays, at the end of the Decade of the Brain, we would call cognitive neuroscience. Freud began by studying pharmacology (the therapeutic effects of cocaine), neurology (juvenile aphasia), and basic neuroscience

1

(staining techniques for visualising neurones). However, he eventually abandoned these pursuits, and what we now would call neuropsychiatry, at a time when psychiatry and neurology diverged, is only nowadays beginning, 100 years later, once again to converge. Throughout the intervening period the two disciplines have employed different languages to describe essentially similar processes; thus the denial of the dementing or psychiatric patient unable to perform a task is very similar to the anosognosia of the neurologist (Starr & Sporty, 1994). However, the psychiatrist traditionally assumes the absence of organicity, while the neurologist, on the basis of imaging, will assume the opposite, even though practitioners of the two disciplines may merely be encountering different aspects of disorders of the same systems. Indeed, this is particularly true of the neurodevelopmental disorders of the frontostriatal system with which this book is concerned. Thus the symptoms of obsessive compulsive disorder, though regarded as psychiatric, frequently emerge after insult to the basal ganglia. Antischizophrenic (neuroleptic) medication commonly results in neurological movement disorders, whereas antiparkinsonian medication can cause psychotic disturbances of thought processes. Electroconvulsive therapy can help both (psychiatric) depression (itself, as we shall see, not uncommonly a consequence of left-sided frontal lesions) and (neurological) Parkinson's disease. The "neurology" of prosopagnosia similarly has its counterpart in the "psychiatry" of Capgras syndrome, while the ictal phenomena of temporal lobe epilepsy and the disturbances of schizophrenia may both involve complex visual hallucinations and be amenable to the same medications. Indeed, most patients experience emotional factors that impinge upon the expression of neurological symptoms, while neurological deficits in turn contribute to psychological and psychiatric symptoms (Starr & Sporty, 1994).

NEUROPSYCHOLOGY, NEUROPSYCHOLOGY, AND BEHAVIOURAL NEUROLOGY

There is, nowadays, a new rapprochement of cognitive psychology, neuropsychology, psychiatry, neurology, and clinical and basic neuroscience, resulting from studies of animals, people (in sickness and in health), neuroimaging, neuroanatomy and neuropharmacology, all aimed at identifying the neural mechanisms of normal cognitive processes, and how they are injured in mental illness; such is the broad field, and scope, of cognitive neuroscience (Andreasen, 1997).

In some respects the historical split between neurology and psychiatry reflects the philosophical distinction between brain and mind. Thus mental illnesses have long been distinguished from corporeal maladies, as affecting "higher" mental or cognitive processes, "the mind". The brain/mind problem of course is still unresolved and is debated at many levels (in terms of reductionism) and by many disciplines. Is mind "simply" the expression of activity of the brain (Andreasen, 1997)? We now know that each can affect the other, in either direction. Thus the brain is highly plastic, even into adulthood, and its operations and local functioning are highly amenable to the effects of experience (Merzenich, 1998); as we shall see, abnormal patterns of metabolic activity correlate with the symptoms of obsessive compulsive disorder, and may be normalised with treatment be it pharmacological or "simply" cognitive behavioural. Cognitive neuroscience, a new discipline, is one attempt at bridging the brain/mind gulf, via a study of the mind in terms of perception, emotion, and behavioural regulation, while cognitive neuropsychiatry addresses mental illnesses as diseases affecting the mind, in so far as the latter are seen to "arise" from the brain.

Cognitive neuropsychiatry, in many ways an offshoot of the far more general discipline of biological psychiatry, is thus a new discipline that is increasingly being applied to the area of overlap between the disciplines of psychiatry, neurology, and cognitive psychology (Baddeley, 1996), though it is not yet perhaps a fully coherent discipline. Just as neuropsychiatry and biological psychiatry, its parent and precursor, went some way towards bridging neurology and psychiatry, cognitive neuropsychiatry seeks to bridge the three "stem" disciplines of recent years—neuropsychiatry, neuropsychology and behavioural neurology:

- *Neuropsychiatry* has sought to address structural and functional aspects and neurophysiological and neuropathological alterations of the central nervous system with respect to mental disease (Mendez, Van Gorp, & Cummings, 1995), and to understand the neurobiological basis, optimal assessment, natural history, and most efficacious treatment of disorders of the central nervous system (Bradshaw & Mattingley, 1995). Neuropsychiatry emphasises the importance of neurochemistry, brain structure, and function at a macromolecular level, and clearly owes much to psychopharmacology, brain biochemistry, and the study of neurotransmitter systems.
- *Neuropsychology* began as a discipline in the late nineteenth century, with the patient studies of Broca, Wernicke, Lichtheim, and Hughlings Jackson, who adopted the principle of functional localisation. According to this doctrine, specific cognitive functions were subserved by discrete brain regions and using the method of anatomical correlation practitioners of the discipline established relationships between damage to particular brain areas, and distinct manifestations of such behavioural anomalies as aphasia or agnosia. Indeed, the localisationist approach itself developed from Gall's original, if misguided, attempt to localise complex behaviours, such as

"philoprogenitiveness", according to the topography of an individual's skull (Bradshaw & Mattingley, 1995). However, as Hughlings Jackson long ago observed, localising a lesion and localising a function are conceptually quite distinct. Neuropsychology nowadays emphasises the relationship between the brain and cognitive functions, mechanisms, and abilities, particularly such aspects as memory, language, visuospatial skills, and executive functions (Mendez et al., 1995). Psychometric measurement of individual differences in such behavioural attributes, rather than treatment, is still a mainstay of neuropsychology, with its older emphasis upon standardised neuropsychological tests and its more recent concern with analysis of cognitive function; it uses, for example, reaction time measures, tachistoscopic or dichotic presentation, electrophysiological indices, and the newer paradigms developed by attentional theorists (Stroop, inhibition of return, negative priming, continuous performance tasks, attentional blink etc.). While neuropsychology is also (like neuropsychiatry) concerned with patient diagnosis and management, the discipline is particularly interested in elucidating the mechanisms that underlie abnormal (clinical) and *normal* behaviour. However, unlike behavioural neurology or neuropsychiatry, information-processing systems may be appealed to, or developed, with relatively little concern for anatomical or physiological instantiation. As such, neuropsychology is clearly far less expensive and technical than, for example, molecular biology, though clearly the molecular and the neuropsychological approaches to the analysis of brain and behaviour are complementary. An adequate conceptualisation of function plays a crucial role in specifying the nature of the problems that the molecular biologist is attempting to understand at a subcellular level; "A poorly-defined phenotype is unlikely to facilitate identification of the underlying genotype" (Baddeley, 1996, p. 186).

• *Behavioural neurology*, the third leg of the tripod supporting the undertaking of cognitive neuroscience, has its roots in the reductionism of neurology, with the latter's emphasis on more peripheral problems such as the control of movement, and a tendency to avoid the "higher" cognitive functions of consciousness, thought, belief, and their disturbance (Baddeley, 1996). As with neuropsychiatry, neurologists increasingly rely on molecular-biological techniques whose relevance to such characteristic issues of cognitive neuropsychiatry as the analysis of hallucinations and delusions is only just beginning to be realised. Like their neurologist predecessors, whose interests may have been largely in diagnosis and treatment, behavioural neurologists use data on the anatomy and physiology of the central nervous system to guide the interpretation of disordered behaviour consequent upon neurological damage. The deficit syndromes of aphasia, agnosia, apraxia, amnesia, amusia, acalculia . . . are all considered neuroanatomically in the context of localisation of function, together with disconnection processes. It is perhaps more descriptive than oriented (as in the case of classical neurology) towards assessment or treatment, though successful management is still important to the discipline (Mendez et al., 1995).

Thus the three disciplines, though displaying considerable overlap and increasing convergence, nevertheless diverge in theoretical orientation and originate from different parent disciplines, historical backgrounds and professional organisations, even though they are all concerned with brain–behaviour relationships. However, only neuropsychiatry and, recently, neuropsychology, have moved away from strict localisation/disconnection theory, and have come to grips with a view of brain function as involving dynamic organisation, reorganisation (e.g. with changes of, or increasing, experience), or disorganisation of patterns or networks of activity across or between whole brain regions. Hopefully, cognitive neuropsychiatry, by studying the much more dramatic (than in normality) modulations in cognitive function that accompany psychiatric disease, might eventually form the basis for a more complete understanding of the neurobiological processes that underlie the emotional and motivational determinants of cognitive function (Baddeley, 1996). For this enterprise, we need the combined expertise of the psychiatrist, neurologist, neuropsychologist, and cognitive scientist.

The general aims of biological psychiatry, the parent discipline of neuropsychiatry, to identify potentially useful markers of various disorders, and to determine the latters' aetiology and hence possible remediation, interact in the context of state versus trait aspects of a disorder. Thus markers may reflect either the *state* (present or absent) of an illness, or the *trait* of a predisposition (see, for example, Anderson & Cohen, 1996). State markers may or may not be genetic, and should revert to normal on recovery or remission; presumably they relate in some fashion to symptomatology rather than to the basic aetiology. However, trait markers must relate somehow to underlying genetic substrates, being present always, even perhaps in the family members of probands. They may be dichotomous, discrete, or continuous. Biological psychiatry is particularly interested in trait markers that are easily and reliably measured, with little overlap between normal and affected groups, and that are useful in diagnosis, subtyping, pedigree and family analysis, establishing a prognosis, and selecting appropriate therapy.

While the experimental (or even the clinical) neuropsychologist will be interested in cognitive function and dysfunction, and the behavioural neurologist perhaps more in motor (and maybe also attentional) aspects, the neuropsychiatrist will tend to address neurotransmitter function (presence, absence, or changes in the neurotransmitters themselves, their metabolites, their receptors, and neurotransmitter-related enzymes) and neuroendo-crinological aspects. All will be interested in neuroimaging correlates of cognitive function or dysfunction, whether morphological or functional (and if the latter, whether "resting" or activational). The many steps from genetic to neuronal functioning have addressed aspects of localisation, cloning, the sequencing of genes for important or relevant enzymes and receptor systems, the assessment of gene activity through measurement of RNA, the elucidation of steps involved in the synthesis, storage, release, and reuptake of neurotransmitters, the mechanisms of coupling between trans-mitters and receptors, and the cascade of events after receptor stimulation; the latter include membrane changes, receptor reconfiguration, and the activation of second messenger systems (Anderson & Cohen, 1996). Also relevant are the genetic factors concerned with the timing and expression of other genes, and the control and development of the central nervous system in normality and pathology. We shall see in this book that the putatively neurodevelopmental disorders Tourette's syndrome, obsessive compulsive and attention deficit hyperactivity disorders, schizophrenia, autism, and depression are particularly amenable to such interpretation and such a programme of study.

HERITABILITY AND GENETICS

For centuries it has been tacitly accepted that a predisposition towards the development of mental disorders is inherited. Nevertheless until recently this acceptance has had few practical consequences, partly because of entrenched beliefs in psychiatry concerning the aetiological importance of life events, and partly because it was long thought that one could not alter the inexorable determination of genetic inheritance (Barondes, 1999). However, with the very considerable recent increases in knowledge about the structure and function of genes, their role in coding for proteins etc., and possible ways of intervening at the molecular level, or pharmacologically, new avenues in neuropsychiatry are increasingly being explored at the level of intervention. It is also now possible sometimes to identify causative alleles to predict individual vulnerability. In this context the *neurodegen-erative* disorder Huntington's disease is particularly interesting, not least as a rare disorder of theoretical, clinical, and practical interest to psychiatrists and neurologists alike. It is maybe simultaneously the easiest to identify as inheritance is autosomal dominant, involving a single abnormal allele (a trinucleotide repeat sequence of varying length, a criterion level of which determines whether or not the disease manifests in an individual's lifetime), and the most difficult to work with. Thus the allele codes for an abnormal protein, huntingtin, whose function is still mysterious but somehow involves glutamatergic neurotransmission.

Unfortunately, matters are much more difficult with the more complex and far commoner *neurodevelopmental* neuropsychiatric disorders with which this book is concerned: Tourette's syndrome, obsessive compulsive disorder, attention deficit hyperactivity disorder, schizophrenia, autism, and depression; they are all clearly familial, but their transmission through the generations is much weaker than is the case with Huntington's disease. Also, unlike the neurodegenerative Huntington's, Parkinson's, and Alzheimer's diseases, all these neurodevelopmental disorders also seem to possess curious, and not always immediately obvious, *adaptive* aspects, often more for clinically unaffected relatives perhaps than for probands themselves; this aspect may of course account for their persistence in the genome despite their clear, immediate, maladaptive aspects. Medicine indeed is nowadays reporting ever more instances of disorders providing positive benefits or protection against some other condition, in instances of low genetic dosage or penetrance. Thus, like other prevalent familial diseases such as diabetes and hypertension, they are "complex diseases" (Barondes, 1999), which reflect the concerted action of particular alleles of several different genes. Such "susceptibility gene" variants do not invariably give rise to disorders in a Mendelian fashion, but instead contribute to *vulnerability* (perhaps in the context of precipitating environmental factors) to complex diseases without necessarily causing them. Also, because variants of multiple susceptibility genes may need to act in concert to give rise to pathology, these diseases may properly be termed "polygenic". Moreover, not only may multiple susceptibility genes be involved, along with environmental factors, but different *combinations* of such susceptibility genes, and maybe even different environmental influences, may operate in different individuals, families, and populations. Such genetic heterogeneity may also account for the very extensive *comorbidity* displayed by the neurodevelopmental disorders; presence in the family of one disorder increases the probability not only of that disorder manifesting, but also of one or more of the others, with or *without* the presence of the "target" or index disorder. Indeed we shall argue that all the neurodevelopmental disorders are closely interrelated, involving merely different loci, or combinations of loci, on the five parallel, segregated fronto-striato-pallido-thalamo-cortical pathways that constitute the frontostriatal system. The disorder one may manifest may be a happenstance, via a particular combination of genetic and environmental circumstances, of the locus or loci of alteration on one or more pathways. That said, all the time new molecular and statistical techniques are being developed that will enable much more rapid and precise localisation and identification of the genetic variants that influence vulnerability to such disorders; hopefully, they will open the way for new diagnostic, therapeutic, management, and preventative approaches (and see Barondes, 1999).

DISEASE, SYNDROMES, SYMPTOMS, AND DIAGNOSIS

The classic deficit disorders of neurology, the aphasias, agnosias, apraxias etc., can often be diagnosed with the help of localising signs such as hemiparesis, visual field defects and so on, while biological markers confirm diagnosis in many medical conditions such as diabetes or cancer. With mental illness there are few reliable or evident biological markers, with (very recently) the possible exception of Alzheimer's disease. Idiopathic Parkinson's disease is notoriously difficult to discriminate from "Parkinson's plus" variants until autopsy, and with the neurodevelopmental disorders with which this book is concerned any diagnostic markers are likely to be complex, small-scale phenomena that will be difficult to quantify or measure. These markers may include anomalies in inter-regional connectivity as measured electrophysiologically or by functional neuroimaging, anomalies in neuronal signalling or transduction, or abnormalities in genes or gene expression (Andreasen, 1997). Such anomalies, however, are likely to be none the less real, producing substantial morbidity and mortality, and in the long run likely to provide objective criteria. As yet, as Andreasen (1997) notes, in the absence of pathological markers current definitions of mental illness are syndromal, based on a convergence of signs, symptoms, outcome, and patterns of familial aggregation. Nevertheless, just as in general medicine, the iterative process of successively refining measurements will continue to be applied in psychiatry.

An apparent difference between psychiatry and many other branches of medicine is the frequent lack, in the former, of clear bounds or distinctions between the "normal" healthy state and the phenotype of a disorder; many forms of mental illness, particularly those involving the neurodevelopmental disorders, involve behaviours or phenomena that extend continuously from normality, with boundaries being placed in an arbitrary fashion or as a matter of convenience. However, as Andreasen (1997) notes, the *risk* factors for many *other* kinds of disease, e.g. cancer, also are continuously distributed, even though the disorder's expression, such as the presence/absence of a tumour, may be discrete. Indeed, precancerous changes themselves, by definition, extend continuously in spectrum fashion between healthy and morbid tissue. In both cases there may be involvement of many genes, in addition to a range of environmental factors, with the probability of expression of a disorder requiring attainment of a criterial number of such genetic/environmental factors, interactions, or combinations; thus there may be levels of vulnerability. In psychiatry, moreover, there may be inordinate focusing on taxonomic categories of disease, with insufficient attention to the symptoms in their own right. Diseases do not exist independently of their signs and symptoms; they are in fact arbitrary constructs or constellations of such symptoms. Useful cognitive models of mental illness provide a general theory of a disease that is consistent with current clinical knowledge, based on observation of signs and symptoms, one which is responsive to treatment, course of illness, genetic, familial, environmental, and epidemiological data—and can be tested experimentally on both human and animal models (Andreasen, 1997).

In the various neurodevelopmental disorders of the frontostriatal system to be dealt with in this book, imaging studies, morphometric or functional, resting or activational, will be seen to provide evidence of departures from normality. What does it mean if, for example, children with attention deficit hyperactivity disorder or obsessive compulsive disorder display abnormal functional magnetic resonance imaging (fMRI) patterns of brain function that normalise with successful treatment (pharmacological or by cognitive behaviour therapy)? Do we now have a diagnostic *test* for the disorder, which may even circumvent the frequent claims (at least in attention deficit hyperactivity disorder) of overdiagnosis, on the basis of behavioural criteria? Does the fMRI pattern somehow even imply *causation*? As Degrandpre (1999) notes, the interrelated problems of causation, correlation, and reductionism relate particularly to the brain/mind problem in general, and psychopathology in particular; is *all* human psychopathology biological, and should we reject the experiential tenets of psychiatry prior to the "neuro-" or biological revolution? While mind, brain, and behaviour inevitably and necessarily share irreducible interconnections, we should not forget that abnormal physical states in patients may stem from factors *other* than the disease itself, such as institutionalisation and social experiences. Is there in fact much to be gained, apart maybe from added certainty (which in the end perhaps should not be lightly dismissed), by an "objective" *biological* diagnosis involving imaging if we can still diagnose the disorder behaviourally, by observation—as indeed has in any case to happen initially on first consultation? Finally, as we shall elaborate further in the following pages, not only are diseases hypothetical constructs (see above), but their very acceptance as abnormal states is itself often a matter of a society's current norms and expectations; under certain circumstances it is *adaptive* to be suspicious, paranoid, obsessive, hyperactive, distractible, over-optimistic. . . . Persistence in the genome of an apparently undesirable trait should make us look for possible hidden advantages.

SUMMARY AND CONCLUSIONS

The historical split 100 years ago between *neurology* and *psychiatry*, in part reflecting the philosophical barrier between brain and mind, is only now beginning to be bridged with the recent emergence of *neuropsychiatry* and *biological psychiatry*. Until now the two disciplines have employed different concepts and vocabularies to address essentially similar issues. Traditionally, the neurologist, but not the psychiatrist, has assumed the presence of organicity. However, psychiatric symptoms can result from neurological insult, and similar modes of treatment can often help patients with disorders managed by both disciplines. Indeed, functional imaging, employed in both disciplines, demonstrates that brain states can reflect current (and changeable) mind sets, and indeed the latter can even determine the former.

The Decade of the Brain sees a rapprochement between *cognitive psychology*, *neuropsychology*, *psychiatry*, *neurology*, and *clinical* and *basic neuroscience*; with this convergence of basic research and clinical management, *cognitive neuroscience* has bridged the brain–mind interface and new disciplines have emerged. *Cognitive neuropsychiatry* is perhaps the most significant, with its overlap between *psychiatry*, *neurology*, and *cognitive psychology*. We still see, however, strong clinical and research traditions continuing in the overlapping disciplines of *neuropsychiatry* (with a greater emphasis on structural, neurochemical, and functional aspects), *neuropsychology* (with its historical emphasis upon the localisation of cognitive functions), and *behavioural neurology* (with its bias towards more peripheral and motor functions, and the deficit syndromes). *Biological psychiatry* generally is concerned with identifying potentially useful markers of disorders and their possible aetiology. In this respect, the discipline observes the distinction between state and trait markers.

Neuroimaging, especially functional, is an important new tool for the cognitive neuropsychiatrist, who is also concerned with a disorder's genetic underpinnings, the relationship between genes and the proteins they code for, and between genes and environment, and the emerging concept of genetic vulnerability. The possibly adaptive aspects of many disorders is a new concept and the question of comorbidity is continuously vexatious. So too is the definition of disease; in mental illness, biological markers are few, the boundaries with the healthy state are vague, and in many ways mental disorders should be seen as arbitrary constructs or constellations of symptoms, or even as in part a consequence of societal demands or expectations. Indeed, what does it mean if in a psychiatric illness we see abnormal brain metabolism in a certain area? Is the relationship causal, and if so in which direction? Is it epiphenomenal? Does it provide a potentially useful marker? Might it be a gold-standard diagnostic test? Might it come to condemn the healthy to an incorrect diagnosis?

These issues are of particular relevance to the neurodevelopmental frontostriatal disorders.

FURTHER READING

Anderson, G.M., & Cohen, D.J. (1996). Neurobiology of neuropsychiatric disorders. In M. Lewis (Ed.), *Child and adolescent psychiatry: A comprehensive textbook* (2nd ed., pp. 30–38). Baltimore: Williams & Wilkins.

Andreasen, N.C. (1997). Linking mind and brain in the study of mental illnesses: A project for a scientific psychopathology. *Science, 275*, 1586–1593.

Baddeley, A.D. (1996). Cognition, neurology, psychiatry: Golden triangle or Bermuda triangle? *Cognitive Neuropsychiatry, 1*, 185–189.

Barondes, S.H. (1999). An agenda for psychiatric genetics. *Archives of General Psychiatry, 56*, 549–552.

Benson, D.F. (1996). Neuropsychiatry and behavioral neurology: Past, present, and future. *Journal of Neuropsychiatry, 8*, 351–357.

Degrandpre, R.J. (1999). Just cause. *The Sciences, March/April*, 14–18.

Mendez, M.F., Van Gorp, W., & Cummings, J.L. (1995). Neuropsychiatry, neuropsychology, and behavioral neurology: A critical comparison. *Neuropsychiatry, Neuropsychology, and Behavioral Neurology, 8*, 297–302.

Starr, A., & Sporty, L.D. (1994). Similar disorders viewed with different perspectives. *Archives of Neurology, 51*, 977–980.

CHAPTER TWO

The frontal cortex and the control of behaviour

By their fruits shall ye know them.

Bible, St Matthew, 7: 20

INTRODUCTION

The frontal regions, perhaps achieving their greatest evolutionary development in our species, are slow to mature and vulnerable to the kinds of neurodevelopmental disorders with which this book is concerned. In this chapter we shall note the largely anterior- posterior hierarchical control of preparation for and execution of action, via the prefrontal cortex (dorsolateral, orbitofrontal, anterior cingulate), the premotor areas (lateral and mesial), and the primary motor cortex. Executive decisions will be seen to be taken by the dorsolateral regions, the anterior cingulate mediating intentionality and aspects of directed attention, and the orbitofrontal regions providing inhibitory control or self-monitoring aspects. The lateral premotor areas will be seen to respond more to externally directed action, and the mesial supplementary motor area to mediate the control of internally initiated complex, sequential behaviour. Circuits involving these cortical regions and the basal ganglia will be described, along with their release of behaviours mediated by the above cortical regions. We shall see that between them preparation for action can be described in terms of decisions about what, how, and when something is to be undertaken, and that breakdown in these circuits can explain the symptoms of a range of common neurodevelopmental frontostriatal disorders. Finally, we shall consider the roles of "gut feelings", attention, and consciousness in preparation for action.

13

PRELIMINARY CONSIDERATIONS

An association between frontal regions and higher intellectual functions was hinted at by the Greeks and Romans two thousand or more years ago (Finger, 1994). In the fourteenth century Guido Lanfranchi was the first to describe the clinical sequelae to frontal damage (Duffy & Campbell, 1994), while Swedenborg (1688–1772) wrote that the frontal lobes are intimately involved in higher cognitive processes. Burdach (1819, cited by Pennington & Ozonoff, 1996) saw them as the "special workshop of the thinking process". The nineteenth century, of course, was the period when localisationist theory perhaps reached its zenith; animal studies, and the celebrated case of Phineas Gage, brought the realisation that these massive (in *Homo sapiens*) "silent" areas may underlie our humanity itself.

HIERARCHICAL ORGANISATION IN PREPARATION FOR ACTION

Along with the realisation that it may be unprofitable to continue to view the brain from the nineteenth-century localisationist viewpoint (or as a collection of discrete encapsulated modules, its modern epiphany; Fodor, 1983), or even as an assembly of fixed and inflexible networks, but rather that it may function as a flexible system of interacting centres whose activity and interrelationships shift dynamically with changing experience, so too we should view brain and brain function in hierarchical terms. Nowhere perhaps is this approach better exemplified than with respect to preparation for action. Fuster (1999) notes that the highest and most global plans and schemes of action are prefrontally elaborated, especially in the dorsolateral prefrontal cortex, with intermediate and more concrete representations (spatial trajectory, temporal sequencing) being mediated via the lateral premotor area and supplementary motor area, with parietal involvement also; elementary motor acts and concrete and specific muscle groups are handled by the primary motor cortex. Each level primes the next level down, though all are at the same time coordinated in parallel, with ongoing interplay at all levels. Fuster sees complex motor functions and their cognitive corollaries of working memory, set, attention, and reasoning being largely elaborated in the dorsolateral prefrontal cortex, while the medial and orbitofrontal cortex sustain the emotional and affective functions that determine our social and "gut" feelings or hunches. Additional to frontal cortex, motor memory also involves the basal ganglia and cerebellum for the more automatic aspects of behaviour, leaving the frontal regions free for the more novel, deliberate, and conscious actions. Speech, the most complex faculty of our species (Bradshaw, 1997), clearly exemplifies these principles; dorsolateral prefrontal cortex damage leads to impoverished linguistic structure and loss of propositionality, fluidity, complex grammar, and ideas. Damage to (left-sided) premotor and supplementary motor areas leads to similar but more severe deficits in linguistic structure: halting speech, monotone, Broca's aphasia and agrammatism, and telegraphic style. Primary motor cortex damage affects the articulatory acts themselves with speech apraxia (Bradshaw & Mattingley, 1995). We should perhaps note at this point that the primary motor cortex may control sets of *synergistic* muscles rather than just a single muscle or a single specific action, so that the classic homuncular somatotopic arrangement is valid only in general terms, in that, for example, the arm *region* lies lateral and ventral to the leg, and dorsal to the face. Moreover, the neurones involved in a given movement may spatially be quite distinct from each other; thus neurones scattered over a relatively wide zone of the motor cortex, and corresponding to a leg or arm, can be activated synchronously to generate a movement sequence involving several muscles *synergistically* (Obeso, Rodriguez, & DeLong, 1997). The primary motor cortex may therefore contain a spatially organised map, in which combinations or patterns of synergistic muscles are arranged almost like books on a library shelf that can be selected at need, in whatever combination is currently optimal to the situation—as determined at hierarchically higher levels. Kakei, Hoffman, and Strick (1999) note that while a substantial group of neurones in the primary motor cortex code for relevant low-level parameters like force in particular muscles, an equal number code for *direction* of limb movement in space *independent* of the muscle activity that might generate such movement. Thus the primary motor cortex may represent both "muscles" and "movements".

ACTION SCHEMATA

The representation and execution of actions is thus mediated, in ascending hierarchical order, by the motor neurones, the anterior roots of the spinal cord, the motor nuclei of the mesencephalon, the cerebellum, parts of the diencephalon (notably, the thalamus and basal ganglia), and the frontal cortex (Fuster, 1999). The latter *itself* is hierarchically organised, the primary motor cortex mediating the representation and execution of elementary skeletal movements, the premotor cortex (premotor area and supplementary motor area) subserving more complex movements defined by goal and trajectory, and the association cortex of the frontal lobe. Here, the broad schemata of action and their enactment are represented at the hierarchically highest level, via distributed networks of neurones whose activity may be "bound" (see Brown & Marsden, 1998) by the temporal coincidence of activity and input via three basic cognitive functions (Fuster, 1999):

- Short-term *motor* memory and preparatory set (perhaps involving the excitatory neurotransmitter glutamate) for the forthcoming action, and involving premovement readiness potentials (*Bereitschaftspotentials*) over the supplementary motor area.
- Short-term *perceptual* memory or working memory for the retention of currently relevant (or expected) sensory information, and involving the "contingent negative variation" over the dorsolateral prefrontal cortex.
- Inhibitory control (perhaps involving the orbitofrontal cortex and the inhibitory neurotransmitter GABA) of interference to suppress whatever is irrelevant.

The frontal cortex is thus constantly active from both external and internal stimuli, generating new schemata for voluntary action, decision, volition, and will. Such action schemata involve the formulation of goals, intention to act, response selection, programming, and the initiation of action (Jahanshahi & Frith, 1998), with higher-order executive or supervisory mechanisms overseeing nonroutine motor processes. Actions are purposeful, goal-directed behaviours, voluntary but not necessarily willed or intentional, with elements of choice, selection, and control. Even automatic actions may become conscious and willed, involving attentional effort; thus walking on ice, via self-monitoring, may lose its automaticity. This is not of course the place to debate the "locus", if any (see above with respect to the localisation debate) of will, intention, or consciousness; suffice it to say that these highest-of-all "human" faculties merely involve the frontal cortex as a "final common path" from many circuits that may ultimately tap much if not most of the brain. Indeed the prefrontal cortex is one of the most highly interconnected (with other regions) of the entire brain, as well as being the latest structure to develop both phylogenetically and ontogenetically (Bradshaw, 1997). Thus it exhibits massive interconnections with parietal, temporal, and limbic regions, brainstem, basal ganglia, and cerebellum, with ascending dopaminergic, noradrenergic, and serotonergic neuromodulatory input. These three neurotransmitters participate in ascending pathways that project widely through the frontal lobes, are highly interconnected, and also modulate other less well understood transmitter systems such as the opioid peptides, as well as the cholinergic and GABAergic (see, for example, Anderson & Cohen, 1996):

- *Serotonin* (5-HT) is important in sleep, mood, appetite, perception, and hormone secretion; it is produced after hydroxylation and decarboxylation of tryptophan, in cell bodies of neurones in the raphe nuclei of the hindbrain.

- *Dopamine* plays an important role in functions relating to reward, and modulates movement and cognition; synthesised from tyrosine, it is produced in cell bodies of the substantia nigra and ventral tegmental area of the midbrain.
- *Noradrenaline* is produced from dopamine by action of the enzyme dopamine β-hydroxylase; most noradrenaline-containing neurones project from the locus coeruleus in the brainstem to innervate the midbrain and cortex. It critically modulates stress responses, central and peripheral arousal, learning, and memory.

This necessarily over-simplistic and incomplete account will suffice as an initial, orienting guide; in the following chapters the various roles of these and other neurotransmitters will be more fully elaborated.

THE PREFRONTAL CORTEX

Structurally and neurochemically, the prefrontal cortex is subject to the neurodevelopmental disorders with which this book is concerned. Essential for the temporal organisation of behaviour, rational thinking, executive functions, and creativity, and constituting about one-third of the adult human neocortex, the prefrontal cortex does not achieve full structural or functional maturation until late adolescence. Its inputs cover the gamut of the internal and external milieu, along with the stored representations of long-term memory (Fuster, 1999). Decisions to act are the result of competition between diverse conflicting influences converging upon the region; the course that an individual may choose can be seen as the vector that results from such multitudinous and largely unconscious influences.

While there is little dispute about the importance, to our species, of the prefrontal cortex, its role, and its comparatively late phylogenetic and ontogenetic appearance, there is debate as to its size relative to the rest of the brain. Adolphs et al. (1996) note that "the large increase in prefrontal cortex in primates and during their development supports the idea that that is where our advanced reasoning lies" (p. 157), and Changeux and Dehaene (1996) observe that "the prefrontal cortex is a critical region whose surface area has increased relatively the most in mammalian evolution, from 3.5 percent (cat) to 17 percent (chimpanzee) and 29 percent (ourselves)" (p. 125). Conversely Damasio (1996), while acknowledging that the frontal lobe is both the largest sector of the telencephalon and has the clearest borders, nevertheless claims that it is not *disproportionately* large, occupying 30% of the telencephalon in the macaque, 35% in the gibbon, orangutan and gorilla, and 35–40% in ourselves; only the white-matter core in the sector anterior to the basal ganglia is larger in humans. Thus our remarkable cognitive abilities may be due less to volumetric mass per se, and more to patterns of internal connectivity, which are indeed different between the frontal lobe and other regions.

As a region, the frontal lobe may be particularly vulnerable, in view of its late maturation, to maturational or *neurodevelopmental* disorders of the type addressed in this book. It is also vulnerable to the *neurodegenerative* disorders of ageing, notably Parkinson's, Huntington's, and Alzheimer's diseases, with which we shall not be dealing directly, but which nevertheless exhibit many phenomenological similarities to the neurodevelopmental disorders. Its location makes it vulnerable to closed head injury (deceleration in traffic accidents and falls) and penetrating head wounds, leading to diffuse axonal injury and focal cortical contusions (Stuss, Alexander, & Benson, 1997). Infarctions of the middle cerebral artery, although especially damaging the dorsolateral prefrontal cortex, may also involve the basal ganglia and white matter; infarctions of the anterior cerebral artery especially affect the orbitofrontal cortex, limbic basal ganglia, anterior cingulate, supplementary motor area, and corpus callosum—and are often bilateral, as both anterior cerebral arteries originate from the same internal carotid artery. Tumours include slow, "benign" space-occupying meningiomas, "benign" ependymomas, oligodendrogliomas, and cystic astrocytomas, whereas gliomas are rapid and malignant, and disrupt both blood supply and cerebrospinal fluid. Observational, clinical, and neuropsychological assessment information from such events has indicated that the signs and symptoms of the *neurodevelopmental* disorders involve analogous dysfunction of frontostriatal pathways. In both cases, traditional neuropsychological assessment procedures have included (Stuss et al., 1997): the Halstead Category Test, Stroop interference, the Wisconsin Card Sorting Test, Trail Making B, Verbal Fluency, Porteus Maze, WAIS subscales (Block Design, Picture Assessment, Memory, Drawing, Serial 7s), Brown–Peterson Memory Interference, Conditional Associative, Serial Order Pointing, and Tower of London. They indicate the potentiality for vulnerability to interference, problems with delay in responding, working memory deficits, and defective problem-solving strategies. On the other hand, real-life problems (deficits in self-awareness, problems in coping, phenomena such as reduplicative paramnesia) are usually far more disabling than laboratory performance might indicate.

The frontal lobes are essential for conceptual thought, drawing abstractions from perceptual experience, manipulating abstract ideas, and the ability to shift or maintain sets, or to maintain two or more antithetic sets simultaneously, where necessary, when for example in appreciating works of art. Damage (see, for example, Gualtieri, 1995) is associated with an inability to initiate an action sequence (akinesia), to withhold a response (defective response inhibition), to sustain an action (motor impersistence), and to stop a no-longer-appropriate response (perseveration, or incorrect repetition of an action); there is an inability to maintain set in the face of distraction (Stroop test) or to self-monitor, or to sustain attention; there is reduced insight, spontaneity, initiative or motivation; a tendency to blame others (autonomy), to be over-dependent on or responsive to environmental stimuli (compulsive utilisation behaviour), to demand immediate gratification, and to confabulate; patients may seek the concrete in place of the abstract, exhibit inappropriate behaviour or loss of empathy, be insensitive or egotistic, exhibit argumentativeness concerning irrelevancies, and manifest impulsivity, perseveration or stereotyped thinking, anosognosia (unawareness or denial of deficit), or outright unilateral neglect.

FIVE PARALLEL, SEGREGATED CIRCUITS

Running through the basal ganglia, a series of five semi-independent, parallel, frontal–subcortical circuits have been identified (Weiner, 1997) that provide a unifying framework for understanding similarities of behavioural changes associated with diverse anatomical lesions (Cummings, 1993). Thus there are commonalities of cognitive, motor, and emotional aspects of disorders involving the frontostriatal system (Foti & Cummings, 1997), whether neurodegenerative (Parkinson's and Huntington's diseases) or neurodevelopmental (Tourette's syndrome, obsessive compulsive, and attention deficit hyperactivity disorders, schizophrenia, and even autism and depression). Cognitive, motor, and emotional changes in all these disorders are an expression of the interruption of specific components of the five frontal–subcortical circuits (Foti & Cummings, 1997; Weiner, 1997): the skeletomotor, oculomotor, dorsolateral prefrontal, lateral orbitofrontal, and anterior cingulate (see Figures 2.1 and 2.2). The latter three originate in the prefrontal cortex, and are responsible for distinct neurobehavioural/neuropsychiatric syndromes involving cognition and emotion. All five share common structures and organisation, originating in the frontal lobe and with sequential projections to the striatum, globus pallidus/substantia nigra, thalamus, and back to the cortex. Each circuit has a direct (facilitatory) and an indirect (inhibitory) pathway between striatum and globus pallidus/substantia nigra; they are all mutually adjacent but anatomically segregated. Generally, the inputs to the circuit are broad and may involve functionally related structures outside the circuit, whereas the output is more localised to specific cortical areas (Foti & Cummings, 1997). Thus the circuits function in both a closed- and open-loop mode, permitting both tuning of processing, and input from and output to other structures:

- The *skeletomotor circuit* originates in cortical motor and premotor fields and the parietal somatosensory cortex. It passes through the

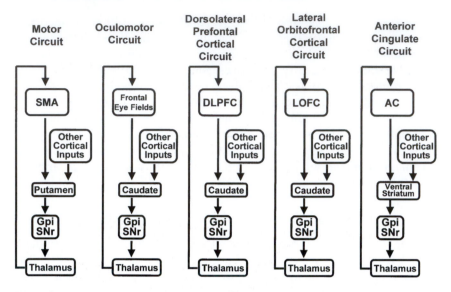

Figure 2.1.   Five frontostriatal circuits: motor (supplementary motor area: SMA), oculomotor, dorsolateral prefrontal (DLPFC), lateral orbitofrontal (LOFC), and anterior cingulate (AC). Each circuit begins and ends in the same cortical location, passing through the striatum (caudate or putamen), globus pallidus pars interna (GPi), and substantia nigra pars reticulata (SNr), and thalamus.

putamen, dorsolateral globus pallidus, and the ventrolateral nucleus of the thalamus, returning primarily to the supplementary motor area. Damage results in the classical akinesia and bradykinesia of Parkinson's disease.

- The *oculomotor circuit* originates in the frontal and supplementary eye fields, with a striatal component within the body of the caudate nucleus. It passes through the dorsomedial globus pallidus and the ventral anterior and dorsomedial thalamic nuclei before returning to the frontal eye fields. Damage leads to problems in voluntary fixational control.

- The *dorsolateral prefrontal circuit* originates in the dorsolateral prefrontal cortex, projects to the dorsolateral head of the caudate, and passes via the dorsolateral globus pallidus and the ventral anterior and dorsomedial thalamic nuclei back to the dorsolateral prefrontal cortex. Damage leads to the dysexecutive syndrome, with problems maintaining or shifting set, generating organisational strategies, retrieving memories, and production of fluent verbal or nonverbal activity.

- The *lateral orbitofrontal circuit* originates in the inferolateral prefrontal cortex, projecting to the ventromedial caudate nucleus and

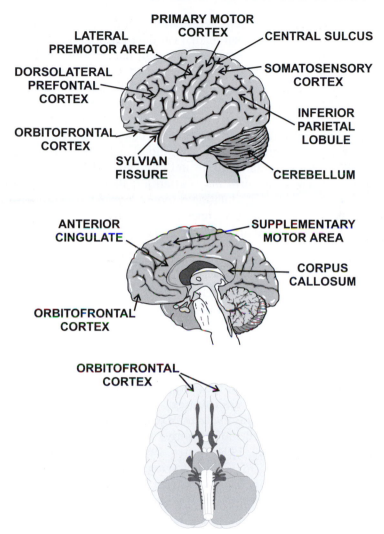

Figure 2.2.   Approximate locations of the dorsolateral prefrontal cortex, orbitofrontal cortex, lateral premotor area, primary motor cortex, somatosensory cortex, anterior cingulate, and supplementary motor area. From top to bottom: lateral (left hemisphere), mesial, and inferior views.

dorsomedial globus pallidus, returning via the ventral anterior and medial dorsal thalamic nuclei. Projections are very similar to those of the previous circuit, but are more medial throughout. The circuit is important in aspects of personality and social restraint, empathy, in the inhibition of interference from external cues, and in self-monitoring. Damage results in disinhibition and irritability, as in early Huntington's disease when medial caudate neurones are damaged.

- The *anterior cingulate circuit* originates in the anterior cingulate, and projects to the ventral (limbic) striatum (nucleus accumbens), olfactory tubercle, and parts of the ventromedial caudate and putamen. There are also multiple additional inputs to the ventral striatum. The circuit returns via the rostrolateral globus pallidus and the dorsomedial thalamic nucleus to the anterior cingulate. Damage is associated with apathy, reduced initiative and akinetic mutism. It is clearly important for maintaining drive and motivation. Indeed, Cohen et al. (1999), reviewing impairments of attention after cingulotomy, see the anterior cingulate as modulating *response intention* (the propensity to respond via behavioural readiness, anticipation, and response maintenance), and *focused attention*, response selection, and control.

THE DORSOLATERAL PREFRONTAL CIRCUIT

The dorsolateral prefrontal cortex clearly closes the gap between sensation and movement (Damasio, 1996), integrating with long-term memory structures in the inferotemporal (visual) cortex and the parietal (spatial, praxic) cortices, and providing a working or active memory, a buffer for response schemata and action plans, and a basis for the establishment of prospective or preparatory set. In many ways the executive functions that it mediates reflect and encompass the role of the prefrontal cortex as a whole, in view of its capacity to maintain an overall strategic or executive overview of adaptive behaviour as a whole. Thus the term "executive functions" is an attempt at capturing our highest order of cognitive functions or abilities (see, for example, Duffy & Campbell, 1994; Fuster, 1999; Mega & Cummings, 1994; Pennington & Ozonoff, 1996). The following list from the above authors reflects some of the diversity of the construct:

- Capacity for autonomous behaviour without external guidance.
- Capacity to persevere in the absence of external direction.
- Directed behaviour when a goal is remote or abstract.
- Self-direction, self-regulation, self-monitoring.
- Ability to organise a behavioural response to solve a new or complex problem.
- Mental synthesis for nonroutine actions.
- Planning and regulation of adaptive and goal-directed behaviour.
- Problem solving, reasoning, generation of solutions to novel problems.
- Initiative, motivation, spontaneity, judgement, planning, insight, strategic decision making.
- Spontaneity and fluency of thought and action.

- Cognitive flexibility.
- Ability to search memory systematically.
- Ability to shift or maintain set as appropriate.
- Ability to withhold or inhibit responses as appropriate.
- Ability to focus or sustain attention.

Inevitably, many of these concepts overlap, and they also overlap with the functions of the other two major prefrontal regions: the lateral orbitofrontal cortex and the mesial anterior cingulate. However, the attentional and set aspects (maintaining and shifting) are often quantified by the Wisconsin Card Sorting Test. In this test, a pack of cards with symbols differing in the dimensions of colour, shape and number (four colours, four shapes, and four numbers) lies before the subject, who must place each response card in front of one of four reference cards also before the subject, who is told "correct" or "incorrect" at each attempt. The sorting is determined arbitrarily by the examiner in terms of a particular dimension, colour, shape, or number. However, when the subject is systematically correct for a criterion number of trials, the rule is changed to a different value (e.g. from red to green) or dimension (e.g. from colour to number). The test is particularly sensitive to perseveration.

THE LATERAL ORBITOFRONTAL CORTEX

Damage to the lateral orbitofrontal cortex (Fuster, 1999; Mega & Cummings, 1994; Pennington & Ozonoff, 1996) results in disinhibitory deficits in both social and cognitive domains. There may be irritability, lability of mood, tactlessness, facetiousness, jocularity, fatuous euphoria, sporadic hypomania, insensitivity, inappropriate responses to social cues, inappropriate lewdness, hypersexuality, outbursts of explosive aggression, sociopathy, pseudopsychopathy, obsessions, and compulsions. In the cognitive or motor domains, lateral orbitofrontal cortex damage may be associated with distractibility, hyperreactivity (Fuster, 1999), echobehaviour (involuntary copying of others' actions, as in Tourette's syndrome), utilisation behaviour (failure to inhibit prepotent but currently inappropriate and often stereotyped responses such as combing the hair in the presence of a comb; see, for example, Jahanshahi & Frith, 1998), inability to make good real-life judgements on the basis of probabilities (Adolphs et al., 1996), inability to inhibit alternative associations, leading to confabulation (Schnider & Ptak, 1999), and general failure of self-monitoring.

The ability to suppress irrelevant or interfering stimuli, thoughts, memories, or impulses is of course a fundamental executive function essential for successful thought, action, and living, and imaging studies have indeed implicated the lateral orbitofrontal cortex in tasks involving the suppression of prepotent responses. However, many studies have also revealed cerebral activation that extends beyond this region. A distributed network that may underlie response inhibition may also include the supplementary motor area, anterior cingulate, and dorsolateral prefrontal cortex (Garavan, Ross, & Stein, 1999), though these additional regions may not actually be necessary for response inhibition per se; they may reflect additional cognitive processes recruited when one is performing inhibition tasks. Indeed Garavan et al. (1999) found that additional regions identified during neuroimaging included the middle and inferior frontal gyri, frontal limbic area, anterior insula, and inferior parietal lobe, with a pronounced right bias. Thus although the lateral orbitofrontal cortex may play a crucial role, it may be part of a distributed cortical network responsible for the broader aspects of response inhibition.

Zald and Kim (1996) provide a detailed review of the physiology of the orbitofrontal cortex, dividing it into lateral and medial orbitofrontal cortex sections. They note that it is located at the interface between sensory association cortices, limbic structures, and subcortical regions involved in the control of autonomic and motor effector pathways. Much of the region, with the exception of olfaction where many of the cells respond very selectively to only one or two smells, is largely responsive to the *behavioural significance*, rather than to the *identity*, of stimuli. They propose four roles for the region which are relevant to the aims of this book:

- *Recognition of reinforcing stimuli.* Lesioned animals are hyper-oral, indiscriminately mouthing or attempting to eat nonfood items, and will work hard in operant tasks to obtain them. The region is involved in a network (amygdala, lateral hypothalamus) of structures (a "reward network") that support intracranial self stimulation. Dopamine antagonists injected directly into the region attenuate, in a dose-dependent fashion, operant responding for intracranial self-stimulation. Increased metabolic activity here in humans correlates with the level of craving for cocaine in addicts undergoing withdrawal.
- *Stimulus-reinforcer learning.* Some orbitofrontal cortical cells in animal studies show activity dependent upon the behavioural significance of stimuli. Lesions to the amygdala, orbitofrontal cortex, or the mediodorsal nucleus of the thalamus, which interconnects these two structures, affect the ability to recognise stimuli associated with appetitive characteristics. The system therefore seems important in the mediation or expression of direct associations between stimuli and reward. Animal studies show that the orbitofrontal cortex plays a critical role in modulating readiness to perform operant responses

as a function of a subject's appetitive (or satiety) state, and the reinforcing value of a stimulus.

- *Coding for changes in reinforcement contingencies.* Cells in the orbito-frontal cortex change firing patterns when reinforcement contingencies change, as when a previously reinforced response is no longer rewarded, or vice versa. Lesions within the *medial orbitofrontal cortex* lead to continued responding during an extinction paradigm in animal studies, whereas lesions in the *lateral orbitofrontal cortex*, on the inferior convexity, result in impaired acquisition of spatial and object reversals and alternations, i.e. perseveration. Overall, orbitofrontal lesions lead to problems in appropriately modulating behaviour in the face of changing contingencies of reinforcement.
- *Emotionality, personality, and autonomic functions.* Lesions in humans (and, where behaviourally appropriate, in animals) lead to dislike of novelty, reduced aggressiveness, increased euphoria, exuberance, irritability and anxiety, increased global emotionality, and emotional expressions disconnected from the relevant social situation. Thus there may be laughing or crying in inappropriate contexts. Lateral-isation may be associated with release of negative emotions with damage on the right, and of positive emotions with left-sided damage. In the extreme case, there may be social or sexual disinhibition, lack of empathy, coarseness, tactlessness, excessive involvement in pleas-ure seeking and sexual behaviour, with reduced sensitivity to negative risks. While such individuals might be impulsive, irresponsible, and antisocial, there is nevertheless absence of intentional viciousness or organisation of a true antisocial personality disorder. Such *pseudo-psychopathy* is associated with intact moral or social reasoning and intellectualisation of risk and of what is morally right or wrong, in the presence of failure to experience appropriate sensations of guilt or anxiety, and a tendency to go ahead and act inappropriately. Interestingly, when instead such lesions occur in *early childhood*, rather than in *adulthood*, there is also loss of moral and social reasoning, and failure to acquire even the factual knowledge that relates to accepted social standards of moral behaviour, as in *true* psychopathy (Anderson, S.W., et al., 1999; see also Dolan, 1999).

Thus Zald and Kim (1996) see the orbitofrontal cortex as relevant to the recognition of behaviourally relevant stimuli, and the regulation of auto-nomic and goal-directed responses. Its position lies anatomically as the interface between sensory association areas, limbic regions involved in the evaluation of stimuli, and limbic efferent pathways. It is involved in a heterogeneous and diverse range of functions, such as the modulation of goal-directed behaviour during changing reinforcement contingencies, stimulus-reinforcement associations, and the regulation of autonomic responses to social stimuli. Damage to *the lateral orbitofrontal cortex* affects the ability to perform alternation and reversal tasks, and go/no-go paradigms; damage to the *medial orbitofrontal cortex* affects stimulus–response learning, extinction, and changes in emotional and autonomic responses. Nevertheless the two subregions, and sets and functions, are probably best seen as mutually complementary. The region as a whole is clearly particularly relevant to the kinds of neurodevelopmental neuropsychiatric disorder with which this book is concerned, especially perhaps to obsessive compulsive disorder (where the region may be hyperactive), and attention deficit hyperactivity disorder, where the reverse situation may occur. In this context Damasio's (1994) somatic-marker hypothesis is particularly relevant; he proposes that behavioural deficits following orbitofrontal damage reflect an inability to involve emotional processing in responding to complex task situations. Emotional influences are held to act as biasing signals, so that when one contemplates options for an action the orbitofrontal cortex engages knowledge related to feelings engendered by previous, similar situations. Such information helps select the action likely to be optimal or most advantageous—a biasing signal that is most influential under conditions of future uncertainty. In conclusion, inhibitory functions of the orbitofrontal cortex may not be restricted to the social context, and the region may code the likely significance of future behavioural options on the basis of whether such options in the past were associated with reward or punishment.

THE MESIAL AND ANTERIOR CINGULATE CIRCUIT

Damage to mesial and anterior cingulate regions (Duffy & Campbell, 1994; Mega & Cummings, 1994; Pennington & Ozonoff, 1996) is, as we saw in the earlier summary, associated with disorders of motivation, exploration, attention, or action. The patient exhibits hypokinesia, apathy, abulia without true dysphoria or depression (i.e. pseudodepression, or simple indifference or disinterest), lack of spontaneity, blunted emotional responsivity, or outright akinetic mutism. Paus, Koski, Caramanos, and Westbury (1998) review 107 blood flow positron emotion tomographic (PET) studies involving the anterior cingulate in normal healthy individuals. They found that task difficulty and the nature of the behavioural response were important determinants of anterior cingulate activity, with increased blood flow with difficult tasks especially in paralimbic and limbic portions of the anterior cingulate. The anterior cingulate was also apparently involved in the control of hand movements, though in a manner distinct from that of the adjacent supplementary motor area. *Supracallosal* regions of the anterior cingulate (connecting primarily with the premotor cortex and dorsolateral prefrontal cortex) were active with hand and other movements, tasks which were difficult or involved recent memory, the early phases of learning, and, especially, the spontaneous initiation of action—all perhaps a function of arousal and attention and involving dopaminergic and noradrenergic modulatory systems. On the other hand, the *subcallosal* region of the anterior cingulate, connecting with the orbitofrontal cortex, amygdala, ventral striatum, and other limbic structures, was apparently more involved in the regulation of autonomic functions such as respiration and heart rate—a visceral motor cortex balancing sympathetic and parasympathetic tone. Thus the anterior cingulate, particularly perhaps its supracallosal regions, may be particularly active under demanding situations that require executive control, divided attention, conflict resolution, error detection, response monitoring, and the initiation and maintenance of appropriate ongoing behaviours (see Awh & Gehring, 1999; Turken & Swick, 1999).

SUPPLEMENTARY MOTOR AREA AND PREMOTOR AREA

In this review of the function of relevant cortical structures, mention has been made of the supplementary motor area and the lateral premotor area, regions which clearly interact (upstream) with the anterior cingulate, and (downstream) with the primary motor cortex. Both, especially perhaps the supplementary motor area, also receive, as we shall see, major input from the globus pallidus of the basal ganglia. The lateral premotor area, mesial supplementary motor area, anterior cingulate, and primary motor cortex all project in an excitatory fashion (glutamatergically) to the ventral horn of the spinal cord via the medullary pyramids (Alexander, 1997). The *lateral premotor area* is particularly active during closed-loop voluntary movements requiring external sensory guidance; lesions result in problems in using sensory cues in the preparation of movement. The (mesially located) *supplementary motor area*, mediating internally generated, intentional movements in the absence of external stimulation, appears to exert an inhibitory effect on the primary motor cortex, with lesions resulting in the release of inhibitory control and alien hand signs. Here, the patient complains of unwelcome, uncontrolled, "autonomous" behaviour of the (often, left) hand. Other manifestations include utilisation behaviour and involuntary grasping. Lesions also lead, conversely, to akinesia and mutism, and parkinsonian deficits. Otherwise the supplementary motor area, from lesion, imaging, and activation studies, is involved in complex motor functions, preparation for movement, motor set (see below), the coordination of bimanual movements, the control of sequential movements, and motor sequence learning. Motor areas exist also (see above) in the anterior cingulate; they are little understood (Alexander, 1997) and seem to involve complex, self-generated, self-initiated movements.

So far the supplementary motor area has been treated as a unitary structure; there are suggestions (Marsden et al., 1996) that anterior regions may be more concerned with self-selection and planning of movements, whereas posterior regions may mediate complex, sequential movements. Similarly, the somatotopically organised caudal area may be more involved in motor *execution*, and the rostral area (with prefrontal input) may be more involved in motor *preparation* (Luppino, Matelli, Camarda, & Rizzolatti, 1993; Marsden et al., 1996).

At this point a note of caution is in order. There may be other fronto-striatal circuits, yet to be identified, additional to the five described here, and mediating just the motor, cognitive, and emotional aspects. There is also probably considerable anatomical and functional interconnectivity between these frontostriatal loops, if only at the cortical level. The same areas, moreover, are likely to be involved in a range of cognitive functions; this may be particularly true of the anterior cingulate. Thus the idea that the latter circuit is essentially facilitatory, and the orbitofrontal inhibitory, is almost certainly going to prove an oversimplification, as neuroimaging evidence is beginning to indicate the involvement, though to varying degrees, of both circuits in both kinds of behaviour. At best we should perhaps view the proposed model as a heuristic guide for explanatory and predictive purposes, and their patterns of functional interconnectivity are almost certainly going to prove more illuminating than a picture of static localisation of function. Finally, we must be wary of reducing the biological substrate of the neuro-developmental disorders exclusively to the frontostriatal loops on a one-to-one basis; several loops are likely to be co-involved in most of the disorders, along with other brain structures or loops, for example frontocerebellar, frontoparietal, and temporolimbic, to name a few.

ACTION, CONSCIOUSNESS AND ATTENTION

Jahanshahi and Frith (1998) note that during learning of a new motor task there is activation of the lateral premotor area, anterior cingulate, dorso-lateral prefrontal cortex, and parietal cortex; deployment of attention increases striatal and cerebellar activation, whereas caudate activity drops when learning is established. When prelearned sequences are run off, the supplementary motor area activates. Thus when subjects *internally* decide on the precise timing of a voluntary, regular, self-initiated action, there is increased activation of the dorsolateral prefrontal cortex, anterior cingulate, supplementary motor area, inferior parietal cortex, putamen, and thalamus. Conversely with *externally* triggered, regular actions where the subject can anticipate, the lateral premotor area, anterior cingulate, inferior parietal cortex, cerebellum, and putamen activate. Generally, the supplementary motor area, putamen, ventrolateral thalamus, anterior cingulate, and dorsolateral prefrontal cortex are all involved in the timing of willed actions. In particular, the supplementary motor area mediates self-initiated, voluntary actions *not* in response to an external signal. Such voluntary actions need to address three strategic questions (Deecke & Lang, 1996):

- *What* to do; the lateral orbitofrontal cortex may eliminate or inhibit what *not* to do.
- *How* to do it; the dorsolateral prefrontal cortex along with the lateral premotor area may mediate goals taking into account the latest sensory information, and the cerebellum may program aspects of automatic execution.
- *When* to do it; this aspect is likely to be mediated by the anterior cingulate (motivational aspects) and supplementary motor area (timing and intentionality).

Change from *reflective*, effortful, deliberate processing to *reflexive*, effortless, routine processing clearly has dramatic correlates in imaged activity. Although the anterior cingulate and dorsolateral prefrontal cortex are active during focused attention, for whatever reason, on a task, or when new rules have to be developed, habit diminishes conscious attention. Although areas active during naive performance become prime candidates for the neural correlates of consciousness (Raichle, 1998), no single unique architecture has emerged as a unifying feature of conscious, reflective performance. Raichle (1998) sees the cortex as being like sections of a symphony orchestra: No one section (or individual) is at all times necessary for the conscious production of music. Rather, there is a distributed process, with participants changing as a function of the strategy adopted (by the dorsolateral prefrontal cortex). Consciousness does not cease when task performance changes from naive, effortful and attention focusing to a practised, effortless response sequence requiring no attention.

Reason, logic, cost–benefit analysis, working memory calculations, and conscious unemotional weighing-up of the pros and cons of a situation are clearly one way, via the dorsolateral prefrontal cortex, of intelligent problem solving in real-life situations. Damasio (1994), however, notes that we also operate in terms of gut feelings, or emotions; he invokes the role of the limbic structure, the amygdala, whose activity can automatically draw our attention, emotionally, to the positive or negative valency associated with a situation's various outcomes. This rapid pathway may allow us unconsciously to avoid or dismiss various alternatives immediately, without further analysis, thereafter allowing the rational dorsolateral prefrontal cortex to perform a final analysis or choice. He sees it as a biasing device that derives from ancestral limbic mechanisms, and which explains intuition (in comparison to the potentially fallible reason); it cannot be excluded from any analysis of apparently intelligent behaviour. Patients with damage here seem unable to make good decisions, in life or experimental situations, even though able otherwise to describe what should be done, and typically show little emotion when choosing bad strategies (Bechara, Damasio, Tranel, & Damasio, 1997; Vogel, 1997). We shall see that the amygdala often has close functional links with the frontostriatal system, especially perhaps in the context of lowered mood and depression.

Thus reasoning follows both rules (explicit or implicit) and hunches triggered by visceral or somatic memory (Adolphs et al., 1996) from background context. Such visceral feelings or hunches may be far more important in real-world problem solving than artificial after-the-event formal logic. Nevertheless the dorsolateral prefrontal cortex integrates both formal rules and informal "gut" feelings, in preparation for action.

No account of the mechanisms of preparation for action would be complete without reference to attentional processes, known to be defective in such a prototypical neurodevelopmental disorder of the frontostriatal system as attention deficit hyperactivity disorder, to say nothing of schizophrenia, autism, and probably Tourette's syndrome. Harris (1995) notes that an attentional system is a basic prerequisite for the selection of information for conscious processing and the deliberate choice of action. Consciousness may be actively (externally) or passively (internally) focused on experience, in a voluntary (by choice) or involuntary (by attraction) fashion. There may be overt orienting, or covert (re)focusing. While attention is not co-extensive with consciousness, the two concepts are clearly interrelated; attention is impossible without full consciousness, though with the latter varying degrees of attention are still possible. Both attention and consciousness seem to imply a unitary focus, as simultaneous states of divided attention or consciousness seem inconceivable, except maybe with division of the forebrain commissures. Attention may drop with fatigue, boredom, intoxication, or reticular damage, and increase with stimulants. A network of regions, rather than any single system, is involved for orientation, selective detection, and sustained alert vigilance:

- Posteriorparietal damage → "sticky" problems of disengagement from a locus.
- Superior collicular damage → problems in shifting attention to a new locus.
- Damage to the lateral pulvinar nucleus of the thalamus → problems in covert orienting and the "engage" function.

SUMMARY AND CONCLUSIONS

Long held to be functionally silent, though also long suspected to play a role in higher cognitive processes, the frontal regions may be the seat of our personalities, and underlie the very essence of our humanity. Although there is debate as to whether they have in fact undergone relatively the greatest evolutionary development of the brain in our species, there is no denying their importance in the frontostriatal neurodevelopmental disorders of profound psychiatric importance. In preparation for action, there is an anterior–posterior gradient or hierarchy, each level priming the next one "down": The dorsolateral prefrontal cortex may be responsible for the highest and most global plans, strategies, and schemata; the lateral premotor area for control of spatial trajectory and sequencing, particularly in response to external events; the supplementary motor area for internally driven release of sequential behaviour; the primary motor cortex for elementary motor acts, control of specific muscle groups, and response synergies; the basal ganglia and cerebellum (the old "extrapyramidal" motor system) for the more automatic aspects, in contrast to deliberate, conscious, volitional action of largely novel behaviours.

Thus schemata for purposeful action are subject to the above hierarchical levels of control, for volition, decision making, and voluntary action, with, progressively, the formulation of goals, intention to act, selection of responses, programming of behaviour, and initiation of action. To achieve such behaviour, the frontal structures are massively interconnected with parietal, temporal, and limbic regions, basal ganglia and cerebellum, with ascending modulatory control from at least three major neurotransmitter systems: dopaminergic, noradrenergic, and serotonergic. Essential as they are for conceptual thought, abstraction from perceptual experience, the manipulation of abstract ideas, the maintenance or shifting of set and attention, and the initiation or withholding of responses, the frontal regions seem particularly vulnerable, perhaps via relatively late maturation, to a range of neurodevelopmental disorders. It is these frontostriatal disorders with which this book is concerned: Tourette's syndrome, attention deficit hyperactivity disorder, obsessive compulsive disorder, schizophrenia, autism, and depression.

Five parallel, segregated circuits have been identified in the above frontostriatal system. They mediate the cognitive, motor, and emotional aspects of higher human behaviour, and all possess a common structure and organisation in the form of a closed loop from a particular cortical origin, via the basal ganglia (striatum to globus pallidus, via a direct, facilitatory, or indirect, inhibitory pathway), and back to the particular locus of cortical origin; specific cortical inputs from other regions add to the specificity and diversity of processing of each of the five parallel, segregated, frontostriatal circuits. Changes, structural or more commonly perhaps functional, in specific pathways or groups of pathways characterise the six frontostriatal disorders—"disorders" which in low "dosage" or penetrance may even play an adaptive role with respect to environmental pressures, and may therefore be perpetuated in the genome. At the very least, a particular frontostriatal configuration may characterise each of our own highly individual personalities, as cautious, risk taking, obsessive, paranoid, hypomanic, salacious, "rude", and so on.

Of the above five circuits, we shall not be greatly concerned with the skeletomotor or oculomotor, with their control of motor reactivity, though we should note, in the context of the former, an important division between two premotor areas: the (mesially located) supplementary motor area and the (lateral) premotor area. The *supplementary motor area* may mediate internally generated, intentional movements in the absence of external stimuli. It is responsible for complex motor functions including bimanual coordination, motor set, and preparation for action; an anterior compartment has been identified, which may mediate self-selection and movement planning, and a posterior compartment, which may be more concerned with complex movement sequences. Damage generally is associated with corresponding deficits, together with alien hand signs and utilisation behaviour. Similarly, a somatotopically organised caudal region may mediate motor execution, and a rostral region with prefrontal input may handle motor preparation. The *lateral premotor area*, with its extensive cerebellar and parietal input, may be concerned more with closed-loop voluntary movements requiring external sensory guidance.

The remaining three parallel, segregated circuits with which we are directly concerned include the dorsolateral prefrontal, the (lateral) orbitofrontal, and the (mesial) anterior cingulate. The *dorsolateral prefrontal* circuit is concerned with the highest cognitive or "executive" functions, which include the capacity to operate via self-direction or without external guidance, the organisation of new behaviours, goal direction, strategy, planning, cognitive flexibility, the maintenance or shifting of set and attention, problem solving, and judgement. Damage, not surprisingly, is associated with the "dysexecutive syndrome".

The *lateral orbitofrontal* circuit is involved with social restraint, empathy, inhibition of interference from external cues, self-monitoring, and the social aspects of personality. Damage or dysfunction in one or other direction results in disinhibition, tactlessness, lack of empathy, inappropriate behaviour, sociopathy, hypomania, explosive aggression, and obsessions or compulsions. Located at the interface between sensory and association cortices, limbic structures, and the autonomic nervous system, this circuit is also important in dopaminergically mediated reinforcement processes, the modulation of behaviour in the face of changing contingencies of reinforcement, emotionality, and positive and negative (i.e. depressed) mood.

The mesially located *anterior cingulate* circuit mediates initiation of action, response intention, and focused attention, with damage resulting in reduced initiative, apathy, disorders of motivation, attention, and exploration.

Between them, these five circuits, which constitute the frontostriatal system, enable us when performing deliberate voluntary actions to decide *what* to do, and *how* and *when* to do it. Clearly they participate in the experience of consciousness, though none is likely to be unique to that subjective state, and other regions are likely to be involved. Nor are all actions governed by deliberate, conscious choice; "gut feelings", via the amygdala, a structure closely associated with the frontostriatal system, unconsciously bias our choices when they are available. Nor can we identify attention with consciousness, though equally clearly the two concepts have much in common; at the very least both seem to involve a unitary focus, as it is difficult to conceive of simultaneous states of divided consciousness or attention, except perhaps in split-brain preparations or patients with divided forebrain commissures.

FURTHER READING

Alexander, G.E. (1997). Anatomy of the basal ganglia and related motor structures. In R.L. Watts & W.C. Koller (Eds.), *Movement disorders: Neurologic principles and practice* (pp. 73–83). New York: McGraw-Hill.

Changeux, J.-P., & Dehaene, S. (1996). Neuronal models of cognitive functions associated with the prefrontal cortex. In A.R. Damasio, H. Damasio, & Y. Christen (Eds.), *Neurobiology of decision-making* (pp. 125–140). New York: Springer.

Deecke, L., & Lang, W. (1996). Generation of movement-related potentials and fields in the supplementary sensorimotor area and the primary motor area. In H.O. Lüders (Ed.), *Advances in neurology: Supplementary sensorimotor area* (Vol. 70, pp. 127–146). Philadelphia: Lippincott-Raven.

Duffy, J.D., & Campbell, J.J. (1994). The regional prefrontal syndromes: A theoretical and clinical overview. *Journal of Neuropsychiatry, 6*, 379–387.

Foti, D.J., & Cummings, J.L. (1997). Neurobehavioral aspects of movement disorders. In R.L. Watts & W.C. Koller (Eds.), *Movement disorders: Neurologic principles and practice* (pp. 15–30). New York: McGraw-Hill.

Frith, C., & Dolan, R. (1997). The role of the prefrontal cortex in higher cognitive functions. In M. Ito (Ed.), *Brain and mind* (pp. 323–337). New York: Elsevier.

Fuster, J.M. (1999a). Synopsis of function and dysfunction of the frontal lobe. *Acta Psychiatrica Scandinavica, 99*, 51–57.

Fuster, J.M. (1999b). *The prefrontal cortex: Anatomy, physiology and neuropsychology of the frontal lobe* (3rd ed.). Philadelphia: Lippincott-Raven.

Gualtieri, C.T. (1995). The contributions of the frontal lobes to a theory of psychopathology. In J.J. Ratey (Ed.), *Neuropsychiatry of personality disorders* (pp. 149–171). Oxford: Blackwell Science.

Hauser, M. (1999). Perseveration, inhibition and the prefrontal cortex: A new look. *Current Opinion in Neurobiology, 9*, 214–222.

Jahanshahi, M., & Frith, C.D. (1998). Willed action and its impairments. *Cognitive Neuro-psychology, 15*, 483–533.

Jonides, J., & Smith, E.E. (1997). The architecture of working memory. In M.D. Rugg (Ed.), *Cognitive neuroscience* (pp. 243–276). Cambridge, MA: MIT Press.

Mega, M.S., Cummings, J.L., Salloway, S., & Malloy, P. (1997). The limbic system: An anatomic, phylogenetic and clinical perspective. *Journal of Neuropsychiatry, 9*, 315–330.

Mesulam, M.-M. (1998). From sensation to cognition. *Brain, 121*, 1013–1052.

Miller, B., & Cummings, J.L. (1999). *The human frontal lobes: Functions and dysfunctions.* New York: Guilford Press.

Parkin, A. (1998). The central executive does not exist. *Journal of the International Neuropsychological Society, 4*, 518–522.

Pennington, B.F., & Ozonoff, S. (1996). Executive functions and developmental psychopathology. *Journal of Child Psychology and Psychiatry, 37*, 51–87.

Petrides, M. (1998). Frontal lobes and behavior. In L. Squire & S. Kosslyn (Eds.), *Findings and current opinion in cognitive neuroscience.* Cambridge, MA: MIT Press.

Posner, M.I., & DiGirolamo, G. (1998). Executive attention: Conflict, target detection and cognitive control. In R. Parasuraman (Ed.), *The attentive brain* (pp. 401–423). Cambridge, MA: MIT Press.

Roberts, A.C., Robbins, T.W., & Weiskrantz, L. (Eds.) (1998). *The prefrontal cortex: Executive and cognitive functions.* Oxford: Oxford University Press.

Roland, P.E., & Zilles, K. (1998). Functions and structures of the motor cortices in humans. In L. Squire & S. Kosslyn (Eds.), *Findings and current opinion in cognitive neuroscience* (pp. 247–256). Cambridge, MA: MIT Press.

Smith, E.E., & Jonides, J. (1999). Storage and executive processes in the frontal lobes. *Science, 283*, 1657–1661.

Stuss, D.T., Alexander, M.P., & Benson, D.F. (1997). Frontal lobe functions. In M.R. Trimble & J.L. Cummings (Eds.), *Contemporary behavioral neurology* (pp. 169–186). New York: Butterworth-Heinemann.

Tanji, J. (1998). New concepts of the supplementary motor area. In L. Squire & S. Kosslyn (Eds.), *Findings and current opinion in cognitive neuroscience.* Cambridge, MA: MIT Press.

Zald, D.H., & Kim, S.W. (1996). Anatomy and function of the orbitofrontal cortex II: Function and relevance to obsessive compulsive disorder. *Journal of Neuropsychiatry and Clinical Neurosciences, 8*, 249–261.

CHAPTER THREE

The basal ganglia

We never do anything well till we cease to think about the manner of doing it.
—*On Prejudice*, William Hazlitt, 1778–1830

INTRODUCTION

The compartments of the frontal lobes, described in the previous chapter, constitute part of the frontostriatal system; the rest comprise the basal ganglia, which, along with the cerebellum, are commonly referred to as the extrapyramidal system. In this chapter we shall describe the direct (facilitatory) and indirect (inhibitory) pathways that make up each of the five parallel, segregated, frontostriatal circuits. We shall review the likely roles of the basal ganglia in selecting and amplifying wanted movements, action, and thought patterns, and inhibiting unwanted activities, via these two pathways respectively. We shall also address other, probably related, roles that have been proposed for basal ganglia function, such as optimising patterns of motor activity in target attainment, sequencing movement complexes in terms of tonic "set" and phasic "cue" functions, respectively for controlling movement amplitude and for mediating serial release, and "chunking" and "binding" functions. Although many of these proposed functions are both hypothetical and mutually overlapping, they go some way towards explaining breakdown of function in the neurodegenerative disorders of ageing, such as Parkinson's and Huntington's diseases, and the neurodevelopmental, "psychiatric" conditions with which this book is concerned.

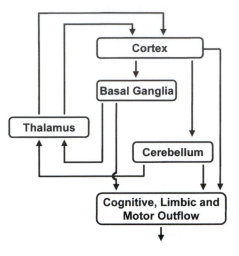

Figure 3.1.   Cortico-thalamo-cortical re-entrant loops of the basal ganglia and cerebellum.

PRELIMINARY CONSIDERATIONS

As Brown and Marsden (1998) observe, so little is known about the dark basements of the mind, the basal ganglia. The basal ganglia and cerebellum constitute two, parallel, re-entrant processing stations that receive separate but largely similar inputs from widespread cortical regions, particularly the motor, premotor, and somatosensory cortices, and return their own influences on response processes to specific and largely separate portions of the precentral motor fields, via the ventrolateral motor thalamus (Alexander, 1997) (see Figure 3.1). There is also some outflow from both basal ganglia and cerebellum to brainstem descending pathways. However, while the basal ganglia may play a more inhibitory role, the cerebellum is essentially excitatory or facilitatory (Mink, 1998). Although both systems are traditionally regarded as extrapyramidal and modulatory, with respect to the (cortical) pyramidal motor system, the cerebellum is likely to be phylogenetically the more ancient.

Both systems, basal ganglia and cerebellum, are organised for parallel processing, with multiple, functionally segregated channels passing through each of the constituent nuclei. Thus in the cerebellum, the vestibular/oculomotor, spinal, and cerebral systems each possess characteristic inputs and outputs through corresponding functional channels via cerebellar output nuclei (Alexander, 1997); these functional subdivisions are maintained along the re-entrant cerebellothalamic pathways.

PHYSIOLOGY OF THE BASAL GANGLIA

Although the possible roles of the basal ganglia are still a matter of debate (and see below), the structure clearly is important in scaling the size of initial agonist bursts in limb movements, reinforcing the voluntary command and inhibiting inappropriate electromyographic activity (Berardelli, Hallett, Rothwell, & Marsden, 1996). The corticospinal tract also has a role in determining the spatial and temporal recruitment of motor units, whereas the cerebellum may be involved in timing voluntary bursts and in the physical implementation of muscle force. Cerebellar damage thus results in deficits in motor sequence learning. The structure may operate as an error detector or comparator (Hazeltine, Grafton, & Ivry, 1997), comparing expectancies with actual movements; as learning proceeds and expectancies increasingly match the required movements, less cerebellar processing may be engaged, with the actual representations of the motor sequences and concomitant increases in brain activity moving elsewhere, to the basal ganglia and supplementary motor area (though see Ceballos-Baumann & Brooks, 1997, and following).

The current anatomical model (see Parent & Cicchetti, 1998) proposes that the striatum (caudate and putamen) constitutes the input stage of the basal ganglia and receives glutamatergic excitatory input. The globus pallidus interna and substantia nigra reticulata constitute the major output nuclei, exerting, as far as the motor system is concerned, a tonic inhibitory influence on the excitatory premotor neurones in the ventral thalamus (see Figure 3.2).

The striatum itself is divided into a matrix compartment (80% of the striatum), the remaining 20% consisting of striasomes or island patches that interdigitate throughout the matrix (Young & Penney, 1998). Limbic and paralimbic inputs from regions including the orbitofrontal cortex project via the ventral pathway (see later) to the striasomes, whereas matrix neurones receive largely motor, sensory and supplementary motor area cortical input along dorsal pathways. Thus organisation of the striatum allows extensive axon collaterals to surround and inhibit other striatal neurones; unwanted behaviours can be inhibited in the striatum, and desired ones facilitated, thereby coordinating complex behaviours or motor programs (Young & Penney, 1998).

The ventral system of the basal ganglia involves nuclei lying ventrally to the striatum, including the nucleus accumbens, olfactory tubercle, and ventral pallidum. It receives input from limbic and olfactory areas of the cortex, including the amygdala and hippocampus. It receives noradrenergic, serotonergic, and dopaminergic input like the striatum, but (in the case of dopamine) from the ventral tegmental area rather than from the substantia nigra compacta, as in the case of the motor system. The ventral pallidum is

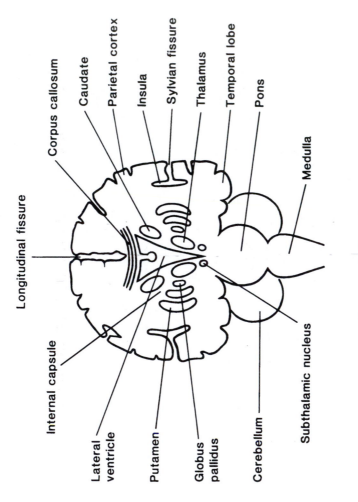

Longitudinal fissure

Corpus callosum

Caudate

Parietal cortex

Insula

Sylvian fissure

Thalamus

Temporal lobe

Pons

Medulla

Internal capsule

Lateral ventricle

Putamen

Globus pallidus

Cerebellum

Subthalamic nucleus

Coronal Section

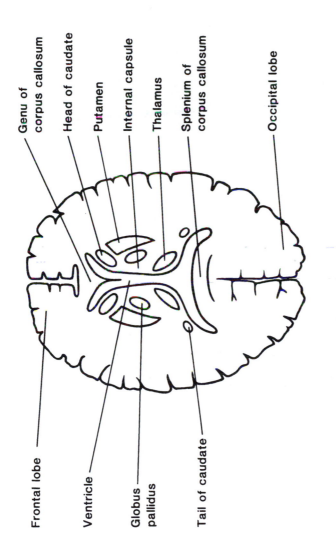

Genu of
corpus callosum

Head of caudate

Putamen

Internal capsule

Thalamus

Splenium of
corpus callosum

Occipital lobe

Frontal lobe

Ventricle

Globus
pallidus

Tail of caudate

Horizontal Section Through The Striatum

Figure 3.2. Structures in the basal ganglia: coronal section (top) and horizontal section (bottom). The representation is schematic only.

analogous to the globus pallidus. The system outputs via the dorsomedial nucleus of the thalamus and thence to the limbic cortex. It is involved in motivation and emotion, and, analogously to the motor role of the basal ganglia, it may act to suppress or select potentially competing limbic mechanisms (Mink, 1998).

Stimulation of the ventral striatum (including the nucleus accumbens) may elicit locomotion, licking, chewing, swallowing, and other stereotypic behaviours which we shall encounter in Tourette's syndrome (Groenewegen, Wright, & Beijer, 1996). Ventral striatopallidal pathways thus project ultimately to a mesencephalic locomotor region, a major rhythmogenic area regulating locomotion, mastication, and sleep/waking activity, and which may be conceived of as an emotional motor system through which limbic forebrain structures influence the premotor regions (supplementary motor area and premotor area). In association with the periaqueductal grey, it mediates species-specific emotional, social, reproductive, nest-building, and hygienic behaviours, all of which have correlates in obsessive compulsive disorder.

DIRECT AND INDIRECT PATHWAYS

All five circuits, perhaps most clearly in the archetypal skeletomotor circuit, according to the traditional scheme are additionally seen to be constituted by a direct pathway, responsible for initiating responses and an indirect, inhibitory pathway (Parent & Cicchetti, 1998) (see Figure 3.3). (Note that here and elsewhere in this book the terms "inhibitory" and "excitatory" refer to functional effects upon other systems, and not to the nature of postsynaptic potentials. Thus we shall see that these effects are mediated by striatal dopamine receptors.) The direct pathway originates from inhibitory striatal neurones that project monosynaptically (via GABA, dynorphin, and substance P) to the globus pallidus interna and substantia nigra reticulata. The indirect pathway similarly arises from inhibitory (GABA and enkephalin) striatal neurones that project polysynaptically via the globus pallidus externa and subthalamic nucleus to the globus pallidus interna and the substantia nigra reticulata. This pathway therefore comprises inhibitory projections from the striatum to the globus pallidus externa, followed by similar inhibitory projections to the subthalamic nucleus, and excitatory glutamatergic projections from the subthalamic nucleus to the globus pallidus interna/substantia nigra reticulata. At the level of the striatum, dopamine acting on medium spiny neurones facilitates transmission along the direct pathway, reducing the inhibitory output of the basal ganglia and thereby increasing thalamocortical output; dopamine similarly inhibits transmission along the indirect pathway, increasing the inhibitory basal ganglia output and thereby reducing thalamocortical output. Thus these two

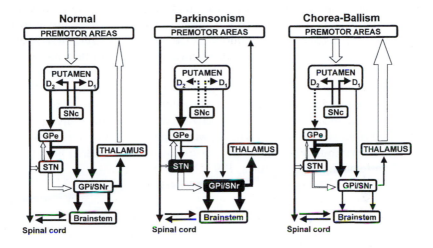

Figure 3.3.   The direct (facilitatory, open connections) and indirect (inhibitory, filled connections) pathways through the basal ganglia under normal healthy conditions (left), parkinsonian hypokinesia (middle), and huntingtonian chorea or ballism (right). D_1, D_2 = dopamine D_1 and D_2 receptors; SNc = substantia nigra pars compacta; SNr = substantia nigra pars reticulata; GPe = globus pallidus externa; GPi = globus pallidus interna; STN = subthalamic nucleus. [Adapted, modified and redrawn from Obeso, J.A. & Rodriguez, M.C. (1997). Basal ganglia pathology: A critical review. In J.A. Obeso, M.R. DeLong, C. Ohye, & C.D. Marsden (Eds.), *The basal ganglia and new surgical approaches for Parkinson's disease: Advances in neurology* (Vol. 74, pp. 3–16). Philadelphia: Lippencroft-Raven.]

opposing and normally balanced effects, mediated respectively by dopamine D1 and D2 receptors, result respectively in positive and negative feedback effects; nigrostriatal dopamine will enhance positive and suppress negative feedback, whereas its absence, as in Parkinson's disease, will have the opposite, hypokinetic effect. Hyperkinesia, as in the chorea of early Huntington's disease, is conversely seen as due to degeneration of inhibitory striatal neurones projecting via the indirect pathway to the globus pallidus externa; resultant globus pallidus externa hyperactivity, due to loss of inhibition, will lead to subthalamic nucleus inhibition, reduced excitatory drive to the globus pallidus interna/substantia nigra reticulata, and reduced GABAergic inhibition of the thalamus (Alexander, 1997; Parent & Cicchetti, 1998; Wichmann & DeLong, 1997). (Later in the disorder, parkinsonian hypokinesia will result from additional degeneration of inhibitory striatal output neurones to the globus pallidus interna, whose resultant disinhibition will reduce the chorea; thus both the direct and indirect pathway come to be affected in Huntington's disease.) Similarly, disturbances of the circuitry of the ventral striatum or pallidum may result in failure of the basal ganglia to suppress a range of motor, cognitive, or limbic responses, with release of tics or ritualistic behaviour of Tourette's syndrome and obsessive compulsive disorder. In this way, the healthy basal ganglia are seen to select and amplify wanted movements and action patterns via the direct pathway, and to inhibit unwanted movements via the indirect pathway. The system thus modulates corticostriatal transmission and fine-tunes large portions of the frontal cortex responsible for movement, cognitive, and limbic functions. Mechanisms are best understood in the motor circuit, but are presumed to operate similarly in all the rest. Thus, as we saw in the last chapter, five parallel segregated circuits have been identified, which mediate motor, cognitive, and emotional behaviour. They all project via specific thalamic nuclei back to the frontal cortex (Foti & Cummings, 1997; Mink 1998):

- Skeletomotor—ventralis lateralis, pars oralis and medialis.
- Oculomotor—ventralis anterior, pars magnocellularis, and medialis dorsalis, pars paralamellaris.
- Dorsolateral prefrontal—ventralis anterior, pars parvocellularis, and medialis dorsalis, pars parvocellularis.
- Lateral orbitofrontal—ventralis anterior, pars magnocellularis, and medialis dorsalis, pars magnocellularis.
- Anterior cingulate—medialis dorsalis, pars posteromedialis.

The above model clearly explains in a reasonably satisfactory fashion the slowness of movement initiation (akinesia) in Parkinson's disease, and slowness of execution (bradykinesia). Aberrantly enhanced inhibition of thalamocortical activity may also explain parkinsonian rigidity and tremor (Berardelli et al., 1996). Drug-induced dyskinesia from chronic dopaminergic medication may shift the balance of activity towards the direct pathway (Wichmann & DeLong, 1997), introducing "noise" into the motor system. Dystonia, also due to chronic medication, may similarly result from inappropriate overactivity of the basal ganglia, with failure to suppress unwanted muscle contraction during limb movement; it is, however, less well understood (Wichmann & DeLong, 1997).

Parent and Cicchetti (1998) note that the above model is nevertheless probably an oversimplification, anatomically, functionally, and clinically. Thus lesions (destructive, or functional, by deep brain stimulation) to the ventral thalamus may abolish contralateral parkinsonian tremor, dyskinesia, and rigidity, and even improve bradykinesia by reducing excess inhibition of the supplementary motor area—and indeed such surgery is employed therapeutically. Theoretically, however, symptoms should worsen through destruction of the positive cortical feedback element of the (excitatory) direct pathway. Moreover the intervention has very little effect on movement initiation (akinesia) in Parkinson's disease. Conversely, similar subthalamic nucleus lesions relieve bradykinesia and induce dyskinesia. It is possible that the motor thalamus functions better with no pallidal input than with misinformation. Alternatively, once optimised by the basal ganglia, a motor program may be moved to the cerebellum, with its future automatic running no longer requiring pallidal output (Ceballos-Baumann & Brooks, 1997). Thus parkinsonian patients can still perform *previously learned* tasks, and pallidotomy may alleviate rigidity without impairing the automatic running of a motor program.

FUNCTIONS OF THE BASAL GANGLIA

What then might be the general functions of the basal ganglia? Clearly the structures receive a broad spectrum of inputs, and information conveyed to them is processed to produce a focused output to areas of the frontal lobes and brainstem that are involved in the planning and production of movement. It used to be believed that the basal ganglia store motor programs, which are then called up and sent to the motor cortex for execution. However, the basal ganglia are active too late in relation to movement and the brain mechanisms known to be involved in its initiation. They clearly modulate, facilitate, and fine-tune the activity of large portions of the frontal cortex involved in movement, cognitive function, and emotional limbic activity. They are also clearly involved in planning, initiating, and executing movements, in terms of speed, sequencing, and fluidity, though their exact operations are not fully understood, and the basic parameters of movement are likely to be mediated by the cerebellum (Brooks, 1996; Ceballos-Baumann & Brooks, 1997).

One role may be to act as a filter, via the direct (facilitatory) and indirect (inhibitory) pathways, selecting certain courses of action for release and inhibiting others. (As we saw, an overactive direct pathway would result in unwanted movement sequences or maybe thoughts, and an overactive indirect pathway in poverty of movement.) Hayes, Davidson, Keele, and Rafal (1998) extend this concept when they argue that the basal ganglia are involved in shifting attentional set, at both a motor and cognitive level. However, they note discrepancies in the literature (Parkinson's patients seem to have problems *holding* attention) and debate whether the basal ganglia may mediate set-switching efficiency, while the closely associated frontal and prefrontal structures may mediate the quality of execution and strategic control. Set switching, they observe, may require both inhibiting (via the indirect pathway) prior sets and activating (via the direct pathway) new sets.

Another role of the basal ganglia may be to optimise the pattern of muscular activity employed by a limb to reach its target once a motor decision has been taken at a higher cortical level, whether the movement is in response to an external cue or event, or is self-initiated (Brooks, 1996). Once a program has been so optimised, it can be released through the supplementary motor area and relayed to the primary motor cortex for execution, and also to the cerebellum for it to be automated (Ceballos-Baumann & Brooks, 1997). Damage to the basal ganglia through Parkinson's disease will impair such optimisation or scaling of amplitude or velocity, resulting in ineffective muscular contractions and co-contractions (rigidity and dyskinesia). Hence pallidotomy *may* help such performance as long as patients perform previously learned rather than novel movements, as pallidotomy may reduce rigidity without affecting the automatic, cerebellar running of learned motor programs. While the cerebellum is also likely to help control the basic parameters of movement (force, velocity, and amplitude), along with the sensorimotor cortex, a continuing involvement of the basal ganglia in amplitude scaling seems probable (Wichmann & DeLong, 1997). This may also be achieved by altering the relative balance of the direct and indirect pathways.

In this way the basal ganglia may also function, as many have proposed, in sequencing movements or movement complexes, particularly in response to internal rather than external cueing events (Middleton & Strick, 1997; Wichmann & DeLong, 1997). Indeed the supplementary motor area, when signalled by the basal ganglia, may be the locus for such internally generated volitional release, whereas the lateral premotor area may respond to external sensory events in release of sequential activities, whether cognitive or motor (Cunnington, Bradshaw, & Iansek, 1996).

Iansek et al. (1995) combine the ideas of amplitude scaling and internal cueing into a model of "set" and "cue"; according to this account, the basal ganglia scale the magnitude (large or small amplitude) of movements to fit the immediate context (*set*), together with the provision of an internally generated *cue* in the form of a premovement potential. This cue may be employed by cortical motor areas to guide the termination of ongoing movement and the initiation of subsequent movements in a sequence. In the absence of external cues, individuals with Parkinson's disease will generate premovement potentials over the supplementary area that are delayed relative to those of controls, and show a prolonged peak and slower decline from peak than controls (Cunnington, Iansek, Bradshaw, & Phillips, 1995). Delayed and prolonged cueing may explain progressive slowing in an automatic movement sequence.

At a neuronal level, according to this model (Iansek et al., 1995), motor set may thus be represented by a sustained (*tonic*) neuronal discharge, the premovement or readiness potential (*Bereitschaftspotential*) over the supplementary motor area, while *cue* is represented by *phasic* neuronal activity generated towards the end of a cued movement, preparatory to the release

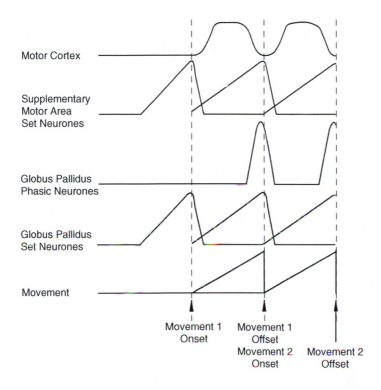

Figure 3.4.   Hypothetical activity level changes over time in a sequence of movements (Movement 1 onset; Movement 1 offset, Movement 2 onset; Movement 2 offset), at the levels of the globus pallidus (set and phasic neurones), supplementary motor area (set neurones), and motor cortex.

of the next upcoming movement (see Figure 3.4). When movement is *externally* cued or driven, supplementary motor area neurones demonstrate discharge increments (set-related activity) that terminate at about the time of the external cue signalling the initiation of the motor event. Around the end of a given submovement, cue-related phasic discharge from the globus pallidus acts to internally signal the end of that motor event. This phasic activity is only generated for a predictable event, and development of the strength of the discharge occurs over a number of repetitions of the task. This discharge intensity is dependent upon the automatic nature of the sequence, disappearing for novel events. The phasic discharge of globus pallidus neurones for a current motor event terminates set-related activity in the supplementary motor area for the *next* motor event, to enable that motor event to execute. Thus the correct sequence can be run in automatic mode. The globus pallidus neurones also discharge in a *tonic* manner in anticipation of a motor event, in a similar fashion to the set-related pre-movement potential over the supplementary motor area occurring only for predictable events under automatic control. Thus a movement plan, once selected by the premotor area, is held in readiness until completely executed in the premotor area or supplementary motor area by tonic neuronal activity. The supplementary motor area has the appropriate neuronal infrastructure to initiate running of the motor plan: set, cue, and movement. Once the plan is initiated, the basal ganglia are activated; tonic activity from the globus pallidus contributes to the preselected level of cortical set and provides the additional necessary internal cue to run the movement sequence to completion, by interaction with the supplementary motor area. The basal ganglia are, however, only utilised for automatic movement sequences—those aspects of movement that are most compromised in Parkinson's disease, where provision of appropriate external cues and/or attentional set can partly compensate for deficit. The electroencephalo-graphic correlates of set and cue in normality and disease, and the effects of attention and of imagining movement, have been documented by Cunnington, Iansek, Bradshaw, and Phillips (1995, 1996), Cunnington, Iansek, Johnson, and Bradshaw (1997), and Cunnington, Iansek, and Bradshaw (1999a, b). In summary, according to this hypothesis, the motor functions of the basal ganglia are:

- To provide the motor (and probably also cognitive and limbic) cortical regions with set-related activity to maintain movement plans in readiness.
- To provide internal cues to enable components of the movement plan to be read in the correct order and timing.

Graybiel (1998) also addresses the concept of control of sequential motor or cognitive activity when she argues that a function of the striatum may be to "*chunk*" action (or thought) repertoires, without conscious supervision. (Indeed, just as introspection is said to spoil an otherwise perfect golf swing, so supervisory attention, necessary only in the acquisition of a motor or "thought" program, will disrupt an acquired and practised train; conversely, when performance of an acquired and practised train is detrimentally affected by Parkinson's disease, partial compensation may, as we saw earlier, be possible by the patient deliberately deploying conscious supervisory attention.) Thus Graybiel sees the basal ganglia as promoting the auto-matised building-up of performance units that can be implemented in a particular temporal order—a sensorimotor form of chunking. She sees the basal ganglia as functioning in some forms of implicit or habit learning that is characterised by a lack of awareness of the algorithm that is learned, and is distinct from the explicit learning mediated by the hippocampus and medial temporal cortex. Thus, as evidenced by imaging, different regions of the basal ganglia and frontostriatal circuitry may be important for the production of habitual or automatic responses (putamen, premotor cortex, supplementary motor area), and for the acquisition of new learning or *conscious monitoring* of old (caudate, anterior prefrontal cortex, anterior cingulate).

Brown and Marsden (1998) promote a related idea, that the basal ganglia are involved in a "binding" function, by facilitating the synchronisation of cortical activity that underlies the selection and promulgation of appropriate sequences or groupings of thoughts or actions. Binding has long been hypothesised to operate via coherent electrical activity in the gamma band (30–50 Hz) to synchronise the processing of the various disparate but temporarily co-occurring sensory qualities ("qualia"); these qualia go to make up or characterise a particular object (heavy, metallic, shiny, valuable, supports candles, used during romantic dinners, a possible heirloom—a silver candlestick). Thus Brown and Marsden (1998) invoke the need for a form of binding of input to output, to permit a sequence of thoughts to call up a motor program. Under the agency of the basal ganglia, via gamma band activity, appropriate processing elements in the sensorimotor cortex, lateral premotor area, mesial supplementary motor area, anterior cingulate, dorsolateral prefrontal cortex, and orbitofrontal cortex may be "bound" and synchronised. The authors cite electrophysiological evidence (e.g. the "Piper" rhythm) in support of such a hypothesis, and invoke activity of the direct and indirect pathways and the ventrolateral thalamus (which normally is active at approximately 40 Hz) in the realisation, or break-up, of such binding. Quite independently, Plenz and Kital (1999; see also commentary by Wichmann & DeLong, 1999) propose that within the basal ganglia a pacemaker is formed by a loop through the subthalamic nucleus and globus pallidus externa, to synchronise rhythmic oscillatory bursting; such activity is seen to underlie both parkinsonian tremor and binding processes. We shall subsequently consider whether basal ganglia involvement in schizophrenia reflects breakdown of the binding process in that disorder.

In conclusion, a variety of roles, not mutually exclusive, have been proposed for the basal ganglia:

- Filtering, selecting, and inhibiting action sequences.
- Optimising (scaling) the pattern of activity to reach a target.
- Movement sequencing, particularly in response to internal cues.
- Provision of "set" and "cue" for the automatic control of behaviour.
- Chunking of repertoires.
- Binding or synchronising cortical activity, to achieve coherent responding.

SUPPLEMENTARY MOTOR AREA AND BASAL GANGLIA

In view of the close anatomical and functional association between the basal ganglia and the supplementary motor area, we should briefly review the latter's possible role in the elaboration of behaviour. In any action, a decision has to be made as to *what* to do, *how* to do it, and *when* it should be done (Deecke & Lang, 1996). All three strategic decisions involve the frontal cortex. With respect to what to do, the lateral orbitofrontal cortex, maybe via eliminating what not to do, may be involved, as damage can lead to inappropriate behaviour. With respect to *how* it should be done, the dorso-lateral prefrontal cortex and premotor cortex are likely to be involved. *When* to do it is very much the province of the supplementary motor area and anterior cingulate, with respect to intention, preparation, and voluntary self-initiation of actions. Thus the supplementary motor area, as evidenced by electrophysiological and lesion studies, is involved in the timing of initiation of complex voluntary movements, and their preparation, temporal co-ordination and sequencing, unimanual and perhaps especially bimanual. While supplementary motor area lesions may result in akinesia and mutism, the region may also have a separate, inhibitory effect upon the primary motor cortex, as supplementary motor area lesions can result in release of inhibitory control, utilisation behaviour, and involuntary grasping (Alexander, 1997). Although the supplementary motor area was tradition-ally considered to manage complex movements, and the primary motor cortex discrete, simple, single muscular responses, recent evidence (Obeso, Rodriguez, & DeLong, 1997) indicates that the primary motor cortex is responsible for controlling sets of synergistic muscles, and may be arranged almost like a library of books, any one or several of which may be selected for the mediation of a range of quite complex action sequences.

SUMMARY AND CONCLUSIONS

The two major constituents of the extrapyramidal motor system—the basal ganglia and the cerebellum—both constitute closed parallel, segregated, re-entrant loops from and back to largely cortical places of origin. The basal ganglia, phylogenetically the more recent, may play a relatively more inhibitory role, via their inhibitory output to the thalamus; the more ancient cerebellum, conversely, may play a more facilitatory role, and act as an error detector or comparator. In both cases, multiple, functionally segre-gated channels each pass through their own specific sets of nuclei. In the basal ganglia, the striatum (constituted by the caudate with its largely cognitive and limbic functions, and the largely motor putamen) acts as an input stage, while the globus pallidus serves as output to the thalamus. While the motor functions, compromised in Parkinson's disease, are fairly easy to model, the limbic basal ganglia are involved in considerably more complex emotional, social, reproductive, hygienic, and stereotypic behaviours that may be caricatured in such disorders as Tourette's syndrome and obsessive compulsive disorder.

Through each of the five segregated frontostriatal circuits—the motor, oculomotor, dorsolateral prefrontal, lateral orbitofrontal, and mesial anterior cingulate—run two pathways between striatum and globus pallidus: the direct and the indirect. The direct pathway, with dopamine D1 striatal receptors, is excitatory in its overall thalamocortical influence, whereas the indirect, with dopamine D2 striatal receptors, has an overall inhibitory effect. Normally these two influences are maintained in a balanced equilibrium for the release of wanted and inhibition of unwanted behaviour or action patterns; frontostriatal disorders may thus result in hyperkinetic release of unwanted behaviours (e.g. tics in Tourette's syndrome, chorea in Huntington's disease) through relative excess activity in the direct pathway, or hypokinetic retardation, as in melancholic depression or parkinsonian or schizophrenic akinesia. Simplistically, the basal ganglia thus serve to select and amplify wanted movements, action, or thought patterns, or inhibit unwanted behaviours; however, this may prove to be an oversimplification anatomically, functionally, and clinically, as evidenced by recent therapeutic lesion studies.

Apart therefore from acting as a filter, to modulate, facilitate, and fine-tune activity within the frontal cortex, and thereby control motor, cognitive, and emotional reactivity, the basal ganglia, in conjunction with the frontostriatal system proper, may also perform a range of other related, overlapping functions. These include planning, initiating, and executing movements in terms of speed, sequencing, and fluidity; optimising (along with the cerebellum) patterns of muscular activity in target attainment, in terms of such parameters as force, velocity, and amplitude; sequencing movement complexes; "chunking" action or thought repertoires without conscious supervision; and, finally, "binding". With respect to sequencing, it may be noted that the (mesially located) supplementary motor area is responsible more for internally generated movement sequences, whereas the (lateral) premotor area responds more to external sensory events. In correctly ordering and timing predictable, automatic sequences of events (motor, cognitive, or limbic/emotional) two processes may operate: set and cue. Tonic set-related activity, originating from the globus pallidus and projecting to the supplementary motor area, may maintain plans in readiness by scaling output amplitude to fit environmental contexts; the electrophysiological manifestation is the *Bereitschaftspotential* (readiness potential). Phasic, cue-related activity, also originating from the globus pallidus, may act to terminate ongoing movement, and initiate each next subsequent stage. The concepts of "binding" and "chunking", on the other hand, are related and refer to another possible role of the basal ganglia in automatically linking together either thought or action sequences (chunking) without conscious feedback, control, or supervision, or in synchronising (binding) cortical activity via gamma band frequencies. Such binding or chunking will serve to label and link together co-relevant qualities or attributes of a percept or concept. This latter process may possibly break down in schizophrenia.

FURTHER READING

Alexander, G.E. (1997). Anatomy of the basal ganglia and related motor structures. In R.L. Watts & W.C. Koller (Eds.), *Movement disorders: Neurologic principles and practice* (pp. 73–83). New York: McGraw-Hill.

Brooks, D.J. (1996). Basal ganglia function during normal and parkinsonian movement: PET activation studies. In L. Battistin, G. Scarlato, T. Caraceni, & S. Ruggieri (Eds.), *Advances in neurology* (Vol. 69, pp. 433–441). Philadelphia: Lippincott-Raven.

Brown, P., & Marsden, C.D. (1998). What do the basal ganglia do? *The Lancet, 351,* 1801–1804.

Ceballos-Baumann, A.O., & Brooks, D.J. (1997). Basal ganglia function and dysfunction revealed by PET activation studies. In J.A. Obeso, M.R. DeLong, & C.D. Marsden (Eds.), *The basal ganglia and new surgical approaches for Parkinson's disease: Advances in neurology* (Vol. 74, pp. 127–139). Philadelphia: Lippincott-Raven.

Graybiel, A.M. (1998). The basal ganglia and chunking of action repertoires. *Neurobiology of Learning and Memory, 70,* 119–136.

Groenewegen, H.J., Wright, C.I., & Beijer, A.V. (1996). The nucleus accumbens. In G. Holstege, R. Bandler, & C.B. Saper (Eds.), *The emotional motor system* (pp. 485–512). New York: Elsevier.

Hayes, A.E., Davidson, M.C., Keele, S.W., & Rafal, R.D. (1998). Toward a functional analysis of the basal ganglia. *Journal of Cognitive Neuroscience, 10,* 178–198.

Middleton, F.A., & Strick, P.L. (1997). New concepts about the organization of basal ganglia output. In J.A. Obeso, M.R. DeLong, C. Ohye, & C.D. Marsden (Eds.), *The basal ganglia and new surgical approaches for Parkinson's disease: Advances in neurology* (Vol. 74, pp. 57–68). Philadelphia: Lippincott-Raven.

Mink, J.W. (1998). Basal ganglia. In M.J. Zigmond, F.E. Bloom, S.C. Landis, J.L. Roberts, & L.R. Squire (Eds.), *Fundamental neuroscience* (pp. 951–971). San Diego: Academic Press.

Obeso, J.A., Rodriguez, M.C., & DeLong, M.R. (1997). Basal ganglia pathophysiology: A critical review. In J.A. Obeso, M.R. DeLong, C. Ohye, & C.D. Marsden (Eds.), *The basal ganglia and new surgical approaches for Parkinson's disease: Advances in neurology* (Vol. 74, pp. 3–18). Philadelphia: Lippincott-Raven.

Parent, A., & Cicchetti, F. (1998). The current model of basal ganglia organization under scrutiny. *Movement Disorders, 13,* 199–202.

Wichmann, T., & DeLong, M.R. (1997). Physiology of the basal ganglia and pathophysiology of movement disorders of basal ganglia origin. In R.L. Watts & W. Koller (Eds.), *Movement disorders: Neurologic principles and practice* (pp. 87–96). New York: McGraw-Hill.

Young, A.B., & Penney, J.B. (1998). Biochemical and functional organization of the basal ganglia. In J. Jankovic & E. Tolosa (Eds.), *Parkinson's disease and movement disorders* (pp. 1–13). Baltimore: Williams & Wilkins.

CHAPTER FOUR

Tourette's syndrome

Le cook d'un steamer était un latah des plus corsés. Il berçait un jour, sur le pont du navire, son enfant dans ses bras, lorsque survint un matelot qui se mit, à l'instar du cook, à bercer dans ses bras un billot de bois. Puis ce matelot jeta son billot sur un tendelet et s'amusa à le faire rouler sur la toile, ce que fit immédiatement le cook avec son enfant. Le matelot, lâchant alors la toile, laissa retomber son billot sur le pont; le cook en fit de même pour son petit garçon qui se tua sur le coup.

—Jumping, Latah, myriachit, *Archives of Neurologie*, *8*, 68–84, Gilles de la Tourette (1884)

INTRODUCTION

Tourette's syndrome is the archetypal hyperkinetic disorder with a range of other unwanted behaviours that have long led to beliefs in witchcraft or possession. In this chapter we shall examine the natural history of tics and tic disorder, the comorbid conditions that may accompany Tourette's syndrome and obfuscate research findings, and the intertwined genetic and environmental factors. We shall also describe the condition's pathophysiology, neuropsychology, and neurochemistry. Finally, we shall review evidence for it as a syndrome of developmental delay, to which most children may in fact almost be subject in subclinical form, and shall refer to the possibly adaptive aspects of the disorder that may have served to maintain its presence in the genome.

PRELIMINARY CONSIDERATIONS

Movements may be classified along a continuum, ranging from the voluntary to the involuntary:

- Voluntary—intentional, prepared, planned, and exhibiting a readiness or premovement potential (*Bereitschaftspotential*).
- Semivoluntary—in response to an "irresistible" urge, e.g. yawning, the "restless legs" or Ekbom's syndrome, and tics.
- Involuntary—tremor, chorea, and the abnormal postures of dystonia; choreiform movements and possibly tics appear usually without a corresponding *Bereitschaftspotential*.

Tics and tic disorders, with which this chapter is concerned, are involuntary to the extent that they cannot be indefinitely inhibited, but are nevertheless under partial inhibitory control, at least for a short duration, and may be extensively modified in their expression. They belong to the category of hyperkinetic movements, where involuntary and undesired movements occur, typically to excess, and contrast with the hypokinetic, bradykinetic, or akinetic state, so typical, to varying degrees, of Parkinson's disease.

Thus hypokinesia (movement insufficiency) encompasses:

- Akinesia—problems or slowness in *initiating* movement, very often in the absence of an external or triggering stimulus or event; increased reaction time (RT) is a typical index.
- Bradykinesia—problems or slowness in *executing* a movement; increased movement time (MT) is a typical index.
- Hypometria—movements of insufficient duration or, typically, insufficient extent.
- Catatonia—a complex behavioural syndrome, with psychological components, that involves altered motor function with akinesia, posturing, and waxy flexibility; bizarre postures may be sustained for long periods against gravity, almost as if motor function is totally frozen.

Conversely hyperkinesia (movement excess) encompasses:

- Hyperkinesia proper—movements of excessive duration or, typically, extent, as may occur with cerebellar dysfunction.
- Tremor—repetitive, rhythmic movements that are consistent in time and place, which may be designated as resting (as in Parkinson's disease), action (as in cerebellar disease), or postural, and which may involve alternate action of groups of muscles and their antagonists.
- Dystonia—sustained contractions often involving twisting and repetitive movements or abnormal postures. Rigidity may involve co-contractions of agonist and antagonist muscle pairs, and such co-contractions may be painful.

- Dyskinesia—any involuntary movement, including dystonia (above, and those listed below); however, the term is perhaps most commonly employed in the context of the complex, choreatic, and dystonic movements that may occur iatrogenically after prolonged neuroleptic treatment for schizophrenia (tardive dyskinesia), or L-dopa treatment for idiopathic Parkinson's disease.
- Athetosis—peripheral dystonic movements often of a writhing nature, and usually iatrogenic.
- Chorea—irregular, generalised movements, often superficially appearing purposive or semi-purposive, but which like tics are largely involuntary and flit and flow; choreiform movements are characteristic of Huntington's disease.
- Tics—repetitive, stereotyped jerks or movements of limited duration that can often be suppressed at cost of increased inner tension; if multiple and simultaneous, they merge into multifocal myoclonus or chorea or both; they are characteristic of Tourette's syndrome.
- Myoclonus—brief (less than 100 ms) shock-like jerks that lack the precursor sensations and partial capacity for deferral of tics; depending upon frequency, they may merge with tremor.
- Ballismus—gross unilateral irregular choreic movements, usually of the upper limb, often due to lesions of the contralateral subthalamic nucleus, and ameliorated by dopamine antagonists.

A form of dyskinesia that bears certain strong similarities to the tics of Tourette's syndrome, with which this chapter is concerned, and which is present in 5% or more of the population, is restless legs (or Ekbom's) syndrome. Originally described by Thomas Willis in 1685 (Tarsy, 1992), it is characterised by strong, subjective lower-limb discomfort that may only be relieved, temporarily, by movement. It occurs mostly late in the day or at night, after prolonged sitting or lying. The abnormal sensations or paraesthesias are deep-seated and usually localised to the lower legs. They are variously described as crawling, creeping, pulling, itching, tingling, cramping, aching, drawing, or stretching sensations within the muscles. These paraesthesias are closely similar to the premonitory sensations and urges that may characterise the tics of Tourette's syndrome, and are momentarily alleviated by movement, or massage, before the urge returns—again as in Tourette's syndrome. Age of onset is typically in early adult life, with an equal gender distribution and a strong family history (Bucher et al., 1997; Chokroverty & Jankovic, 1999). Its cause is unknown, the condition is lifelong, mild or severe, static or progressive, remitting or unremitting, and a variety of drug treatments, notably dopamine agonists, may help. Basal ganglia involvement seems probable, and the disorder otherwise resembles drug-induced tardive dyskinesia, where there are similar feelings of unease in the legs, a compulsion to move, with fidgety, restless, and repetitive limb movements, which like tics can be briefly controlled by an effort of will.

According to Lees and Tolosa (1993), the word *ticq* appears in seventeenth-century French, meaning "an unsightly muscular caprice" and may be connected with the idea of goats, as indeed also is the word *caprice* (*caper*—Latin for "goat"). Indeed, the Old German word *ziki* itself means "goat", while the Italian *ticchio* is related to *capriccio*, itself a form of *capro* (Italian for "goat"). Maybe bewitchment by the goat god Pan is the common thread.

The first clear medical description of tic disorder was made by Itard (1825, cited in Comings, 1990), a French physician, who reported the case of a French noblewoman, the Marquise de Dampierre, who developed persistent body tics, barking sounds, and uncontrollable utterances of obscenities. He describes:

> Madame de D____ at the age of 7 was affected by convulsive movements of the head and arms . . . After each spasm, the movements of the head became more regular and better controlled, until a convulsive movement would again interrupt her work. It soon became clear that these movements were indeed involuntary in nature . . . [and] involved the shoulders, the neck and the face, and resulted in contortions and extraordinary grimaces . . .

Elsewhere (Shapiro, Shapiro, Young, & Feinberg, 1988, cited in Arzimanoglou, 1998) Itard is cited as recounting the Marquise's profanities (coprolalia, see below, which may also include motor tics in the disorder now known as Tourette's syndrome) as described below:

> Thus in the middle of a conversation, suddenly and without being able to avoid it, she interrupts that which she says or hears with bizarre cries and extraordinary words which make deplorable contrast to her distinguished manner. These words are mostly rude oaths or obscenities, which are no less embarrassing for herself as for others.

However, descriptions of such "bewitched and possessed" individuals go back centuries. Thus Sprenger (1489; see, for example, Lohr & Wisniewski, 1987, p. 191) described:

> A sober priest without any eccentricity . . . No sign of madness or any immoderate action [who was said to be possessed of the devil] . . . When he passed any church, and genuflected in honour of the Glorious Virgin, the devil made him thrust his tongue far out of his mouth; and when he was asked whether he could not restrain himself from doing this, he answered: I cannot help myself at all, for he so uses all my limbs and organs, my neck, my tongue

and my lungs, whenever he pleases, causing me to speak or to cry out; and I hear the words, as if they were spoken by myself but I am altogether unable to restrain them.

Gilles de la Tourette, however, gave the first, full characterisation of the syndrome, now bearing his name, as a separate entity. Born in the kitchen of his uncle's home in the small French village of St Gervais les Trois Clochers, George Albert Edouard Brutus Gilles de la Tourette (1857–1904), like George Huntington and James Parkinson, was brought up in a family of physicians. A neurologist at the famous Parisian Hôpital de la Salpêtrière in Charcot's department in 1884, he became the latter's registrar in 1886. He wrote many books and papers in the fields of both neurology and psychiatry (and indeed Tourette's syndrome still straddles the artificial and now vanishing boundary between neurology and neuropsychiatry). In his later life, a young paranoid female patient shot him three times in a consulting room. One of the bullets hit him in the head, and although it was removed he never fully recovered (Stevens, 1971, cited in Finger, 1994). Depressive episodes and mania manifested in his later years, and there are indications that he died from syphilis (Guilly, 1982, cited in Finger, 1994).

According to DSM-IV, Tourette's syndrome is a disorder characterised by multiple motor and one or more vocal tics occurring in bouts many times a day, most days, for at least a year; their number, frequency, complexity, and severity change over time; they are not due to intoxication, and their onset is prior to 18 (Leckman & Cohen, 1996). The disorder is often accompanied by behavioural, emotional, and cognitive problems, and its manifestations cross the boundaries between voluntary and involuntary behaviour (Peterson, Leckman, & Cohen, 1995). It is a disorder of neurochemical regulation with complex genetic and environmental determinants, the latter acting at critical developmental stages, and just as Parkinson's disease acts as a disease model of basal ganglia disorder and hypokinesia, Tourette's syndrome acts as a model for other, often hyperkinetic, disorders, such as attention deficit hyperactivity disorder (ADHD), mania, and the stereotyped movements of obsessive compulsive disorder (OCD). It is open to behavioural, genetic, epidemiological, clinical, molecular, and neuroimaging study. It lies on a spectrum of related disorders according to DSM-IV (see Arzimanoglou, 1998):

- *Transient tic disorder of childhood*, involving single or multiple motor and/or vocal tics that occur many times a day, nearly every day, for at least 4 weeks but for no longer than 12 consecutive months, with onset before 18 years, causing impairment of social, academic, or occupational functioning, and not a consequence of psychoactive intoxication or known central nervous system disease; the disorder is

self-limiting, commoner in boys, affects 2–4% of children, with an onset between ages 3 and 10 (see Leckman, King, & Cohen, 1999).
- *Chronic motor or vocal tic disorder*, as above, except that *only* motor or vocal tics (not both) must occur intermittently for more than a year.
- *Tourette's syndrome*, as above, except that both multiple motor and one or more vocal tics must be present at the same time, in a waxing and waning character, with changing anatomical location, number, frequency, complexity, and severity.

We have already seen that tics are repetitive stereotyped jerks or movements of limited duration that may be briefly suppressed. They clearly belong to a class of movements that include also mannerisms, stereotypies, and rituals, and that relate to the compulsive behaviours of OCD with which we shall deal in a subsequent chapter. However, it may be useful to contrast tics with those three other related phenomena (Arzimanoglou, 1998):

- Mannerism—a bizarre mode of performing a purposeful act, usually as a result of incorporating a stereotyped movement into goal-directed behaviour.
- Stereotypy—a purposeless movement of a whole body area that is a fragment of normal behaviour and which is executed in a uniformly repetitive fashion, often for long periods of time, and at the expense of all other activities, e.g. head nodding or banging, or the restless pacing of a caged animal.
- Ritual—a seemingly purposeless repetitive action of a complex nature which occurs as a result of an irresistible urge and which significantly interferes with normal living but nevertheless relieves internal anxiety or stress; examples include pirouetting or bowing before an open door (for example, the lexicographer Samuel Johnson), or, ultimately, many apparently superstitious or religious beliefs.

TICS

Tics, which are preceded by increasing sensations of tension, with short-lived relief upon their release, encompass an enormous range of sudden, repetitive, recurrent, nonrhythmic, stereotyped movements, expressions, gestures, or utterances, and seem to represent poorly modulated fragments of normal behaviour (Leckman et al., 1997). Occurring in paroxysmal bouts, and bouts of bouts, each tic rarely lasts more than 1 second, though longer, well-orchestrated tics may merge with compulsions. Often forceful and potentially self-injurious, they are perceived as involuntary, purposeless, and meaningless; indeed often in the early stages the patient is anosognosic, only later experiencing characteristic premonitory sensations, urges, and tension, or displaying an affective, aggressive aspect. They are exacerbated by both boredom and stress, reducing with distraction and sleep. The sufferer may employ distracting manoeuvres (*gestes antagonistes*) to reduce them, or to incorporate them into strategically appropriate points or breaks in voluntary activity so as to mask them. While they can be briefly suppressed, this is at the cost of a rapid rise in feelings of tension or discomfort, leading to an explosive outburst and only transient relief. They can be simple or complex, motor or phonic, though motor tics usually come first. Simple tics appear meaningless, abrupt, brief, repetitive, single, and isolated, whereas complex tics involve apparently more purposeful, distinct, coordinated patterns of sequential movements requiring multiple muscle groups and seeming to perform a common stereotypical motor act (Leckman et al., 1999; Shytle, Silver, & Sanberg, 1996). Onset may be gradual and subtle, often in the head, neck, face, or eyes, with a cephalocaudal progression. However, unlike dystonia or athetosis, they typically fluctuate in form, region, and time. Commonest simple motor tics include abrupt eye blinking, facial twitches, head or arm jerks, and shoulder shrugs, whereas complex motor tics include touching, licking, rubbing, spitting, jumping, hitting, smelling, squatting, facial expressions, head or hand gestures, dystonic postures, and adjustments for symmetry. Common vocal/phonic tics include squealing, sniffing, throat clearing, snorting, yelping, speech fragments or phrases (Robertson & Eapen, 1995). Speech may also acquire unusual rhythms, tones, accents, volume, or speed. Although they are not common, later they may develop as a range of repetitive or obscene gestures, actions, or speech, which are performed compulsively. These include copropraxia (obscene gestures or behaviour), coprolalia (obscene, aggressive, or socially inappropriate words), echopraxia (imitating others' behaviour), echolalia (repeating others' speech) and palilalia (repeating one's own words or phrases). Although inappropriate, such actions, behaviours, or language are usually more or less devoid of true emotive content; indeed, the content of any obscenity is itself often largely determined by the society's current norms, and may be political, religious, or even racial. While such behaviours are largely compulsive, repetitive, or ritualistic they may be deliberately left incomplete ("fu. . .h") or camouflaged or otherwise somehow substituted into the ongoing discourse or action. Thus as automatisms they may be slipped in at syntactically (though not necessarily semantically) appropriate junctures or breaks. Coprolalia may even occur in sign with congenitally deaf users of that medium, when a term such as perhaps copropraxia may be equally appropriate. With echopraxia, the patient may feel compelled to mimic another, even to the extent of possibly injurious consequences, e.g. while driving, climbing, or flying, though sufferers may still be successful as mechanics, surgeons, or pilots. With palilalia, a phrase may be repeated a set number of times until it feels "just right" (vocal rituals), whereas with speech, atypicalities, unusual rhythms, tones, accent, volume or speed may be adopted. Figures of 30% (coprolalia), 20% (copropraxia), and 10–40% for echolalia and palilalia have been reported (Robertson & Eapen, 1995).

Gilles de la Tourette (1884) himself reports a fatal example (*latah*) of echopraxia (pp. 179–180):

> The cook on a steamer had long-standing *latah*. One day, on the bridge, he was cradling his child in his arms. Then a sailor began to copy the cook's action with a piece of wood. He threw it on a sail, amusing himself rolling it down the canvas. The cook immediately did the same with his infant. The sailor then lowered the canvas and allowed the wood to fall on the bridge. The cook, in doing the same, killed his little boy instantly. (My translation)

Normally, before a voluntary movement occurs, a premovement potential (*Bereitschaftspotential*, readiness potential; see, for example, Cunnington, Iansek, Bradshaw, & Phillips, 1996) is detectable over the supplementary motor area. Such potentials are said to be absent in Tourette's syndrome, though there is a suggestion that they may occur with tics preceded by strong urges to move, over the lateral premotor area (see Peterson et al., 1995; Karp, Porter, Toro, & Hallett, 1996).

External events, as with the echophenomena, may easily "capture" the patient, suggesting abnormal responsivity to external cues, just as in Parkinson's disease patients may come to rely upon such cues and may also be captured, freezing in doorways. Indeed it is possible that in genetically or otherwise susceptible individuals local irritation or allergies can sow the seeds for subsequent functionless perpetuation of initially adaptive reflexes like blinking, sniffing, or throat clearing. Thus, just as in dystonia, tics may commence as voluntary movements, only later becoming stereotyped and automatic. Indeed, latent tic activity may be reactivated or triggered as with partially controlled addictive behaviours, by environmental stimuli like hearing someone clearing the throat, or seeing a yawn. Yawns are of course universally, and inexplicably, infectious. Stress, excitement, premenstrual tension, and fever may exacerbate the condition, just as stressed animals (or animals or humans given dopaminergic stimulants) can exhibit stereotypic behaviour; however, boredom and fatigue can also have similar effects, whereas the condition typically ameliorates with sleep, relaxation, or enjoyable or absorbing pastimes (Shytle et al., 1996).

RATING SCALE OF SEVERITY

The rating scale of severity for Tourette's syndrome is Tourette's Syndrome Global Scale (Harcherik, Leckman, Detlor, & Cohen, 1984).

AGE OF ONSET AND PREVALENCE

The onset of Tourette's syndrome is typically between 5 and 10 years, though a range of 2–14 years has been reported (Leckman et al., 1997). While 4–5% of school-age children may experience chronic tics at some point in their development, true Tourette's syndrome may have a prevalence of around 1 to 8 per 1000 boys, and 0.1 to 4 per 1000 girls (Leckman & Cohen, 1999a). Tics may worsen towards puberty, with thereafter the possibility of some relief (Robertson & Eapen, 1995). However, estimates of the prevalence of Tourette's syndrome and tic disorder vary widely, due to problems of criteria, ascertainment, and diagnostic instruments. Thus in chronic tic disorder the appearance and disappearance of tics, as a function of fatigue, stress, anger, anxiety, or interest, may represent a *forme fruste* of true Tourette's syndrome. Tics, however, of one sort or another do tend to be much commoner in boys than in girls, by a ratio of around 4 : 1.

COMORBIDITY

A number of disorders are comorbid with Tourette's syndrome: OCD, inattention, hyperactivity, ADHD, impulsivity, disruptive behaviour and learning difficulties, depression, anxiety, sleep disturbances, speech problems, and agoraphobia, all often more annoying than the Tourette's syndrome itself (Walkup, Scahill, & Riddle, 1995; Zohar et al., 1999). These disorders can also occur in isolation, as can Tourette's syndrome, though the latter is itself characterised by mood swings, temper outbursts, and aggression. Indeed the boundaries between Tourette's syndrome and its often comorbid disorders are blurred, and manifestations and mechanisms are likely to be common. An aggressive or sexual quality is often present in the urges to action, and the behaviours are often redolent of an obsessive or compulsive quality (Peterson et al., 1995). OCD is possibly an alternative manifestation of a common gene causative for Tourette's syndrome and OCD, when accompanied by Tourette's syndrome tends to be more violent, sexual, and aggressive and to involve more symmetrising behaviours, than when pure, when anxiety may more characterise the disorder. While more males may exhibit pure Tourette's syndrome, more females may have pure OCD; around half of Tourette's syndrome sufferers also experience OCD (Shytle et al., 1996), whereas 30% of OCD patients have a personal (and another 10–15% a family) history of Tourette's syndrome (Peterson et al., 1995). In any case, patients often describe both tics and compulsions as a need to perform an action until a feeling of tension is relieved, or until it feels "just right".

Comorbid ADHD usually occurs earlier than comorbid OCD, and may even be prodromal to Tourette's syndrome; 40% of Tourette's syndrome patients also have ADHD-like symptoms (Leckman et al., 1997; Robertson & Eapen, 1995). Its core features, many of which resemble those of

Tourette's syndrome, are *attentional* (problems in initiating and maintaining on-task behaviour), *impulsivity* (failure to consider consequences before action), and *motor hyperactivity* (see, for example, Walkup et al., 1995). It is unclear whether attention deficits can occur without hyperactivity, or vice versa, and whether Tourette's syndrome predisposes to the development of ADHD, or whether both syndromes are due to shared genetic variance. In any case individuals seeking treatment are more likely to have compound, comorbid conditions and multiple problems, such that clinical samples may overestimate the frequency of comorbidity. Be that as it may, OCD and ADHD could well be expressions of the same aetiology or aetiologies that produce Tourette's syndrome, with all three conditions due to frontostriatal pathology at varying, if related, sites. Yet again, the matter could all be an artefact of taxonomy; thus as Towbin, Peterson, Cohen, and Leckman (1999) note, when we seek to equate our constructed diagnoses with actual diseases, problems arise with patients whose symptoms seem to cross boundaries, or where the patients themselves seem to have more than one disease. Thus the concept of comorbidity presumes that a patient has two or more simultaneous, independent diseases, while strictly he or she may instead have one underlying disease that displays features of two of our arbitrarily differentiated diagnoses.

Patients with Tourette's syndrome typically have short temper and may exhibit rage attacks, aggression, oppositional and confrontational behaviour, lying, stealing, and pyromania. Thus oppositional defiant syndrome disorder is often comorbid with Tourette's syndrome, with its negativistic, hostile, defiant behaviours lasting more than 6 months. Especially common in boys, it involves stubbornness, resistance, argumentativeness, testing of the limits, verbal aggression, and refusal to follow verbal directions. Otherwise, anxiety, depression, and learning disabilities also can co-occur with Tourette's syndrome, the latter involving a significant discrepancy between presumed ability and scores on standardised tests of achievement. This underachievement is not due to inadequate education, reduced motivation, or depression, and is particularly common in males. As with ADHD, decrements are evident in executive functions, especially planning, selective attention, response inhibition, and problem-solving skills (Walkup et al., 1995). All these comorbid disorders are suggestive of common genetic mechanisms.

FAMILIAL AND GENETIC ASPECTS

Family studies indicate a major genetic component, though environmental factors may determine *how* (as Tourette's syndrome, OCD or ADHD . . .) and *when* (and indeed *if*) a putative gene is expressed. As monozygotic twins do differ in severity, other factors must also operate; thus the worse-affected twin may typically weigh less at birth, indicating that pre- and perinatal risk factors may also be important. Indeed animal studies indicate the effects of maternal stress on offspring's neurotransmitter (especially dopamine) levels and functions in adulthood (Peterson et al., 1995) and the number of striatal dopamine D2 receptors (Leckman & Cohen, 1996). Multiple, intertwined neuroanatomical, neurochemical, and neurodevelopmental processes are therefore probably involved. Since, as we shall see, any Tourette's syndrome gene is neither necessary nor sufficient on its own to cause Tourette's syndrome, we must invoke the concept of genetic vulnerability (Peterson et al., 1995), with tic behaviours maybe on a continuum with normal behaviour. Thus normal copies of vulnerability genes may be turned on and off at specific developmental points; abnormal copies may alter this development by changing the timing or degree of expression of specific gene products, in response to environmental influences. Alternatively, abnormal genes may influence the development of basal ganglia and limbic regions under sex hormone control, with, perhaps, excessive expression or abnormal persistence of normal developmental characteristics (Palumbo, Maughan, & Kurlan, 1997). Thus genes may cause certain frontostriatal circuits to be selectively and differentially disinhibited in Tourette's syndrome, OCD, and ADHD. This may perhaps be particularly true of the orbitofrontal cortex and anterior cingulate, both of which are involved in emotional behaviours, the former playing an inhibitory role and the latter a facilitatory role. Thus the anterior cingulate may be overactive in all three disorders, and the orbitofrontal cortex also in OCD, though it must be admitted that these suggestions are hypothetical, and have not been supported by neuroimaging evidence; indeed, the anterior cingulate may even be underactive during inhibitory, Stroop and timing tasks in ADHD (Garavan, Ross, & Stein, 1999). Disregulation of neuromodulatory systems (dopaminergic, serotonergic, noradrenergic, and even cholinergic) may mediate these effects, under genetic influence. Leckman and Cohen (1999a) suggest dopaminergic hyperinnervation or dopamine D2 receptor hypersensitivity in the striatum in Tourette's syndrome, with, additionally, gonadal steroids modulating frontostriatal circuits and influencing sex-related differences in the disorder, and changes at puberty.

Autosomal dominant inheritance with high but incomplete penetrance and variable expression was originally suggested by the family studies, the concordance for monozygotic twins exceeding 50%, but only reaching 18% for dizygotic twins and male first-degree family members (Leckman & Cohen, 1996). Within monozygotic twins discordant for severity, differences in dopamine D2 receptor binding (super)sensitivity in the head of the caudate were found to predict phenotypic severity (Wolf et al., 1996). Moreover the dopamine D2 A1 allele has increased frequency in Tourette's syndrome, impulsive, compulsive, and addictive disorders (Comings, 1995), and haloperidol, a competitive antagonist of the dopamine D2 receptor, ameliorates Tourette's syndrome symptoms. However, according to Leckman and Cohen (1999b) the most promising candidate gene is an allelic variant of the dopamine D4 receptor gene, though it may only operate modestly and in a few families. According to Pauls, Alsobrook, Gelerntner, and Leckman (1999) we should not perhaps anyway be invoking autosomal dominance, but rather an additive model involving major gene inheritance. Lichter, Jackson, and Schachter (1995) reported that maternal transmission of Tourette's syndrome was related to greater motor tic complexity, and more frequent noninterfering rituals, whereas paternal transmission was associated with increased frequency of rituals, earlier onset of vocal tics, and more prominent ADHD behaviours. The authors concluded that the findings are consistent with genomic imprinting in Tourette's syndrome.

Although Tourette's syndrome, ADHD, and schizophrenia may be neurodevelopmental disorders involving inherited defects in brain development, environmental factors (pre- and perinatal events, obstetrical complications, infections, altered immune processes) may also play an important role. Thus tics and OCD symptoms may develop after streptococcal infection by a process of molecular mimicry; antibodies directed against bacterial antigens may cross-react with brain targets, especially the caudate and subthalamic nucleus, producing a spectrum of childhood neurobehavioural disorders (paediatric autoimmune neuropsychiatric disorders, or PANDAs; see Kurlan, 1998) arising by postinfectious autoimmune mechanisms. Tourette's syndrome, OCD, Sydenham's chorea, and maybe even ADHD may occur this way, in the presence of a genetically determined predisposition or susceptibility.

PATHOPHYSIOLOGY OF TOURETTE'S SYNDROME

Within the basal ganglia two pathways have been identified, direct and indirect, which are normally kept in balance by dopaminergic and possibly serotonergic activity. Release in the striatum of dopamine from terminals of the nigrostriatal projection appears to facilitate transmission over the direct pathway (which acts to release behaviours) via activation of D1 receptors, and to inhibit transmission over the indirect pathway (which acts to inhibit behaviours) via activation of D2 receptors. The net effect in Tourette's syndrome appears to be a reduction of basal ganglia inhibitory output leading, by disinhibition, to increased activity of thalamocortical projections and (possibly unwanted) movement facilitation. Conversely, reduction of striatal dopamine, as occurs in parkinsonism, should increase inhibitory basal ganglia outflow and inhibit movement (Wichmann & DeLong, 1997). There is therefore normally a negative correlation between striatopallidal activity, and that of these structures' thalamocortical targets. However, activity in both of these regions may positively correlate in Tourette's syndrome (Juncos & Freeman, 1997), indicating a failure of basal ganglia gating of motor, cognitive, and limbic pathways, with resultant inability to suppress movement, impulsivity, and inattention. Leckman et al. (1997) see this pattern as mediated by a dopaminergic hyperinnervation of the striatum and/or a supersensitivity of striatal D2 receptors; this would result in increased inhibition of the indirect and stimulation of the direct pathway, with consequent increase, from both sources, of thalamocortical stimulation.

Electrostimulation of the anterior cingulate can produce complex tic-like coordinated patterns that are difficult to inhibit (Peterson et al., 1999a). Typical responses include touching, leaning, stretching and rubbing, which are often preceded by a "feeling" that may be compared to the sensory phenomena often experienced by Tourette's syndrome patients before initiation of tics. The paraesthesias associated with tics, and the tics themselves, may thus be due to disinhibition of the basal ganglia–thalamocortical circuit, whereas the highly emotional aspects which often co-occur with tics in Tourette's syndrome may indicate the additional involvement of limbic components (Leckman et al., 1997). Similarly, dopaminergic stimulants applied to basal ganglia nuclei can cause tic-like stereotypies in previously normal animals or humans, or exacerbate symptoms in patients (Peterson et al., 1999a). Appropriately placed lesions to the thalamus, cingulum, or lateral orbitofrontal cortex can ameliorate OCD (Peterson et al., 1995), whereas lesions to the ventral, medial, or intralaminar thalamic nuclei, or neuroleptics, can attenuate tics (Leckman et al., 1997). Volumetric and metabolic studies of brain regions in Tourette's syndrome have proved conflicting (Eidelberg et al., 1997; Robertson & Yakely, 1996; Sheppard, Bradshaw, Purcell, & Pantelis, 1999b), though the basal ganglia have been repeatedly implicated, with reduced volumes or activation and abnormal asymmetries (Peterson et al., 1999a). These abnormal structural or functional asymmetries tend to be associated with such behavioural consequences as loss or reversal of normal asymmetries in line bisection, turning biases, dichotic ear effects, and patterns of verbal–manual concurrent task interference (Yazgan, Peterson, Wexler, & Leckman, 1995), though findings are confused (Hyde et al., 1995; Petersen et al., 1993; Singer et al., 1993). If one can draw any general conclusions, they are that frontal, cingulate, caudate, and thalamic activity tends to be altered, thereby presumably leading to a disinhibitory release of behaviour.

NEUROPSYCHOLOGICAL DEFICITS

A disinhibitory release of behaviour is even apparent at a cognitive level; in a Stroop-like task involving the Simon effect, Georgiou et al. (1995) reported that Tourette's syndrome patients had problems inhibiting the more natural response of movement in accordance with stimulus location, when it was incongruent with arrow direction. However, there is debate as to whether or not there is a general deficit in the performance of executive function tasks involving set and attention (Schultz, Carter, Scahill, & Leckman, 1999). With respect to visuomotor integration, there seem to be consistent deficits in accurate copying of geometrical designs such as the Rey Osterrieth Complex Figure; there is also compelling evidence of deficits in finger tapping and motor coordination, e.g. with the Purdue Pegboard task, though these problems could possibly stem from the difficulties with visuomotor integration. On the other hand there is less persuasive or con- sistent evidence for visuospatial or visuoperceptual deficits. It is noteworthy that Tourette's syndrome, OCD, and ADHD are all associated with deficits in visuomotor integration. This would seem to point to a common abnor- mality in the basal ganglia, a region important for cognitive and motor control processes, and one reported to exhibit anomalies in all three disorders. However, it is possible that it is the ADHD that is driving the deficits in visuomotor integration, especially since it is notoriously difficult to obtain "pure" samples of Tourette's syndrome, without additional ADHD comorbidity.

Eye movement control may also be deficient in Tourette's syndrome, with intrusive saccades during smooth pursuit, failure of antisaccades (deliberate eye movements in the direction opposite to a stimulus event), and impaired performance of sequences of memory-guided saccades (Narita et al., 1997; Straube et al., 1997).

NEUROCHEMISTRY, PHARMACOLOGY, AND TREATMENT

In line with evidence that dopamine D2 receptor antagonists (e.g. halo- peridol, pimozide, sulpiride) ameliorate Tourette's syndrome symptomatol- ogy, and dopamine agonist stimulants exacerbate it, though ameliorating attention deficit hyperactivity disorder (Leckman & Cohen, 1996), there may be dopamine D2 receptor hypersensitivity, dopaminergic hyperinner- vation of the striatum, or increased number of dopamine transporter sites. Such situations would lead to disinhibition of thalamocortical projections. However, Anderson, Leckman, and Cohen (1999) note that in Tourette's syndrome there is as yet no clear evidence of global alterations in dopamine turnover, altered presynaptic metabolism, or altered dopamine D2 receptor functioning, apart from some recent claims of increased density of pre- synaptic dopamine uptake sites, and of increased binding of a dopamine transporter ligand in the striatum of people with Tourette's syndrome. These very recently reported findings may reflect an upregulation of transporters in response to excessive dopamine activity. At present there is little evidence of serotonergic involvement, except that selective serotonin reuptake inhibitors (which ameliorate OCD) may worsen tics; however, noradrenergic pathways may also be involved. Thus clonidine, an α_2-noradrenergic receptor agonist, ameliorates both Tourette's syndrome and ADHD; Tourette's syndrome is of course a stress-sensitive disorder.

Shytle, Silver, Newman, and Sanberg (in press) have explored the use of nicotine in the treatment of Tourette's syndrome. After initial trials with Nicorette chewing gum (2 mg) twice a day, and noting profound obtundation of tics, they trialled transdermal nicotine patches, which produced a gradual rise in serum nicotine levels, peaking in 3–5 hours, and achieving plasma concentrations of 10–20 μg L^{-1}. They found that 7 mg transdermal nicotine patches, daily, resulted in steady-state plasma concentrations within 3 days, and very significant improvement, especially if the nicotine treatment was undertaken in conjunction with ongoing neuroleptic medication, though side effects (nausea, headache, sedation) were sometimes a problem. They argue that nicotine promotes the presynaptic release of various neurotransmitters, especially acetylcholine, and potentiates the action of dopamine D2 antagonists by activating disinhibited striatal cholinergic interneurones; the latter then activate the striatopallidal GABA neurones, which in turn inhibit the globus pallidus. Thus in Tourette's syndrome they believe that striatal cholinergic interneurones and striato-pallidal GABA output neurones are abnormally shut down due to hyper-innervation of dopaminergic neurones acting via D2 receptors. As a result, the globus pallidus is unable to gate neuronal activity of the thalamocortical projections to motor areas. Neuroleptics would then reinstate inhibitory control over thalamocortical fibres by disinhibiting striatopallidal output neurones.

TOURETTE'S SYNDROME A SYNDROME OF DEVELOPMENTAL DELAY?

We have noted that normal copies of vulnerability genes may turn on and off at specific developmental points, with abnormal copies altering this development by changing the timing or degree of expression of specific gene products, perhaps in concert with environmental influences. In that case Tourette's syndrome may be seen as an excessive expression or abnormal persistence of normal developmental characteristics, involving arrest or delay of key developmental aspects involving neuroregulatory centres important for sensorimotor, cognitive, and affective behaviour. In the context of closely related OCD and ADHD, normal childhood is replete with disinhibition, collecting mania, scatology, repeated checking, fear of and fascination with dirt, short attention span, and tantrums (Kurlan, 1994; Peterson et al., 1995; Palumbo et al., 1997), although tic-like behaviour is also a near-universal phenomenon during normal development (Kurlan, 1994). Kurlan (1994) concludes that a putative Tourette's syndrome gene or genes influences the development of the basal ganglia and limbic regions that are under sex hormone control, with Tourette's syndrome an excessive expression or abnormal persistence of otherwise normal developmental characteristics.

ADAPTIVE ASPECTS OF TOURETTE'S SYNDROME

Sacks (1992) suggested that Mozart may have suffered from Tourette's syndrome; he was hyperactive, given to tics, sudden impulses, odd motor behaviours, echolalia, and palilalia, with a love of nonsense words and a head full of melodies—like Samuel Johnson (1709–1784), the lexicographer and compiler of the first English dictionary, with a head full of words. According to contemporary accounts, Johnson suffered from what we would now call akathisia (motor restlessness), unusual, complex compulsions, and various vocal and motor tics. He was said to be "awkward" at 7 years, and later exhibited facial grimacing, finger twirling, head tilting, shoulder shrugging, gesticulations, loud vocalisations, and bizarre rituals on going through doorways. He even commented upon the compulsive life of a lexicographer in his own dictionary. Other idiosyncrasies of Johnson were his continual picking at his fingers, cutting at the knuckles, biting the nails to the quick, and repeatedly hitting and rubbing his legs.

We can ask, with Sacks, whether Johnson and Mozart were creators and innovators in their fields *despite* Tourette's syndrome, or *because* of it. Tourette's syndrome may therefore be a continuum; at one end, simple motor tics, vocalisations, iterations, perseverations, and stereotypies are largely a nuisance and an irrelevance. At the other end we may see elaborations, playful mimicry, extravagant impudent inventiveness, audacious dramatisations, surreal associations, uninhibited inventiveness, incontinent reactivity, stimulus hunger, imagery, and exuberant art. Sacks saw this latter extreme to be a source of inspiration, of "ticcy witticisms and witty ticcisisms" in language, music, art, athletics, and games, a usefully harnessed disorder. Indeed jazz and "tic dancing" are extremely popular at Tourette Syndrome Association socials, and Sacks reminds us of a patient who renounced his medication because it destroyed his creativity.

SUMMARY AND CONCLUSIONS

In a continuum of movement volitionality between voluntary and involuntary, tics may be seen almost as semi-voluntary. In a continuum of disorder ranging from hypokinesia (akinesia, bradykinesia, hypometria and catatonia) to hyperkinesia (tremor, chorea, athetosis, dystonia, dyskinesia, ballismus, and myoclonus) tics are clearly hyperkinetic, whose nearest analogue may be Ekbom's restless legs syndrome. Similarly, tics relate to but can be contrasted with mannerisms, stereotypies, and rituals. In a spectrum ranging from the extremely common transient tic disorder of childhood, through chronic motor and vocal tic disorder, Tourette's syndrome, with its long social history of bewitching and possession, may be seen as a particularly severe form of the latter; thus it involves a range of additional symptoms that include echophenomena and coprolalia and copropraxia. As with the delusions of schizophrenia, the manifestations of such coprophenomena are often culture dependent. The disorder is in many ways a model for other hyperkinetic disorders of release, disinhibition, or excess, as for example attention deficit hyperactivity disorder.

Tics may be simple or complex, motor or vocal, and occur in bouts, with additional behavioural, emotional, and cognitive problems. They involve a huge range of sudden, repetitive, recurrent, nonrhythmic, stereotyped movements, expressions, gestures, or utterances, presenting as poorly modulated fragments of normal behaviour. Perceived by all parties as involuntary, purposeless, and meaningless, they can nevertheless be briefly postponed, though at the cost of increasing tension, usually followed by explosive release. Indeed they are exacerbated by both stress and boredom, and are normally preceded by sensations of increasing tension, and followed by short-lived relief. They fluctuate in form and time, like the obsessions and compulsions of that disorder, and the delusions of schizophrenia, and the sufferer, often initially anosognosic, may learn how to camouflage them by incorporating them into other ongoing activities. Often with a subtle, gradual onset in face or extremities during childhood, they may even be behaviours "captured" by environmental triggers (hayfever → sniffing, eye irritation → blinking, infections → throat clearing), just as environmental objects may capture behaviour in parkinsonian freezing, and induce the complex mannerisms of obsessive compulsive disorder. With a prevalence in boys of 1 to 8 per 1000 (much less in girls, who instead may manifest more obsessive compulsive symptomatology), the disorder is frequently comorbid with OCD, ADHD, disruptive behaviour, learning difficulties, depression, anxiety, and speech problems. Indeed there is often a hyperactive, aggressive, sexual quality in the disorder, with obsessive components.

Its familial characteristics suggest autosomal dominant transmission, with high but incomplete penetrance and variable expression. An additive genetic model, perhaps with genomic imprinting, is also a possibility. However, environmental risk factors (obstetric complications, prenatal events, infections, postinfectious streptococcal autoimmune processes targeting the striatum) also suggest an inherited genetic vulnerability; thus vulnerability genes may be turned on and off at various developmental phases. Differences in dopamine D2 receptor binding sensitivity in the head of the caudate may predict phenotype severity, and the dopamine D2 A1 allele has increased frequency in the disorder, and indeed also in other impulsive, compulsive, addictive disorders. The dopamine D2 receptor antagonist haloperidol, moreover, ameliorates Tourette's syndrome. However, the theoretically most promising candidate gene so far may be an allelic variant of the dopamine D4 receptor gene, though it may in fact only operate modestly, and in a few families.

Pathophysiology, together with the above considerations, suggests a failure of striatopallidal gating of motor, cognitive, and limbic pathways, with resultant inability to suppress impulsivity; this situation may be due to dopaminergic hyperinnervation of the striatum, and/or supersensitivity of striatal D2 receptors, leading to increased inhibition of indirect and stimulation of direct basal ganglia pathways. Notably, dopaminergic stimulants lead to tic-like stereotypies, whereas dopamine D2 antagonists like haloperidol ameliorate the condition. However, there is as yet no clear evidence of global alterations in dopamine turnover, altered presynaptic metabolism, or altered dopamine D2 receptor functioning, though some recent evidence does suggest upregulation of dopamine transporters in response to excessive dopamine activity.

Electrostimulation of the anterior cingulate can also lead to release of tic-like behaviour, which is complex, coordinated, and difficult to inhibit, with prior paraesthesias resembling those that precede the tics of Tourette's syndrome. Conversely, lesions to the ventral, medial, or intralaminar nuclei of the thalamus can attenuate tics. Imaging findings (morphometric and metabolic) are conflicting, though there is evidence of reduced volume and activation, and of abnormal asymmetries, in the basal ganglia. These abnormal physiological and anatomical asymmetries are mirrored in abnormal behavioural asymmetries.

Apart from the above abnormal behavioural asymmetries, neuropsychological studies indicate disinhibitory release of behaviour in Stroop and Simon effect tasks, a possible deficit in executive functions, deficits in visuomotor function and in certain aspects of motor coordination and saccadic control, though many of these apparent deficits may stem from the co-presence of highly comorbid ADHD.

Although dopamine antagonists are clearly useful in treatment, there is little evidence of serotonergic involvement, except that selective serotonin reuptake inhibitors may worsen tics. On the other hand clonidine, an α_2-noradrenergic receptor agonist, ameliorates both Tourette's syndrome and ADHD, suggesting additional involvement of noradrenergic pathways. Cholinergic pathways may also be involved, as nicotine helps (as it also seems to in schizophrenia and Huntington's disease), perhaps by promoting presynaptic release of various neurotransmitters; it may also potentiate the action of dopamine D2 antagonists by activating disinhibited striatopallidal GABA neurones. Thus in the disorder, striatal cholinergic interneurones and striatopallidal GABA output neurones may be abnormally shut down, due to hyperinnervation of dopaminergic neurones, with resultant failure to gate thalamocortical projections.

Tourette's syndrome is thus to be seen as a syndrome of developmental delay or arrest. Vulnerability genes may be turned on by environmental factors, with excessive expression or abnormal persistence of normal developmental characteristics; most normal children are at risk for exhibiting disinhibited, tic-like behaviour. Nevertheless there may be adaptive aspects in a "usefully harnessable" disorder, as many sufferers seem to be good at music, art, games, and athletics; *deficits* in motor coordination, if present, may instead be due to any comorbid ADHD.

FURTHER READING

Arzimanoglou, A.A. (1998). Gilles de la Tourette syndrome. *Journal of Neurology*, *245*, 761–765.

Eidelberg, D., Moeller, J.R., Antonini, A., Kazamuta, K., Dhawan, V., Budman, C., & Feigin, A. (1997). The metabolic anatomy of Tourette's syndrome. *Neurology*, *48*, 927–934.

Juncos, J., & Freeman, A. (1997). Pathophysiology and differentiated diagnosis of tics. In R.L. Watts & W.C. Koller (Eds.), *Movement disorders* (pp. 561–568). New York: McGraw-Hill.

Kurlan, R. (1998). Tourette's syndrome and "PANDAS". Will the relation bear out? *Neurology*, *50*, 1530–1534.

Leckman, J.F., & Cohen, D.J. (1996). Tic disorders. In M. Lewis (Ed.), *Child and adolescent psychiatry: A comprehensive textbook* (2nd ed., pp. 622–629). Baltimore: Williams & Wilkins.

Leckman J.F., & Cohen, D.J. (Eds.) (1999). *Tourette's syndrome: Tics, obsessions, compulsions.* New York: Wiley.

Leckman, J.F., Peterson, B.S., Anderson, G.M., Arnsten, A.M.F.T., Pauls, D.L., & Cohen, D.J. (1997). Pathogenesis of Tourette's syndrome. *Journal of Child Psychology and Psychiatry*, *38*, 119–142.

Palumbo, D., Maughan, A., & Kurlan, R. (1997). Hypothesis III: Tourette syndrome is only one of several causes of a developmental basal ganglia syndrome. *Archives of Neurology*, *54*, 475–483.

Robertson, M.M., & Eapen, V. (1995). Gilles de la Tourette syndrome. In M.M. Robertson & V. Eapen (Eds.), *Movement and allied disorders* (pp. 1–29). New York: Wiley.

Robertson, M.M., & Yakeley, J. (1996). Gilles de la Tourette syndrome and obsessive-compulsive disorder. In B.S. Fogel, R.B. Schiffer, & S.M. Rao (Eds.), *Neuropsychiatry* (pp. 827–870). Baltimore: Williams & Wilkins.

Sheppard, D.M., Bradshaw, J.L., Purcell, R., & Pantelis, C. (1999). Tourette's and comorbid syndromes: Obsessive compulsive and attention deficit hyperactivity disorder. A common aetiology? *Clinical Psychology Review*, *19*, 531–552.

Shytle, R.D., Silver, A.A., & Sanberg, P.R. (1996). Clinical assessment of Tourette's syndrome. In P.R. Sanberg, K.P. Ossenkopp, & M. Kavaliers (Eds.), *Motor activity and movement disorders* (pp. 343–360). Totowa, NJ: Humana Press.

CHAPTER FIVE

Obsessive compulsive disorder

Doctor: What is it she [Lady Macbeth] does now? Look, how she rubs her hands.

Gentlewoman: It is an accustomed action with her to seem thus washing her hands: I have known her continue in this a quarter of an hour.

—*Macbeth*, Act V, Scene I, Shakespeare

INTRODUCTION

Obsessive compulsive disorder (OCD) has clear affinities with Tourette's syndrome, though it is less of a movement disorder, and more of a cognitive or psychiatric condition. In this chapter we shall see how its particular pattern of loss of self-regulation and control, and problems with the natural inhibition of thought and action, can be devastating for the sufferer, who knows how irrational are his/her obsessive thoughts and consequent compulsive actions. We shall see that OCD lies within a spectrum of related conditions and, further, is comorbid with a range of other neuropsychiatric, developmental, and frontostriatal disorders. We shall in this context note that many of the obsessions and compulsions are natural extensions of the preoccupations of normal childhood, and indeed in nonclinical form are clearly adaptive or protective. We shall discuss the genetics of the condition, and how genetic factors may interact with environmentally predisposing agents in the form of vulnerability genes. We shall note the neuropsychological consequences of the disorder, and the associated neuropathology, which affects aspects of the frontostriatal system and related circuitry. After discussing the neurochemistry of the disorder, which involves a range of modulatory neurotransmitters and neuropeptides, many of which are known from animal studies to play a role in obsessive compulsive behaviours in humans, we shall briefly address the treatment options.

71

PRELIMINARY CONSIDERATIONS

Shakespeare, ever observant of the manifold foibles of humanity, provides us with an early example of Lady Macbeth's obsessions and hand-washing rituals.

According to Boswell, his contemporary biographer, the eighteenth-century English lexicographer Samuel Johnson behaved in a fashion indicative of a modern diagnosis of comorbid Tourette's syndrome and OCD. A man otherwise known for the subtlety of his intellect and philosophical predisposition, he also appeared to suffer from uncontrolled eating compulsions, akin perhaps to bulimia, a condition allied to OCD. Thus Chapman (1953, cited by Parry-Jones, 1992, p. 851) records in modern English Boswell's account of Johnson's gustatory infelicities:

> When at table, he was totally absorbed in the business of the moment: his looks seemed riveted to his plate: nor would he, unless when in very high company, say one word, or even pay the least attention to what was said by others, till he had satisfied his appetite, which was so fierce, and indulged with such intenseness, that while in the act of eating, the veins of his forehead swelled, and generally a strong perspiration was visible. To those whose sensations were delicate, this could not but be disgusting: and it was doubtless not very suitable to the character of a philosopher, who should be distinguished by self-command . . . and not only was he remarkable for the extraordinary quantity which he ate, but he was, or affected to be, a man of very nice discernment in the science of cookery.

OCD is a poorly understood condition exhibiting considerable heterogeneity of content and variation over time, for which there is no pathognomic test. It is associated with problems in the natural inhibition of repetitive thoughts and action (Rosenberg et al., 1997), and with loss of self-regulation and control, compromised volition, stereotyped and perseverative ideas, obsessions, and behaviour (compulsions) (Koziol, 1994a). Patients know their obsessions are irrational and their compulsions excessive, but they persist despite all objective evidence to the contrary, manifesting a dissociation between knowing and doing. The pattern of disability changes and evolves over time, evincing a waxing and waning quality, often as a function of stress (Towbin & Riddle, 1996). Indeed it is currently classified according to DSM-IV as an anxiety disorder; very high anxiety ratings are typical, and it may be comorbid with other anxiety disorders. Performance of compulsions leads to temporary reductions in anxiety, and resistance to them is associated with increased anxiety and obsessions (Altemus, 1995).

For a diagnosis of OCD, obsessions and compulsions must be experienced as inappropriate, and sufficiently intense, frequent, or lengthy as to cause distress (to distinguish the condition from valid, real-life worries).

They must be recognised as a product of one's own mind (Parkin, 1997), even though they may be held with almost delusional strength. Thus although patients may recognise their thoughts and fears as absurd, they nevertheless often find it hard to believe that the feared consequences of not carrying out a ritual will not actually happen. The repetitive behaviours, which cannot easily be resisted, ignored, or suppressed, must be performed according to rigid "rules", and must not be gratifying, but done to reduce anxiety or distress (Carter, Pauls, & Leckman, 1995). In summary, there must be functional impairment, a feeling of force or invasion by the symptoms, and some level of insight into the senselessness or excessiveness of the thoughts or actions (Towbin & Riddle, 1996). Should this insight be lost, the condition clearly merges with the psychotic paranoia of schizophrenia. Should the actions be pleasurable, they no longer should be diagnosable as involving OCD, though the boundary again may be unclear, as with sexual obsessions, shoplifting, gambling, and eating disorders, and compulsive thrill seeking, all of which may also involve dysregulation of similar dopaminergic and serotonergic mechanisms (Blum, Cull, Braverman, & Comings, 1996; Wise, 1996).

ONSET AND PREVALENCE

The disorder's onset tends to be gradual rather than abrupt, and usually occurs after 7 years of age, and typically shortly after puberty, when in any case symptoms may increase. Manifestations may, however, first appear in adulthood, or after orbitofrontal or striatal damage. It tends to manifest earlier in males (20 years, versus 22 in females; see Jenike, Baer, & Minichiello, 1998), with a longer preclinical duration before presentation, perhaps being preceded by micro-episodes (Carter, A.S., et al., 1995). Its prevalence (which may be even higher in certain communities, such as the religious) is now estimated to reach 2–3% (Jenike et al., 1998; though see also Carter, A.S., et al., 1995; Niehaus & Stein, 1997; Koziol, 1994a; Towbin & Riddle, 1996; Wilson, 1998). It is the fourth most common psychiatric disorder after the phobias, substance abuse, and major depression, and ranks before schizophrenia. It occurs in roughly equal frequency between the sexes, though compulsive slowness may be commoner in males, and obsessions about hygiene and food in females (Parkin, 1997). Otherwise, obsessions may be more frequent in males and compulsions in females (Piacentini & Graae, 1997).

Tic-related OCD tends to start earlier then "pure" (nontic-related) OCD, and to affect more males (King, Leckman, Scahill, & Cohen, 1999). When, as it may, it manifests in children (AACAP Official Action, 1998), it does so in about one third to one half before 15 years, maybe as early as 5 years, with a mean age of onset at 10 years. Again boys tend to start earlier, though later there may be a corresponding female preponderance, and boys are more likely also to have tic disorder or Tourette's syndrome. Early onset is likely to be familial. Onset may be abrupt or insidious, with or without a precipitating event or trigger. The childhood form, moreover, may be chronic or remitting, though the majority tend to remain symptomatic. AACAP Official Action (1998) estimate a prevalence of 1–3.6% in adolescents, though they note that many young people "normally" exhibit a broad range of mild rituals and obsessions with similar content and form to the "pathological" variety, but differing significantly in frequency, intensity, and consequences. Such "normal" preoccupations are typically rarer, briefer, more easily dismissed, less vivid or disturbing, and less likely to provoke efforts at neutralisation or to be accompanied by compulsive acts. Thus there may be a lifetime prevalence, across the community, of self-reported intrusive images (6%), disturbing thoughts (8%), hoarding (29%), repetitive actions (27%), urges to repeat (30%), ritualised routines (34%), orderliness (49%), and extreme neatness (72%). Most individuals agree that these preoccupations are senseless but only 3.5% (the clinically affected individuals?) find them distressing.

OBSESSIONS AND COMPULSIONS

Patients often attempt to camouflage OCD behaviours, and may even be able, temporarily, to inhibit them, though at the cost of increased tension and rebound effects. *Obsessions* are defined as repetitive, intrusive thoughts, images or ideational impulses, with contents frequently seeming to be unrelated to the activities of daily living; they often appear pointless, bizarre, nonsensical, repulsive, obscene, sexual, or aggressive. The patient tries to resist, ignore, suppress, or neutralise them with another thought or action—a compulsion. Common obsessions (King et al., 1999) include:

- Aggression—fear of harming oneself or others, violent images, fear of blurting out obscenities or insults, fear of acting on impulses or of stealing, fear that one will be responsible for terrible happenings or events.
- Concern as to whether such an unacceptable act (sexual, aggressive, inappropriate, antisocial) was actually committed.
- Fears about a possible disaster to a loved one, or general safety.
- Fears of dirt and contamination, involving hygiene, waste, excretion, dirt, germs, the environment, animals and insects, and sticky residues; these fears are often accompanied by anxiety, disgust, guilt, and shame.
- Anxieties concerning possible separation from significant attachment figures.

- Sexual concerns, with respect to children, incest, forbidden thoughts, impulses, or images.
- Religious scrupulosity and concerns about possible sacrilege or blasphemy.
- Need for symmetry, exactness, perhaps accompanied by magical thinking or beliefs about lucky numbers or numerosity.
- Concerns about hoarding, saving or collecting.
- Somatic obsessions involving the body, illness, disease, or appearance.
- Pathological doubt—*folie de doute*.

Just as the obscenities or socially unacceptable behaviours of Tourette's syndrome, and the paranoid beliefs concerning thought control by the schizophrenic patient, are largely determined by the current societal standards, beliefs, or technological complexity, so too cultural factors strongly influence the nature of obsessions in OCD; in the Middle Ages there was fear of the plague, later was fear of syphilis, then of cancer, and nowadays of HIV/AIDS. At any one time, the patient may experience multiple obsessions and compulsions, though obsessions on their own, sexual, aggressive, or self-injurious, are perhaps commoner than unaccompanied compulsions.

Compulsions may, paradoxically, sometimes precede obsessions. Compulsions, actions, not intrinsically rewarding, in response to perceived internal obligation to follow certain rituals and rules, are normally typically motivated by obsessions or by efforts to ward off certain thoughts, impulses, or fears. Subjects may elaborate a variety of precise rules for the chronology, rate, order, duration, and number of repetitions of acts (Towbin & Riddle, 1996). Performance of compulsions leads to temporary reduction of anxiety, while resistance results in increased anxiety and obsessional mentation. Common compulsions (Carter, A.S., et al., 1995; King et al., 1999; Towbin & Riddle, 1996) include:

- Repetitive checking (acting out of *folie de doute*) of, for example, locks, stoves, heaters, irons, and other appliances, to avert possible harm to oneself or others.
- Repetition of rituals, repeating ritualised actions, words, or phrases, repetitive praying, which may merge with religious scrupulosity.
- Counting compulsions.
- Continual requests for reassurance.
- Ordering and arranging objects, "evening up" of sleeves, laces, dress etc. until everything is "just right".
- Cleaning and washing (especially of hands).
- Hoarding.

In childhood, when OCD emerges early, essentially similar findings are reported (AACAP Official Action, 1998); the commonest childhood symptoms involve obsessive contamination fears accompanied by compulsive washing and avoidance of "contaminated objects". Also found is compulsive checking, praying, scrupulosity, or worries concerning imagined sins, counting, arranging, touching in patterns or repetitions until things are "just right", and symmetrisation. The child may be unable to specify what may be the dread consequences their compulsive rituals are intended to avert, other than vague premonitions of something bad about to happen.

Of course, in nonpathological form, many obsessions and compulsions are adaptive, relating to safety, security, and health. It is possible that OCD may subdivide into a predominantly *obsessional* subtype, with excessive preoccupation with sexual or religious matters or violent imagery, a predominantly *compulsive* subtype (counting or checking rituals, ordering, and symmetry balancing), and a *mixed* subtype. It is also possible that these subtypes involve different structures within, for example, the frontostriatal circuitry (see below).

RATING SCALES OF SEVERITY

Scales and instruments for diagnosing and assessing OCD include the following:

- *Self rated*: Maudsley Obsessional Compulsive Inventory (MOCI) (Hodgson & Rachman, 1977); Leyton Obsessional Inventory (LOI) (Snowdon, 1980).
- *Observer rated*: Yale–Brown Obsessive-Compulsive Scale (Y-BOCS) (Goodman & Price, 1998); NIMH Global Obsessive-Compulsive Scale (Goodman & Price, 1998).

All are reviewed in Pato, Eisen, and Pato (1994) and Goodman and Price (1992).

OBSESSIVE COMPULSIVE PERSONALITY

We should distinguish obsessive compulsive *disorder* from the anxious and perfectionist obsessive compulsive *personality*, characterised, according to DSM-IV criteria, by hoarding, list making, rigid scheduling, a preoccupation with orderliness, perfectionism and control at the expense of flexibility, openness, and efficiency. There is a preoccupation, to the extent that the major point of the activity is lost, with details, rules, lists, schedules, order, and organisation; there is overconscientiousness, scrupulousness, morality, ethical values, a devotion to work, an inability to discard old, worn-out, and worthless objects, a reluctance to delegate authority, a lack of generosity, with miserliness, rigidity, and stubbornness to the extent that work and quality of life suffer. The obsessive compulsive personality is also reminiscent of the so-called parkinsonian (preclinical) personality of rigidity and excessive orderliness. Conversely, many people with true OCD are not especially neat, compliant, or attentive to details outside their specific symptoms. Perhaps the main difference between OCD and obsessive compulsive personality is that the former is characterised by feelings of inappropriateness and intrusiveness, while patients with obsessive compulsive personality maintain that their thoughts and actions are consistent with their own self image (Wilson, 1998).

A NEURODEVELOPMENTAL DISORDER

Like Tourette's syndrome, OCD may be partly a neurodevelopmental disorder. While children lack the metacognitive capacities sufficient for self-report on obsessive ideation, they often engage in rituals and apparent compulsions, with repetitive thoughts and words, a hatred of dirt though with scatological fascinations, and a worry about cleanliness, and they fuss and are indecisive (Carter, A.S., et al., 1995). Their ritual games and perseverative behaviours are reminiscent of frontal dysfunction. They exhibit a passion for sameness and uniformity with respect to clothing, food, stories, and bedtime routines, especially when stressed; they obsessively collect and engage in rituals to a "just so" level, and to magically ward off uncertainty. Their repetitious play (seen to excess in autism also) and superstitious behaviour merge with adult OCD routines (Evans, Gray, & Leckman, 1999). Again, however, unlike the adult phenomenology, much of this childhood activity is more or less pleasurable. During childhood there are massive developmental changes in the prefrontal cortex: an initial increase in prefrontal neuropil perhaps corresponding to the emergence of obsessional behaviours, followed by synaptic pruning in the striatum, orbitofrontal cortex, and anterior cingulate (Rosenberg & Keshavan, 1998), perhaps corresponding to these behaviours' normal disappearance. Thus OCD may be a neurodevelopmental disorder, with benign manifestations affecting many of us, even in adulthood. Thus a tune which one cannot get out of one's head and a passion for collecting stamps, wine labels, or cigarette packets may represent forms of obsession or compulsion far below clinical levels.

COMORBIDITY

OCD often overlaps, or is comorbid, with anxiety and depression (though not mania), hypochondriasis, panic attacks, and social and other phobias and substance abuse (Jenike et al., 1998; Niehaus & Stein, 1997). Indeed about half of OCD probands also have anxiety and/or depression, and the same is true in the reverse direction (AACAP Official Action, 1998). Anxiety rates are also elevated in the relatives of OCD probands. Obsessional thinking, moreover, is common in major depression (where it manifests as intrusive, persistent rumination); indeed the pharmacology and neurosurgical procedures (disruption of white matter tracts between the frontal lobes, basal ganglia, and thalamus) are essentially similar in both circumstances. Obsessional thinking is also common in schizophrenia, though such sufferers tend not to view their ruminations as intrusive and unpleasant (Parkin, 1997). Children with pervasive developmental disorders (e.g. autism and Asperger's disorder) also often manifest stereotypic behaviour, preoccupations, and fixed interests, though these experiences seem not to occasion the same level of distress as is the case with OCD (AACAP Official Action, 1998). Moreover, high rates of OCD have been reported in the first-degree relatives of probands with autism and Asperger's disorder. There is likewise considerable comorbidity between OCD and attention deficit hyperactivity disorder, and conduct disorder, both of which tend to manifest earlier than OCD itself.

However, OCD is particularly comorbid with Tourette's syndrome, and may even be an alternative (for motor tics) manifestation of a Tourette's syndrome gene. Indeed it is often difficult to distinguish between complex tics and compulsions, both of which may be preceded by similar premonitory sensations (King & Scahill, 1995), though only OCD may possess the ideational component. There is also a suggestion that OCD comorbid with Tourette's syndrome is more likely to involve touching, symmetrisation, and violent or sexual urges, while OCD without Tourette's syndrome tends to involve fears of contamination (Niehaus & Stein, 1997). In some ways, of course, OCD is a cognitive counterpart of the motor manifestations of Tourette's syndrome: both disorders involve disinhibition of repetitive behaviours that, while "involuntary" (like a yawn), nevertheless are still amenable to some voluntary control; both involve a prior feeling of increasing tension until the action is "correctly" performed, followed by temporary relief; both are exacerbated by stress, fatigue, and emotion; both involve scatological or obscene cognitive material, contamination, excretory, or sexual behaviours. There are, however, also important differences: although the intrusive thoughts of OCD may result, like Tourette's syndrome, from lack of cognitive inhibition, there is also an important element of *overfocusing* of attention in OCD, with inhibition of other possibly more relevant behaviours. This situation is rather different from Tourette's syndrome and attention deficit hyperactivity disorder, both disorders of motoric disinhibition, with an inability to sustain or focus attention. Importantly, the ritual of OCD often seems more "purposeful" than the tic of Tourette's syndrome; moreover, whereas sensory phenomena may precede the tics of Tourette's syndrome, complex cognitions and anxiety tend to precede the compulsions of OCD. Some patients have described tics as being preceded by "an itch", and compulsions as by "a want" (King et al., 1999); thus a tic is perhaps more physical, and a compulsion more mental or emotional. That said, the borderline between the complex tics of Tourette's syndrome and simple compulsions in OCD, such as tapping or repetitive symmetrical touching, is very vague, though the onset of motor tics tends to precede that of compulsive actions (King et al., 1999). Complex tics and obsessive thoughts may reflect homologous aberrant neural processes that are manifested respectively in the motor and cognitive behavioural domains (Drevets, 1999a).

OCD occurring in the context of a personal or family history of tics may differ from OCD in their absence, in terms of clinical phenomenology, neurobiological concomitants, responsiveness to pharmacological interventions, gender ratio, age of onset, and number and nature of symptoms (AACAP Official Action, 1998). Thus tic-related childhood-onset OCD has an earlier onset, and is commoner in boys. Moreover the presence or absence of related tics in the families of OCD probands tends to breed true (Pauls, Alsobrook, Gelerntner, & Leckman, 1999). The need to touch or rub, blinking or staring rituals, worries over symmetry and exactness, and intrusive aggressive images are all commoner in OCD with comorbid tics, whereas contamination and hygiene worries and rituals are all more common in nontic OCD. Tic-related OCD responds less well to selective serotonin reuptake inhibitors alone.

Symptoms of OCD may occur in cases of postencephalitic parkinsonism, Huntington's disease, and Sydenham's chorea, and after lesions of the neostriatum or pallidum, or prefrontal cortex (Blanes & McGuire, 1997).

It may be useful to conceive of a spectrum of disorders related more or less closely to OCD (AACAP Official Action, 1998; Geller, 1998). Such disorders include onychophagia (nail biting), skin and face picking, trichotillomania (compulsive hair avulsion), eating disorders (anorexia and bulimia nervosa), body dysmorphic disorder (preoccupation with imagined defects in appearance that leads to excessive grooming and mirror checking), compulsive shopping and gambling, kleptomania, and pyromania. Some of these should not be included directly under OCD, as participants may get some pleasure from their actions, may not necessarily recognise the senselessness of those actions, and do not necessarily try to resist the compulsions (Jenike & Wilhelm, 1998). Indeed, while all OCD behaviours are characterised by intrusive events, and are accompanied by a drive to perform the intentional, although unwanted, repetitive behaviours, there are nevertheless subtle differences (Rauch, Whalen, Dougherty, & Jenike, 1998):

- OCD and body dysmorphic disorder both involve intrusive cognitive events driven by anxiety.
- Tourette's syndrome and trichotillomania are primarily sensorimotor intrusions driven by urges to relieve sensory tension.

A similar analysis may clearly be performed for other numbers of the spectrum. Compulsive shopping and gambling, kleptomania and pyromania, moreover, may associate with bipolar disorder. In the eating disorders there is a female preponderance, and diet may be restricted by fasting, purging, or excessive exercise (itself an obsession/compulsion in its own right), or by the use of laxatives, enemas, emetics, or diuretics; refusal to maintain minimal normal weight, and fear of weight gain, may lead to persistent amenorrhoea. Clearly, there are additional disturbances of body image, and in bulimia nervosa, where bingeing and dieting alternate, there may be a similar sense that self-esteem depends on body weight and shape.

An obsession-like condition with which many may identify is the state of "being in love", where intrusive thoughts and inappropriate actions may come to dominate the otherwise happy afflicted individual. We shall see that low levels of serotonin may characterise OCD; this state may also characterise the amorous state, according to Marazziti, Akiskal, Ross, and Cassano (1999), just as it does also the anxious, the aggressive, and the sexually overactive, as well as such intrusive emotions as obsessive jealousy. Other factors must obviously also be present to differentiate these various states; nor is the direction of causality necessarily obvious.

GENETICS

Genetic transmission of OCD is implied by its familial nature, with increased prevalence in first-degree relatives (25% of whom may share a diagnosis of OCD; Wilson, 1998), the increased prevalence of Tourette's syndrome in relatives, and increased concordance in monozygotic (>70%) compared to zygotic twins (Alsobrook & Pauls, 1998; King & Scahill, 1995; Towbin & Riddle, 1996). Autosomal dominant transmission seems probable, though no good gene candidates have yet emerged, and it should be noted that whereas OCD prevalence is increased in female relatives of Tourette's syndrome sufferers, tics are more common in male relatives. A model whereby vulnerability genes may be turned on or off at various times during development, as a result of environmental or genetic factors, may be preferred (Leckman & Cohen, 1999b). Thus there may be a range of both risk and protective factors influencing gene expression, including pre- and perinatal events and exposure to bacterial antigens. Similar vulnerability genes may also be associated with other comorbid and frontostriatal disorders, such as depression, bipolar disorder, anxiety disorder, and conduct disorder.

NEUROPSYCHOLOGY OF OBSESSIVE COMPULSIVE DISORDER

There is an increased presence of mild neurological abnormalities and "soft signs", many indicative of frontostriatal involvement, including also deficits in fine motor coordination, involuntary and mirror movements (Cohen, Stein, & Hollander, 1997). Other motor signs include slowed response times (though this could stem from obsessional or meticulous indecisiveness or checking), tics, and/or choreiform movements as in other such putatively neurodevelopmental disorders as autism or attention deficit hyperactivity disorder, and oculomotor irregularities. Thus OCD patients may have difficulty suppressing oculomotor responses to exogenous stimuli, when required, but may be *superior* to normal individuals on oculomotor delayed responses (Rosenberg & Keshavan, 1998), perhaps because they are more focused, less distractible, and less likely to disengage attention—a pattern opposite to that of attention deficit hyperactivity disorder.

Neuropsychological tests reveal deficits in visuospatial and visuoconstructional performance and visual memory as shown by the ability to manipulate objects in two- or three-dimensional space (Purcell, Maruff, Kyrios, & Pantelis, 1998; Savage, 1998); tasks have included Block Design, Cube Copying, Money's Road Map Test, Figure Matching Test, and Mental Rotation. Deficits in nonverbal memory manifest in the context of the ability to learn and recall new visual objects, pictures, or items that cannot be easily labelled. Deficits have been shown at the levels of encoding and retrieval rather than of storage, and tests have included the Wechsler Memory Scale, the Delayed Recognition Span Test, the Benson Visual Retention Test, Korsi's Block Test, and Stylus Maze Learning.

Language and general intelligence seem relatively unaffected, although there is considerable evidence of executive dysfunction, reduced verbal fluency and problems with set or attention shifting, planning, abstract thinking, problem solving, response inhibition, and trial and error learning. Thus patients show deficits in the strategic organisation of complex responses, and the ability flexibly to adapt to novel situations, indicative of involvement of the dorsolateral prefrontal cortex (Purcell et al., 1998; Rosenberg et al., 1997). The Wisconsin Card Sorting Test, the Cambridge Neuropsychological Test Automated Battery, Trail Making, and the Stroop all attest to problems with perseveration, set, and attention, though it should be noted that we can partition the latter into at least five components:

- Detection of novel events.
- Sustained vigilance.
- Selectivity or focusing.
- Disengagement.
- Shifting of attention.

These components are likely to be differentially affected, along with motor aspects, in Tourette's syndrome, OCD, and attention deficit hyperactivity disorder. The focusing aspect may largely involve the anterior cingulate and orbitofrontal cortex, the sustained aspect the diffuse ascending reticular formation and noradrenergic mechanisms, and a switching component (encompassing both disengagement and shifting), respectively the parietal cortex and the superior colliculus, with perhaps greater involvement of the right hemisphere. The pulvinar may mediate attentional engagement (Posner & Raichle, 1994).

Disordered, sensorimotor gating in OCD, with frontostriatal involvement, is further suggested by problems with saccadic eye movement programming (problems with smooth tracking, overshooting, and reversal saccades), with prepulse inhibition of the startle reflex, and with inhibition of return (Wilson, 1998). People can normally suppress the startle reflex when a startling stimulus (e.g. loud noise burst) is preceded by a weaker "cueing" prepulse; this suppression is reduced in OCD. In Posner-type tasks precues as to location of an upcoming event normally benefit reaction times when valid; when, however, a second event happens to occur in the location of a previous event, there is a cost (increase in reaction time)—"inhibition of return". This cost of "returning" to a previously "visited" location is reduced in OCD, especially with events in the right visual field, suggesting disruption of a normal novelty bias.

The distributed nature of the cognitive and motor dysfunctions in OCD has led to the suggestion (Blanes & McGuire, 1997) that there may be two subtypes of the disorder: One is a late-onset (largely female) variant characterised by obsessional thoughts and preoccupations, including anorexia nervosa, body dysmorphic disorder, depersonalisation, hypochondriasis, anxiety, and mood disorder. The other (largely male, and of early onset) is associated with neurological dysfunctions of a more clearly frontostriatal nature; it is characterised more by motor symptoms, stereotyped, ritualistic or driven behaviours, tics, trichotillomania, Sydenham's chorea, and other pervasive (neuro)developmental disorders like autism and schizophrenia. This subtype has more severe symptomatology that is more resistant to serotonergic antidepressants, and is more likely to be associated with neuroimaging anomalies, a history of obstetric complications, and neurological soft signs. Blanes and McGuire (1997) even speculate that common neurodevelopmental mechanisms may lead either to schizophrenia or OCD.

NEUROPATHOLOGY OF OBSESSIVE COMPULSIVE DISORDER

OCD-like behaviour may be reported with disorders involving damage to the basal ganglia, notably the striatum, as in Huntington's disease (Purcell et al., 1998; Rosenberg et al., 1997). Indeed autoimmune OCD, perhaps in genetically vulnerable individuals, with antineuronal antibodies formed after childhood streptococcal infection and involving the corticostriatothalamic pathways, as in Sydenham's chorea, is not uncommon (Leckman & Cohen, 1999b). Thus Jenike, Baer, and Minichiello (1998) see OCD as a PANDA (a paediatric autoimmune neuropsychiatric disorder), which as a group may also encompass tic disorder and even some cases of attention deficit hyperactivity disorder. PANDAs typically have a prepubertal onset, an episodic course of symptom severity, a dramatic exacerbation of symptoms after a group A β-haemolytic streptococcal infection, and a range of neurological abnormalities. Pathways affected in OCD are thought to mediate key mammalian behaviour routines of grooming, cleaning, nesting, reproduction, and avoidance of danger. We have already seen that cingulate damage in rats can affect nest building, maternal care, and affiliative and sexual behaviours of the sort found excessively in human OCD (Peterson et al., 1999a). Similarly the neuropeptides oxytocin and arginine-vasopressin are important in repetitive, affiliative grooming and maternal behaviour (Anderson, Leckman, & Cohen, 1999; Jenike, 1998). Consequently OCD behaviour (hygiene, checking, hoarding etc.) may represent an exaggeration or disinhibition of such normally adaptive species-specific behaviours (King & Scahill, 1995; Koziol, 1994a; Wilson, 1998). However, many compulsions, e.g. counting and praying, are not really of this sort.

Abnormal volumes and activity of various frontostriatal regions have been reported in OCD (for reviews, see Drevets, 1999a; Peterson et al., 1999a; Rauch & Baxter, 1998; Rosenberg et al., 1997). Thus there may be an overall reduction in caudate volume in OCD. At a functional level and in the neutral, resting state, there is prominent hyperactivity in the orbitofrontal cortex and probably also in the striatum (especially perhaps on the right) and anterior cingulate, which reduces with successful treatment. Under symptom provocation, the orbitofrontal cortex, caudate, and anterior cingulate are further activated in many but not all studies. Thus there are many inconsistencies in the literature, stemming in part from procedural differences, depending upon whether measurements were taken during resting state, with symptom provocation, or during (or after) treatment (Wilson, 1998). Nevertheless if the orbitofrontal cortex is crucial for suppressing behavioural responses to irrelevant stimuli, and OCD onset after 7 years corresponds to the period of normal development of such structures, then OCD may be seen as a neurodevelopmental disorder of an overactive orbitofrontal warning system (Piacentini & Graae, 1997). This would account for the abnormal caution and checking activity, whereas a hyperactive striatum would explain abnormal release of obsessions and compulsions (Koziol, 1994a; Purcell et al., 1998). Thus the key to OCD may be hyperactivity of the anterior cingulate (driving the behaviour) and of the orbitofrontal cortex (perhaps an attempt at focusing, inhibiting, or "warning", with defective striatal filtering). Conversely, in Tourette's syndrome we may see hyperactivity of the sensorimotor cortex and putamen, and in anxiety and affective disorders disturbance of the limbic and paralimbic structures including the anterior cingulate, ventral striatum, and nucleus accumbens (see Rauch & Baxter, 1998). Other evidence for orbitofrontal involvement in OCD comes from the finding (Barnett et al., 1999) of a deficit in olfactory function in the disorder.

NEUROCHEMISTRY OF OBSESSIVE COMPULSIVE DISORDER

Dopamine agonists and stimulants (cocaine, amphetamine) can cause response stereotypies, perseverative behaviour, and hoarding in animals, and repetitive ritualistic behaviour (and improved performance on delayed response tasks) in humans, whereas OCD is ameliorated by dopaminergic blocking agents (pimozide, haloperidol) (see, for example, Rosenberg & Keshavan, 1998; Towbin & Riddle, 1996). Indeed such medication may even result in loss of interest in collecting hobbies, suggesting that the latter may themselves represent a benign form of the disorder. However, serotonin, which has an inhibitory effect on dopaminergic neurones, is also implicated in the disorder, as selective serotonin reuptake inhibitors, which may act on the head of the caudate and on the nucleus accumbens, ameliorate the condition. These drugs (fluoxetine, fluvoxamine) take time to act via auto-receptor downregulation (Rauch et al., 1998) and may also affect other neurotransmitters, whereas clonidine stimulates α_2-noradrenergic receptors on serotonergic terminals (Altemus, 1995). The reciprocal relationship between dopamine and serotonin levels, and the observation that dopamine agonists can improve delayed responding, supports the possibility (Rosenberg & Keshavan, 1998) that reduced prefrontal serotonin levels in OCD may account for patients' superior performance in delayed responding; performance in delayed responding, in animal studies, is moreover known to involve orbitofrontal mechanisms.

In addition to dopamine and serotonin, the neurosecretory peptides arginine, vasopressin, somatostatin, and oxytocin have also been implicated (King & Scahill, 1995; Piacentini & Graae, 1997), many of which seem to play a role in grooming, affiliative, maternal, sexual, and aggressive behaviour (Anderson, G.M., et al., 1999). Changes in OCD severity at puberty may relate to the modulating effect of gonadal hormones on vasopressin projections from amygdala to regions involved in generating repetitive behaviours and stereotypies.

FRONTOSTRIATAL CIRCUITRY AND OBSESSIVE COMPULSIVE DISORDER

We have already seen that the orbitofrontal cortex (especially the anterior and lateral division) is involved in response inhibition and the social regulation of behaviour; the anterior cingulate (and maybe the poster-omedial division of the orbitofrontal cortex; see Rauch et al., 1998) as a component of the limbic and paralimbic systems is probably concerned with drive, motivation, and affect, integrating abstract representations of the outside world (derived from the dorsolateral prefrontal cortex) with inner emotional states. In this way priority may be assigned during infor-mation processing. The role of the striatum is to intervene as a filter or switch, to process information automatically and without conscious rep-resentation, particularly for stereotyped, rule-governed, or repetitive behav-iour. In OCD, the orbitofrontal cortex and anterior cingulate appear simultaneously hyperactive, maybe via positive feedback loops through the direct and indirect pathways of the basal ganglia. Thus (see, for example, Rosenberg & Keshavan, 1998) OCD may stem from increased activation of the *direct* (compared to the *indirect*) basal ganglia pathway, with a consequent inability to inhibit intrusive thoughts. (The direct pathway plays a generally activating role, and the indirect an inhibitory role.) Conversely, a defect in the inhibitory indirect pathway may lead to overactivity in the direct pathway, again with consequent overactivity (and increased volume) in the anterior cingulate. Serotonin and dopamine set the balance between the two pathways, with dopamine D1 receptor stimulation activating the direct and dopamine D2 receptor stimulation inhibiting the indirect pathway. Disturbance, of course, of this arrangement with nigrostriatal dysfunction in Parkinson's disease leads to hypokinesia and rigidity. It is also possible that OCD stems from delayed serotonergic maturation, along with normal, premature, or excessive dopaminergic maturation or activity, with similar consequences to those outlined above. Either way, effects would be further mediated, and modulated, by excitatory glutamate, whose levels may increase during stress, which itself is known to exacerbate the disorder. The combination of stress and genetically mediated fronto-striatal anomalies may lead to a glutamatergically driven hyperdopami-nergic state in the anterior cingulate and orbitofrontal cortex (Rosenberg & Keshavan, 1998).

Rauch et al. (1998) suggest a possible additional role for the amygdala in OCD. This structure within the medial temporal lobe responds to biologically relevant stimuli and mediates increased arousal or emotional reactivity. Important for rapid, automatic "gut" responses, it receives input widely from the cortex, thalamus, hypothalamus, and hippocampus, and projects to the dorsolateral prefrontal cortex, orbitofrontal cortex, cingulate, insula, striatum, thalamus, and hypothalamus. It is therefore well placed to activate autonomic responses, potentiate motor releases, and regulate overall arousal. It is also clearly relevant to conditioned fear, vigilance behaviour, and anxiety, driving repetitive behaviour via the corticostriatal system. Performing these behaviours is perhaps anxiolytic and inhibits the overactive amygdala. According to such a model, these behaviours then become conditioned and self-perpetuating.

Zald and Kim (1996) address essentially the same point, in the context of the overall functioning of the orbitofrontal cortex, and indeed see a fourfold relevance of that structure to OCD:

- It is involved in neural networks otherwise implicated, from animal studies, in the coding of stimuli of behavioural significance or relevance to the individual; because it is anatomically and functionally associated with paralimbic regions and the amygdala, it is well placed to assess the aversive properties of stimuli that trigger OCD symptoms such as fear and anxiety.
- It is involved in neural substrates mediating operant responses to reward, intracranial self-stimulation, and craving for addictive substances; in these respects it is clearly relevant to the compulsions of OCD, whose performance, via ritualised behaviour, leads to a temporary reduction in anxiety and distress.
- It is involved in social-affiliative behaviour, with lesions resulting in the pseudopsychopathy of risky behaviour despite full knowledge of the risks involved. In this respect patients with OCD show excessive concern for others (compared to the pseudopsychopath's lack of concern), and worry that their actions will negatively affect others. Guilt, shame, and anxiety are all heightened, and reduced with therapeutic lesions to input structures to the orbitofrontal cortex.
- It is involved in the maintenance of appropriate response sets in delayed responding and reversal learning; overactivity in the orbitofrontal cortex may therefore lead in OCD to ritualised and repetitive responding to get things "just right".

Such considerations may help to resolve the apparent paradox of overactive orbitofrontal regions in OCD, when the latter may seem to involve inability to inhibit the unwanted cognitions; the overactivity may be an attempt to inhibit an overactive "drive" from the anterior cingulate and/or direct basal ganglia pathways. Such an account would also fit with the overfocused quality of the disorder.

TREATMENT

In the Middle Ages exorcism may have been the only resort, but nowadays there is a range of pharmacological, surgical, and behaviour therapy treatments. Orbitofrontal outputs, as we have just seen, drive the caudate, which in turn inhibits the globus pallidus. Weakened activity in the globus pallidus may fail to inhibit the thalamus, which is therefore more excitatory to the orbitofrontal cortex. Treatment may weaken the inhibitory activity from the caudate so that the globus pallidus inhibits the thalamus and decreases excitatory return input to the orbitofrontal cortex (Towbin & Riddle, 1996). Stereotaxic surgery (anterior capsulotomy, anterior cingulotomy, subcaudate tractotomy, limbic leukotomy) is one way of achieving this (Piacentini & Graae, 1997), as is medication and even behaviour therapy. In the latter case, provoking situations are rank ordered, and the therapist starts with the weakest and gradually works up, with gradual confrontation and response prevention (delaying ritualisation) (King and Scahill, 1995; Piacentini & Graae, 1997). There is some evidence of normalisation of area metabolism with relief of symptoms from behaviour therapy.

With respect to drug treatment, serotonergic agents (selective serotonin reuptake inhibitors) are clearly the medication of choice in OCD, acting maybe via the ventromedial striatum (including the nucleus accumbens), where there is much direct serotonergic innervation. Drugs such as fluoxetine (Prozac), sertraline (Zoloft), paroxetine (Paxil), and fluvoxamine (Luvox) are all selective serotonin reuptake inhibitors, whereas clomipramine (Anafranil, a serotonin reuptake inhibitor) also affects other neurotransmitters (Jenike, 1998). All five are equally effective, for OCD and for the usually concurrent depression. The opiate antagonists naloxone and naltrexone are efficacious against trichotillomania and self-injurious behaviour. As noted above, successful treatment also tends to normalise metabolic anomalies, suggesting the presence and operation of state rather than trait factors.

SUMMARY AND CONCLUSIONS

Obsessions and compulsions have long aroused the interests of literary observers of the human condition. The disorder itself, like all the neuropsychiatric developmental disorders of the frontostriatal system, is poorly understood in its aetiology and heterogeneous in its manifestation. However, there is a common difficulty with the natural inhibition of repetitive or perseverative thoughts and actions, and a loss of self-regulation and control. Sufferers know the irrationality of the condition, but are driven to indulge or accommodate it. Like Tourette's syndrome (which it resembles, though the latter lacks the overfocused quality of OCD), and like attention deficit hyperactivity disorder, there is a waxing and waning quality; in schizophrenia and depression, such cycles may be of longer duration. To quantify for diagnosis, behaviours must be inappropriate, intense, and lengthy enough to cause distress; they must not be gratifying, otherwise an obsessive compulsive *personality* should be ascribed. Similar considerations apply to a spectrum of related disorders, bulimia, trichotillomania, pyromania, compulsive shoplifting and gambling, and thrill seeking, where an element of (often vicarious) pleasure is experienced. Thus performance follows rigid rules, accompanied by a feeling of invasion, though with preservation of insight concerning the situation's intrinsic futility, an insight which is typically absent with similar behaviour in schizophrenia. Other comorbid or accompanying conditions include anxiety, depression, bipolar disorder (as with compulsive shopping and gambling), phobias, substance abuse, and, especially, Tourette's syndrome, which may even be a variant of a gene common to both disorders. Thus complex motor tics lie on a continuum with simple compulsions, and the latter may be regarded as cognitive, mental, or "semi-purposeful" counterparts of the former. However, there is a strong element of overfocusing in OCD that is absent in Tourette's syndrome and attention deficit hyperactivity disorder. Obsessional thinking is of course also present in schizophrenia, autism, and Asperger's disorder.

The disorder manifests in childhood or at puberty, a little later in females (as in schizophrenia), and usually gradually, though sometimes abruptly, with a 2–3% prevalence. *Obsessions* involve repetitive, intrusive thoughts, images, or ideational impulses, which are recognised even by the sufferer as pointless, bizarre, nonsensical, repulsive, obscene, sexual, or aggressive; there may frequently be fear of harm to oneself, or to loved ones either from one's own or others' actions. *Compulsions* are not intrinsically rewarding, but are anxiolytic attempts motivated by the obsessions, in an attempt to neutralise the distress with another thought or action, or to ward off certain thoughts, impulses, or fears. Hygiene, hoarding, orderliness, symmetry, rearranging, checking, rituals, and counting all feature, as indeed they also tend to in many normal children, with their ritual games, perseverative behaviours, and fascination with dirt, excretion, and sexual matters, and their passions for collecting. The neurodevelopmental arrest which may thereby feature in the disorder is attested to by such childish obsessions; the obsessive quality of adult sexual love or attraction may be a relic to which we are all potentially subject. Indeed, most of the behaviours in nonpathological form are clearly adaptive in the maintenance of health, hygiene, safety, an adequate food supply, and a sexual or reproductive partner; a successful scientist, physician, or home-maker must display many of these behaviours in moderation.

The condition is clearly familial, and possibly heritable via autosomal dominant transmission, though no good candidate gene has yet been identified. Symptoms may appear after exposure to various environmental events, such as postencephalitic parkinsonism, pre- and perinatal events, and childhood streptococcal infection, as with Tourette's syndrome and possibly attention deficit hyperactivity disorder, which suggests a role for antineuronal antibodies, targeting the striatum. Vulnerability genes may perhaps be turned on and off at various times during childhood. Apart from striatal lesions triggering such behaviours, cingulate damage in rats may affect nest building, maternal care, and sexual behaviours, all of which are reminiscent of the behaviours over-expressed in human OCD. There are reports of reduced caudate volume, and hyperactivity of the orbitofrontal cortex (excessive focusing?), anterior cingulate (compulsive drive?), and the right striatum (all the neurodevelopmental disorders of the frontostriatal system involve some anomalies of lateralisation). However, there are many inconsistencies in the literature.

Neuropsychologically, there is evidence of soft signs, mild neurological impairment, and deficits in fine motor coordination; increased reaction times may reflect meticulous obsessionality. There are executive dysfunctions, and problems with visuospatial and visuoconstructive performance and visual memory. Sufferers are less likely to disengage attention—a pattern opposite, for example, to what is found in Parkinson's disease, and indicative of the role of dopamine in attentional focusing. There are anomalies of behavioural lateralisation, inhibition of return, and prepulse inhibition. Conversely, performance on delayed response tasks may be superior.

Neurochemically, stimulants such as the dopamine agonists cocaine and amphetamine lead in animals to stereotypies, perseverative behaviour and hoarding, and in humans to ritualistic behaviours. Dopamine blockers such as haloperidol, conversely, ameliorate the condition, as do the selective serotonin reuptake inhibitors. The neurosecretory peptides arginine, vasopressin, oxytocin, and somatostatin are all involved in grooming, affiliative, sexual, maternal, and aggressive behaviour—behaviours that are all reminiscent of those found in OCD; the gonadal hormones may modulate the above mechanisms.

For treatment, stereotaxic surgery (anterior capsulotomy, anterior cingulotomy, subcaudate tractotomy, limbic leukotomy) severs a range of tracts relevant to the expression of the disorder; success, however, is not assured. The selective serotonin reuptake inhibitors, acting on the nucleus accumbens, have the added advantage of also alleviating the usually concomitant anxiety. Behaviour therapy is often efficacious, even normalising area metabolism, leading to the question as to whether abnormal metabolic function causes or accompanies the disorder—and, if the latter, may even be an attempt at compensation. Either way, abnormal area metabolism seems to be a state rather than a trait factor.

Clearly, frontostriatal mechanisms are involved: limbic mechanisms of drive, motivation, and affect; faulty striatal filtering or switching, in the context of repetitive, rule-governed behaviour; increased orbitofrontal (overfocusing? attempts at compensation? rumination?) and anterior cingulate (compulsive quality?) activity, both reflecting a glutamatergically driven (stress response) hyperdopaminergic state; and, finally, amygdaloid involvement, responding to biologically relevant stimuli, with its role for rapid, automatic, "gut" responses and its links to the orbitofrontal cortex. There may of course also be an additional imbalance of direct (over-activity?) and indirect (underactivity) pathways within the basal ganglia, as a consequence of dopaminergic and serotonergic involvement.

FURTHER READING

AACAP Official Action (1998). Practice parameters for the assessment and treatment of children and adolescents with obsessive compulsive disorder. *Journal of the American Academy of Child and Adolescent Psychiatry, 37* (Suppl. 10), 27S–45S.

Altemus, M. (1995). Neuroendocrinology of obsessive compulsive disorder. In J. Panksepp (Ed.), *Advances in biological psychiatry* (Vol. 1, pp. 215–233). London: JAI Press.

Blanes, T., & McGuire, P. (1997). Heterogeneity within obsessive compulsive disorder: Evidence for primary and neurodevelopmental subtypes. In M.S. Keshaven & R.M. Murray (Eds.), *Neurodevelopment and adult psychopathology* (pp. 206–214). Cambridge, UK: Cambridge University Press.

Carter, A.S., Pauls, D.L., & Leckman, J.F. (1995). The development of obsessionality: Continuities and discontinuities. In D. Cicchetti & D.J. Cohen (Eds.), *Developmental psychopathology: Risk disorder and adaptation* (Vol. 2, pp. 609–632). New York: Wiley.

Hollander, E., & Stein, D.J. (Eds.) (1997). *Obsessive compulsive disorders: Diagnosis, etiology, treatment*. New York: Marcel Dekker.

Jenike, M.A., Baer, L., & Minichiello, W.E. (1998). An overview of obsessive compulsive disorder. In M.A. Jenike, L. Baer, & W.E. Minichiello (Eds.), *Obsessive compulsive disorders: Practical management* (pp. 3–11). St Louis: Mosby.

King, R.A., & Scahill, L. (1995). Obsessive compulsive disorder in children and adolescents. In M.M. Robertson & V. Eapen (Eds.), *Movement and allied disorders* (pp. 43–56). New York: Wiley.

Koran, L. (1999). *Obsessive-compulsive and related disorders in adults: A comprehensive clinical guide*. Cambridge, UK: Cambridge University Press.

Parkin, R. (1997). Obsessive compulsive disorder in adults. *International Review of Psychiatry, 9*, 73–81.

Rosenberg, D.R., & Keshavan, M.S. (1998). Toward a neurodevelopmental model of obsessive compulsive disorder. *Biological Psychiatry, 43*, 623–640.

Rosenberg, D.R., Averbach, D.H., O'Hearn, K.M., Seymour, A.B., Birmaher, B., & Sweeney, J.A. (1997). Oculomotor response inhibition abnormalities in pediatric obsessive compulsive disorder. *Archives of General Psychiatry, 54*, 831–838.

Tallis, F. (1997). The neuropsychology of obsessive compulsive disorder: A review and consideration of clinical implications. *British Journal of Clinical Psychology, 36*, 3–20.

Towbin, K.E., & Riddle, M.A. (1996). Obsessive compulsive disorder. In M. Lewis (Ed.), *Child and adolescent psychiatry: A comprehensive textbook* (pp. 684–693). Baltimore: Williams & Wilkins.

Wilson, K.D. (1998). Issues concerning the cognitive neuroscience of obsessive compulsive disorder. *Psychonomic Bulletin and Review, 5,* 161–172.

Zald, D.H., & Kim, S.W. (1996). Anatomy and function of the orbital frontal cortex, II: Function and relevance to obsessive compulsive disorder. *Journal of Neuropsychiatry and Clinical Neurosciences, 8,* 249–261.

CHAPTER SIX

Attention deficit hyperactivity disorder

It is one thing to praise discipline, and another to submit to it.
—*The Dialogue of the Dogs*, Cervantes (1613)

INTRODUCTION

Attention deficit hyperactivity disorder (ADHD) is in some respects a cognitive analogue of Tourette's syndrome, with respect to impulsivity and disinhibition; similarly, it contrasts with the focused preoccupations of obsessive compulsive disorder (OCD), and the inertia of melancholic depression. However, unlike these other disorders, it perhaps impacts rather more upon other members of society than upon the affected individual. In this chapter we shall review criteria and problems in diagnosis (and possible over-diagnosis), the existence of two possible variants of the disorder, comorbidities, how it may continue into adulthood, and possible environmental determinants. We shall see that, like so many of the neurodevelopmental frontostriatal disorders, there is probably an inherited susceptibility, with vulnerability genes perhaps able to be turned on or off at various developmental phases. We shall review possible genetic mechanisms, and the role of modulatory neurotransmitters, particularly dopamine, serotonin, and possibly noradrenaline. Although there may be morphometric correlates of the disorder, we shall see that a neurochemical imbalance may be a more important factor, as perhaps with Tourette's syndrome, OCD and depression, though as with schizophrenia we cannot discount possible structural changes. We shall review the neuropsychology of the disorder, particularly with reference to executive functions and inhibitory processes. As with Tourette's syndrome and OCD, many of the characteristic features of ADHD are normally present in most children younger than a certain age; we shall finally, therefore, address the possibly adaptive aspects of the "disorder" in certain selective or environmental contexts.

PRELIMINARY CONSIDERATIONS

ADHD may be seen as an externalising disorder in that its effects maximally impact upon others in the community, particularly carers and educators, and perhaps relatively less upon the individual concerned, at least directly (Diamond & Mattsson, 1996). In this respect it is perhaps rather different from Tourette's syndrome, OCD, autism, schizophrenia, and depression, where the direct effect upon the individual patient is hardly less severe than upon other concerned individuals.

Descriptions of what we now know as ADHD date back more than 100 years (Diamond & Mattsson, 1996). Thus in the nineteenth century a German physician described the cartoon character Zappel-Phillip ("Fidgety Phil") as a "child who twitched and 'twittled' back and forth on a chair, and was unable to sit still" (Zametkin, 1995); in 1904 Meyer reported inattention and impulsivity after brain trauma, and in 1937 the benefits of amphetamine sulphate (benzedrine) were noted. Indeed, by the First World War it was observed that the sequelae of von Economo's encephalitis included hypokinetic symptoms of Parkinson's disease (a *neurodegenerative* disorder of the frontostriatal system) in adults and, paradoxically perhaps, hyperkinesia in children; consequently a neurological role was assumed, and we now see the hallmarks of basal ganglia involvement. Hyperactivity was ascribed to minimal brain damage, and by 1980 inattention, impulsivity, and hyperactivity were linked. Various synonyms have been applied to what we now refer to as ADHD, including hyperkinetic impulse disorder, organic driveness, hyperactive child syndrome, minimal brain damage, or minimal brain dysfunction (Ratey, Middledorp-Crispijn, & Leveroni, 1995). All the different names were to reflect the presumed aetiology, or the most important or salient functions perceived.

We now see ADHD as a complex, inherited neurological syndrome; a syndrome, unlike a disease the symptoms and course of which are relatively consistent, has a set of characteristic symptoms and a course that may vary widely. Thus ADHD is a poorly understood, heterogeneous (even more so than Tourette's syndrome and OCD), idiopathic disorder that encompasses a diversity of related behavioural and cognitive manifestations, and clinical subtypes. As yet there are no firm diagnostic criteria or even definitions. Thus, as with most psychiatric disorders, diagnosis is generally made on the basis of history, and little is known about the validity of diagnosis, which anyway clearly should take into account normal age-related development and ability to pay attention, inhibit impulses, and control restlessness. In any case signs of ADHD may not be evident in highly structured one-to-one situations as during assessment (Zametkin & Ernst, 1999).

DIAGNOSTIC CONSIDERATIONS

There has in fact in recent years been a huge increase in diagnosis of ADHD, and consequent initiation of treatment; thus there has been over the last decade an eightfold increase in the use of psychostimulants in the United States, and consequent concern about over-diagnosis with respect to boisterous, exuberant children. (Conversely, as it is so easily confusable with other disorders that share its symptoms, such as personality disorder, anxiety, depression, and conduct disorder, it may even be *under*-diagnosed; see, for example, Ratey et al., 1995.)

Such considerations highlight the problem that diagnoses are concepts that evolve over time, whose usefulness is judged by their ability to inform concerning relevant pathophysiology, treatment, possible prevention, or prognosis. In psychiatry, most diagnoses continue to be based upon symptomatology and course of illness, with no absolute gold standards or clear predictivity (Sachdev, 1999). Consequently there is a tension between *categorical* (yes, there is a disease process occurring, versus no, the propositus is in fact healthy) and *dimensional* (a continuum from normality to pathology) approaches to classification. Clinicians, perhaps wrongly, may find the categorical approach more appealing, just as there is a universal human tendency to "carve nature at the joints", to seek neat dichotomies where a continuum or some other relationship may exist (Bradshaw & Nettleton, 1981). Neurodevelopmental disorders, maybe *par excellence*, lend themselves to an approach based on a continuum with normality, if we view their manifestations as merely interruptions or delays in a normal, ongoing, ontogenetic, or neurodevelopmental process. Should the delay prove permanent, and/or detrimental to either the individual or society, then clearly the appellation "disorder" proves appropriate, and maybe even a categorical approach likewise. That said, we must again recognise that nomenclature should reflect rather than drive our interpretations of the real world. We impose, through language, our own taxonomic, hierarchical, or categorical structure upon our view of reality; by our artificial concepts we reify processes that may not necessarily have a real, independent existence, or which, by another discipline or civilisation, might be viewed quite differently.

SYMPTOMATOLOGY

Core behavioural symptoms include inattention along with impulsiveness and hyperactivity (Tannock, 1998), though hyperactivity may not always be present, and clearly it may not always be easy to decide where to draw the line along the continuum with normal behaviour. However, for a diagnosis to be made, it must be viewed in a developmental context, with behaviour generally worse than that of children of that age (Golden, 1995), both in absolute degree of the symptomatology (persistence and severity) and in terms of a circumstantially and developmentally inappropriate nature. Thus ADHD should be seen as a classical neurodevelopmental disorder; most children are more impulsive and distractible than adults (Barkley, 1998), just as they are more prone to compulsions (cf. OCD) and tic-like mannerisms (cf. Tourette's syndrome). Symptoms must begin before 7 years, be present in most social, school, or work situations, and not be due to drugs, mood, anxiety, or personality disorders (Boliek & Obrzut, 1997). Inattention here is seen as failure to attend to details, or distractibility; hyperactivity manifests as excessive locomotion, motility, fidgetiness, or restlessness, whereas impulsivity, the symptom of greatest significance, involves lack of patience, inability to inhibit or delay responses, inappropriately or prematurely responding, recklessness, impetuosity, or interruptions. Similarly, there may be excessive attention to immediate gratification or reward. All these symptoms may ameliorate in novel, controlled, interesting, or challenging circumstances or situations. Associated features are poor social skills, low frustration tolerance, temper outbursts, stubbornness, dysphoria, and demanding behaviour. Diagnostic differences may explain its apparently high incidence in certain parts of the Western world (Swanson, 1997).

Disturbed attentional regulation (inattention, or inability to sustain attention) underlies many aspects of the disorder (Barkley, 1997), with or without symptoms of hyperactivity and impulse control, though the latter may typically be the earlier to emerge. Indeed in the final analysis, ADHD may be primarily a disorder of inhibitory dyscontrol. Problems of impulsivity and lack of behavioural inhibition may be pervasive (Weiss, 1996), with inability to take turns, continuous and impatient interruptions, and the blurting out of interjections. There are associated tendencies to seek immediate reinforcement or gratification, with poor investment and maintenance of effort towards future goals. All of these aspects we shall see imply orbitofrontal–striatal dysfunction. Three subtypes of the disorder have been identified (Tannock, 1998): predominantly inattentive, predominantly hyperactive *and* impulsive (earlier, these two aspects were separated), and a combined type. Note that although ADHD may therefore be diagnosed in the absence of inattention, the latter is necessary for the diagnosis of hyperkinetic disorder. Alternatively, patients, on the basis of response to stimulant medication, may differentiate into aggressive and anxious. Such issues and the problem of comorbidity with other disorders (Tourette's, conduct, and oppositional defiance) have resulted in cross-national differences in diagnostic criteria and alternative names, e.g. hyperactivity, hyperkinesia.

If ADHD is characterised by inattention, impulsivity, and hyperactivity, and is typically accompanied by disinhibition, poor self-control, a tendency to aggressive or delinquent behaviour and conduct disorder, to over-reaction, immaturity, low self-esteem, and a propensity to be easily distressed, then we should perhaps accept the diagnostic category of a variant, attention deficit disorder (ADD). Thus Fisher (1998) warns against misdiagnosis. This variant, ADD, is characterised by cognitive sluggishness, a tendency to day dreams, withdrawal, confusions, mental "fogginess", slowness to respond, a capacity to be lost in one's own inner world, a reticence, apprehensiveness, passivity, avoidance of engagement, poor social integration, procrastination, poor concentration and reduced processing capacity, and, frequently, depression. Such individuals, perhaps often girls, while boys may clearly predominate in the other subgroup of ADHD proper, are easily distracted by extraneous stimuli, have difficulty sustaining attention and in following through others' instructions, tend not to "hear" what was said, and not to pay close attention to detail; they may lose important things, have difficulty organising goal-directed activity, and tend to keep switching between incompleted activities (Fisher, 1998). If ADHD is to be seen as a deficit of *selective* attention and a disorder of dyscontrol, maybe ADD is more a deficit of *sustained* attention. Thus ADD may involve dysfunction of posterior parietal activity, and ADHD instead a dysfunction of anterior, frontal (dorsolateral prefrontal cortex, orbito-frontal cortex) activity; in both subtypes there may be a greater involvement of right hemisphere structures, given the role of that hemisphere in attentional processes (Posner & Raichle, 1994). However, it is not clear whether the ADD subgroup is really synonymous with the alternative, standard classification of "attention deficit hyperactivity disorder predominantly inattentive", with all other individuals falling into the other two standard subtypes, predominantly hyperactive and impulsive, or combined.

RATING SCALES OF SEVERITY

The rating scales of severity for ADHD are: The Attention Deficit Hyperactivity Disorder Parent Interview (Barkley, 1990); the Attention Deficit Hyperactivity Disorder Behaviour Coding System (Barkley, 1990); Achenbach Child Behavior Checklist Direct Observation Form (Achenbach, 1986); the Attention Deficit Hyperactivity Disorder Rating Scale (Barkley, 1990). Note that all of the above scales seem to be based on DSM-III-R criteria. The Achenbach seems to be the most used clinically, because it also checks out various other disorders. One scale based on DSM-IV criteria that concentrates exclusively upon ADHD is the Attention Deficit Disorders Evaluation Scale (McCarney, 1995).

PREVALENCE

According to DSM-IV criteria, symptoms must appear before 7 years, and be present for at least 6 months. Peak onset is between years 3 and 4 (Boliek & Obrzut, 1997)—possibly later in the predominantly inattentive (attention deficit disorder?) subtype. With a prevalence of between 2% and 10% (Barkley, 1997; Tannock, 1998; Zohar et al., 1999), there is a boy : girl ratio of around 4 : 1. Boys, however, are the more aggressive and so are more often referred, whereas females may frequently exhibit the "inattentive" (attention deficit) subtype, which is also more prevalent among relatives and children with developmental learning disabilities. Apparent differences in prevalence rates between the United States, United Kingdom, and Australia may disappear if common (DSM-IV) criteria are used. Figures of 7% (primarily inattentive), 2.5% (primarily hyperactive), and 4.5% (combined subtype) have been proposed (Sachdev, 1999), as have a male : female ratio of 4 : 1 for the predominantly hyperactive–impulsive subtype, and 2 : 1 for the predominantly inattentive subtype (Zametkin & Ernst, 1999).

The disorder persists, according to Barkley (1997), through to adolescence in 50–80% of childhood diagnoses, and to adulthood in 30–50%, though its manifestations may change. In any case such adults, who may be successfully treated in a similar fashion to children, tend to hold down lower-status occupations. Indeed, for such individuals, life has often by then become a series of crises in meeting demands and keeping up (Fisher, 1998). Thus as problems become more complex, there may be an increasing build-up of anger and hostility. All this can result in low frustration tolerance, emotional lability, confusion, excessive sensitivity and fragility, and a sense of being overwhelmed. Not surprisingly, this can lead to attempts at self-medication, alcoholism, and substance abuse, anxiety and depression, conduct disorder, and antisocial behaviour merging with oppositional defiant disorder. On the other hand some individuals *do* become high-flyers, fanatically pursuing a chosen career and seeking relief from an ever-increasing and distracting progression of confusing thoughts (Ratey et al., 1995). Yet others may choose, for relief, dangerous hobbies such as hang-gliding, sky-diving, and bungee-jumping.

ADULT ONSET

Can ADHD have adult onset? Not, strictly, according to current diagnostic criteria, and if we view the syndrome as a *neurodevelopmental* disorder of childhood onset, under (see later) a complex interplay of genetic and environmental (perinatal trauma, infection) factors. Of course insults in adulthood (brain trauma, infection) may *simulate* ADHD. The situation is analogous to the close parallelisms between, but mutual independence of, the various acquired (adult-onset) syndromes of dyslexia and corresponding developmental dyslexias of childhood. Although one should perhaps reserve the diagnosis of ADHD proper for onset in childhood, the diagnosis anyway in adulthood is likely to be confounded by comorbid disorders of substance abuse and personality disorder, and high levels of mood, anxiety, and somatiform disorder. Then again, there is the problem as to whether childhood-onset ADHD may *predispose* towards the development of such comorbid disorders in *adulthood* (Sachdev, 1999).

COMORBIDITY

It is thus the case that other disorders are often comorbid with ADHD; oppositional defiant and conduct disorder are perhaps the commonest, followed by anxiety and depression, and specific learning disability (reading disorder) (Tannock, 1998). Indeed ADHD is a major risk factor for later conduct and oppositional defiant disorder, delinquency, substance abuse, and personality disorder. Children are often in trouble, unpopular, and underachieving, with scholastic difficulties, poor self-esteem, anxiety, and depression (Barkley, 1997; Weiss, 1996). Later in life, as adults, as we have seen, they may be over-represented among social rebels, thrill-seekers, dare-devils, hang-gliders and sky-divers, bungee-jumpers and drug users (Ratey et al., 1995). Alcoholism, drug abuse, and sociopathy may also be prevalent among relatives of probands. Although around 50% of Tourette's syndrome sufferers may also have ADHD (Golden, 1995), the reverse is not necessarily the case (Ratey et al., 1995); indeed Eapen and Robertson (1996) reject the view that ADHD is an alternative expression of a putative Tourette's syndrome gene, even though symptoms of the two disorders are phenomenologically similar, due in both cases to focally disinhibited frontostriatal function. Golden (1995) also rejects the idea that ADHD, learning, speech, and stuttering problems are variants of Tourette's syndrome, even though relatives of Tourette's syndrome patients may be at increased risk of developing ADHD; in some cases ADHD (and even OCD) may be secondary to Tourette's syndrome, but otherwise it might be quite independent.

Jensen, Martin, and Cantwell (1997) argue that individuals suffering from ADHD should in fact be grouped into more homogeneous subgroups on the basis of comorbidity patterns, especially if, as seems to be the case, such subgroups exhibit distinctive characteristics of age of onset, sex ratio, and patterns of familiality, and if they respond differentially to specific treatments, have different clinical correlates, and demonstrate unique clinical outcomes. They admit, however, that some apparent comorbidity patterns may in fact be artefactual, a manifestation merely of severe psychopathology or impairment that results in an increased probability of referral. Although conduct disorder and oppositional defiant disorder both occur extremely commonly with ADHD, especially in boys (and rarely in girls, though conduct disorder itself is rare in girls), there is little evidence that ADHD on its own increases the risk of criminality; Jensen, Martin, and Cantwell (1997) believe that all three conditions—ADHD, conduct and oppositional defiant disorders, along with antisocial personality disorder— are distinct or at least semi-independent conditions, each with their own unique constellations of genetic and environmental aetiologies. (At this point we might note the critique of DSM diagnoses generally that is offered by Kutchins & Kirk, 1997; odd or socially disapproved behaviour, usually in the absence of any physical marker, leads to the invention of a diagnostic label that is then used in a circular fashion to explain the behaviour. Persons who compulsively steal are labelled kleptomaniacs, and we know they are kleptomaniacs merely because they steal compulsively.)

Conduct disorder, according to DSM-IV, is a "repetitive and persistent pattern of behaviour where the basic rights of others or major age-appropriate societal norms or rules are violated". Three of the following four categories of antisocial behaviour must be met: aggressiveness, property destruction, deceitfulness or theft, and serious rule violation, e.g. truancy. Thus although maybe 50% of normal teenagers will occasionally transgress the law, there must be multiple instances of antisocial behaviour that are repetitive and persistent. Prevalence is similar to that of ADHD: 4–10% of the population, with a 3:1 male:female ratio, with earlier male onset (Pennington & Ozonoff, 1996). However, unlike ADHD, where onset is early and may stem from neuromaturational delay rather than from temperamental, family, or social adversities, onset is usually at adolescence in the case of conduct disorder; rarer childhood onset is associated with a poorer prognosis. In addition to ADHD, conduct disorder has a high comorbidity with learning (reading) disorders, depression and anxiety. Unless ADHD is comorbid, there seems to be little evidence of the deficits in executive function that otherwise are so characteristic of ADHD (Pennington & Ozonoff, 1996). Thus the core deficit in pure conduct disorder seems to lie outside of the domain of executive function, though note that Moffit (1993) reports some executive function deficits in conduct disorder. An X-linked gene involving the monoamine oxidase A gene may be present, along with disorders of serotonin and noradrenaline, and low psychophysiological arousal; birth complications have also been invoked.

The symptomatologies of conduct disorder (persistent violation of others' basic rights or of age-appropriate societal norms) and of oppositional defiant disorder (negativity, defiance, disobedience, hostility towards authority figures) correlate more highly with the hyperactivity and impulsivity aspects of ADHD than with its inattentional aspects (Swanson et al., 1988b). Indeed children with *intentional* problems (*refusal* to pay attention, rather than "mere" inability to do so) are likely to be disruptive, restless, overactive, or disturbance provoking, with a low tolerance of frustration and frequent mood swings—and to be wrongly diagnosed as having ADHD.

ADHD and anxiety, bipolar disorder and depression often co-occur, with synergistic or interactive effects, and increased probability of occurrence in relatives of any of these disorders (Faraone & Biederman, 1998; Fisher, 1998). Thus the additional presence of depression is associated with an increased probability of failure to respond to traditional stimulant medications, and a better therapeutic response to antidepressants (Jensen, Martin & Cantwell, 1997a). Note, however, that while ADHD typically has an early onset, and continues with a largely unremitting course and worsening of symptoms with increased environmental demands, mood and anxiety disorder usually have an episodic, remitting course of later onset. Learning (reading) disorders and ADHD also very commonly co-occur, but while the diagnosis of the latter is typically on the basis of inattention, impulsivity, and hyperactivity, that of the former involves the discrepancy between intelligence tests and performance achievement. Moreover, whereas deficits in naming and linguistic fluency may reflect reading disability, deficits in verbal learning and memory are generally linked to disorders of attention. Thus although some behaviours are undoubtedly common to ADHD and learning disorders generally, the two disorders or disorder clusters do not represent the same diagnosis; both may be susceptible to learning problems, but with different causes and genetic bases.

GENETICS OF ATTENTION DEFICIT HYPERACTIVITY DISORDER

Environmental factors have been associated with ADHD, such as complications of pregnancy or delivery, especially toxaemia, eclampsia, poor maternal health, increased maternal age, fetal prematurity, prolonged labour, fetal distress, reduced birth weight, and antepartum haemorrhage (Faraone & Biederman, 1998). Other such potential factors have included maternal use of alcohol or tobacco, brain injuries, or exposure to lead in childhood (Barkley, 1998). High blood levels of lead are certainly associated with neurological damage, and distractibility, hyperactivity, and restlessness, but are not likely to be implicated in the bulk of cases. Similarly, it was widely believed that certain foods such as sugar, or artificial food additives, may be instrumental in precipitating the disorder, but again there is little hard evidence. A genetic susceptibility to the autoimmune consequences, in the striatum, of childhood streptococcal infections may also play an adventitious role (Peterson et al., 1999b), as in Tourette's syndrome and OCD (Leckman & Cohen, 1999b). Indeed, as with all the neurodevelopmental frontostriatal disorders, an interaction between an inherited genetic predisposition and precipitating environmental factors is an appealing hypothesis. Thus vulnerability genes may be turned on and off at various times during development, as a result of both environmental and (other) genetic factors. There may even be *protective* factors influencing gene expression. The pre-, peri-, and early postnatal period of neurodevelopment may be a particularly sensitive time in this respect.

There is very strong evidence of a familial involvement in ADHD, a disorder that clearly displays complex relationships between genetic, biological, and environmental factors. The siblings of probands are six times as likely as controls to develop the disorder, whereas the child of a proband parent has a 50% chance (Barkley, 1998). Conversely, one in four diagnosed children has a biological parent similarly affected (Zametkin, 1995), suggesting a single dominant or single major gene or, more probably, several genes operating in an oligogenic or polygenic fashion (Tannock, 1998). Noteworthy also is the high incidence of alcoholism, depression, sociopathy, and even psychopathy in parents of attention deficit hyperactivity probands. Tannock (1998) notes the increasing specificity of modern studies of familiality, heritability, mode of transmission, and actual gene locus. Concordance rates for monozygotic twins (around 0.66) are certainly greater than for dizygotic (around 0.28), and see also Sherman, Iacono, and McGue (1997), suggesting a heritability factor of around 0.80. Thus up to 80% of the differences in attention, hyperactivity, and impulsivity between individuals with and without ADHD can be explained genetically. Genetic heterogeneity, moreover, is indicated by the high levels of comorbidity. There may be a genetic predisposition towards dopamine depletion in or underactivity of the prefrontal–striatal–limbic system (Teeter & Semrud-Clikeman, 1995), or towards an imbalance of dopamine and serotonin (see below) whose actual nature and locus may determine whether Tourette's syndrome, OCD, or ADHD (or some combination) manifests. Swanson (1997; see also Sachdev, 1999) notes that there is some evidence of a transmission disequilibrium for alleles on chromosome 5 of the dopamine transporter gene, with effects via enhanced dopamine reuptake, with other evidence of reduced sensitivity in the dopamine D4 receptor gene on chromosome 11. Faraone and Biederman (1998) note that a 7-repeat allele of the dopamine D4 receptor gene is associated with novelty seeking, impulsivity, exploratory behaviour, excitability, and quick temper; this variant, moreover, mediates a blunted response to dopamine. There seem to be increased rates of this variant in children with ADHD, and reduced rates in Asians who as a group tend to have reduced numbers of such individuals. It is also noteworthy that dopamine depletion in rats may lead to ADHD-like behaviour that responds to stimulant medication, and which abates after puberty (Sachdev, 1999). Knockout of the dopamine transporter gene in mice, moreover, may lead to incessant hyperactivity, whereas noradrenergic depletion in neonatal rats may lead to inattentive-like behaviour. Conversely, serotonergic deficiency may be associated with impulsivity and aggression. Clearly, multiple neurotransmitter systems may be involved, probably in a mutually modulatory fashion. However, dopamine depletion may perhaps be more important in ADHD proper, and noradrenaline depletion in the ADD variant (Fisher, 1998), where arousal is compromised.

Contrary to popular belief, the effectiveness of dopaminergic psychosti-mulants upon children with ADHD is not "paradoxical" (i.e. they do not exacerbate the hyperactivity); *normal* children respond in the same way to such medication with improved cognitive function and reduced motor activity, further emphasising the continuum between normality and (ADHD) pathology (Sachdev, 1999).

In any event, dopaminergic involvement is certainly indicated because of the symptom reduction effects of pharmacological agents operating on dopaminergic and noradrenergic systems (Tannock, 1998); methylpheni-date, dextroamphetamine, pemoline, and buproprion all inhibit the dopamine transporter. Moreover dopamine D4 receptors are present in the striatum and the dorsolateral prefrontal cortex, areas (see later) known from imaging studies to be functioning abnormally, and which mediate atten-tional and novelty-seeking behaviour also known to be abnormal in ADHD (Tannock, 1998). A faulty dopaminergic system in ADHD may, further-more, explain the frequently reported extrapyramidal symptoms of clumsi-ness, slowed responding, and poor timing. LaHoste et al. (1996) note that the dopamine D4 receptor gene displays a very high degree of variation in the human population, and may be associated with novelty-seeking behav-iour, characterised by increased exploratory drive, excitability, and impulsivity. They found that the distribution of dopamine D4 gene alleles was significantly different in children with ADHD, and conclude that although the disorder may well be multifactorial in its aetiology, its heritability is likely to be polygenic; a polymorphic variation in the gene encoding the dopamine D4 receptor may contribute to the expression of symptoms associated with ADHD.

NEUROIMAGING STUDIES

Neuroimaging studies in ADHD are noteworthy for their contradictory findings. Morphometric (*structural*) studies indicate a 5% reduction in brain volume, especially perhaps of right hemisphere frontal regions, reductions in various regions of the corpus callosum and cerebellum, and absence or reversal of normal patterns of asymmetry (themselves disputed) in the striatum, notably the head of the caudate, and possibly of the globus pallidus. These regions are all involved in higher, executive cognitive function, such as working memory, rule-based learning, and planning. Thus the prefrontal cortex, especially perhaps on the right, is important in "editing" one's behaviour, spatially focusing attention, resisting distractions, and developing an awareness of self and of time; the basal ganglia play a major role in switching off automatic responses, in coordination, and in selecting deliberate, voluntary actions, whereas the cerebellum, in addition to motor functions, is now known to modulate a range of cognitive and emotional behaviours (see Barkley, 1998; Pennington & Ozonoff, 1996). As ventricular volumes are unaffected, pathology must be early in development.

At a *functional* level, frontal and striatal anomalies are again frequently reported, including reduced metabolism; these regions of course are rich in the catecholamines thought, as discussed below, to be relevant to ADHD. Several studies report hypoperfusion of the right striatum. Good reviews of the structural and functional findings are given by Baumgardner et al. (1996), Castellanos, Giedd, Marsh, and Hamburger (1996), Faraone and Biederman (1998), Filipek (1999), Giedd and Castellanos (1997), Mataro et al. (1997), Peterson et al. (1999a), Sachdev (1999), and Tannock (1998).

Although striatal damage is known to be associated with hyperactivity and attentional deficits (Kado & Takagi, 1996), reduced frontostriatal metabolism (Koziol, 1994b; Ratey et al., 1995; Tannock, 1998; Teeter & Semrud-Clikeman, 1995) probably accounts for much of the disorder's disinhibitory loss of control and cognitive deficit. Swanson et al. (1998a) speculate, in particular, that the motor excesses of ADHD may stem from caudate hyperactivity, whereas the cognitive problems may be associated more with anterior cingulate hypoactivity. It is of interest that parents of ADHD probands have also been reported to have reduced glucose metabolism in right frontal areas, and that Ritalin may normalise both behavioural and metabolic anomalies (Pennington & Ozonoff, 1996).

Asymmetrically reduced metabolic activity in frontal and parietal regions (Tannock, 1998; see also Boliek & Obrzut, 1997; Castellanos et al., 1996) may all have behavioural consequences in terms of abnormal laterality (Swanson, 1997; and see later). Electrophysiologically, increased slow wave (θ) activity (especially in frontal regions) has been reported, indicative of decreased cortical arousal, especially during tests of cognitive function, along with increased β and reduced δ activity over the left hemisphere; alterations in evoked responses, especially the P300 stimulus evaluation potential, have been noted (Tannock, 1998), along with increased latencies and reduced amplitudes to target events. Such findings are suggestive of problems of both sustained and selective attention.

NEUROPSYCHOLOGY OF ATTENTION DEFICIT HYPERACTIVITY DISORDER

Although there is little evidence of neurological hard signs, there may be nonlocalising soft signs such as poor coordination and synkinesia (Golden, 1995). Cognitively and behaviourally, executive dysfunction is prominent in the five developmental psychopathologies—ADHD, conduct disorder, Tourette's syndrome, schizophrenia, and autism (Tannock, 1998), with problems of working memory, self-regulation, sequencing of behaviour, flexibility of thought or responding, information-processing capacity, and planning and organisation of behaviour—quite independently of attentional dysfunction, itself another aspect of putative dorsolateral prefrontal executive control. Separate again are the inhibitory dysfunctions and poor self-regulation of ADHD—impulsiveness, inability to delay responding, excessively fast responding, and errors of *commission* (whereas errors of *omission* tap distractibility and deficits of sustained attention and of information processing); such errors are quantifiable by the Continuous Processing Task and Wisconsin Card Sorting Test (Boliek & Obrzut, 1997; Golden, 1995; Ratey et al., 1995; Teeter & Semrud-Clikeman, 1995). All of these deficits are reminiscent of prefrontal and orbitofrontal damage. (The Continuous Processing Task requires speeded detection of letter or letter combination targets, within a background of similar distractors, whose presentation rate can be varied; see, for example, Strandburg et al., 1996; Weiss, 1996). Other paradigms sensitive to ADHD impulsivity are stop signal, Stroop, and go/no-go tasks. In the former, a measure of efficiency of inhibitory processes, a just-initiated motor response to a target (e.g. in a continuous processing task) must be interrupted on the occasional appearance of a stop signal, which may occur at various intervals after the initial "go" signal; patients with ADHD typically inhibit fewer responses, perhaps reflecting compromise of anterior cingulate, dorsolateral prefrontal, and orbitofrontal cortices. Indeed in this task orbitofrontal activation correlates with a fall in false alarms, and anterior cingulate activation with an increase (Casey et al., 1997). Thus inhibition may be mediated by the orbitofrontal cortex, and response execution by the anterior cingulate. Poor ADHD performance on these tasks may be normalised by methylphenidate.

In go/no-go tasks, where some categories of stimuli require response withholding, patients typically exhibit high levels of errors of commission. Patients, moreover, typically have problems in tasks requiring fixational eye movements to laterally occurring flashes to be delayed or reconfigured (see, for example, Quay, 1997, for review).

ATTENTIONAL PROBLEMS

In the ADHD subtype, which is characterised more by inattention and day-dreaming, without the hyperactivity and impulsivity, problems of sustained attention may tend to manifest more in slow than in excessively fast responding (Tannock, 1998). Other cognitive deficits include difficulties with the Tower of Hanoi task (Barkley, 1997), where hypotheses must be tested before responding. In an auditory and visual selective attention task (Jonkman et al., 1997), where an infrequently occurring event has to be detected in the relevant channel, children with ADHD have reduced hit rates, increased false alarm rates, reduced P300 amplitude to nontargets, and reduced early frontal positive activity to targets. Van der Meere (1996) reviews derailment by children with ADHD in dichotic listening tasks.

In a letter cancellation task, children with ADHD made more left-sided errors than right, a pattern otherwise found with left-neglect patients suffering from right hemisphere damage (Voeller & Heilman, 1988; see also Manly, Robertson, & Verity, 1997). In a visual–spatial endogenous orienting task, Carter, C.S., et al. (1995) found that unmedicated children with ADHD showed a loss of normal reaction time costs on attentional orienting to invalidly cued (by a central arrow) targets in the left visual field, which is indicative of an abnormal hemispheric asymmetry of "controlled" spatial orienting. (Normal control subjects showed costs on invalid trials on *both* sides.) In addition, in an exogenous or automatic orienting task, where target location was now peripherally cued by illumination changes on one or other side, Carter, C.S., et al. (1995) found that invalid cues for left-side targets (i.e. where the cues appeared on the right) were more disruptive than invalid cues on the left for targets subsequently appearing on the right. This performance asymmetry, absent in the normal controls, is commonly found in left-neglect patients with right-sided damage. Increased costs of invalid cues for left-sided targets were also found in a group of adult patients with ADHD (Epstein et al., 1997). In another exogenously cued orienting task (Nigg, Swanson, & Hinshaw, 1997), children with ADHD were slower to uncued left (compared to right) targets; this abnormal asymmetry was normalised with methylphenidate medication. In a computerised line bisection task (Sheppard, Bradshaw, Mattingley & Lee, 1999a), children with ADHD, off medication, bisected lines significantly further to the right compared to controls, who showed a small leftward error. Again, methylphenidate normalised performance. Note, however, that Ben-Artsy et al. (1996) did not find that children with the disorder bisected lines further to the right. However, it is unclear whether their sample also contained children with comorbid learning disorders and/or oppositional defiant disorder, whose difficulties may be different from those of children with a diagnosis of ADHD per se.

In summary, frontal structures regulate attentional and intentional processes such as strategic planning and response selection, and provide continuity over time. They are involved in temporal sequencing, prioritising, goal setting, and avoiding "capture" by irrelevancies. With their links to limbic structures mediating emotion, they modulate affective, interpersonal, and social aspects, monitoring, evaluating, adjusting, and supervising. These executive or supervisory functions are particularly prominent in situations where planning and decision making are important; where strong, habitual responses have to be overcome; where temptation must be resisted; where potential danger or technical difficulty may occur; and where the individual must engage in error correcting or trouble shooting—all situations "at risk" for sufferers from ADHD (Fisher, 1998). All children below a certain developmental age exhibit limitations in their capacity to process information, to allocate attention appropriately, and to inhibit inappropriate responses; in ADHD these limitations may merely be more severe, just as all children tend to show the obsessions and compulsions of OCD, and the mannerisms of Tourette's syndrome, in attenuated form. The capacity to allocate attention may be limited by both structural capacity and energetic (motivational) factors, with the latter partly under voluntary control. Prefrontal executive control may mediate the strategic aspects of selectivity, set, and attention, whereas capacity limitations may also stem from sub-cortical determinants.

Attention itself may be:

- Divided, when multiple channels or inputs require monitoring.
- Focused or selective, in the face of distracting competition.
- Sustained, involving vigilance or the maintenance of effective attentional set over extended periods.

With the ADD subtype there may be reduced capacity, problems with concentration, and with divided, focused, and sustained attention, reduced alertness, and problems with concurrent tasks and operation at both an automatic and controlled level (see Fisher, 1998).

In their model of attention, Posner and Raichle (1994) see three distinct neural networks accomplishing the component processes of alerting, orienting, and executive control:

- An alerting mechanism for sustained attention; background "noise" is suppressed by inhibiting ongoing or irrelevant activity, to produce a state of readiness to react or a state of vigilance. Mental effort is required, along with involvement of the frontal and parietal lobes on the right, and the noradrenergic system. Attention deficit hyperactivity disorder deficits in sustained attention will manifest from disorders of such a system.

- An orienting system for selecting and mobilising specific neural resources or processors, and inhibiting others, so as to prepare to process an expected type of input. Posterior parietal cortex, thalamus, and superior colliculus are likely to be involved, in covertly disengaging, moving and engaging an internal "spotlight"; they are also likely to be compromised in those aspects of ADHD that involve deficits in selective attention or distractibility.

- An executive control system for divided attention, for coordinating multiple specialised neural processes, for detecting the presence of a target, for starting and stopping mental operations, and for ordering multiple responses so as to direct behaviour toward a goal. The anterior cingulate, dorsolateral prefrontal cortex on the left, and basal ganglia, are likely to be involved in resolving conflict between competing systems and targets, and appropriately coordinating and regulating behaviour. In ADHD, a deficit in such an executive control network is likely to manifest in impulsivity.

INHIBITORY, REWARD, AND ACTIVATION SYSTEMS

According to an alternative formulation, Quay (1997) sees the hyperactive, impulsive variant of ADHD as due to an underactive behavioural inhibitory system (BIS), rather than to deficits in divided, selective, or sustained attention, or to a failure to be able to shift from a controlled to an automatic mode of processing, or to a limited capacity to perform dual tasks; patients may of course still be generally less efficient in information processing, or less able to bring processing resources to bear. Quay places the BIS in the septohippocampal complex together with the prefrontal (orbito-frontal) cortex, and under largely noradrenergic (from the locus coeruleus) and serotonergic (from the raphe nuclei) control. The BIS may be impaired by anxiolytics; it controls passive avoidance (inhibition of responding learned under threat and nonreward), and acts in opposition to a (dopaminergic) reward/activation system, which responds to conditioned stimuli for reward and underlies active avoidance and escape. Damage to the BIS is therefore seen to result in an inability to inhibit responding in the face of probable punishment or nonreward, and sufferers from ADHD are likely to be less responsive to conditioned stimuli. In many respects, therefore, ADHD is seen as the opposite of OCD, where the BIS may be overactive. However, Quay (1997) notes that this model does not apply to the predominantly *inattentive* type of ADHD.

Taylor (1998), on the other hand, places more emphasis on, in effect, Quay's reward/activation system, seeing hyperactivity as being associated with a need to respond for immediate reward or gratification, rather than as an inability to defer gratification. Of course such behaviour, including hyperkinesia itself, may on occasions be an adaptive or even an appropriate strategy. Both approaches, however—that of Quay and that of Taylor— would see the hyperkinetic variant of ADHD as stemming from an under-lying deficit in reinforcement processes, and resulting in a lack of behav-ioural inhibition. This would manifest in an inability to withhold a planned response, to interrupt a response once initiated, or to delay a response, along with a generalised style of impulsiveness, sensation seeking, risk taking and over-reactivity to frustration. Sagvolden and Sergeant (1998), in this context, invoke a genetically based, hypofunctional, dopaminergic system as responsible, in ADHD, for such impulsivity, overactivity, and even deficient sustained attention. Leckman and Cohen (1999b) develop this idea further; genes may make certain frontostriatal circuits tend to be selectively and differentially disinhibited, not just in ADHD, but also in OCD and Tourette's syndrome. The orbitofrontal cortex may be especially involved, along with the anterior cingulate, both of which are of course involved with emotional or "limbic" behaviours. Thus disinhibition of pre-wired behaviours will occur, probably via dysregulation of the catecho-lamine neuromodulatory systems (dopaminergic, serotonergic, noradrenergic, and maybe even cholinergic). This dysregulation would operate differen-tially, in terms of frontostriatal locus and the particular mix of neuro-transmitters involved, for the various disorders, including also perhaps schizophrenia, autism, and depression. With ADHD there is likely to be chronic underarousal, reflected in the search for arousing stimulation, which may be partly corrected by the administration of psychostimulants.

NEUROCHEMISTRY AND TREATMENT OF ATTENTION DEFICIT HYPERACTIVITIY DISORDER

As noted earlier, the disorder may be heterogeneous; moreover blood concentrations of neurotransmitters or of related substances may not necessarily reflect brain status, the neurotransmitters may all interact, and there may be positive and negative feedback mechanisms affecting the consequences of medication (Kado & Takagi, 1996). Nevertheless ADHD (like OCD and Tourette's syndrome) may perhaps be more likely to be due to a transmitter imbalance, a chemical rather than a physical lesion (Koziol, 1994b), though at this stage such a hypothesis is purely speculative. A dopaminergic dysfunction, perhaps of ventral tegmental area origin, pro-jecting to prefrontal, orbitofrontal, basal ganglia, and limbic regions, is likely to be involved, as dopamine regulates frontal and frontostriatal function. However, noradrenaline and serotonin are probably also implicated, with serotonin also modulating the synthesis of noradrenaline from dopamine. One possibility (Swanson et al., 1998b) is a noradrenergic deficit of the right hemisphere, coupled with a dopaminergic deficit of the left.

The successfully used psychostimulants dextroamphetamine, methylphenidate (Ritalin) and magnesium pemoline (which produce a dose-related improvement in ADHD symptoms, but may worsen tics; see, for example, Walkup, Scahill, & Riddle, 1995) are primarily dopaminergic, though they may also affect the reuptake of noradrenaline (Koziol, 1994b). Methylphenidate affects primarily the dopamine transporter, preventing synaptic reuptake of dopamine; it therefore may act by correcting a hyperefficient dopamine transporter and thus in turn correcting a hyperefficient dopamine reuptake (Swanson, 1997), particularly in the striatum. Alternatively, it may operate by counteracting a supersensitive dopamine receptor. Side effects include tachycardia, hypertension, anorexia, and insomnia. Clonidine, an α_2-noradrenergic receptor agonist, ameliorates ADHD without worsening tics (Walkup et al., 1995); it is especially effective with comorbid aggression, conduct, and oppositional defiant syndrome (Weiss, 1996). The tricyclic antidepressants imipramine (Tofranil) and desipramine (Norpramin) block the reuptake of both serotonin and noradrenaline (Boliek & Obrzut, 1997), and also help alleviate comorbid anxiety and depression, whereas the monoamine oxidase inhibitors deprenyl and clorgiline increase dopamine release and inhibit the noradrenergic locus coeruleus (Boliek & Obrzut, 1997; Golden, 1995). Nicotine, even from smoking, may help by facilitating dopamine release by nigrostriatal and mesolimbic neurones; it also stimulates noradrenaline release, thereby promoting regulation of attention (Faraone & Biederman, 1998).

EVOLUTIONARY ADAPTIVE ASPECTS OF ATTENTION DEFICIT HYPERACTIVITY DISORDER

All the neurodevelopmental disorders may be seen as involving altered or extreme variants of normal behaviours, perhaps with perpetuation or prolongation of juvenile phenotypes into developmentally later phases of ontogeny. Clearly, aspects of ADHD may prove adaptive if you are a migrant, nomadic, hunter-gatherer, whereas OCD-like behaviour may be more adaptive for a settled agriculturist who has to look to the future. Thus the behavioural and emotional responses of a "disorder", especially if relatively common, persisting in the genome, and possessing an inherited component, may not just be "symptoms" (as viewed from a particular societal perspective), but may instead be adaptive responses to environmental demands (see also Jensen et al., 1997b). Our ancestral environments varied in resource availability and safety, and ADHD's classic triad of symptomatology—hyperactivity, disturbed attentional processes, and impulsivity—are all potentially and independently adaptive in certain circumstances (Jensen et al., 1997b):

- Hyperactivity is adaptive for exploring the environment, especially during times of scarcity.
- Rapidly shifting attention is clearly adaptive for monitoring for possible danger or threats, while overfocusing as in OCD could be dangerous in a risky environment.
- Impulsivity, or a rapid reflexive response to environmental stimuli while not considering alternatives, may also be advantageous in risky, rapidly changing circumstances. Thus we might need to adjust the threshold and timing of responses as functions of the likelihood of pay-off as a result of immediate, delayed, or withheld responding; costs and pay-offs of false-positive or withheld responses also need assessing. Thus there may sometimes be advantages with impulsive, hair-trigger responses, maybe more in times of war than of peace, when hypervigilance is essential. Impulsive behaviour is adaptive when time is critical. Indeed the personality characteristics of the good warrior (impulsive) and the good strategist (reflective) are very different, probably based on dopaminergic striatal mechanisms, and equally valuable to a society.

Schools and educational establishments demand focused, reflective, non-impulsive, and measured behaviour, whereas the opposite is required by many forms of games and entertainment of a risk-taking nature, and is favoured by those of a certain personality profile. Of course, as Jensen et al. (1997b) observe, many modern occupations also still demand ice-age impulsivity and response readiness, for example those of the soldier, air traffic controller, entrepreneur, emergency ward physician, or salesperson. ADHD is not the only "disorder" that is a product of society's norms, and which would be considered adaptive in a simpler and more dangerous society; thus anxiety, depression, bipolar disorder (hypomania), Tourette's syndrome, and schizophrenia all convey additional adaptive advantages, and involve probable neurodevelopmental and lateralisation anomalies of the frontostriatal system.

SUMMARY AND CONCLUSIONS

ADHD disorder is an externalising disorder in that, unlike for example depression or OCD, it affects others far more than the individual concerned. Although something like the condition has been recognised for 100 years, only recently have the hallmark symptoms been identified: inattention, hyperactivity, and above all impulsivity. Its status as a *frontostriatal* disorder therefore seems assured, and its status as a *neurodevelopmental* disorder is affirmed by the diagnostic requirement that the symptomatology be over and beyond what otherwise might be expected for a child of that chronological age. Thus nearly *all* children below a certain age may tend to be inattentive, hyperactive, and impulsive, just as they may all tend to exhibit behaviours that, in an adult, might be regarded as indicating the presence of Tourette's syndrome or OCD.

A complex, heterogeneous, neurological syndrome, it exhibits a widely varying course without firm diagnostic criteria; indeed diagnosis can only be made on the basis of history. A recent major increase in diagnosis (currently between 2% and 10% of the population) suggests possible over-diagnosis, though much may depend upon criteria adopted and societal expectations. Diagnosis should be made before 7 years of age; peak onset is between 3 and 4 years, and clinical manifestations should not be due to drugs, anxiety, or the presence of other disorders. Maybe four times as many boys present as girls, and the condition may persist to adulthood. In such instances, affected individuals typically take up low-status occupations, and their lives pass through a series of crises. Such adults may exhibit considerable hostility and aggression (the boundaries with comorbid conduct disorder and oppositional defiant syndrome are unclear), or choose to undertake a range of "dangerous" hobbies. Similar, if milder, patterns of behaviour may also manifest in close relatives.

Impulsivity may be the most significant or disruptive symptom—an inability to inhibit or delay responses or gratification, impetuosity, and a low tolerance of frustration. However, all symptoms may decrease in an interesting or appropriately challenging environment. Two variants of the disorder have been suggested: ADHD proper, with its hyperactivity, distractibility, and dyscontrol, which may be particularly common in boys, and as a deficit of *selective* attention may involve the dorsolateral prefrontal and orbitofrontal cortices; conversely, attention deficit disorder (*without* hyperactivity), involving sluggishness, withdrawal, passivity, and a failure to engage, may be relatively more common in girls, and as a deficit of *sustained* attention may involve additional posterior parietal mechanisms. The latter variant may be less likely to be associated with aggressive dyscontrol, conduct disorder, or oppositional defiant syndrome. Both variants may additionally be comorbid with anxiety, depression, reading, and learning disorders.

Familial and twin studies indicate a high degree of heritability, probably via several genes operating in an oligogenic or polygenic fashion. As environmental factors have also been implicated (obstetric complications, maternal use of alcohol or tobacco, but probably not an effect from artificial food additives), a genetic vulnerability may predispose towards development of the syndrome, with vulnerability genes maybe being turned on or off during development. As with Tourette's syndrome and OCD, there may also be a genetic vulnerability to the autoimmune consequences of childhood streptococcal infection.

The dopamine transporter gene on chromosome 5 has been implicated, and there is evidence of reduced sensitivity in the dopamine D4 receptor gene on chromosome 11. Indeed a 7–repeat allele of the dopamine D4 receptor gene, mediating a blunted response to dopamine, has been associated with novelty seeking, impulsivity, exploratory behaviour, and excitability. Conversely, inhibition of the dopamine transporter by dextroamphetamine or methylphenidate is pharmacologically beneficial, whereas knockout of the dopamine transporter in mice, or dopamine depletion in rats, leads to attention deficit hyperactivity-like behaviour that responds to stimulant medication. There are of course dopamine D4 receptors in the striatum and dorsolateral prefrontal cortex—regions that are involved in attention and novelty seeking, and which appear abnormal in ADHD. However, other neurotransmitters may also be involved, as a serotonin deficiency is associated with impulsivity and aggression; although dopamine depletion may be important in ADHD proper, noradrenaline depletion may be a significant factor in ADD *without* hyperactivity.

Neuroimaging studies indicate reduced brain volume, especially in right prefrontal regions, abnormalities in the corpus callosum and cerebellum, and abnormal morphometric asymmetries in the striatum and globus pallidus. Functionally, there are indications of right striatum hypoperfusion and frontal anomalies, which may account for disinhibitory loss of control and abnormal behavioural lateralities. Neuropsychologically, there are non-localising soft signs, poor coordination, synkinesia, executive and inhibitory dysfunctions, impulsivity and errors of commission (orbitofrontal?) and of omission (anterior cingulate?) as indexed by Continuous Processing, Stroop, Wisconsin Card Sorting, stop signal and go/no-go tasks. The subtype that includes hyperactivity may generally tend to respond in a rapid error-prone fashion, whereas the subtype without hyperactivity may be associated with excessively slow responses. Abnormalities in performance on the Posner task indicate altered performance asymmetries, and deficits in sustained and selective attention and executive control. Indeed, in certain respects the disorder seems to be the opposite of the highly overfocused OCD. Thus, genes and environmental factors may differentially affect frontostriatal circuits, and/or modulate neurotransmitters, to maintain certain childhood behaviours; the latter may later manifest inappropriately as ADHD, OCD or Tourette's syndrome—or even as schizophrenia, autism, or depression. Indeed normal children all show behaviour reminiscent of ADHD (distractibility, impulsivity, hyperactivity), or of OCD (obsessional overfocusing), or even of Tourette's syndrome (tics, a fascination with dirt, patterns and sex, and stereotypies).

Neurochemically, the disorder, like most of the other neurodevelopmental frontostriatal disorders, is less one of a structural, physical lesion or dysgenesis, and perhaps more one of a chemical imbalance, in view of the effects of successful medication, though it cannot be denied that there are indications of morphometric changes or altered asymmetries in all the related disorders. Although alterations in dopamine function seem to play a major role, serotonin and noradrenaline are also probably implicated; one hypothesis is of a noradrenergic deficit of the right hemisphere, and a dopaminergic deficit of the left. Psychostimulants (e.g. dextroamphetamine and methylphenidate) are all primarily efficacious via the dopaminergic pathways, though they may also affect the noradrenergic system—and worsen tics in the presence of comorbid Tourette's syndrome. However, clonidine (an α_2-noradrenergic receptor agonist) inhibits release of noradrenaline and ameliorates the condition without worsening tics. Smoking may be employed to self-medicate via the nicotinic cholinergic system.

As with the other neurodevelopmental frontostriatal "disorders", we should perhaps view the condition more in terms of a personality bias than as a pathology, at least perhaps when present in "low doses" or incomplete penetrance, as in clinically "unaffected" close relatives. Such individuals may be at a selective advantage when there is a need for exploration, rapid shifts of attention or of responding, impulsive, "hair trigger" reactions, or risk-taking behaviour.

FURTHER READING

Barkley, R.A. (1997). Behavioral inhibition, sustained attention, and executive functions: Constructing a unifying theory of ADHD. *Psychological Bulletin, 121*, 65–94.

Barkley, R.A. (1998). Attention-deficit hyperactivity disorder. *Scientific American*, September, 44–49.

Boliek, C.A., & Obrzut, J.E. (1997). Neuropsychological aspects of attention deficit/hyperactivity disorder. In C.R. Reynolds & E. Fletcher-Janzen (Eds.), *Handbook of clinical child neuropsychology* (2nd ed., pp. 619–633). New York: Plenum Press.

Faraone, S.V., & Biederman, J. (1998). Neurobiology of attention-deficit hyperactivity disorder. *Biological Psychiatry, 44*, 951–958.

Fisher, B.C. (1998). *Attention deficit misdiagnosis*. Boca Raton, FL: CRC Press.

Jensen, P.S., Martin, D., & Cantwell, D.P. (1997a). Comorbidity in ADHD: Implications for research, practice and DSM-V. *Journal of the American Academy of Child and Adolescent Psychiatry, 36*, 1065–1079.

Jensen, P.S., Mrazek, M.D., Knapp, P.K., Steinberg, L., Pfeffer, C., Schowalter, J., & Shapiro, T. (1997b). Evolution and revolution in child psychiatry: ADHD as a disorder of adaptation. *Journal of the American Academy of Child and Adolescent Psychiatry, 36*, 1672–1679.

Koziol, L.F. (1994). Attention deficit disorder, frontal lobe syndromes, and related psychiatric disturbances. In L.F. Koziol & C.E. Stout (Eds.), *The neuropsychology of mental disorders* (pp. 52–79). Springfield, IL: C.C. Thomas.

LaHoste, G.J., Swanson, J.M., Wigal, S.B., Glabe, C., Wigal, T., King, N., & Kennedy, J.L. (1996). Dopamine D4 receptor gene polymorphism is associated with attention deficit hyperactivity disorder. *Molecular Psychiatry, 1*, 121–124.

Quay, H.C. (1997). Inhibition and attention deficit hyperactivity disorder. *Journal of Abnormal Child Psychology, 25,* 7–13.

Ratey, J.R., Middeldorp-Crispijn, C.W., & Leveroni, C.L. (1995). Influence of attention problems on the development of personality. In J.J. Ratey (Ed.), *Neuropsychiatry of personality disorders* (pp. 79–119). Oxford: Blackwell Science.

Sachdev, P. (1999). Attention deficit hyperactivity disorder in adults. *Psychological Medicine, 29,* 507–514.

Sagvolden, T., & Sergeant, J.A. (1998). Attention deficit/hyperactivity disorder: From brain dysfunctions to behavior. *Behavioural Brain Research, 94,* 1–10.

Sandberg, S. (Ed.) (1996). *Hyperactivity disorders of childhood.* Cambridge, UK: Cambridge University Press.

Swanson, J., Posner, M.I., Cantwell, D., Wigal, S., Crinella, F., Filipek, P., Emerson, J., Tucker, D., & Nalcioglu, O. (1998). Attention-deficit/hyperactivity disorder: Symptom domains, cognitive processes, and neural networks. In R. Parasuraman (Ed.), *The attentive brain* (pp. 445–459). Cambridge, MA: MIT Press.

Tannock, R. (1998). Attention deficit hyperactivity disorder: Advances in cognitive, neuro-biological, and genetic research. *Journal of Child Psychology and Psychiatry, 39,* 65–99.

Taylor, E. (1998). Clinical foundations of hyperactivity research. *Behavioural Brain Research, 94,* 11–24.

Weiss, G. (1996). Attention deficit hyperactivity disorder. In M. Lewis (Ed.), *Child and adolescent psychiatry: A comprehensive textbook* (pp. 544–563). Baltimore: Williams & Wilkins.

CHAPTER SEVEN

Schizophrenia: A disorder of thought

Whom the gods love, they first make mad.
—Old Greek Proverb

INTRODUCTION

Although considerably less prevalent than depression, schizophrenia is the archetypal, serious psychiatric disorder of our times, because it affects so many functions and individuals other than the patient. In this chapter we shall review its symptomatology, paying particular attention to hallucinations, delusions, disordered thought and affect, and negative aspects. Although structural and functional studies will be seen to reveal widespread brain involvement, the major frontostriatal circuits will all be shown to be intimately involved in the various symptoms. Cognitive and executive problems will be seen to be widespread, along with difficulties with attention and inhibition; in these latter respects certain commonalities will be apparent with attention deficit hyperactivity disorder. We shall review the evidence for schizophrenia as a fetal neurodevelopmental disorder, with certain preclinical signs possibly long antedating the appearance of florid symptomatology. Like the other frontostriatal disorders, it will be seen to have a strongly heritable component, even though the genetic mechanisms are far from clear. Although disturbances of dopamine neurotransmission may play a major role, the neurochemical mechanisms are complex and involve other neurotransmitters also, especially perhaps serotonin and probably glutamate and maybe nitric oxide. Even the modes of action of medication, with the increasingly efficacious, newly developed atypical neuroleptics, are far from being fully understood. However, its importance for the individual and society make schizophrenia perhaps the most significant, if the most complex, of the neurodevelopmental frontostriatal disorders.

PRELIMINARY CONSIDERATIONS

Schizophrenia, a common disorder with a lifetime risk of around 1%, ruins careers, personal relationships, and lives. Before neuroleptic treatment was introduced in the 1950s, at least half of all hospital beds in advanced countries were occupied by psychiatric cases. Now, less than one quarter are so occupied, even though the disorder accounts for nearly half of all long-term care days, and around half of all mental illness involves schizophrenia. There is an overall suicide rate of around 10–15% (Barondes et al., 1997). Increased incidence in lower socioeconomic classes and the unmarried may suggest potentiation by stress, though war is not associated with any increase in incidence. Nevertheless social interaction probably plays a moderating role, and though psychosis is increasingly seen as organic rather than psychosocial, psychosocial factors may influence how and when it manifests. It is typically a disorder of young adulthood, though disablement may manifest in the late teens, with patients becoming highly dependent on and disruptive of society. With males it typically begins in the mid twenties, and with females 6 or 7 years later. Later female onset suggests a hormonal contribution, though it could merely reflect better social skills in women. Subtle social, behavioural, facial, or motor signs may be apparent in, for example, home movies years before clinical diagnosis; however, a sudden acute onset in an older individual with previously good personal adjustment, prominent affective symptoms, and no previous history offers a better prognosis.

SYMPTOMATOLOGY OF SCHIZOPHRENIA

This complex, intractable, and poorly understood disorder affects emotional reactivity, interpersonal relations, perceptual processes (hallucinations), attention, information processing and thought (delusions and disordered thinking), motivation (avolition) and speech (tangentiality, alogia) (see, for example, Schultz & Andreasen, 1999). Heterogeneity marks its phenotypic expression, its multiple aetiological pathways, its fluctuations at different stages in its development, and in its responsiveness or otherwise to treatment (Goldman-Rakic & Selemon, 1997). As we shall see, no one brain system and no one dysfunction seem central to its pathophysiology; there is a considerable range of overlap with what may be considered normal, and none of the findings are pathognomic, restricted to or even sufficient for an indisputable diagnosis of schizophrenia. Its symptoms aggregate into relatively independent complexes, so there may in fact be distinct neural substrates to each complex (Buchanan & Carpenter, 1997); indeed the use of symptoms to define schizophrenia subgroups began in the early days of the twentieth century with Kraepelin and Bleuler.

Three models have historically been proposed to explain the clinical variability of schizophrenia's manifestations (Gooding & Iacono, 1995): a single neurological insult that can manifest in various ways; a heterogeneous condition with various causations leading via a final common pathway to a single outcome; or a condition that is heterogeneous in both aetiology and manifestations—the presently preferred approach. Characterised by hallucinations, delusions, thought disorder, and cognitive deficit in the acute phase, and by apathy, social withdrawal, reduced initiative, blunted affect, and poverty of speech and ideation in the chronic phase, schizophrenia presents, as we saw, with multiple and variable symptoms that encompass almost every aspect of cognition and behaviour. However, not every patient manifests signs and symptoms in every area; nor does the clinical presentation remain stable throughout the course of the illness.

Not only is schizophrenia heterogeneous with respect to its symptomatology, but there is also considerable diversity, with respect to age of onset, premorbid history, course and outcome of the disease, familial risk, environmental determinants, response to medication, and location and even the presence of brain anomalies. Not only do males, as we saw, tend towards earlier onset, but they may also typically have poorer premorbid histories and outcome, and more deficit symptoms; conversely, females may have more relatives with schizophrenia, fewer abnormal neurological signs, and may be less likely to have experienced perinatal complications, than males (Pearlson & Pulver, 1994).

A recurrent pattern of affective change is uncommon in schizophrenia, unlike the mood disorders, and its psychotic symptoms tend to be more bizarre and less intuitively understandable than those of affective disorders. Gradual development of the disease, incomplete remissions between psychotic episodes, and prolonged social and occupational impairment, all contribute to a diagnosis of schizophrenia (Carpenter & Buchanan, 1994).

According to DSM-IV criteria, for a diagnosis of schizophrenia, temporal lobe epilepsy, dementia, metabolic disturbances, the effects of toxic substances and psychoactive drugs must be excluded, along with affective disorders and recurrent mood disturbances. There must be significant social or occupational dysfunction, which typically persists even after control of other, more severe symptoms, and the patient must exhibit at least two of the following for some substantial period of time, typically 6 months or more:

- *Positive symptoms*, which include delusions, hallucinations, disorganised or incoherent thought and speech, grossly disorganised or catatonic behaviour.

- *Negative symptoms*, which include flattening of affect, alogia and avolition, and typically result in loss of the ability to interact meaningfully with others or the environment; negative symptoms are usually the most resistant to treatment.

Diagnosis is thus based purely on observation, and usually will also take account of deterioration of work performance, interpersonal relationships, self-care etc., and failure to reach an appropriate level of interpersonal, academic, or occupational achievement (Schultz & Andreasen, 1999). Alternatively, symptoms may be categorised into three classes (Buchanan & Carpenter, 1997):

- Hallucinations and delusions.
- Negative symptoms of blunted affect, anhedonia, and avolition, poverty of speech and movement, and curbing of interests and social activity.
- Disorganised behaviour, formal thought disorder, bizarre behaviour, and inappropriate affect.

Frith (1992) proposes an essentially similar tripartite taxonomy to that of Buchanan and Carpenter (1997), but with a more elaborately developed theoretical basis:

- Disorders of willed action, leading to alogia and avolition.
- Disorders of self-monitoring, leading to auditory hallucinations, and delusions of alien control.
- Disorders of monitoring the intentions of others ("mentalising"), leading to formal thought disorder and delusions of persecution.

While we shall later return to the question of faulty monitoring, all of the above may be seen as special cases of a single underlying mechanism, a disorder of consciousness or self-awareness that impairs the ability to think with "metarepresentations"—higher-order abstract concepts that are representations of mental states (Andreasen, 1997). In this respect schizophrenia resembles autism in involving a deficit in understanding the boundaries of belief, thought, and action between oneself and others.

However we cluster the symptomatology, which clearly merges with the continuum of behaviours that would be judged as "normal", there is the question as to whether different brain regions are involved in each symptom complex; as we shall see, limbic, temporal, prefrontal, anterior cingulate, and striatal mechanisms are both theoretical and empirical candidates. Thus Buchanan and Carpenter (1997) speculate that hallucinations and delusions are associated with anterior cingulate, basal ganglia–thalamocortical structures and language circuits, whereas the dorsolateral prefrontal cortex, basal ganglia, and thalamocortical circuit may be concerned with negative symptoms. Although perhaps only a minority of patients with schizophrenia exhibit the trait of avolitional pathology captured by the deficit symptom concept, most nevertheless experience some negative symptoms at some point in the course of their disorder.

Pantelis and Brewer (1996) offer perhaps the most ambitious neuro-anatomical model in their attempt to link the various factors (above) with prefrontal syndromes consequent upon damage to specific prefrontal regions and circuits. Thus they link the dysexecutive syndrome of dorso-lateral prefrontal impairment with psychomotor poverty, social withdrawal and depression in schizophrenia. They link orbitofrontal disinhibition with disorganisation, thought disturbance, and antisocial behaviour in schizophrenia. They link the apathy of anterior cingulate dysfunction with schizophrenic disorganisation, social withdrawal, and thought disturbance, and the ideomotor syndrome of supplementary motor area damage with delusions of control. Clearly there is considerable overlap, and potentiality for rearranging or reassigning responsibility to different areas, often with joint involvement. Temporal regions probably also contribute their own flavour with respect, for example, to delusional beliefs. It is also clear that schizophrenia is a heterogeneous disorder, with perhaps several different aetiological processes, and intertwined genetic and environmental factors, giving rise to the disorder's characteristic signs and symptoms (Knoll et al., 1998).

Negative symptoms are perhaps the most persistent, intractable, and disabling aspect of schizophrenia (McPhillips & Barnes, 1997), and may differentiate, better than positive symptoms, the various categories of the disorder. They are, however, also present in bipolar disorder and depression, and may be confused with depressive features and drug-induced parkinsonism. (Schizoaffective disorder may indeed lie between schizophrenia and affective disorders along a continuum, and it is probable that relatives of propositi with either disorder have an increased risk of developing the other; see, for example, Leboyer & Gorwood, 1995.) Moreover anhedonia, poverty of speech and action, social withdrawal, or poor social functioning can all occur in other prefrontal syndromes, probably reflecting frontal involvement in schizophrenia. Morphometric anomalies, too, in these regions, correlate with the degree of negative symptoms present, and persistence of the latter may be a more reliable predictor of continued functioning than those elicited during a single acute episode. Indeed the longer the psychosis proceeds unchecked before treatment, the worse the negative symptoms, the poorer the prognosis, and the poorer the response to neuroleptics. Although social impairment may possibly be an independent factor in its own right, as some factor-analytic studies have suggested (e.g. Harvey et al., 1996), it may also of course be a consequence of the other deficits, acting either independently or in an interactive fashion.

A fundamental characteristic of the disorder, implicit in its very name, is a break with reality, or a separation of cognitive from emotional functions, such that inappropriate affect may result in laughter while discussing a family tragedy. Otherwise, however, there have been numerous attempts to identify homogeneous subtypes. Traditionally, a distinction has been made between *catatonic* (involving largely a psychomotor deficit), *hebephrenic* (with disorganised behaviour and flat, inappropriate affect), and *paranoid* (with hallucinations and delusions). However, patients often move between paranoia, catatonia, and hebephrenia, and neither genetic nor neuropsychological studies now support such a subtyping (Gourovitch & Goldberg, 1996). Later, patients were dichotomised into type 1 with largely positive symptoms (such extra or "supernormal" behaviours as delusions, hallucinations, and disorganised speech and behaviour), and type 2. The latter type was characterised by negative symptoms or deficits in behaviour, e.g. poverty of action, speech, and thought, blunted affect (anhedonia), and emotional and social withdrawal. Type 2 patients were thought to be long term and chronic, less amenable to medication, and with evidence of pathological brain changes, unlike type 1 patients for whom the prognosis, and response to neuroleptics, was held to be better (Crow, 1980).

It may well be the case, as we shall see below, that negative symptoms reflect irreversible brain changes (frontal lobe?), and positive symptoms a potentially reversible neurochemical or receptor imbalance (temporolimbic?), but the type 1/type 2 distinction may at best only reflect a patient's state at a particular point in time, as patients may shift between the two types during the progression of the disease. Thus three phases may occur (Buchanan & Carpenter, 1997):

- An exacerbating phase of largely positive symptoms.
- A plateau phase, where the severity and frequency of positive symptoms stabilise.
- Remission of hallucinations, delusions, and disorganised behaviour, with evolution or worsening of negative symptoms.

(Note, however, that according to Stevens, 1997, apparently minor disturbances in motivation, attention, perception, and affect may precede the onset of frankly psychotic symptoms, and may set the stage for the emergence of the positive symptoms of hallucination and delusion.) Indeed the disorder may exhibit three types of trajectory (Stevens, 1997):

- A single attack, with more or less total recovery.
- Repeated attacks, with subtotal recovery.
- A course progressing to chronic disability.

Unfortunately, the last is all too common. However, it does not seem possible to predict the future course of the disease with any certainty from a knowledge of the type and distribution of the symptoms in its early stages. Frequently, patients in later stages exhibit "late" or "tardive" dyskinesias. It is often thought that this irreversible phenomenon is solely a consequence of prolonged neuroleptic medication; however, as we shall see, motor anomalies of a progressive nature have been noted from before the days of such treatment, and may well be integral to the evolution of the disorder, reflecting basal ganglia involvement.

HALLUCINATIONS

Schizophrenia is popularly associated with florid, hallucinatory, and delusional behaviour. However, hallucinations are not uncommon in normal healthy individuals. When we drop off to sleep we may experience hypnagogic imagery, maybe "hearing" a few brief words, typically well formed grammatically but otherwise senseless, which we ignore. Experiments in the 1960s at the dawn of the Space Age investigated the effects of restricted sensory environments ("sensory deprivation") for would-be astronauts; many had to be terminated because of unwanted hallucinatory experiences, typically visual. People with failing vision may experience the Charles-Bonnet syndrome, named from the description by an eighteenth-century Swiss naturalist of his blind grandfather's visual hallucinations. The difference is, of course, that unlike patients with schizophrenia we do not normally *misattribute* such experiences to a real or external source. Indeed, patients' hallucinatory experiences seem often to have a precise, highly personalised content which is consistent with the current semantic context (David, 1999), such that the experience *personifies* them. Thus, just as with the coprolalia of Tourette's syndrome, cultural factors help determine the content; conversely, listening to music may help, either by blocking out the intrusive signals or redirecting attention. Hallucinations tend to be auditory in schizophrenia rather than visual, and may manifest as a form of inner speech that is so intense that it is interpreted as being of external origin. However, visual hallucinations do also occur, though they tend to be less common or disturbing (Stein & Richardson, 1999), possibly because we rely more on auditory language as a channel for thought and communication. When they do occur, visual hallucinations may take the form of elongation, truncation, dilation, or constriction of perceived environmental objects, or experiential swirling, iridescence, looming, retiring, or disintegration. Stein and Richardson (1999) speculate that the mechanism may involve impairment in the development and operation of the visual magnocellular system, in a manner that has also been proposed for visuoperceptual deficits in developmental dyslexia. (It may be no accident, as we shall shortly see, that both disorders may be construed as *neurodevelopmental*.) Indeed there is evidence that many developmental dyslexic families may be at increased risk for schizophrenia, and many families of schizophrenic probands likewise of developmental dyslexia. As Stein and Richardson (1999) observe, the visual magnocellular system also projects to pontine nuclei and on to the cerebellum, another structure known (see later) to be abnormal in schizophrenia (and autism), and a centre where comparator and reafference operations may occur. (We shall shortly review the evidence for schizophrenia as a disorder of misattribution or reafference.) Stein and Richardson (1999) also propose that the magnocellular system may mediate "binding" (the hypothetical process whereby the disparate sensory, perceptual, or even emotional qualities of, for example, shape, colour, size, value . . . of objects are correctly associated and assigned to their respective objects). Binding may thus be defective in schizophrenia, thereby accounting for disordered perception and thought—a proposal also made earlier by Bradshaw (1998).

If, however, hallucinations in schizophrenia are predominantly auditory, we might wonder what are the experiences of patients who also happen to have been profoundly deaf from a very early age. A study by du Feu and McKenna (1999) addressed this issue, finding that symptoms in such patients, who were prelingually and profoundly deaf, were broadly comparable to those in hearing patients with schizophrenia, even with respect to *auditory* hallucinations. It is of course difficult to imagine how such symptoms could be experienced by individuals who have either never heard speech, or who have lost hearing before they have acquired the ability to comprehend spoken language. Thus, surprisingly, there is a very long tradition of profoundly deaf patients reporting the hearing of voices. *Are* they really hearing voices, or experiencing some other phenomenon? Although some may indeed turn out to be *visually* hallucinating signing and finger spelling, nevertheless many do still insist that they are *hearing* something. Du Feu and McKenna (1999) studied 21 patients fulfilling all necessary criteria (schizophrenia, profound prelinguistic deafness). Some experienced nonverbal auditory hallucinations, but many were emphatic that they heard voices in the second or third person offering comments on them or instructions to them, and they could give no reasonable explanation how they could hear, being deaf. Voices were single or multiple, located inside or outside of the head, verbal or nonverbal, exactly like the voices of hearing patients. Accounts were clear and well articulated of material that was neutral, pleasant, or derogatory in nature, and ranged from single words to lengthy conversations and discussions. There was, however, a perhaps unusually high frequency of the normally rare *visual* hallucinations.

Abnormal subcortical and limbic activation may produce the hallucinatory activity via activation of auditory (or even visual) association areas in the temporal lobe (Zipursky & Kapur, 1998). Thus there is evidence (for reviews, see David, 1999; du Feu & McKenna, 1999; Vogeley & Falkai, 1999) of increased perisylvian activation during hallucinatory episodes, especially of Broca's area, and anterior cingulate, along with failure to activate supplementary motor area and middle temporal gyrus regions on the left. These areas are probably important in monitoring and correctly attributing self-generated speech to endogenous rather than exogenous sources. Others, however, suggest increased medial temporal lobe, anterior cingulate, and basal ganglia activation, with reduced frontal involvement. Be that as it may, the final common pathway for experiencing auditory hallucinations in schizophrenia does seem to involve areas subserving normal speech perception, with anomalies in midtemporal and subcortical regions perhaps facilitating or failing to inhibit auditory activation. Indeed Johns and McGuire (1999) found that patients who hallucinated were more likely than nonhallucinators or controls to misattribute the electronically altered sound of their *own* voices to *other* people, further supporting the idea that hallucinations stem from misattributing one's own inner speech to an external source.

DELUSIONAL BELIEFS

The schizophrenic phenomenon of unfounded or delusional beliefs of persecution or control clearly relate in some way to hallucinatory experiences, and may be the origin of folk beliefs in witchcraft. False delusional beliefs may include the following (see, for example, Frith, 1992):

- Thought insertion, as from an outside source into one's head.
- Thought broadcast, from one's own mind to others'.
- Thought withdrawal, from one's own mind by someone else.
- Hearing one's own thoughts spoken aloud.
- Hearing voices either addressing one (in the second person) or commenting about one.
- Delusions of control, where an external force makes one act.
- Delusions of persecution, where someone is out to get one.
- Delusions of reference, where the actions and gestures of strangers are believed to be of special significance.

Both hallucinations and delusions may also occur in Huntington's disease, though such patients tend to be more cautious and guarded about them, and less likely to admit to them. It is also noteworthy that many of the above delusional beliefs, so characteristic of schizophrenia, have their counterpart in the pretend play and mythology of children; in the neurodevelopmental disorders it is often a short step, via arrested development, from normal childhood behaviour to adult psychopathology.

Delusional disorders generally are characterised by more or less bizarre, chronic and content-encapsulated false beliefs that are held in the context of generally intact affect, speech, and general behaviour—a situation that clearly does not necessarily apply in the specific context of schizophrenia. The subject matter may vary with persecutory, jealous, grandiose, eroto-maniac, and somatic subtypes, according to Charlton and McClelland (1999), who propose three major defining characteristics:

- The delusional belief is false.
- It is behaviourally dominant.
- It is resistant to counter-argument.

Charlton and McClelland (1999) note that human social intelligence has arisen to understand, predict, and manipulate the behaviour of others (see Bradshaw, 1997); as a result of social competition, huge demands are placed upon cognitive structures. We normally interpret others' behaviour in the light of inferred mental states (the theory of mind hypothesis: autistic individuals may have failed to develop an adequate understanding of others' beliefs, desires, or intentions). Thus we normally use our own emotional reactions as indicators of another's mental state, so as to model behavioural consequences. Charlton and McClelland (1999) propose that delusions (generally, or in the context of schizophrenia) occur with intact theory of mind, but with misapplied logic, or reasoning based on false premises. Because we are such intensely social animals, the subject matter of delu-sional disorder relates closely to important aspects of contemporary social interaction. All the delusions are social, and involve making mental state inferences with respect to the dispositions, motivations, or intentions of others; however, there are mistakes in logic, and false premises are adopted with respect to one's own emotional responses and those of others, and the links between such emotional responses and the hypothesised mental states.

A closely related concept is one, explored earlier in the context of hallu-cinations, of a failure of reality monitoring; patients misattribute self-generated processes to external sources, though now the social aspects are de-emphasised. An empirical demonstration of such an operation may be made when patients review lists of items (words, pictures, or objects pre-sented visually or aurally), and then must recognise these items from among a larger list. Patients tend to report new items as old, and to misattribute self-generated items to the outside source (Surguladze & David, 1998). Thus faulty monitoring may extend to intentions, especially perhaps in the social context, with the patient thinking his/her thoughts, emotions, and actions are controlled by someone else. Whether it is subvocal speech, as in hallucinations, or thought processes, as in delusions, the patient may be unable to recognise them as their own (Frith, 1992), due to a failure of self-monitoring and of the feedforward (reafference or corollary discharge) system that comes into play whenever any voluntary activity is undertaken. Various structures (cerebellum, parietal lobe) have at different times been proposed as the site of such a comparator system, whereby we match forward projections (neural copies) of likely experiences of upcoming responses with the actual consequences, fed back, of those actual actions; in the event of a mismatch, the behaviour is attempted again, with appropriate variations, to achieve a target goal. Thus we continuously and economically build up and update internal predictive models on the basis of past experience. The system clearly must be able to distinguish sensations caused directly by the body's own movement, from those arriving extraneously from the environment. Our ability to do this and to predict the consequences of our actions may explain why we cannot tickle ourselves, unless we introduce a 200 ms time lag into a device that then enables us to tickle ourselves. We shall see that in addition to disorders of self-attribution patients with schizophrenia may have a cerebellar deficit—and *can* experience self-tickling (Wolpert, Miall, & Kawato, 1998)! Clearly such a reafference system requires the capacity appropriately to gate internally or externally generated input, a capacity that may be defective in both schizophrenia and autism, where patients may be hyper- or hyposensitive to external stimuli, or display fascination with internally generated behaviours or repetitive events. Whether, in schizophrenia, there is a *local* failure (e.g. cerebellar) or there is instead a failure of various systems (anterior and posterior) adequately to *interact* is yet to be determined (see Friston, 1999).

Nor is it entirely clear how (or whether) delusional beliefs should be related to formal thought disorder in schizophrenia. Thus patients may have problems with abstract concepts, and tend to give literal rather than metaphorical interpretations to proverbs. They may produce bizarre, inappropriate, oblique, loose, or indirect associations, or frankly "derail". Spitzer (1997) addressed this issue with the technique of semantic priming in a lexical decision task. Normally "black" would be recognised faster if preceded by "white"; this effect was particularly pronounced with patients with schizophrenia, indicating perhaps increased strength of associative links in semantic memory (see Surguladze & David, 1998). Other associated signs include incoherence of speech, with repeated shifts of topic, lack of organisation, and lack of logical connectivity between phrases and sentences. There may be incongruity of affect, with the expressed emotion (e.g. laughter) not fitting the gravity of the topic (e.g. death of a spouse).

RATING SCALES OF SEVERITY

Rating scales of severity for schizophrenia are: Abnormal Involuntary Movement Scale (AIMS) (Department of Health, Education and Welfare, 1974). The Positive and Negative Syndrome Scale (PANSS) for Schizophrenia (Kay, Fiszbein, & Opler, 1987). Scale for the Assessment of Negative Symptoms (SANS) (Andreasen, 1989). Scale for the Assessment of Positive Symptoms (SAPS) (Andreasen, 1984).

STRUCTURAL AND FUNCTIONAL ANOMALIES OF THE BRAIN IN SCHIZOPHRENIA

The neuropathology of schizophrenia has been described as the graveyard of neuropathologists (Plum, 1972, cited in Harrison, 1999), which still fascinates and exasperates researchers, generating more heat than light, and being notable for memorable quotations rather than for durable data. Major recent reviews of this controversial area have been provided by Arnold (1999), Harrison (1999), and Weinberger (1999). The triad of most consistent findings are ventricular enlargement, reduced hippocampal volume, and hypofrontality. Thus temporal and frontal lobes and related subcortical limbic structures are especially affected, with schizophrenic symptoms similar to those when tumours, trauma, infections, or neurodegeneration affect these same regions. Structural or anatomical findings may correlate with trait variables, whereas functional findings may correlate with trait vulnerability or with state-dependent factors. Trait vulnerability correlations may be best examined during periods of clinical remission, to reduce state-dependent fluctuations.

Reductions in whole-brain volume have been reported, especially perhaps on the right side. Increased ventricular size, perhaps correlating with negative symptoms, is of course also found with other disorders such as Huntington's and Alzheimer's diseases. It may be especially prominent in the lateral horns on the left, but is probably not diagnostic, in view of the considerable overlap with normal values. However, in discordant monozygotic twins, the affected twin seems always to have the larger ventricles; unaffected close relatives may also exhibit ventricular enlargement.

Reductions in temporal lobe volume may be greater on the left, and include the hippocampus, related structures, and the amygdala. Such reductions may also be apparent in currently unaffected close relatives, though to a lesser degree (Lawrie et al., 1999), a finding that we shall see is concordant with a neurodevelopmental model for schizophrenia in which structural anomalies may precede the clinical syndrome by many years. Grey matter reductions, again more perhaps on the left, may be more prominent than white matter changes. These temporal regions of course are important in declarative and verbal memory, known to be affected in schizophrenia (see later), and are likely to be closely involved in positive symptoms and delusional and hallucinatory behaviour. There are disputed reports of abnormalities in neuronal density and size and of neuronal processes in the entorhinal cortex, hippocampus, and superior temporal gyrus; Ammon's horn is most consistently said to be affected. Increased density and reduced size of neuropil and dendritic arborisation may be intrinsic to schizophrenia, or possibly a consequence of associated stress.

The dorsolateral prefrontal cortex mediates executive functions (working memory, decision making) and attention along with the anterior cingulate; these functions, and regions, are known to be affected in schizophrenia. Reductions in frontal lobe volume are reported somewhat less consistently than is the case with the temporal lobes, though at a functional level hypofrontality, both in "resting" and activation studies, is commonly reported, particularly when negative symptoms are evident (Travis & Kerwin, 1997)—though of course the patient may simply be no longer trying! Indeed Heckers et al. (1998) claim that under other more demanding circumstances we may see in schizophrenia a prefrontal *over*activation along with hippocampal underactivation, suggesting that the former effect may be an attempt to control (or compensate for) hippocampal malfunction, with the disorder perhaps better characterised as an inter-regional (frontotemporal) disintegration (see later, and Fletcher, 1998). Thus hypofrontality, when it occurs, may stem from later, negative symptomatology, a sense of hopelessness, or even the effects of chronic medication.

Olfactory dysfunction has also been reported in schizophrenia, just as it has in obsessive compulsive disorder, Parkinson's and Alzheimer's diseases, indicating involvement of the orbitofrontal cortex, medial temporal lobe, and basal forebrain.

Elsewhere in the brain, abnormalities have been reported in neurone density, number, and size in the nucleus accumbens, substantia nigra, thalamus, locus coeruleus, and pedunculopontine nucleus. In the basal ganglia, reduced left lenticular activation and increased volume have been reported in some components, though this may be due merely to neuroleptic medication. The clinical efficacy of neuroleptics is, as we shall see, linked to the dopamine D2 receptors present in high concentrations in the striatum. There is evidence in schizophrenia of increased dopamine receptor density, which is perhaps responsible for motor and affective symptoms. Metabolism may, however, be reduced in the striatum, with neuroleptics normalising this state of affairs. The thalamus, a structure important in filtering sensory input—and we have already seen that this function may be defective in schizophrenia—may exhibit reduced metabolism and volume, especially dorsally. In the corpus callosum, there is a range of inconsistent findings with respect to anomalies of size (in either direction) in various subregions. The septum pellucidum is a structure consisting of two laminae, which separate the two frontal horns of the lateral ventricles; consistent findings of abnormalities in this region may indicate abnormal midline development, itself supportive of the neurodevelopmental failure hypothesis of schizophrenia (see below).

A current debate (Andreasen, Paradiso, & O'Leary, 1998) centres on whether "cognitive dysmetria" in schizophrenia stems from cerebellar involvement. The disorder presents with a diversity of symptoms representing multiple psychological domains—perception, inference, concept formation, language, volition, motor activity, social interaction, and emotion—though not all patients have symptoms that express all these domains. Executive functions, attention, memory, emotion, and motor activity may be core aspects, and the term "cognitive dysmetria" (by analogy with motor dysmetria in cerebellar disorder, where there is a poor control of reach and aim) may encompass them. *Cognitive* dysmetria may manifest as difficulty in coordinating the processing, prioritisation, retrieval, and expression of information, leading to hallucinations, delusions, disorganised behaviour, alogia, affective blunting or incongruity, avolition, anhedonia, and attentional impairment. Andreasen et al. (1998) note that the cerebellum plays a major role (along with the prefrontal cortex, with which it is interconnected) in cognitive processes, including functions known to be compromised in schizophrenia. Like the prefrontal cortex, the cerebellum is greatly increased in size in humans and is well suited to perform massive parallel processing; it is constructed of multiple modules, extensively interconnected with the rest of the cortex, particularly the dorsolateral prefrontal cortex, parietal, temporal, and mesocortical (limbic) regions, the nucleus accumbens (the limbic basal ganglia), the anterior cingulate, and orbitofrontal cortex (Katsetos, Hyde, & Herman, 1997). There are hints of cerebellar dysfunction in schizophrenia, just as there is increasing evidence of the same in autism, a disorder of earlier, childhood, onset which nevertheless exhibits some interesting parallels with schizophrenia, including a possible neurodevelopmental pathology *in utero*. As in autism, there are suggestions of pathology of the vermis of the cerebellum (Martin & Albers, 1995), generalised cerebellar atrophy and abnormal metabolism, mild gait ataxia, disturbed coordination of the upper and lower limbs, a mild intention tremor, and dysmetric saccades. In this context of cognitive dysmetria, Nopoulos, Ceilley, Gailis, and Andreasen (1999) report smaller vermis area of the cerebellum, noting further that the vermis is a midline structure; there are other suggestions that schizophrenia may involve midline anomalies.

Selemon and Goldman-Rakic (1999) review the evidence for the hypothesis of neuropil reduction in schizophrenia, which is likely to be related to increased neuronal densities in prefrontal (and possibly occipital) regions in this *neurodevelopmental* disorder. This situation may possibly seem paradoxical, given the cell loss in *neurodegenerative* disorders like Alzheimer's and Huntington's diseases. It may perhaps be explained in terms of reduced *distances* between neurones, because of neuropil reduction, whereas the *number* of neurones remains unchanged. Thus schizophrenia would be seen as involving atrophy of neuronal processes without actual cell loss—the reduced neuropil hypothesis. The hypothesis clearly is congruent with evidence in the dorsolateral prefrontal cortex of decreased volume and increased neuronal density and may relate, as we shall see below, to abnormalities of synaptic pruning during adolescence. There is apparently little evidence of cell loss per se, as any increase in glial density is approximately commensurate with increase in cell packing. There is also apparently some evidence of a selective reduction in cell size of large pyramidal neurones, which may possibly undergo atrophic changes in the disorder. Intercellular communication could consequently suffer. Much of the neuropil consists of dendritic processes and presynaptic terminal input. Synaptic contacts may be especially affected on pyramidal cells, particularly thalamic inputs, with a reduced complement of dopaminergic or GABAergic terminals in the prefrontal cortex where glutamatergic (see later) pyramidal cells abound. Thus, as we shall see, glutamate receptor antagonists can induce psychosis, thereby leading to the glutamate hypothesis of schizophrenia.

This reduced neuropil hypothesis of schizophrenia (Selemon & Goldman-Rakic, 1999) departs from the current model of depleted cell populations due either to neurodegeneration (unlikely) or neurodevelopmental (more likely) processes. The authors also note that small changes in the level of dopamine D1 receptor stimulation in the dorsolateral prefrontal cortex can greatly alter a neurone's responsivity to extrinsic input, and a patient's ability to perform working memory tasks, and that the spines and distal dendrites of pyramidal neurones are key loci for dopamine modulation. So even small changes in dendritic arborisation could affect the ability of the dorsolateral prefrontal cortex to respond to extrinsic stimuli.

SCHIZOPHRENIA: A DISORDER OF INTERCONNECTIVITY

Buchsbaum and Hazlett (1998; see also Arnold, 1999; Friston, 1999; Graybiel, 1997; Waddington, Lane, Larkin, & O'Callaghan, 1999) observe that we should not view hypometabolism of the anterior cingulate and dorsolateral prefrontal cortex (even though it may correlate with negative symptom severity) and hypermetabolism of the temporolimbic cortex (which may correlate with positive symptomatology) in mutual isolation. Instead, anomalous patterns of activation, both at rest and during information processing, should be seen as a failure of coordinated connectivity or coactivation. Indeed it is easy to see how disorganised thought processes and bizarre associations could arise from such a process. Thus we should not necessarily look for local failure of structures or locally impaired functional specialisation, but rather for a failure of interaction. This may not necessarily mean structural loss of white matter tracts (though see Arnold, 1999, for consideration of reduced density of inhibitory inter-neurones in the anterior cingulate), but rather maybe a loss of moment-to-moment functional interaction between centres, perhaps as modulated by the modulatory monoamine systems dopamine, noradrenaline, acetylcho-line, and serotonin. Such a view is supported by the relapsing and remitting course of schizophrenia, and its responsivity to medication. Thus in a verbal fluency task, we might *normally* find activation of the dorsolateral pre-frontal cortex and anterior cingulate, and bitemporal, medial prefrontal, and posterior cingulate deactivation (Dolan et al., 1999), whereas *patients* may instead demonstrate simultaneous dorsolateral prefrontal and temporal activation with failure of anterior cingulate activation; dopamine in the cingulate cortex may act to facilitate integration of information processing via attentional modulation of cortico-cortical integration. If this model is correct, there are interesting parallels with obsessive compulsive disorder (OCD), where again there are anomalous interregional correlations that are normalised by medication. Both disorders are profitably seen as being disorders of the basal ganglia and frontostriatal circuitry, though whereas schizophrenia may be characterised as essentially hypofrontal, OCD is essentially hyperorbitofrontal. Medication may work by normalising the frontostriatal–thalamic circuitry via the basal ganglia, rather than by directly targeting cortical areas.

Increasingly, therefore, schizophrenia is viewed as a disorder of the frontotemporal and frontostriato-pallido-thalamo-cortical pathways; we shall later discuss whether the disorder is neurodevelopmentally of very long standing (and so may have precluded acquisition, during subsequent devel-opment, of normal cerebral structures) or whether there may be continuing neurodegeneration. Thalamic involvement in the circuit would account for clinical anomalies of sensory gating and overload (Buchsbaum et al., 1999; Jones, 1997); involvement of the mediodorsal nucleus in particular, with its links to the dorsolateral prefrontal cortex, temporolimbic cortex, and basal forebrain, would account for breakdown of connectivity, functional as well as structural, and runaway positive symptoms and hallucinations, whereas prefrontal deactivation would explain the negative symptoms. In addition, however, to involving the thalamus per se, schizophrenia should perhaps be seen generally as a circuit disease of the basal ganglia as a whole (Graybiel, 1997), of the mesocortical and mesolimbic dopaminergic mechanisms, and even of the nigrostriatal motor system. Thus, as we have seen, the basal ganglia influence motor, cognitive, and limbic processes of the forebrain via the *dorsal* system (dorsolateral prefrontal cortex, supplementary motor area, caudate, putamen, and globus pallidus, mediating movement sequencing and cognitive planning), and the *ventral* system (nucleus accumbens, amygdala, temporolimbic cortex, for reward, reinforcement, and drive); two prominent neurochemically defined tissue compartments in the striatum—matrix and striosomes—correspond to these two divisions above. In this way we may again see the basal ganglia as playing a role in cognitive binding, analogous to motor sequencing, and schizophrenia as a disorder of binding.

Anomalies in basal ganglia functioning of the sort described above, at the cognitive and motor level, may also explain some of the anomalies of behavioural asymmetry in schizophrenia, which have been likened to a subtle form of right neglect (Downing et al., 1998a; Maruff & Currie, 1996): a slowness to initiate rightward movements, especially in the absence of external cues. Maruff and Currie (1996) review the evidence for biased turning behaviour in individuals with schizophrenia, and its relationship to the asymmetrical effects of dopamine agonists (amphetamine) on basal ganglia function, and behaviour, in rodents. Many of these anomalous behavioural asymmetries may be ameliorated or eliminated with neuroleptic medication (dopamine blockers).

COGNITIVE DEFICITS IN SCHIZOPHRENIA

Nearly all aspects of cognitive function may be affected in schizophrenia (Heinrichs & Zakzanis, 1998; Nestor & O'Donnell, 1998). The disorder was seen as an *attentional* dysfunction as early as 1919 (Kraepelin, and, separately, Bleuler, cited by Buchanan, Buckley, Tamminga, & Schulze, 1998), both in terms of maintaining concentration and of screening out intrusive irrelevant stimuli from the environment (Jeste et al., 1996; Maruff & Currie, 1996). Indeed considerable similarity is evident between the positive and negative symptoms of the disorder, and the effects of frontal lobe lesions, with in both cases intrusions of irrelevant cognitions. Attentional deficits therefore make an early appearance in the symptomatology, in terms of maintaining/switching set, slowed simple reaction times, problems with advance information and warning signals, with processing multiple stimuli or searching for multiple targets or over a large array of potential distractors, with mobilising or allocating attentional resources, lengthened backward-masking susceptibility, reduced vigilance, and problems with continuous processing tasks; with the latter, predetermined targets, or especially target sequences, must be detected in the presence or absence of distractors. Patients show increased errors of omission and commission, and in Posner-type precue tasks have problems redirecting attention to the right side after an invalid cue on the left (Posner et al., 1988). Many of the above attentional deficits also manifest during remission (Jeste et al., 1996), suggesting a *core* or *trait* rather than a *state* deficit, perhaps of processing resources, due to a defective cortico-striato-pallido-thalamo-cortical re-entrant loop.

Such considerations would also explain *executive* dysfunctions, which anyway overlap with disorders of attention. Thus there are problems in concept attainment, holding/shifting hypotheses and set in the Wisconsin Card Sorting Test, problems in abstract reasoning, in monitoring ongoing behaviour, in making antisaccades (deliberate eye movements in the direction opposite to that of a suddenly occurring signal), in performing Stroop tasks and rapid alternation responses, with reduced fluency of thought, language, and behaviour, poor planning, and impaired insight and social judgement (Gourovitch & Goldberg, 1996; Jeste et al., 1996; Maruff & Currie, 1996; Pantelis & Brewer, 1996). Indeed close relatives who are therefore at high genetic risk of developing the disorder may also be poor in executive and general intellectual functions (Byrne et al., 1999). Other problems experienced by patients, and reviewed by Nestor and O'Donnell (1998), involve abnormal latent inhibition, and negative and flanking priming. Latent inhibition is a form of inhibitory conditioning, with repeated presentation of a trivial, irrelevant stimulus; if it subsequently becomes a conditional stimulus, conditioning is faster in patients than in controls, indicative perhaps of faulty inhibitory processes. With negative priming, response times normally increase to targets that in the last trial were distractors; this effect is reduced in schizophrenia, perhaps indicative of a deficit in strategic controlled inhibition. With flanking priming, flanking stimuli that are incompatible or incongruent with a centrally located target lead to reduced interference in patients, though only at very short stimulus onset asynchronies; this effect, as with negative priming that may involve slower-controlled inhibition, suggests a disturbance of fast, automatic attentional inhibition.

At the level of *memory*, there are deficits at all stages—encoding, consolidation, retrieval, and recognition—in verbal and visuospatial working memory, declarative and semantic memory (Rossell & David, 1997). This is again suggestive of frontal and temporal involvement (Egan & Weinberger, 1997; Gourovitch & Goldberg, 1996). There is failure to use, normally, semantic categorical clustering in learning scrambled word lists, or to show normal levels of release from proactive interference/inhibition. Thus there is failure to spontaneously perform necessary semantic (re)organisation. However, procedural skills may be preserved, along with automated (through practice) perceptual and motor skills, including performance of the Tower of Hanoi Test (Jeste et al., 1996), which might not be expected with impairment (see earlier) of the basal ganglia.

Language also shows impairments often manifesting as illogical or bizarre, with loss of continuity, problems in discourse editing, and an inability to inhibit inappropriate perseveration of ideas, words, or sounds (Gourovitch

& Goldberg, 1996). Priming studies suggest that multiple meanings of ambiguous words are often simultaneously available (in a potentially confusing and conflicting manner) to patients, who cannot inhibit inappropriate associations. Thus semantic priming is enhanced in patients when target words are preceded by semantically related primes (Spitzer, cited by Buchanan et al., 1998).

Apart from problems in performing antisaccades, i.e. in inhibiting and reversing normal saccadic reflexes, there may also be intrusions, into smooth pursuit tracking, of small anticipatory saccades in schizophrenia, correlating with reductions in frontal eyefield metabolism (Javitt, 1997). This phenomenon is distributed in the families of patients in the form of an autosomal dominant trait (Adler et al., 1999), just as is also the P50 deficit described later; both involve failure to inhibit intrusions, and may be normalised by high doses of nicotine. Adler et al. (1998) in fact note heavy tobacco use in patients with schizophrenia, suggestive of self-medication, and cholinergic transmission as a potential therapeutic target. (In our work with Huntington's disease patients, we have also informally noted heavy tobacco use as a form of self-medication.) Thus in schizophrenia there may be a deficit in sensory gating (see above) that is not normalised by neuroleptics, and which stems from anomalies, noted at autopsy, of nicotinic receptors in the hippocampus (Adler et al., 1998).

Distractibility, strangely, is not listed as a diagnostic criterion for schizophrenia in DSM-IV, even though it is for mania and attention deficit hyperactivity disorder (ADHD); there are repeated claims of distractibility in schizophrenia, problems in maintaining attentional focus, and intrusions of unwanted sensory information, all of which correlate with the level of psychosocial decline (Adler et al., 1999). An electrophysiological index of such phenomena is the *prepulse inhibition effect*; loud noises normally produce electrophysiological (and observable) startle responses, which reduce or are inhibited when preceded by lower-intensity prepulses or sound bursts; such effects are reduced in patients with schizophrenia or OCD (Javitt, 1997). Loss of inhibitory function in this context in schizophrenia is also demonstrable by the conditioning–testing P50 paradigm (Adler et al., 1999). Auditory stimuli are presented in pairs, the first activating excitatory inputs that evoke the P50 response; the latter is a positive wave with a 50 ms latency that activates or conditions inhibitory pathways, such that if a second signal occurs soon after it is suppressed by the still-active inhibitory mechanisms associated with the first stimulus. In patients with schizophrenia, and certain close relatives with clinically evident symptoms, in a manner consistent with autosomal dominant transmission P50 suppression is reduced. Impaired P50 suppression is most pronounced in patients evidencing abnormal attentional or linguistic functions. Patients treated with atypical (but not typical) neuroleptics like clozapine, or with nicotine, show gradual normalisation of their P50 ratios coincident with clinical improvement. This P50 gating deficit is also found in bipolar patients, though in the *manic* phase only, suggestive of a *state* rather than a *trait* phenomenon; patients with schizophrenia, however, show the effect whether their symptoms are predominantly positive or negative. In manic patients, P50 gating normalises as plasma levels of the noradrenaline metabolite 3-methoxy-4-hydroxyphenylethylene glycol (MHPG) decrease towards normality with medication (lithium or neuroleptics). Thus loss of inhibition of the P50 potential is associated with noradrenergic transmission.

In life, it is of course vital to be able to detect unusual or possibly dangerous events. The mismatch negativity (MMN) is an early-stage event-related potential that is elicited when infrequent ("deviant") sounds occur in a sequence of repetitive ("standard") sounds, even in the absence of attention to these sounds (Gené-Cos, Ring, Pottinger, & Barrett, 1999). The mismatch negativity may form part of an acoustic detection system involved in survival. It occurs early in processing, peaking at 100–200 ms from stimulus onset, and exists at an early age, persisting throughout adult life. Such event-related potentials are EEG changes reflecting at a neurophysiological level the neuronal processing of sensory and motor events; their components recorded during cognitive tasks allow assessment of cerebral information processing with millisecond temporal (but very poor spatial) resolution, compared to functional imaging where spatial resolution (at the millimetre level) has poor temporal characteristics. The best-known event-related potentials component in neuropsychiatric studies is the odd-ball P3, a positive wave (P300) appearing 300 ms after a target stimulus. However, the MMN reflects even earlier cortical events in auditory pre-attentive or "echoic" memory, and may be generated by an automatic, attention-independent, preconscious process that contrasts ongoing sensory inputs with a memory trace that encodes the physical features of preceding ("standard") stimuli. As abnormalities of auditory information processing have been associated with psychopathology, the MMN may provide an objective measure of information-processing deficits (Gené-Cos et al., 1999). It may have at least two subcomponents—supratemporal and frontal—in its generation. The process generating the MMN may represent a "call" from preattentive mechanisms, to focus attention on a sudden and unexpected change in the (auditory) environment, so as to facilitate switching of attention or orientation. The P300 occurs within 200 ms after the MMN, reflecting additional, attentional-dependent, controlled cortical processing, whereas the MMN is elicited by all deviant stimuli, whether or not attended to, or task relevant or irrelevant. The P300 amplitude is largest to attended, task-relevant stimuli. In schizophrenia, generation of both the MMN and the P300 is disturbed (Javitt, 1997; Gooding & Iacono, 1995).

An information-processing deficit at the level of attention is clearly apparent in schizophrenia. However, a growing number of studies have applied a transient (magnocellular) or sustained (parvocellular) explanation to account for deficient processing of briefly presented or moving visual stimuli (Schwartz, Maron, Evans, & Winstead, 1999). Thus the earliest phase of normal visual processing may be regulated by two distinct types of ganglion cells in the peripheral and foveal regions of the retina, which act as tuned spatiotemporal filters or channels. One channel, composed of Y cells, responds primarily to briefly presented, low-spatial-frequency visual information. In the presence of stimulus onset or offset, these cells respond with a sudden burst of activity, and so are referred to as the *transient* channel of the *magnocellular* pathway, whose function it is to orient attention to the appearance or presence of stimuli. By contrast, the X cells of the *sustained* channel respond to high-spatial-frequency information. In the presence of a stimulus, these cells of the *parvocellular* pathway characteristically respond with a long response latency and a slower rise time; they remain relatively unresponsive to brief stimulus presentation, such as flickering or flash of light. The parvocellular pathway functions to orient attention for semantic identification and object recognition. Schwartz et al. (1999) report and review evidence for a deficit in schizophrenia in the transient ("where is it?") magnocellular pathway, but not in the sustained ("what is it?") parvocellular pathway. In the *neurodegenerative* disorder of the frontostriatal system—Parkinson's disease—there also is a disturbance of visual function, at the level of the retina.

In a major meta-analysis, Heinrichs and Zakzanis (1998) report 22 mean effect sizes from 204 studies, to index the deficits of patients with schizophrenia in global and selective verbal memory, nonverbal memory, bilateral and unilateral motor performance, visual and auditory attention, general intelligence, spatial ability, executive functioning, and language. Moderate to large effect sizes appeared for all variables, and the authors conclude that the disorder is characterised by a broadly based cognitive impairment involving most neurocognitive tasks in common use. Interestingly, biggest effects were for global verbal memory, bilateral motor skill, and performance IQ—and not for prefrontal executive performance. Nestor and O'Donnell (1998), in their review, conclude that involvement of many brain regions seems likely, but emphasise a disturbance in both sustained and selective attention, both of which involve suppression of irrelevant stimuli. There may therefore be a weakening of attentional inhibitory processes at all information-processing levels, from preconscious and automatic to higher-order, controlled, and strategic.

In conclusion, we should note that cognitive problems in schizophrenia are highly resistant to treatment, unlike the positive symptoms. Are they due to a global dysfunction or to failure of a number of basic cognitive processes, such as attention or working memory? As yet, we do not have an answer to this question, but might note with Goldman-Rakic (1994) and Goldman-Rakic and Selemon (1997) a fundamental working-memory impairment in schizophrenia, in the ability to "guide behaviour by representations" so as to manipulate current information on-line; this would permit one to respond flexibly and appropriately on the basis of internal representations, rather than being driven by external stimuli or events. Such a defect would account for disorganised speech (because the *discourse* plan cannot be held in mind) and thought disorder, together with negative symptoms (because of failure to maintain an *action* plan), hallucinations, and delusions (because of the patient's inability to reference a specific external or internal experience, as compared to emergent associated memories). It would also perhaps explain perseveration in schizophrenia, the contextually inappropriate repetition of a response or behaviour unit, which may take three forms (Crider, 1997):

- *Continuous perseveration*—a failure to terminate a discrete response, which is therefore repeated without interruption, e.g. of letters, numbers, words, or shapes.
- *Stuck-in* perseveration, where the patient fails to switch response modes, after a shift in response outcome contingencies, as in the Wisconsin Card Sorting Test; the patient continues to sort on the basis of a previously relevant but currently irrelevant attribute.
- *Recurrent* perseveration, where there is repeated intrusion of an initial response into a subsequent response sequence, e.g. AbcAdeAfghiAjkA. . .

Perseveration in discourse and speech (particularly of words, phrases and ideas) is common in schizophrenia, along with tasks involving guessing; it also occurs (in appropriate response form) in animal models treated with dopamine agonists; this suggests a failure of frontal specification of striatal outputs during capacity-demanding tasks, with continued re-eliciting of previously activated but no longer appropriate response schemata (Crider, 1997).

Working memory is of course a distinctively human attribute, a work-space for recalling, manipulating, and associating old and new information. Problems with working memory do not of themselves result in the instrumental deficits of aphasia, agnosia, apraxia, or amnesia, but rather in problems in retrieving and processing information *appropriately* in terms of a goal, concept, or strategy, with the end result being impoverished, repetitive, anomalous, and perseverative thought. Many of the cognitive and executive dysfunctions of schizophrenia can therefore perhaps be attributed to problems with working memory and the dorsolateral prefrontal cortex, where a running record must be kept of recent events or instructions. Attentional gating problems, with which this section commenced, would therefore be seen as part, along with executive dysfunction generally, of a wider deficit in working memory; they would therefore also explain problems with the Continuous Performance Task, Stroop, Tower of London, categorisation performance, and delayed responding tasks.

MOTOR DEFICITS IN SCHIZOPHRENIA

At a motor level, deficits appear to be an inherent part of schizophrenia spectrum disorders, and not just a reflection of neuroleptic medication status (Malla et al., 1995). Indeed, motor impairment correlates closely with thought disorder, suggesting an interaction between cognitive and motor functions. Slowed response times in schizophrenia correlate with increases in task complexity and cognitive load (Malla et al., 1995). In more complex movement tasks, kinematic measures quantified the difficulties of patients with schizophrenia in programming movements, particularly with low levels of advance information (external cues), as in Parkinson's disease (Downing et al., 1998b). Thus in schizophrenia, as in Parkinson's disease, there is a cue-dependent akinesia indicative of underlying basal ganglia dysfunction.

In a study of our own (Bellgrove et al., 2000), involving the kinematics of bimanual coordination (cranking), we found that patients were considerably impaired in their ability to maintain proper coordination between the hands; unlike controls, they were quite unable to achieve 180° anti-phase movements, locking instead into in-phase control.

SCHIZOPHRENIA AS A NEURODEVELOPMENTAL DISORDER

Gooding and Iacono (1995) propose that for schizophrenia to develop a genetic liability or diathesis may be necessary, along with an environmental stressor, perhaps operating at or above a threshold level; genetic endowment may determine the threshold above which psychopathology eventuates. Candidate stressors include obstetric complications and season of birth (and resultant maternal viral infections), along with possible environmental agents.

There is a raised incidence of intrauterine adversity and obstetric complications in schizophrenia, all of which can independently lead to ventricular enlargement, widening of cortical sulci, cerebellar atrophy, hypofrontality, and reduced interneuronal densities. Waddington et al. (1999) review the evidence for intrauterine adversity in schizophrenia:

- Birth in winter or spring; correlations with incidence of schizophrenia are modest, but as we shall see later in further detail, a seasonally varying factor (perhaps maternal exposure to infectious agents) may act *in utero* to increase the risk of later emergence of psychosis.

- Urban birth, which may interact with or be related to factors involved with seasonality of birth, such as maternal influenza infection during the second trimester; Mortenson et al. (1999) in a sample of 2669 patients found that individuals born in spring had a 10% risk elevation, those in autumn a 10% reduction, and that those born in a capital city had a 2.4-fold increase compared to those born in the country.
- Maternal dietary insufficiency, maybe particularly during the first trimester.
- A mixed bag of obstetric complications, which may be causal, or may merely appear as complications due to an already compromised fetus (Buckley, 1998). Geddes et al. (1999), in a meta-analysis of 700 patients with schizophrenia, found significant associations between the disorder and premature rupture of the membranes, gestational age less than 37 weeks, and use of resuscitation or an incubator. There were associations of borderline significance with low birthweight and forceps delivery.

As we shall see, structural abnormalities in the brain that may stem from these or other factors are more consistent with a neurodevelopmental disturbance in early or mid gestation than with continuing neurodegenerative processes. Indeed, the hippocampus and globus pallidus are particularly vulnerable to hypoxia (Gur & Pearlson, 1993), and obstetric complications may interact with other possibly more fundamental agents for neurodevelopmental disorder, such as genetic predisposition or maternal infection. Thus Tsuang and Faraone (1999) propose a multifactorial, polygenic version of the diathesis–stress theory, according to which all schizophrenia-related disorders arise from a single pool of genetic and environmental variables, each of small effect, that act in additive fashion to produce a vulnerability to schizophrenia; if an individual's vulnerability exceeds a certain threshold, he or she will manifest signs and symptoms of the disorder, whereas at lower thresholds some *other* neurodevelopmental disorder may manifest, such as bipolar. All such interactive factors will lead to early maldevelopment of the brain (especially, perhaps, of the frontostriatal and frontotemporal circuits)—the neurodevelopmental hypothesis.

Although old home videos of infancy may suggest early behavioural signs, schizophrenia may be floridly expressed when relevant structures or behaviours have "unfolded", or the frontal cortex comes "on line" in a deficient fashion, due to long-standing abnormalities of the prefrontal cortex, anterior cingulate, and temporolimbic regions that may interact with currently occurring environmental stressors. Indeed, in primate studies, prenatal prefrontal injury only manifests symptoms much later in development, often in the presence of environmental stressors (Gooding & Iacono, 1995). Moreover, the prefrontal cortex is the last region to mature during adolescence, when schizophrenia may manifest. Various neurochemical systems also change rapidly in adolescence, along with the manifestations of other, movement and attention, disorders such as Tourette's syndrome, OCD and ADHD. It is noteworthy that the peak incidence of schizophrenia is around 7 years earlier in males, who exhibit an overall higher incidence and greater severity, perhaps reflecting their later puberty, which may be associated with greater apoptosis. Conversely, oestrogens have an anti-dopaminergic effect (Gooding & Iacono, 1995). Indeed, there are several experimental treatment procedures currently under way involving oestrogen treatment, even with male patients.

Nor might maternal infection be limited to influenza; other viral agents acting during the second trimester such as diphtheria, pneumonia, measles, and polio have also been implicated, and these factors, along perhaps with deficits in maternal nutrition, may prevent the full elaboration of neuronal development, as reflected in the reduced neuronal size and altered shape in the hippocampus, and reduction in neuropil and increase in neuronal density in the hippocampus and prefrontal cortex (Raedler, Knable, & Weinberger, 1998). The mechanism may involve abnormal neuronal migration during development, due to improper functioning of proteins that regulate such migration, apoptosis, and synaptogenesis. The apparent absence of gliosis (see later) is held to suggest (though there is some dispute) that the disorder is not progressive.

The traditional viewpoint is clearly that schizophrenia is a "neurodegenerative" disorder, which is nonprogressive beyond a certain developmental stage. Absence of gliosis and little evidence (though see later) of continuing brain changes generally support this viewpoint. Rund (1998) reviews longitudinal studies of cognitive deficit, and finds no evidence of continuing decline, in the majority of cases, whose cognitive performance may remain remarkably stable over time, apart from normal ageing effects; thus the cognitive evidence seems to concur with the neuropathological, that schizophrenia is not a continuing degenerative process, like dementia, but rather a static encephalopathy due to a neurodevelopmental fault or arrest. Moreover cognitive deficit is in any case by no means universal in schizophrenia. However, Rund (1998) also notes a problem in drop-out rate; cognitive decline may *not* in fact remain stable in those patients who fail to remain in a study.

However, Arnold (1999) and Buchanan et al. (1998) review the evidence for a *progressive* form of the disorder, at a *functional* level, in at least *some* patients, with declining social adjustment and level of cognitive and daily functioning over the first 5–10 years of the illness; in these instances there may then be progressive development of the more severe subtypes of the disorder, such as hebephrenia, catatonia, and the deficit forms. Duncan, Sheitman, and Lieberman (1999) speculate that pathological sensitisation may occur in schizophrenia, as in depression and epilepsy—a "kindling" phenomenon with progressively more severe bouts, and the longer the psychosis the worse the treatment outcome. Neurodegenerative disorders of course usually occur in individuals previously deemed healthy, as in Parkinson's, Huntington's and Alzheimer's diseases, HIV/AIDS, multiple sclerosis, and Creutzfeldt–Jakob disease. Although the progress is typically steady and remorseless, exacerbations, remissions, and *formes frustes* of the disorder may occur that temporarily return the patient to the premorbid state; schizophrenia is of course like that. Although we do not know why perhaps only some patients with schizophrenia show continuing neuro-psychological deterioration and degenerative processes, it is noteworthy that the same brain areas are involved as in the classical degenerative disorders of age, such as the entorhinal cortex, hippocampus, anterior cingulate, and dorsolateral prefrontal cortex; schizophrenia is like an early dementia, and may amplify other independent degenerative processes. However, it is debatable whether Alzheimer's disease has increased prevalence in older patients with schizophrenia.

The question as to whether schizophrenia may ever be progressive is also complicated by the problem of the long-term effects of medication, together with uncertainty concerning whether a given cognitive test acts as a *trait* or a *state marker*. Thus we need to distinguish between:

- Vulnerability or *trait* markers, i.e. stable characteristics that constantly deviate from normal levels, independently of medication or remissions, and which are present in vulnerable individuals even when asymptomatic; they therefore may reflect structural abnormalities.
- Episodic or *state* markers, which are present largely during symptomatic episodes, and return to normal with remission; they may reflect underlying neurochemical disturbances.

Heinrichs and Zakzanis (1998) note that although significant cognitive deficit is common in schizophrenia, substantial numbers of patients are neuropsychologically normal or even superior. (A mathematician, John Nash, even won the Nobel Prize for his work on game theory while struggling with schizophrenia.) There may therefore be a continuum of neurocognitive function, with patients varying from those unaffected, through mild and moderate impairment, to severe levels, and from a static to a progressive manifestation. It is of course always possible that the "unaffected" are still really operating below their true potential level. Nor do we know whether a neurocognitive deficit is central or only secondary or peripheral to the illness.

Rund (1998) finds that cognitive stability is most evident for verbal skills (word meaning, word association, verbal fluency), memory (long term, short term, verbal, spatial, visual), and preattentional information processing (backward masking); it is less evident and there is less stability for complex attentional and concentration-demanding tasks, for attentional span and set holding and shifting—i.e. for executive functions. While cognitive deficit may be highest (and most likely to be progressive) in patients with (or developing) negative symptoms, we can also ask whether such deficit (initial, perhaps with little subsequent further decline) is one that occurs during adolescence; alternatively, did the cognitive functions never appear (unfold or develop) in the first place?

Knoll et al. (1998) note that, at a *structural* level, although there may be little or no evidence of ongoing neurodegeneration in many patients, this is certainly not true of all. Thus in some there may indeed be a progressive increase in ventricular size, an accelerating loss of brain tissue (especially in the cerebellum and hippocampus), progressive delays in responsivity to treatment, and neuroimaging and electrophysiological (P300) indices all indicative of ongoing neurodegeneration. They ask what may cause ongoing neurodegeneration in such a subgroup—necrosis or apoptosis:

- *Necrosis* follows injury, and consists of cellular swelling (oedema), lysis, and subsequent spilling of cellular contents into the extracellular space, with a resultant inflammatory response and glial proliferation.
- In *apoptosis*, the nucleus and cytoplasm condense and fragment, with the resultant fragments rapidly undergoing phagocytosis by neighbouring cells or macrophages; there is no inflammation, damage to neighbouring cells from noxious cell contents, or gliosis. This inconspicuous process of programmed cell death is very important in neurodevelopment to permit pruning for the establishment of appropriate connectivities; it continues even after the major termination phase of adolescence. Thus, on receipt of an appropriate signal, cells and neuropil are constantly eliminated via apoptosis, and neuropil is often replenished by regeneration. When regeneration and apoptosis are in equilibrium, tissues are stable, and tissue loss is only apparent when apoptosis is accelerated or regeneration is reduced.

Three major steps are now recognised in the apoptotic process (Ziv & Melamed, 1998):

1. *The triggering stimulus*, which may range from DNA damage, cell cycle perturbations, metabolic or toxic insults, or deprivation of

growth factors, to activation of specific cell death receptors. These triggers converge to activate central death signals, that lead to:

2. *The apoptosis commitment point*, the point of no return beyond which the cell can no longer be rescued by removal of the cell death stimulus. This apoptotic crossroad probably involves the mitochondria.

3. *The execution phase*, where the cell death program operates via catalysis of a chain of reactions leading to the extensive, characteristic structural alterations.

Typically, apoptosis is regulated by patent cellular systems as a strategic tool for the elimination of cells that are potentially harmful to the organism, either as a result of their inherent defects (e.g. cancerous cells), or as a result of their interference with proper tissue integration and function, for example during development. During central nervous system development, apoptosis serves as a major tool for the removal of defective cells, or for the resculpturing of the neuronal networks; apoptosis may, however, proceed inappropriately, as perhaps in schizophrenia.

Knoll et al. (1998) therefore conclude that schizophrenia is largely due to excessive early apoptosis, with, in a minority of cases, continued partial failure of maintenance and regeneration. In the latter instance, patients will suffer continued loss, with pruning continuing up to and through adulthood. (Indeed, Madsen et al., 1999, report continued progression of frontal and central atrophy in their patients.) They ask whether remissions correspond to temporary reversals of such a process, and whether the process itself may be due to an abnormal susceptibility to free radical oxidation of membrane unsaturates and/or to glutamate excitotoxicity from excess activity, as perhaps in stroke, Parkinson's, and Huntington's diseases.

Inappropriate or excessive early apoptosis may therefore be a factor in altered brain development in schizophrenia due to defective ontogenesis. Indeed most neurodevelopmental disorders (mental retardation, ADHD, autism, cerebral palsy, specific disorders of speech or of arithmetic or of motor ability) seem to be associated with abnormal brain morphology, deficits in neural migration, microgyria, lissencephaly, micro- or hydrocephaly, absence or alteration of normal asymmetries of specific brain regions, and specific histological or biochemical abnormalities (Stevens, 1997). Such neurodevelopmental disorders generally manifest in the first decade in the form of delayed motor or cognitive milestones, or disturbances of behaviour, posture, or movement. Moreover, these signs and symptoms rarely progress, and may even show some improvement, with or without treatment. Clearly one must distinguish such neurodevelopmental disorders from perinatal insults such as ischaemia, haemorrhage, or infections in infancy or childhood, and from genetic disorders or errors of metabolism such as phenylketonuria or the lipodystrophies; the latter, like schizophrenia, may be expressed early, or delayed until adolescence (Stevens, 1997). After onset, seizures, behavioural disorders, psychoses, and progressive mental deterioration (as in autism) may develop in disorders predominantly affecting grey matter, whereas disturbances of posture, sensation, and intellect may be more common for disorders predominantly affecting white matter. Thus the typical cause of many types of schizophrenia is compatible with that of many genetic disorders, though many patients with schizophrenia *do* recover spontaneously, which is unusual with other genetic disorders.

A good case therefore may be made that schizophrenia stems from altered brain development due to defective ontogenesis. Such a neuro-developmental hypothesis is supported by the presence of cytoarchitectural abnormalities in regions undergoing maturation during gestation (Duncan, Sheitman, & Lieberman, 1999). Thus anomalies may be found of alignment of hippocampal neurons, together with disorganisation in the entorhinal cortex (Arnold, 1999). Moreover these regions also are subject to profound plastic modification in synaptic organisation during normal adult life, further suggesting that schizophrenia is associated with a defect in cellular processes regulating aspects of such plasticity (Weinberger, 1999). Thus defective ontogenesis in schizophrenia may involve either faulty early migration, or altered subsequent pruning or apoptosis, or both processes (Jones, 1997). *Faulty migration* from the ventricular epithelium towards cortical targets, via neuroglial fibre guides, and occurring mostly in the second trimester, may explain cytoarchitectural anomalies in the medial temporal cortex and hippocampus, with migratory displacement of layer II cells to layer III. *Axon elimination* normally occurs in the early postnatal phase in the commissural and cortico-cortical tracts, to prevent growth towards inappropriate targets. This process may be arrested in schizophrenia, resulting in inappropriate connectivity and maybe even explaining the propensity for disordered thought and excessive cognitive associations. *Synaptic pruning*, between the first year and puberty, is particularly prominent in frontal regions (Jones, 1997; Rison, 1998)—a region known to be affected in schizophrenia—and may be arrested or faulty in that disorder. Indeed this period is when symptoms typically first manifest. High levels of synaptic connectivity (which peaks between 1 and 2 years, decreasing rapidly during adolescence) may in fact underlie juvenile plasticity and the ability to recover after injury. Thus reorganisation of the brain and juvenile pruning may unmask latent schizophrenia. Buchanan et al. (1998) note that neonatal surgical lesions of the hippocampus in monkeys leads in *adulthood* to changes reminiscent of human schizophrenia phenomena, such as altered prepulse inhibition and decremented performance in delayed alternation tasks. The important point is that these changes become evident only at maturity, and are not found in animals lesioned as adults or juveniles. Other evidence in support of a central role of the medial temporal lobe in a neurodevelopmental origin of schizophrenia, and a sensitivity of the hippocampus to putative perinatal risk factors, comes from findings (see, for example, Saunders, Kolachana, Bachevalier, & Weinberger, 1998) that neonatal lesions of the medial temporal lobe disrupt normal regulation of dopamine by the prefrontal cortex; *early* brain lesions thus have substantial *long-term* effects on the function of more distant neurosystems, and early injury of the medial temporal lobe can affect striatal dopaminergic regulation by the dorsolateral prefrontal cortex in adulthood.

Absence of gliosis in schizophrenia is a further argument adduced in support of the position that the disorder is due to faulty ontogenesis of the central nervous system. It is true that gliosis (indicative of past inflammatory processes and therefore of some form of insult) is not generally found in schizophrenia, except where there are also separate, concurrent neuropathological abnormalities as with Alzheimer's disease (Harrison, 1999). However, it is by no means certain that gliosis does not occur until after the second trimester *in utero*; nor is gliosis always evident after postnatal neural injury. Thus the lack of gliosis does *not* mean that schizophrenia *must* be a neurodevelopmental disorder (Harrison, 1999).

MINOR PHYSICAL ANOMALIES IN SCHIZOPHRENIA

Neuropsychiatric anomalies, neurological soft signs, abnormal facies, posture or movement, and physical stigmata may be found in children who go on to develop schizophrenia (Barondes et al., 1997; Egan & Weinberger, 1997). Such children may seem to have preferred solitary play, and to have exhibited a range of neuromotor anomalies and social disturbance. As both brain and skin derive from the same ectodermal tissue (Curtis, Iacono, & Beiser, 1999), it is perhaps not altogether surprising that minor physical anomalies of the face and dermatoglyphs (fingerprints) have been noted in schizophrenia (and Down syndrome) (see, for example, Buckley, 1998).

Waddington et al. (1999) review the evidence for minor physical anomalies (MPAs), in particular, craniofacial dysmorphology, in schizophrenia. They cite the words of Clouston 100 years ago in his book, presciently titled "The Neuroses of *Development*" (my emphasis):

> I had for several years noted that the palates of those labouring under "adolescent insanity" had appeared to be high . . . The most anterior point of the brain is seen to fall in Man through the centre of the hard palate . . . The brain unquestionably deriving its shape and size and qualities from ancestry, and a bad heredity, determining a bad brain, we see how a bad nervous heredity would naturally determine a bad palate.

Waddington et al. (1999) note that over early fetal life cerebral morpho-genesis proceeds in exquisite embryological intimacy with craniofacial morphogenesis, such that classical neurodevelopmental disorders such as Down's syndrome encompass dysmorphic features that also involve skull and face. Such minor physical anomalies constitute biological markers of first or early second trimester dysgenesis. Minor physical anomalies occur excessively in schizophrenia, especially with subtle dysmorphogenesis of the craniofacial areas, and a shift towards more prominent narrowing and vertical elongation of the anterior midface. That this occurs during primary palate formation in the embryonic–fetal stage of development suggests a concomitant impairment of anterior cerebral development. The overall picture, according to Waddington et al. (1999), can include a narrowing and elongation of the mid and lower anterior facial region, a heightening of the palate, reduced mouth width, a widening of the skull base, abnormalities of mouth, ears, and eyes, and general frontonasal dysmorphology. These changes, they say, are all associated with increased size of the third (midline) but not the lateral ventricles, qualitative abnormalities of the mesial temporal lobes and corpus callosum (both midline structures), hippocam-pus, and entorhinal cortex. Quite separately, but yet another instance of skin-related dysmorphology, Curtis et al. (1999) note that in schizophrenia there is a raised incidence of high visibility of the nailfold plexus, the subpapillary plexus into which capillaries drain.

CHILDHOOD SCHIZOPHRENIA

Some cases of autism, another neurodevelopmental disorder, may later apparently progress to schizophrenia (Gooding & Iacono, 1995). Also, many early-onset cases of schizophrenia have previously exhibited autism-like features, though childhood autism is probably not merely a variant of schizophrenia. Childhood schizophrenia is not common, and may in fact be a particularly severe form of the adult version. It is difficult to diagnose because of problems of insight and communication. Thought disorder and other positive symptoms such as hallucinations, delusions, and illogical thinking may be prominent. There may also be very early motor abnor-malities. The earlier the onset, usually the worse the prognosis. The disorder is also characterised by deficits in attention and information processing. Retrospective evidence from individuals later developing childhood schizo-phrenia indicates in infancy a tendency to passivity, low levels of energy, shortened attention span, abnormalities in both gross and fine motor performance and in facial expression, and retardation (Gooding & Iacono, 1995). Rapoport et al. (1999) note that individuals with very early onset schizophrenia exhibit progressive ventricular enlargement and decrease in cortical grey matter volume in parietal and especially frontal and temporal regions during adolescence. While such data do not undermine the neurodevelopmental model of the disorder, they do also underline the probability that in at least some individuals there may be a two-hit process, of continuing as well as early loss of tissue.

LATE-ONSET SCHIZOPHRENIA

Late-onset schizophrenia is a controversial concept, as typically schizophrenia has been defined as a condition for which early onset is an intrinsic criterion. Until recently, the aetiology of late-onset psychoses has generally been attributed to "organic" illnesses, brain lesions, or substance abuse (Jeste et al., 1996). However late-onset schizophrenia is now recognised, and there is no longer any age cut-off for diagnosis, with a fair number of patients demonstrating their first recognisable symptoms after 45 years of age. The late-onset variant is essentially similar to classical schizophrenia, though now there may be a preponderance of women, and auditory or visual impairments have also sometimes been noted. The degree of neuropsychological impairment may also be somewhat milder than when onset is earlier, just as in Huntington's disease, with a more favourable prognosis, though there may be an increased risk of side effects, including extrapyramidal side effects and tardive dyskinesia, associated with neuroleptic treatment in older patients.

GENETICS OF SCHIZOPHRENIA

Family, twin, and adoption studies all indicate a role of genetic factors, with illness clusters (schizophrenia spectrum disorders, schizotypal personality, and schizoaffective disorders) in families, increased risk in biological parents of affected adoptees compared to that in biological parents of normal adoptees, and higher concordance in monozygotic than in dizygotic twins (Leboyer & Gorwood, 1995). Thus the monozygotic co-twin of an affected individual has a nearly 50% risk, whereas that of a dizygotic co-twin is around 14% (Moldin & Gottesman, 1997); this compares with a baseline population risk of around 1%, 8% if a sibling has the disorder, 12% if one, and 40% if both parents are sufferers (see, for example, Gooding & Iacono, 1995).

Nowadays, use of quantitative dimensions (magnitude of certain symptoms), rather than of qualitative differences with respect to categories of psychosis, has clarified thinking about the familial inheritance of schizophrenia (DeLisi, 1999). Thus family and genetic studies are increasingly taking note of the amount and severity of positive and negative symptoms, and the degree of language disorganisation and depression in large cohorts of patients. The dimension of disorganisation and thought disorder seems to show the highest concordance within families, suggesting that it may in fact even be the core genetic syndrome (DeLisi, 1999).

It looks increasingly unlikely that there is one major gene that determines every case of schizophrenia, or that there is a single major gene, differing perhaps in different families, that is responsible for either a single common aspect of the disorder, or for the entire, heterogeneously presenting condition. More likely, there are groups of genes, none of which is sufficient to cause illness, that interact mutually and with the environment, and provide susceptibility. Thus schizophrenia transmission fails to follow normal Mendelian modes of inheritance (Adler et al., 1999), with no clear or simple pattern of dominant or recessive inheritance (Schultz & Andreasen, 1999). Genes and environment may interact additively (or even multiplicatively) to establish susceptibility levels. There may therefore be multiple susceptibility genes, each with small effects, or several such genes each with moderate effects (Maier & Schwab, 1998). Although the word "gene" usually implies a coding defect, a mutation, substitution, deletion, or unstable expanding repeat sequence (as with Huntington's disease, fragile X syndrome, and several movement disorders involving the cerebellum), a gene or genes that therefore manifest variability in the general population may at the extreme end of a distribution lead to schizophrenia; alternatively, interacting in a quantitative fashion with other genes, they may lead to certain symptoms, mild or severe (DeLisi, 1999).

Linkage studies are really designed more for single-locus models of inheritance, rather than for such polygenic accounts (Moldin & Gottesman, 1997). They examine whether a disorder is transmitted together with a gene that is indicated by a genetic marker in families with multiple affected individuals (co-segregation). Genetic markers are polymorphic, with multiple genetic variants and known locations on the genome. Lod scores measure the strength of an association, with values between 1.9 and 3.3 being suggestive of linkage, and values >3.3 being evidence for linkage (Maier & Schwab, 1998). Affected sib-pair analysis is the most robust procedure where, as in schizophrenia, the mode of transmission is unknown. One option for selecting genetic markers is the *candidate gene approach*, examining the contribution of polymorphisms at sites coding for products (proteins) with putative pathophysiological relevance; it has proved so far to be unsuccessful. Another option is a *systematic genome scan*, which may be especially appropriate where, as in schizophrenia, the exact pathophysiology of the disease is unknown. Suggestive susceptibility regions have been found by linkage analysis, using the systematic genome scan strategy; currently 5q, 6p, 8p, 13q, and 22q may be the most promising, especially perhaps 6 and 8, though there have been numerous failures to replicate (Buchanan et al.,

1998; Maier & Schwab, 1998; Schultz & Andreasen, 1999). Adler et al. (1999) note evidence of autosomal dominant inheritance of a single gene in abnormal P50 gating, with linkage to markers in chromosome 15q14, where there may be coding for the α_7-nicotinic acetylcholine receptor. Chromosomes 3, 9, and 20 have also been implicated (Cloninger, 1997; Barondes et al., 1997), along with 2 and 18 (DeLisi, 1999), and the pseudoautosomal region of the sex chromosomes (Leboyer & Gorwood, 1995; Gooding & Iacono, 1995). Indeed the X chromosome is likely to contain genes responsible for brain growth and higher cognitive functioning; it seems also to be involved in cognitive abilities known to be compromised in schizophrenia, which may therefore result from a variant of one of the development genes modulating cognitive maturation (DeLisi, 1999).

Association studies attempt to determine whether a genetic variant is more common among affected than among unaffected individuals. An association between a gene marker and schizophrenia might indicate that the gene or another closely located gene in linkage disequilibrium with the tested genetic marker contributes to the disorder (Maier & Schwab, 1998). There is some evidence, from association studies, for the human leukocyte antigen system, and weaker evidence for the 5-hydroxytryptamine (serotonin) type 2A receptor gene ($5-HT_{2A}$). Concentrations of serotonin may be abnormal in schizophrenia, its biochemical similarities to the hallucinogens are intriguing, and its receptors seem to be targets for the action of atypical neuroleptics such as clozapine, all suggesting a role for serotonin in schizophrenia (DeLisi, 1999); indeed a specific allele has been shown to be associated with clozapine responsivity.

The dopamine receptors segregate into D1 and D5, versus D2, D3, and D4 (Leboyer & Gorwood, 1995), with the therapeutic efficiency of antipsychotics partly deriving from their high-affinity binding to D2 receptors. However, there is no strong genetic evidence for a major role for the genes coding for the D1, D2, D4, or D5 receptors (Adler et al., 1999), though according to Serretti et al. (1999) long-allele variants of the dopamine D4 receptor gene have been associated with high delusional scores in schizophrenia. The D3 receptor gene may be a better candidate for susceptibility to schizophrenia, being expressed almost exclusively in the limbic system, and in fact all the antipsychotics are recognised by it. However, so far no specific D3 receptor gene has been associated with schizophrenia. Indeed, as we saw, it is unlikely that a single gene accounts for most cases, the disorder probably being caused by a nonlinear interaction of multiple genetic and environmental factors influencing brain development and personality. Such a situation would result in the extensive symptomatic heterogeneity within individuals and families, which is so characteristic of the disorder (Cloninger, 1997). However, unstable DNA sequences may also operate in the form of expanded trinucleotide repeats, as in Huntington's disease, as there is evidence of anticipation, with a younger age of onset in successive generations (Bassett & Honer, 1994).

THE NEUROCHEMISTRY OF SCHIZOPHRENIA

Of all the neurodevelopmental frontostriatal disorders, the neurochemistry of schizophrenia is the most complex, possibly merely because it has been the most thoroughly researched. A number of hypotheses, corresponding to a similar number of neurotransmitters, have at various times been proposed, involving most of the major modulatory neurotransmitters known. As so often is the case, a composite model is beginning to emerge, with the leading contender emphasising glutamate (GLU), though in the context also of dopamine and nitric oxide (NO). However, as serotonin received early emphasis, and has since made something of a comeback, we shall commence with that system.

Serotonin

While in recent years the dopamine hypothesis as an explanation for the signs and symptoms of schizophrenia has proven pre-eminent, before then the serotonin hypothesis derived from observations that hallucinogens such as lysergic acid diethylamide (LSD) have serotonin embedded within their structure; moreover because schizophrenia is a disease exemplified by hallucinations, then that transmitter must, it was thought, be involved. This line of thinking was abandoned in favour of the dopamine hypothesis, because of the efficacy of the antidopaminergic neuroleptics, and because the hallucinations of schizophrenia differed (being predominantly auditory) from the (largely visual) hallucinations induced by LSD (Roth, Willins, Kristiansen, & Kroeze, 1999). However, the position is again now being re-evaluated:

- All atypical neuroleptics which are clinically very effective bind with high affinity to various serotonin receptors, especially the 5-HT_{2A} receptor, though also to the 5-HT_{2C}, 5-HT_6, and 5-HT_7 receptors; indeed clozapine, risperidone, and olanzapine have a stronger affinity for the 5-HT_{2A} receptor than for the dopamine D2 receptor (Buchanan et al., 1998; Glenthøj & Hemmingsen, 1999; Harrison, 1999; Roth et al., 1999; Tamminga, 1998).
- Hallucinogens and psychotomimetics like LSD and mescaline are serotonin agonists that act upon 5-HT_{2A} receptors.
- Unlike the dopaminergic system, which innervates a relatively restricted cerebral area, serotonin fibres emanating from the dorsal raphe system project to all areas of the cortex, and especially the basal ganglia.

- In schizophrenia, the serotonergic systems in the limbic striatum, hippocampus, and frontal cortex are altered (Glenthøj & Hemmingsen, 1999; Harrison, 1999; Lieberman et al., 1998).
- Serotonin is involved in the trophic aspects of neurodevelopment (Harrison, 1999; Lieberman et al., 1998), an observation that is compatible with the neurodevelopmental hypothesis of schizophrenia.

Serotonin and dopamine probably interact in the aetiology of schizophrenia, rather than either acting independently; because the serotonin system includes a multiplicity of receptor families with many distinct receptor proteins, data have been conflicting (Glenthøj & Hemmingsen, 1999; Harrison, 1999; Tamminga, 1998), thereby accounting for reluctance until recently to afford serotonin its rightful importance in the disorder. Lieberman et al. (1998) review the role of serotonin in normal brain function. They note that dopamine and serotonin neurotransmission interacts (generally in a negative fashion) at various anatomical levels via a range of receptor subtypes for both neurotransmitters. In its role as a neurodevelopmental regulator of the central nervous system, the serotonin system is the first to innervate the developing brain and to show functional activity. It helps regulate the density of dendritic spines and synapses. Its role in the cerebellum, and the learning deficits resulting from its depletion in the early postnatal period, indicate its significance for autism, a disorder with many commonalities with schizophrenia.

Dopamine

In the 1950s chlorpromazine, originally used as a major tranquilliser, was found to be highly effective, though only after several weeks of treatment, against the positive (but not the negative) signs and symptoms of schizophrenia. Subsequently, it was found that the clinical efficacy of such conventional neuroleptics correlated with their binding affinity for dopamine D2 receptors (Duncan et al., 1999; Glenthøj & Hemmingsen, 1999). Similarly, it was observed that dopamine agonists such as amphetamine led to psychotic symptoms in the previously healthy, similar to those of patients with schizophrenia, or exacerbated their symptoms. So was born the dopamine hypothesis, that schizophrenia was due to excess dopamine, or increased sensitivity to dopamine, or to increased density of dopamine D2 receptors (Harrison, 1999). It was known that the prefrontal cortex received major dopamine innervation, and that dopamine, inhibiting neurones in this region, regulated excitatory neurotransmission (Goldman-Rakic & Selemon, 1997). The question then arose as to whether schizophrenia was due to too little or too much dopamine, or whether that depended upon the disease stage and/or predominance of positive or negative symptoms, or was due to differential involvement of dopamine D1 or D2 receptors, with their differential excitatory or inhibitory roles in the striatum. Other suggestions were that overactivity of mesolimbic (nucleus accumbens, amygdala, cingulate, hippocampus, and entorhinal cortex) neurotransmission from ventral tegmental area cell bodies leads to psychotic symptoms, whereas hypodopaminergia in prefrontal terminals of mesocortical dopamine neurones leads to the negative symptoms of avolition, apathy, alogia, and asociality (see, for example, Duncan et al., 1999; Friedman, Temporini, & Davis, 1999). Alternatively, there may be upregulation of dopamine D2 striatal receptors, which conflicts with a basal hyperdopaminergic state with, in the temporolimbic region, increased dopamine content and upregulation of dopaminergic activity via interactions with glutamate-mediated transmission (Glenthøj & Hemmingsen, 1999)—an issue we shall return to shortly. Sensitisation to dopamine in the temporolimbic system as in the "kindling" phenomenon of epilepsy and perhaps depression was another possibility, perhaps via glutamatergic activity (see below), with patients becoming increasingly sensitised. Similarly, repeated exposure to psychostimulants such as methamphetamine may cause sensitisation, via initial enhancement of dopaminergic activity, leading to positive symptoms, and to degeneration of dopamine neurones, leading to negative symptoms and hypodopaminergia. The problem, however, with the dopamine hypothesis, per se, is that there is little clear and unambiguous evidence of pathological dopamine activity (Duncan et al., 1999), whether in terms of increased dopamine levels or receptor numbers, and the atypical neuroleptics such as clozapine seem to work via their capacity for antagonistic affinity for the 5-HT$_2$ receptor.

Byne and Davis (1999), notwithstanding the above problems with the traditional dopamine hypothesis, note that there is much evidence for dysregulation in schizophrenia, of both subcortical dopaminergic neurotransmission and of prefrontal cortical activity, and ask how these two phenomena might be connected. Input from the mesocortical dopamine projection modulates prefrontal cortical activity, whereas projections from the prefrontal cortex feed back to the midbrain to modulate dopamine release. Indeed, they suggest, subcortical dopamine dysregulation may be *secondary* to cortical (prefrontal) pathology. Release of dopamine, according to this model, may occur via two mechanisms: a *phasic* process triggered by action potentials of dopamine neurones in response to behaviourally relevant stimuli, and a *tonic* or sustained mechanism that mediates background dopamine release. Such tonic release, via glutamatergic projections from the prefrontal cortex, determines the basal concentrations of dopamine in the synaptic cleft, and so sets the tone for responsivity of the dopamine system via homeostatic regulation of the density of pre- and postsynaptic receptors. The phasic mechanism releases transient bursts of dopamine, which do not greatly affect receptor homeostasis. Consequently, Byne and Davis (1999) suggest, prolonged decrease in prefrontal cortex activity would lead to decreased subcortical *tonic* dopamine release, with compensatory effects that include increased dopamine synthesis (due to decreased stimulation of autoreceptors), sprouting of dopamine axons, upregulation of dopamine receptors, exaggerated *phasic* subcortical release of dopamine with behaviourally relevant stimuli, and increased upregulation of postsynaptic receptors. Via such a vicious circle, exaggerated *phasic* dopamine responses will occur to behavioural stimuli in the absence of any net increase in total dopamine release, due to decreased *tonic* release. This model, Byne and Davis claim, nicely explains the efficacy of dopamine receptor blockade in ameliorating the positive symptoms of schizophrenia, without any evident increase in dopamine turnover.

Glutamate

Mention has been previously made of the possible involvement of glutamate in dopamine regulation. Thus Byne and Davis (1999) note that electro-stimulation of the prefrontal cortex leads via glutamatergic projections to increases in dopamine levels from subcortical sites, as such increases are blocked by glutamate antagonists. Glutamate is a key excitatory transmitter involved in learning and memory, and the integration of different brain areas, which also plays a critical role in cellular signalling both during neurogenesis and degeneration, in cell migration with both a guiding and a trophic role, and in apoptosis (Arnold, 1999). Thus any derangements should affect the critical (for schizophrenia) frontal and temporal association areas most, where there is the greatest, longest, and most complicated ontogenesis, connectivity, and plasticity. Such considerations, and the effects of N-methyl-D-aspartate (NMDA) antagonism, have led to the suggestion that schizophrenia may be due to a primary defect of the glutamate system. Thus phencyclidine (PCP, "angel dust"), a psychotomimetic inducing schizophrenia-like symptoms, is a potent noncompetitive inhibitor of the NMDA subtype of the glutamate receptor (Friston, 1999). Similarly ketamine, another noncompetitive NMDA antagonist, induces schizophrenia-like symptoms that are countered by glycine, an NMDA agonist (Buchanan et al., 1998). There are also abnormalities of pre- and postsynaptic glutamate indices in patients with schizophrenia (Friston, 1999; Harrison, 1999), and antipsychotics potentiate glutamate activity (Glenhøj & Hemmingsen, 1999). As we have seen, the glutamate and dopamine systems interact (Duncan et al., 1999; Harrison, 1999), and glutamate is also neurotoxic (excitotoxic) in quantity; thus a good case can be made that schizophrenia is a disorder of glutamate, a disorder of modulation of interconnectivity of brain areas responsible for learning, memory, emotion, and thought

(Friston, 1999). If the psychotomimetic effects of phencyclidine are seen as causing a "transient chemical disconnection" (Friston, 1999), then we have added support for the idea that schizophrenia can be viewed at a cognitive level as a disorder of binding, and that one of the roles of the basal ganglia and thalamocortical system, known to be compromised in schizophrenia, is to mediate binding (Graybiel, 1998).

Stress has long been known to precipitate psychiatric decompensation in schizophrenia (Byne & Davis, 1999), with increased glutamate activity, especially in the prefrontal cortex, and increased dopamine release from both cortical and subcortical dopamine terminals. NMDA receptor antagonists enhance stress-induced sensitisation to dopamine (Duncan et al., 1999). So, in the genetically predisposed, a neurodevelopmental insult to the central nervous system may lead to subtle premorbid impairments of cognitive, motor, and social functions, with altered NMDA receptor function, increased sensitisation of dopamine systems, and increased susceptibility to stress; schizophrenia proper may develop via neurodegeneration if stress is persistent. We see a similar model for the role of stress in the development of depression.

Moore, West, and Grace (1999) develop further the dopamine–glutamate hypothesis, in perhaps the most complete and internally consistent manner to date, invoking also a role for nitric oxide, though otherwise many aspects of their model are similar to what has already been described. As above, dopamine transmission is not seen as altered in schizophrenia due to a primary defect in dopamine neurones, but because of abnormalities in their regulation by prefrontal limbic cortex. They propose that dysregulation of the forebrain dopamine system is due to dysfunction within limbic structures, and a collective dysfunction of these systems leads to profound functional abnormalities of the cortico-striato-pallido-thalamo-cortical circuits, and behaviours. They suggest that in schizophrenia a decrease in activity of glutamatergic frontostriatal pathways leads to a reduction in *tonic* basal ganglia dopamine, and an alteration in the responsivity of striatal output cells to *phasic* dopamine. Frontal and temporal cortical outputs control bursting in dopamine neurones, and thereby regulate phasic dopamine release in forebrain terminals in these regions. Glutamatergic output functions as a homeostatic regulator of both tonic and phasic dopamine release. Tonic dopamine may suppress phasic dopamine neurotransmission. Thus modulation of tonic dopamine levels by cortical afferents may regulate phasic dopamine responses to behaviourally relevant stimuli. Insults to the cortical systems responsible for this homeostatic maintenance of tonic dopamine levels could lead to inappropriate processing (filtering) of sensory stimuli in the frontostriatal system, and to schizophrenia-like deficits. Thus, as before, corticostriatal glutamatergic afferents maintain tonic dopamine levels. At this point, Moore et al. (1999) introduce the role of nitric oxide;

the level, they say, of nitric oxide tone in the striatum may regulate the activity of striatal feedback to midbrain dopamine neurones, although the cortex may also utilise striatal nitric oxide signalling to control subcortical dopamine transmission, with glutamate also possibly involved in these processes.

Frontal and limbic cortices are activated during learning, and are necessary for normal appetitive conditioning, as also is activation of the amygdala. Moreover, projections from these regions can control both tonic and phasic dopamine release. Thus, according to Moore et al. (1999), when behavioural demands recruit prefrontal, hippocampal, or amygdalar inputs to the basal forebrain and midbrain, dopamine cell firing shifts to a burst pattern, resulting in a phasic dopamine signal in the striatum. Simultaneously, glutamate- and nitric oxide-mediated mechanisms can increase dopamine release, increasing tonic dopamine transmission. The prefrontal and limbic cortico-striato-pallidal circuits mediate a range of psychomotor and cognitive processes that are altered in schizophrenia, such as working memory, selective attention, contextual learning, and the formation of associations between stimuli and responses during appetitive or aversive conditioning; all are mediated by dopamine. *Tonic* dopamine transmission may permit the initiation of movements during the formation of such associations, and *phasic* dopamine may modify the corticostriatal microcircuits that mediate the specific stimulus–response associations required for complex learned behaviours; this situation is similar to the basal ganglia–supplementary motor area mediation of the sequential release of serial motor activities. All such processes, say Moore et al. (1999), are likely to be altered in schizophrenia, including also working memory and motor planning. Thus we have ourselves found breakdown of performance, in schizophrenia, in a kinematic task involving serial choice reaction times with varied levels of advance information (Downing et al., 1998b), just as in Parkinson's disease. In both disorders similar mechanisms may result in behaviour that is driven more by immediate perceptual stimuli than by appropriate internal cues (Spitzer, 1997). Cortical regulation of tonic dopamine release in the ventral striatum during aversive learning may be mediated via the amygdala. Abnormalities in cortically mediated tonic dopamine release in the ventral striatum could lead to the maladaptive fear or stress responses seen in schizophrenia.

We should perhaps note at this point the hypothetical nature of the recently advanced models of dopamine, glutamate, and nitric oxide involvement in schizophrenia. Their exact involvement in positive and negative symptomatology and tonic and phasic processes and interactions awaits elaboration and resolution. We should also perhaps note, with caution, the possible dangers of extrapolating from the numerous rodent studies in accounts of dopamine projections to the cortex.

Acetylcholine

There are two cholinergic pathways of cognitive significance (Friedman et al., 1999): the septohippocampal (perhaps more concerned with episodic and working memory), and the pathway that runs from the nucleus basalis of Meynert up to the cortex (which is perhaps more involved in reference or semantic memory). As yet, there is no direct evidence of abnormalities of cells in the latter system in schizophrenia, though deficits in auditory sensory gating have been postulated as due to changes in the α_7-nicotinic cholinergic receptor (Adler et al., 1998). Such changes may account for the heavy tobacco use often found in schizophrenia (McEvoy, Freudenreich, & Wilson, 1999), and suggest cholinergic transmission as a potential therapeutic target. Indeed McEvoy et al. (1999) also noted that smokers showed a significantly greater therapeutic response to clozapine than nonsmokers, and smokers smoked less when treated with clozapine than with conventional neuroleptics. Self-medication by smoking has also been reported in Tourette's syndrome and depression, reflecting the wide distribution of nicotinic receptors in the brain, and their involvement in the modulation and release of dopamine and serotonin (Foulds, 1999). Thus, although acute administration of nicotine may enhance their release or activity, chronically there may be desensitisation to dopamine, thereby alleviating the positive symptoms of schizophrenia, and reduced concentration and synthesis of serotonin in the hippocampus. Finally, the P50 inhibitory deficit in patients and close relatives may be normalised by high doses of nicotine (Adler et al., 1999), whereas cholinomimetic drugs such as acetylcholinesterase inhibitors and M1/M4 muscarinic agonists may enhance cognition in both demented and normal healthy individuals (Friedman et al.,1999).

Noradrenaline

Noradrenaline pathways originate from the locus coeruleus, and are important in responsivity to novel stimuli, vigilance, attention, and filtering out distracting information (Friedman et al., 1999)—a problem in schizophrenia. The prefrontal cortex is rich in noradrenergic terminals, and feeds back to the locus coeruleus. In the prefrontal cortex α_2-receptor activity is important in noradrenergic neurotransmission, which seems aberrant in schizophrenia. Thus noradrenaline levels are depleted in the prefrontal cortices of cognitively impaired patients, whereas the atypical neuroleptic clozapine, which (unlike the conventional neuroleptics) is fairly efficacious against often-recalcitrant negative symptoms, has potent noradrenergic effects; it potentiates α_2-noradrenergic receptor activity, and helps various cognitive functions. Thus α_2-noradrenergic agonists like clonidine and β-adrenergic agonists may prove pharmacologically and therapeutically useful.

MEDICATION

Until recently, pharmacotherapy has concentrated exclusively on controlling positive symptoms, and to this end most conventional neuroleptics block the dopamine D2 receptors (Moore et al., 1999), though such blockade in the *nigrostriatal* system will lead to extrapyramidal side effects (EPSEs); it is the blockade of the *mesolimbic* system (ventral tegmentum, nucleus accumbens, amygdala, hippocampus, cingulate, and entorhinal cortex) that is associated with antipsychotic efficacy. The *mesocortical* system projects from the ventral tegmentum to the prefrontal cortex, and has fewer D2 receptors; perhaps for this reason antipsychotics are less efficacious against negative symptoms, which may have in part a prefrontal origin.

The ability of conventional neuroleptics to prevent psychotic episodes develops over a period of time, with repeated treatment, as a result of inactivation of mesolimbic dopamine neurones, via a mechanism known as depolarisation block. This phenomenon seems to affect both tonic and phasic pools in the striatum, lowering tonic dopamine activity, and preventing phasic activation of dopamine cell activity and release. However, these effects may well also tend to exacerbate the cognitive and negative symptoms, and contribute to the anhedonic effects often reported with neuroleptics. Newer treatment strategies address the negative and cognitive symptoms, due to altered structure and functional activity of dopamine in the medial prefrontal cortex; they selectively increase activation in prefrontal cortical and limbic regions, and modulate, interactively, dopaminergic, serotonergic, and glutamatergic activity. Thus dopamine and serotonin neurotransmission interacts at various anatomical levels, with decreased activity of the latter generally associated with increased activity of the former, though serotonin can have a stimulatory effect on the mesolimbic dopamine system; serotonin neurones in the median and dorsal raphe nuclei innervate dopamine neurones in the substantia nigra, ventral tegmental area, caudate, putamen, nucleus accumbens, medial prefrontal cortex, and amygdala. While blockade of dopamine D2 receptors causes extrapyramidal signs, 5-HT$_2$ *antagonists* release dopamine from inhibition and thus decrease extrapyramidal signs; 5-HT$_{1A}$ *agonists* inhibit serotonin neurones, disinhibiting dopamine in the striatum and decreasing extrapyramidal signs. Clozapine, with its 5-HT$_{2A}$ antagonistic properties, reduces the number of spontaneously active ventral tegmental neurones, but not those in the substantia nigra, while the conventional neuroleptic haloperidol reduces the number of spontaneously active neurones in both regions. Clozapine interacts with a range of dopamine and serotonin receptors. Lieberman et al. (1998) observe that there is no simple explanation relating this mixed neuroreceptor profile to the anatomically selective pharmacological effects of clozapine on neuronal activity in the ventral tegmental area.

The newer atypical neuroleptics, with their serotonin-antagonistic properties, reduce the side effects of parkinsonism and akathisia; they may treat the negative as well as the positive symptoms previously addressed by the older, traditional drugs, as well as the cognitive and depressive symptoms to some degree (Buchanan et al., 1998; Tamminga, 1998), though at the cost of tachycardia, sedation, and orthostasis, and (rarely) the potentially fatal white blood cell condition agranulocytosis. In therapeutic respects, risperidone may be intermediate between clozapine and haloperidol.

According to Moore et al. (1999), the relatively beneficial effects of clozapine on negative and cognitive symptoms stem from their selectively increased activation effects in prefrontal cortical and limbic regions, via modulation of glutamatergic transmission. They argue that atypical neuroleptics, while still able to suppress *phasic* dopamine via inactivation of mesolimbic dopamine neurones, may also normalise *tonic* dopamine transmission in limbic and cortical regions by increasing dopamine and/or noradrenaline in these regions. Similarly, they say, possibly by enhancing cortical dopamine, administration of low doses of dopamine and noradrenaline reuptake inhibitors, such as amphetamine, may enhance the cognitive abilities of patients whose psychosis (positive symptomatology) is controlled by neuroleptics. Additional target molecules in the treatment of schizophrenia may therefore now include intermediaries between the dopamine and the glutamate systems, such as nitric oxide.

Keefe, Silva, Perkins, and Lieberman (1999) report the results of a meta-analysis (15 studies) of the effects of atypical antipsychotic drugs on neurocognitive impairment in schizophrenia. Such drugs, pharmacologically related to clozapine, include olanzapine, risperidone, quetiapine, sertindole, and ziprasidone; they all produce fewer extrapyramidal side effects than typical neuroleptic drugs, and more potent antagonism of 5-HT_{2A} receptors relative to dopamine D2 receptors, though they still antagonise dopamine D2 receptors to varying degrees. Keefe et al. (1999) conclude that the atypicals are significantly more effective than conventionals at improving cognitive function, especially verbal fluency, digit–symbol substantiation, fine-motor, and executive functions. Attentional processes improved less, and learning and memory functions least, and cognitive function was never fully restored to normal. They speculate that conventional antipsychotics impair timing processes in schizophrenia, via extrapyramidal signs, a phenomenon (and consequence) that is absent with atypicals. They conclude that the balance between multiple mutually modulatory transmitter systems (acetylcholine, serotonin, dopamine, noradrenaline . . .), rather than the operation of any one, may be most crucial for optimal cognitive function. Thus one cannot predict the cognitive effects of a drug exclusively from receptor binding studies. Clozapine, the prototypical new-generation antipsychotic, has a high affinity for multiple receptors, generally in an antagonistic capacity, except for muscarinic receptors of the cholinergic system, where it acts as an agonist.

Meltzer and McGurk (1999) review the effects of clozapine, risperidone, and olanzapine, a more restricted group of the newer atypicals, on cognitive function in schizophrenia. They find that clozapine improves attention and verbal fluency, and some aspects of executive function. Risperidone improves working memory, executive function, and attention, whereas olanzapine improves verbal learning, memory, verbal fluency, and executive function, but not attention, working memory, or visual learning and memory.

SUMMARY AND CONCLUSIONS

Schizophrenia, with a lifetime risk of around 1% and a suicide rate of between 10% and 15%, ruins careers, lives, and relationships; although depression may be our most common disabling psychiatric malady, schizophrenia is certainly our most serious. In this respect it resembles the childhood disorder autism. A disorder heterogeneous in presentation if not aetiology, it manifests clinically in young adulthood, perhaps a little earlier in males than in females, though retrospective analysis of old home movies may reveal early evidence of abnormalities of movement or behaviour. Complex, poorly understood and intractable, its course is fluctuating, and it merges with the extremes of what might otherwise be regarded as normality. Indeed the whole spectrum of behaviour may be affected, including emotional reactivity, interpersonal relationships, perceptual and thought processes, and motivation. A gradual development, with incomplete remissions and prolonged impairment, contributes to a diagnosis where overall clinical observation rather than any single criterion must suffice.

Like many neurological and neuropsychiatric disorders, symptoms may be largely positive (an excess) or negative (an insufficiency). The former include delusions, hallucinations, and disorganisation of thought, speech, and behaviour. Negative symptoms, usually the most resistant to treatment, include flattening of affect, alogia, and avolition. Although taxonomies may vary, three classes may usefully be distinguished: hallucinations and delusions, the popular stereotype of the disorder; the negative and rather parkinsonian symptoms of blunted affect, anhedonia, avolition and poverty of speech, movement, and social activity; and disorganised and inappropriate behaviour, thought, and affect. A popular cognitive model, which attempts to encompass such diversity, appeals to a disorder of monitoring one's own and others' intentions—an account with clear commonalities with proposed disturbances of theory-of-mind in autism—or of conscious self-awareness.

In addition to the frontostriatal system, wider limbic and temporal involvement seems likely; however, compartments of the prefrontal cortex provide a useful explanatory model. Thus disorder of the dorsolateral prefrontal cortex may account for psychomotor poverty, social withdrawal, and depression; disorder of the lateral orbitofrontal cortex may explain disorganisation, thought disturbance, and antisocial behaviour; anterior cingulate dysfunction may lead to the apathy and social withdrawal of schizophrenia, whereas altered function of the supplementary motor area may partly explain delusions of control. Note, however, the danger to which I have previously alluded of sticking too closely to a localisationist approach; these (and other) circuits all interact in a dynamic fashion, and are likely to be synergistically activated during many complex, higher-level, cognitive functions. A possibly dubious but still useful distinction is that of type 1 schizophrenia, with its positive symptomatology and with which the disorder may often commence, and type 2 with its negative symptomatology (shared also with Parkinson's disease and depression), which may be more apparent later in the disorder's progression. However, individual patients may indeed move in both directions between the two typologies.

Hallucinations are not of course unique to the disorder, occurring in hypnagogic imagery and during drug intoxication or states of sensory deprivation. However, under such circumstances there is rarely the degree of misattribution seen in schizophrenia with its intense inner speech, inappropriate temporal and anterior cingulate activation, and failure to engage editing processes via the supplementary motor area. Even those patients profoundly deaf from an early age seem to experience auditory hallucinations of speech, whereas in the visual modality impairments of the magnocellular system have been proposed, as in developmental dyslexia, another neuro-developmental disorder sharing risk with schizophrenia. Delusions, like the inappropriate profanities of Tourette's syndrome and the compulsions of OCD, are partly determined by current social context; witchcraft has nowadays given way to beliefs of electronic and CIA manipulation. As bizarre, content-encapsulated false beliefs that are resistant to counter-argument, delusions are largely social, as indeed tends to be the case in other disorders such as Alzheimer's or Huntington's disease. Thought insertion, withdrawal, or broadcasting may be reported, along with hearing one's own thoughts spoken aloud, or those of others. There may be delusions of control, persecution, or reference, with a failure of reality monitoring, an inability to differentiate between one's own and other people's beliefs or actions. A failure of reafference involving cerebellar or parietal systems is possible.

Structural and functional anomalies are small but pervasive, extending also to clinically "unaffected" close relatives. There may be ventricular enlargement, reduced hippocampal volume and hypofrontality, though frontal changes may be less consistent than those of the temporolimbic system. There are contentious reports of abnormalities of neuronal density and size, but not maybe of cell number, and of reduced neuropil in the temporolimbic cortex, especially in the vicinity of Ammon's horn; neuronal density changes may also be present in the limbic striatum and thalamus, whereas anomalies of the septum pellucidum, corpus callosum, and ventricles all suggest abnormal midline development. Cerebellar maldevelopment has been invoked to explain "cognitive dysmetria" and intention tremor, whereas anomalies of basal ganglia and thalamus may explain abnormal sensory gating, attention, and "binding" at both a cognitive (dorsal system) and an emotional (ventral, limbic system) level. Bizarre associations and disorganised thought may reflect functional rather than structural alterations, perhaps via dysregulation of the modulatory neurotranmitter systems (dopamine, noradrenaline, serotonin) and glutamate, in a fashion similar to that perhaps occurring in OCD. Indeed both the latter (*hyper*orbitofrontality) and schizophrenia (*hypo*frontality) may involve anomalous interregional correlation, perhaps via the basal ganglia. Thus schizophrenia may usefully be seen as involving anomalous coordination or integration of frontal and temporal activity.

In cognition nearly all aspects are affected, including holding, shifting, and selecting in attention. Executive dysfunction, which is highly resistant to treatment, extends to concept attainment, set, reasoning, monitoring ongoing behaviour, judgement, and fluency of thought. There are deficits of inhibition, as shown by saccadic dyscontrol and the P50 suppression and prepulse inhibition paradigms, and in all aspects of memory. Priming studies suggest simultaneous availability of competing interpretations, perhaps thereby explaining the pervasive bizarre illogicality and tangential derailments. MMN, an early potential correlated with the detection of infrequent deviant events, may be anomalous, while all levels of motor functioning, including response times and bimanual coordination, may be affected; parkinsonian and other manifestations are not just a consequence of neuroleptic medication.

Effects from seasonality of birth, obstetric complications, and maternal infections, along with a high level of heritability, suggest a genetic liability interacting with environmental stressors. Anomalies of neurodevelopment in the critical second trimester of pregnancy are proposed, though there is debate as to whether there is thereafter a static neuropathy or also continuing neurodegeneration without gliosis. The fact that significant clinical manifestations usually only appear in young adulthood suggests that requisite normal behaviours must first unfold; however, early frontal or temporal damage in animal models can lead to behavioural abnormalities that only manifest in adulthood, and to abnormal dopaminergic activity in distant areas. The same brain areas are affected in schizophrenia as in the classic age-dependent neurodegenerative disorders Huntington's and especially Alzheimer's disease, and indeed continuing cognitive decline is clearest for nonautomatic, complex, attention-demanding tasks. Nevertheless, overt necrosis seems minimal, with developmental abnormalities of cellular migration, synaptogenesis, or apoptosis the most probable, though there is some evidence of excessive apoptosis continuing right up to adulthood. In any case, all neurodevelopmental disorders seem to be associated variously with abnormalities of brain morphology, deficits in neural migration, microgyria, lissencephaly, micro- or hydrocephaly, biochemical abnormalities, or altered asymmetries. The latter, of course, though nearly universal in the neurodevelopmental disorders reviewed in this book, may be merely markers rather than aetiological in their own right. If grey matter is predominantly affected, as perhaps in autism, then we may see seizures, psychoses, progressive cognitive deterioration, and behavioural disorders, while if, instead, white matter is predominantly involved, we may see problems in posture, sensation, and intellect.

Precursor indicators of possible later development of schizophrenia, apart from neurological soft signs and neuropsychiatric changes, include abnormal facies, posture and movement, minor physical anomalies of skin (dermatoglyphs), and dysmorphies of face; cerebral morphogenesis parallels craniofacial development, and neural and skin tissue derive from the same ectodermal origin. Midline abnormalities of palate, midface, mouth, and frontonasal morphology may all be associated with dysgenesis of the third ventricle, corpus callosum, and mesotemporal regions.

Family, twin, and adoption studies all indicate high heritability, though it is unlikely that a single major gene is responsible for all cases, or even that the same gene is operative within a single family. There may be multiple susceptibility genes all interacting in an additive fashion with environmental factors; there is certainly no clear Mendelian dominant or recessive pattern of inheritance. Although there have been numerous failures to replicate, susceptibility regions have been identified by systematic genome scanning in chromosomes 5, 6, 8, 13, and 22, with some evidence also for 3, 9, 20, and possibly 2, 18, and the X chromosome. Association studies suggest involvement of the human leukocyte antigen system, and possibly the 5-HT_{2A} receptor gene; concentrations of serotonin, moreover, may be abnormal. Indeed the atypical neuroleptic clozapine is a highly efficient 5-HT_{2A} blocker, and hallucinogens target the serotonin system. Although the efficiency of conventional neuroleptics is proportional to their capacity to bind to dopamine D2 receptors, as yet there is no evidence for a relationship between schizophrenia and genes that code for any of the dopamine receptors, except maybe D3, which is indeed expressed mainly in the limbic system.

Nevertheless, all neurotransmitters have now been implicated in the disorder, and an interaction between dopamine, serotonin, and glutamate is a favoured hypothesis. Serotonin, in addition to its role in hallucinogens, is important in neurodevelopment and in cerebellar function, and modulates the activity of dopamine. The original dopamine hypothesis stemmed from observations of the antipsychotic effects of dopamine antagonists such as chlorpromazine, and the psychosis-producing effects of dopamine agonists. However, schizophrenia is probably not simply due to excess dopamine or dopamine hypersensitivity. The effects of the dopaminergic system may depend upon the staging of the disorder and the predominance of positive and negative symptoms, with probable prefrontal hypodopaminergia and temporolimbic hyperdopaminergia. A newly emerging hypothesis is that glutamate projections from the prefrontal cortex may normally regulate dopamine levels tonically, whereas behavioural stimuli may regulate dopamine levels phasically. Reduced prefrontal activity in schizophrenia may cause reduced subcortical tonic release of dopamine and thereby increased dopamine synthesis via the autoreceptors, and consequent upregulation of postsynaptic receptors. Such a vicious circle may lead to exaggerated phasic dopamine responses to behavioural stimuli, along with further reductions in tonic dopamine. Glutamate, a major excitatory neurotransmitter, is also involved in neurogenesis, cell migration, guidance and trophism, apoptosis, neurodegeneration and, probably, binding, of which schizophrenia may indeed be a disorder. Schizophrenia may involve a defect of the glutamate system, with prefrontal activation normally acting, via glutamate, to mediate subcortical dopamine release. Stress is known to cause schizophrenic decompensation, probably via glutamatergic mechanisms, and to lead to neurodegeneration of the mesotemporal and limbic regions. Thus reduced prefrontal glutamatergic activity in schizophrenia may lead to reduced tonic dopamine in the basal ganglia, and altered responsivity of striatal output cells to phasic dopamine. Glutamate thus may act as a homeostatic regulator of tonic and phasic dopamine release. Faulty glutamate metabolism in schizophrenia may be associated with both faulty filtering and binding processes. Glutamate afferents may maintain tonic dopamine levels, with striatal levels or tone of nitric oxide regulating striatal feedback to midbrain (ventral tegmental) dopamine neurones. The cortex may use striatal nitric oxide signalling, along with glutamate, to control subcortical dopamine transmission.

Acetylcholine is important in cognition, episodic and working memory. There is no direct evidence of anomalies of this system in schizophrenia, except that α_7-nicotinic receptors are involved in auditory sensory gating, and patients (as in Huntington's disease and Tourette's syndrome) are often heavy smokers in apparent self-medication. Nicotine moreover seems to help the response to clozapine. Clozapine also potentiates α_2-noradrenergic receptor activity, which is abnormal in patients' prefrontal cortices, and ameliorates cognitive deficits. Indeed the prefrontal cortex is rich in noradrenergic terminals, which may be important in regulating responsivity to novel stimuli and vigilance situations.

Until recently, medication has concentrated upon the less recalcitrant positive symptomatology, though at the expense of developing extrapyramidal signs. The 5-HT$_{2A}$ antagonist clozapine decreases such signs by releasing dopamine from inhibition, as well as playing an active antipsychotic role by reducing the number of spontaneously active ventral tegmental neurones. However, its effects are complex and poorly understood, and probably also involve modulation of glutamatergic transmission, with selective prefrontal activation.

FURTHER READING

Andreasen, N.C., Paradiso, S., & O'Leary, D.S. (1998). "Cognitive dysmetria" as an integrative theory of schizophrenia: A dysfunction in cortical-subcortical-cerebellar circuitry. *Schizophrenia Bulletin, 24,* 203–218.

Arnold, S.E. (1999). Cognition and neuropathology in schizophrenia. *Acta Psychiatrica Scandinavica, 99* (Suppl. 395), 41–50.

Buchanan, R.W., Buckley, P.F., Tamminga, C.A., & Schulze, S.C. (1998). Schizophrenia research: A biennium of progress. Proceedings from the sixth international congress on schizophrenia research. Colorado Springs, CO, 12–16 April, 1997. *Schizophrenia Bulletin, 24,* 501–518.

Buchsbaum, M.S., & Hazlett, E.A. (1998). Positron emission tomography studies of abnormal glucose metabolism in schizophrenia. *Schizophrenia Bulletin, 24,* 343–364.

Buckley, P.F. (1998). The clinical stigmata of aberrant neurodevelopment in schizophrenia. *Journal of Nervous and Mental Disease, 186,* 79–86.

Byne, W., & Davis, K.L. (1999). The role of prefrontal cortex in the dopaminergic dysregulation of schizophrenia. *Biological Psychiatry, 45,* 657–659.

DeLisi, L.E. (1999). A critical overview of recent investigations into the genetics of schizophrenia. *Current Opinion in Psychiatry, 12,* 29–39.

Duncan, G.E., Sheitman, B.B., & Lieberman, J.A. (1999). An integrated view of pathophysiological models of schizophrenia. *Brain Research Review, 29,* 250–264.

Friedman, J.I., Temporini, H., & Davis, K.L. (1999). Pharmacologic strategies for augmenting cognitive performance in schizophrenia. *Biological Psychiatry, 45,* 1–16.

Friston, K.J. (1999). Schizophrenia and the disconnection hypothesis. *Acta Psychiatrica Scandinavica, 99* (Suppl. 395), 68–79.

Goldman-Rakic, P.S., & Selemon, L.D. (1997). Functional and anatomical aspects of prefrontal pathology in schizophrenia. *Schizophrenia Bulletin, 23,* 437–458.

Harrison, P.J. (1999). The neuropathology of schizophrenia: A critical review of the data and their interpretation. *Brain, 122,* 593–624.

Heinrichs, R.W., & Zakzanis, K.K. (1998). Neurocognitive deficit in schizophrenia: A quantitative review of the evidence. *Schizophrenia Bulletin, 12,* 426–445.

Jones, E.G. (1997). Cortical development and thalamic pathology in schizophrenia. *Schizophrenia Bulletin, 23,* 483–501.

Katsetos, C.D., Hyde, T.M., & Herman, M.M. (1997). Neuropathology of the cerebellum in schizophrenia—an update: 1996 and future directions. *Biological Psychiatry, 42,* 213–224.

Knoll, J.L., Garver, D.L., Ramberg, J.E., Kingsbury, S.J., Croissant, D., & McDermott, B.

(1998). Heterogeneity of the psychoses: Is there a neurodegenerative psychosis? *Schizophrenia Bulletin, 24*, 365–379.

Lieberman, J.A. (1999). Is schizophrenia a neurodegenerative disorder? A clinical and neurobiological perspective. *Biological Psychiatry, 46*, 729–739.

Lieberman, J.A., Mailman, R.B., Duncan, G., Sikich, L., Chakos, M., Nichols, D.E., & Kraus, J.E. (1998). Serotonergic basis of antipsychotic drug effects in schizophrenia. *Biological Psychiatry, 44*, 1099–1117.

Maier, W., & Schwab, S. (1998). Molecular genetics of schizophrenia. *Current Opinion in Psychiatry, 11*, 19–25.

Moore, H., West, A.R., & Grace, A.A. (1999). The regulation of forebrain dopamine transmission: Relevance to the pathophysiology and psychopathology of schizophrenia. *Biological Psychiatry, 46*, 40–55.

Nestor, P.G., & O'Donnell, B.F. (1998). The mind adrift: Attentional dysregulation in schizophrenia. In R. Parasuraman (Ed.), *The attentive brain* (pp. 528–547). Cambridge, MA: MIT Press.

Rund, B.R. (1998). A review of longitudinal studies of cognitive functions in schizophrenia patients. *Schizophrenia Bulletin, 24*, 425–435.

Schultz, S.K., & Andreasen, N.C. (1999). Schizophrenia. *The Lancet, 353*, 1425–1430.

Selemon, L.D., & Goldman-Rakic, P.S. (1999). The reduced neuropil hypothesis: A circuit based model of schizophrenia. *Biological Psychiatry, 45*, 17–25.

Stevens, J.R. (1997). Anatomy of schizophrenia revisited. *Schizophrenia Bulletin, 23*, 373–383.

Tamminga, C.A. (1998). Serotonin and schizophrenia. *Biological Psychiatry, 44*, 1079–1080.

Waddington, J.L., Lane, A., Larkin, C., & O'Callaghan, E. (1999). The neurodevelopmental basis of schizophrenia: Clinical clues from cerebro-craniofacial dysmorphogenesis, and the roots of a lifetime trajectory of disease. *Biological Psychiatry, 46*, 31–39.

Weinberger, D.R. (1999). Cell biology of the hippocampal formation in schizophrenia. *Biological Psychiatry, 45*, 395–402.

Zipursky, R.B., & Kapur, S. (1998). New insights into schizophrenia from neuroimaging. *Current Opinion in Psychiatry, 11*, 33–37.

CHAPTER EIGHT

Autism

> Some conjurors say the number 3 is the magic number, and
> some say the number 7. It is neither, my friend, it is neither. It
> is number 1.
> —Fagin in *Oliver Twist*, Charles Dickens (1837–1838)

INTRODUCTION

Just as schizophrenia is the most devastating psychiatric condition to affect
adults, and Alzheimer's disease the elderly, autism, sometimes described as a
dementia of childhood, is the most destructive disorder of youth. Indeed
autism bears a number of similarities to schizophrenia, including early,
erroneous ideas about an aetiology from poor parenting. In this chapter we
see the autistic spectrum within the general context of other neuropsychiatric disorders characterised by specific delays, or rather halts, in development, and how a range of medical conditions may be associated with
autism. This disorder, heterogeneous in possible causes and manifestations,
is highly comorbid with the other conditions that involve the frontostriatal
system to varying extents, and with which this book is concerned. We shall
note its peculiar social and communicational deficits, and its tendency to a
stereotyped range of interests and behaviours, along sometimes with
peculiar islands of high ability. We shall also note explanatory accounts
such as a failure of central coherence, or of possession of a theory of mind,
which, however, may be unable of themselves to explain all aspects of the
disorder. As with schizophrenia, we shall see that any neuropathology is
subtle and heritability is high, and that what is inherited may be a
predisposition or susceptibility that also requires the action of certain other
environmental events, perhaps at key points in neurodevelopment. Again,

as with the other disorders, we shall observe that a range of modulatory neurotransmitters, known to be active in the frontostriatal system, may be involved, particularly serotonin, dopamine and the peptides oxytocin and vasopressin. Finally, we shall review Asperger's disorder, which is closely related to autism, and Williams syndrome, which has some surprising similarities and differences.

EVOLVING CONCEPTS IN THE STUDY OF AUTISM

Kanner (1943) in his now classic paper identified what we have come to see as the key features of autism and related disorders, and in an era of "epidemic environmentalism" (Rutter, 1999) initially rejected a purely environmental account. However, he later became influenced by the *Zeitgeist*, seeing autism as an unusually early manifestation of schizophrenia, and caused at least partly by environmental factors, including rearing by "refrigerator parents". He also differentiated autism from other childhood or developmental disorders of a psychiatric nature, and laid the groundwork for seeing it as one of a group of disorders of an immature brain, involving, as we now believe, the cerebellum, frontal and temporal lobes, diencephalic nuclei, basal ganglia and thalamus, and the corpus callosum, along with dysfunction of serotonergic, dopaminergic, and opiate pathways (Rapin, 1999). Kanner thus gave his name to the syndrome whereby children who could handle objects skilfully and often had abnormally good memories, or calendrical, musical, or artistic abilities, nevertheless in other respects appeared retarded. They were unable to engage in normal conversation, and rejected all forms of social contact. They frequently confused personal pronouns ("I" and "you"), had an obsessive desire for sameness with emotional outbursts should any object or routine be in any way changed, and had shown tendencies for solitariness from their earliest days. A year later Asperger (1944) described an apparently milder form, Asperger's disorder, where there is little or no mental retardation but similar deficits in movement and social interaction.

Observations that the personality characteristics of parents resembled in some ways the behavioural difficulties of proband children, which had led to the original beliefs in faulty parenting, slowly were reconciled instead with an approach based on shared inheritance of social and other difficulties (Bailey, Palferman, Heavey, & Le Couteur, 1998). By the 1950s, the first systematic attempts were made to differentiate autism from other psychiatric disorders (Rutter, 1999), and the identification in autism of these characteristic features: failure to develop normal social relationships and interpersonal functioning, language retardation (involving impaired comprehension, echolalia and pronominal reversal), and ritualistic compulsive behaviour and repetitive, stereotyped play. During that period, epilepsy was frequently observed and there arose the first idea that it was a neurodevelopmental disorder based on an organic brain dysfunction, instead of being an acquired psychogenic disorder. As Rutter observes, the emphasis now was on cognitive deficits such as sequencing, abstraction, and meaning. Autism was now differentiated from mental retardation and schizophrenia, and from disintegrative disorders involving profound regression and behavioural disintegration after an initial period of apparently normal development.

From the 1970s to the mid 1980s, according to Rutter's (1999) historical analysis, there was increased realisation of the heterogeneity of autism and its differentiation from other neurodevelopmental disorders such as Rett syndrome and fragile X. There was also the realisation that autism went beyond mere severe language deficit, and that genetics played an important role. Cognitive deficits came to be seen as independent of social withdrawal, and it was realised that both were necessary contributors to the syndrome. It also came to be realised that there were socioemotional problems in terms of a failure to experience empathy and, from false-belief tests, that there was an inability to "read the minds" of others.

Between the mid 1980s and the mid 1990s, twin concordance studies indicated a very high heritability, and polygenic models of inheritance were proposed, with the realisation that "clinically unaffected" relatives may nevertheless share certain characteristics with probands, and that autism belonged to a spectrum of a broader range of social and communicative deficits in individuals of otherwise normal intelligence; links were seen with the other frontostriatal neurodevelopmental disorders such as schizophrenia, obsessive compulsive disorder (OCD) and Tourette's syndrome. Of late, there has been increasing interest in the genetics (autism has been linked now to anomalies in all but three chromosomes!), neuropathology, neurochemistry, and interventional approaches; however, as of now, and unlike schizophrenia, depression, OCD, Tourette's syndrome and attention deficit hyperactivity disorder (ADHD), no drug treatment has emerged that produces major behavioural improvements in autism.

PERVASIVE DEVELOPMENTAL DISORDERS

Autism is one of the autistic spectrum of pervasive developmental disorders (PDDs), neuropsychiatric disturbances characterised by specific delays and deviance in social, communicative, and cognitive development, with onset typically in the first years of life (Volkmar, 1996). Although commonly associated with mental retardation, these disorders do not simply reflect the developmental level attained. Nor does the term imply a specific cause, theoretical orientation, or treatment approach; rather, it indicates that developmental disturbance is so pervasive that it interferes with a range of functions, including language and social development (Harris, 1996). Thus it is not specific to any one deficit. It is still a controversial term, and there is debate as to whether it should apply only to children with social and communicative dysfunction.

The category of pervasive developmental disorders was introduced to classificatory systems in 1980 when it became clear that autism was not a psychiatric disturbance or a consequence of faulty parenting (Minshew, 1997). Nevertheless the relative contributions of nature and nurture continue to be debated (Bauman & Kemper, 1994; Plomin, Owen, & McGuffin, 1994), with both genetic and environmental factors interacting (Ciaranello & Ciaranello, 1995). In addition to impairments in (especially) social interactions, and verbal and nonverbal communication, the PDD category is stipulated for disorders involving impaired symbolic and imaginative play and abstract reasoning (Minshew, 1997). Impairments are disproportionate to age and expected intelligence with distinctive qualitative characteristics. Other aspects include the presence of stereotyped interests and activities, lack of cognitive flexibility, poor organisational skills, poor insight into what others may be thinking, rigidity, perseveration, and increased anxiety (Rapin, 1999). There may also be hyperactivity and/or delayed motor development, and unusual sensitivity (or insensitivity) to sensory stimuli.

Based on the presence, number, and distribution of 12 behavioural descriptors, and age of onset, five types of PDD may be identified according to DSM-IV criteria:

- Classic autism (see below), which requires at least six deficits, two or more in sociability, one each in language and range of interests and activities, and onset before 3 years of age.
- Asperger's disorder or syndrome (see below), which is less severe, requiring at least three deficits, two in sociability, one in range of interests and activities, without language delay or significant cognitive deficit; its distinction from autism is debated.
- Disintegrative disorder, where there is normal early development, followed by severe later language, cognitive, and behavioural regression, in the absence of an obvious degenerative disease of the brain. Also known as Heller's syndrome or infantile dementia, it is rare and is possibly just another variant of autism, with its restricted stereotyped and repetitive behaviour, interests and mannerisms. However, in some respects it clearly resembles adult dementia.
- Rett disorder, a genetic neurological syndrome restricted to girls, and characterised by apparently normal pre- and perinatal development, and psychomotor development, in the first year, followed by deceleration of head growth, and loss of acquired purposeful hand skills and speech by 1–2 years (Harris, 1996). The developing

microcephaly contrasts with the tendency towards macrocephaly in autism. There is gait apraxia, severe mental deficiency, frequent seizures and the development of stereotypies (Fein, Joy, Green, & Waterhouse, 1996; Rapin, 1997). Problems in respiration and swallowing also ensue, with death characteristically occurring in the second or third decade (Minshew, 1997).

- PDD not otherwise specified, where there are severe impairments in sociability, language, and range of activities, but where the criteria for autism, Asperger's disorder, and disintegrative disorder are not otherwise met.

The above five PDDs, by virtue of the involvement of deficits in sociability and tendencies to stereotypies, clearly differ from neurodevelopmental disorders such as specific learning disorder, or nonverbal (developmental) learning disability of the right hemisphere. As Bax (1999) observes, this is a very complex area, the terminology is a morass, and epidemiology and diagnosis are very difficult because of symptomatology changing with development. The study of specific learning disorders tends to fall between educationalists and neurologists, in part because of problems of management. However, there is much comorbidity with and overlap between frontostriatal disorders generally, such as ADHD, and PDDs specifically, such as autism. Nonverbal (developmental) learning disability of the right hemisphere involves a lesser degree of social impairment than autism, abnormal facial expression, abnormal eye contact and face recognition, and impaired arithmetic, visuospatial ability, and attention to left hemispace, all suggesting right parietal involvement.

There are a number of medical conditions also that can cause, or simulate, autistic symptoms. These include the effects of thalidomide, valproate, untreated phenylketonuria, hyperthyroidism, lactic acidosis, neurofibromatosis, Moebius' syndrome, cytomegalovirus, rubella and herpes encephalopathy (Fein et al., 1996). Two, however, are particularly prominent:

- Fragile X syndrome, characterised by a fragile site on the long arm of the X chromosome, is not a common cause of autism, though there are more individuals with this inherited disorder who meet the diagnostic criteria for autism than can be accounted for by chance (Feinstein & Reiss, 1998). The disorder involves mental retardation, hypotonia, tactile defensiveness, motor stereotypies, deficits in social and language abilities with gaze aversion, attentional deficits, hyperactivity, and seizures (Dykens & Volkmar, 1997; Rutter, Bailey, Simonoff, & Pickles, 1997). Individuals are, however, interested in social interactions, while displaying intense social anxiety. They also tend to possess prominent ears, a long narrow face, macro-orchidism (in postpubertal males), hyperextensible joints, flat feet and strabismus. Females may be less affected (Fein et al., 1996), tending instead to exhibit spatial deficits (Cornish, Munir, & Cross, 1998).

- Tuberous sclerosis (TSC) is a common neurocutaneous disorder, characterised by abnormal tissue growth that results in benign tumours, hamartomas and nongrowing lesions (hamartias) in various organs, including eye, skin, brain, heart, and kidney. Tuberous sclerosis is inherited as an abnormal autosomal dominant disease with variable expression. Involvement of the central nervous system is evident in more than 90% of cases. It is genetically heterogeneous, and linkage studies have identified two genes, TSC1 located on chromosome 9q34, and TSC2, on 16p13 (Smalley, 1998). Among families segregating tuberous sclerosis, about half are due to TSC1, and half to TSC2. The TSC2 gene codes for the protein product tuberin, which is important in cell growth, development, and differentiation, and rat studies suggest exceptionally high levels of tuberin in the hippocampus and Purkinje granule cells of the cerebellum. We shall see that these brain regions have been repeatedly implicated in autism. The frequency of autism is very high in tuberous sclerosis, nearly half the cases of tuberous sclerosis meeting criteria for autism or PDD generally (Smalley, 1998). However, among autistic populations the frequency of tuberous sclerosis does not exceed 4%, reaching 8–14% among the subgroup of autistic individuals with seizure disorder. Mental retardation and seizures, especially infantile spasms, are significant risk factors for the development of autism or PDD. Otherwise in tuberous sclerosis hyperactivity, impulsivity, and uncooperativeness are common (Dykens & Volkmar, 1997; Rutter et al., 1997).

Apart from fragile X syndrome and tuberous sclerosis, the XYY syndrome has also been associated with autistic symptoms; in fact many of the behavioural patterns linked with autism seem to suggest a decrease in the influence of the normal female chromosomes (XX), and a corresponding increase in the influence of the male (Y) chromosome (Ciaranello & Ciaranello, 1995). As contributing medical conditions, some authorities also include schizoid or schizotypal disorders, characterised by rigidity of thought, blunted affect, anhedonia, exquisite sensitivity, suspiciousness, poverty of ideas, micropsychotic episodes, and circumscribed interests (e.g. bus routes, railways), along with solitariness, nonconformity, and difficulty with emotional relationships.

It is noteworthy that there is significant familial aggregation in many of the pervasive developmental disorders, and that the risk crosses the subtype distinctions (Szatmari, Jones, Zwaigenbaum, & MacLean, 1998). It is also noteworthy that none of the pervasive developmental disorders, *sensu stricto*, has been unequivocally associated with characteristic discrete focal lesions, or recognised encephaloclastic processes (Filipek, 1999), though there have been numerous attempts to correlate neuroimaging features with disorders. In any case, much less is known about lesion-based brain–behaviour correlations or cerebral reorganisation within the developmental (compared to the adult) realm. Moreover the brains of children are more plastic, and may need relatively more injury than is the case with adults for dysfunction to emerge. Finally, as Filipek (1999) observes, in the developmental realm we may have to reverse the normal procedure of starting with a localised lesion and then seeking behavioural consequences; we may now have to start with anomalies of behavioural development and then seek neural correlates.

AUTISM: GENERAL FEATURES

Clearly, the evolving clinical description of pervasive developmental disorders is generally that of autism, with other PDDs being defined largely in terms of how they deviate from autism. Nevertheless, according to an alternative viewpoint, autism is a heterogeneous disorder that may manifest, in various symptomatic ways, in a range (spectrum) of otherwise only loosely related syndromes and as a consequence of various mechanisms. Autism, like other PDDs, usually presents between the ages of 2 and 5 years, in the form of a developmental delay—impairments manifesting as skills failing to appear at the usual developmental milestones. Language delay is often the major initial concern, but there may also be problems with social and play skills and fine motor praxis, with motor delays as in walking (Minshew, 1997). However, in about one quarter of cases there may instead be regression during or after the second year, with loss of previously acquired skills after a period of largely normal development. Sometimes referred to as disintegrative disorder, this condition, as we have seen, is probably not really distinct from true autism. Although the signs and symptoms of autism are most severe in early childhood, thereafter about half of affected individuals make some developmental gains in language, reasoning, and behaviour, though with major difficulties persisting throughout life. In the remaining half, little or no further progress is ever achieved (Minshew, 1997).

Autism must manifest before the age of 3 years, though abnormalities in movement and/or social interest may be apparent even in the first few months of life (Insel, O'Brien, & Leckman, 1999). Three major criteria define the condition:

- Social impairment, manifesting as a lack of social reciprocity, reduced eye contact, failure to recognise the uniqueness of others, lack of empathy, affection, and sharing of enjoyment, impaired development of peer relationships or friendship, social dysfunction, aloofness, shyness, suspiciousness, odd behaviour, inability to confide.
- Communication abnormalities, delayed or incomplete language acquisition, deficits in nonverbal, prelinguistic, and verbal expression, reduced play.
- Stereotyped, restricted, repetitive behaviours and interests, unusual attachments to objects or parts of objects, rigid adherence to routines or rules, mannerisms like hand flapping and echolalia.

In addition to the above triad (see also Piven, 1997; Volkmar, 1996; Waterhouse, Fein, & Modahl, 1996), there is a general rigidity and constriction affecting thought, memory, emotion, attention, and action, impaired imaginary play and cognitive skills (75% function at a retarded level), especially of abstract reasoning. There may, however, be unusual islands of rote memory or visuospatial ability, or even exceptional talents (Bauman & Kemper, 1995). There may also be a tendency towards hypotonia, dyspraxia, and disordered modulation (hyper- or hyposensitivity) of sensory input, and electroencephalographic anomalies and seizures (see later), though no genetic or metabolic markers are known. Nevertheless the disorder is immediately recognisable at a behavioural level by the clinician.

Intellectual disability is in the range of 75–80% (Sigman, Dissanayake, Arbelle, & Ruskin, 1997), leading to a problem in the selection of an appropriate control group for comparison purposes (Fein et al., 1996). Thus normal children of similar *chronological* age (CA) will invariably score higher, while normal children of similar *mental* age (MA) will be immature and unable to control for years of experience. Moreover children with autism vary in mental age, chronological age, and severity of the disorder, and different functions may be expected to manifest at different mental and chronological ages. The tendency is to use learning-disabled or mentally retarded groups (e.g. children with Down syndrome, except that the latter are usually extremely sociable, quite the opposite to autism), though then there is a problem of heterogeneity (Dawson, 1996). Some studies use only high-functioning autism, but then there is the problem of generalisability. Finally, except for individuals with Asperger's disorder, people with autism almost by definition have grossly discrepant verbal and nonverbal intelligence scores, leading to further problems in matching.

The condition may gradually ameliorate over time, tending more perhaps towards a pattern reminiscent of ADHD, especially in initially higher-functioning cases. However, some residual impairment is common: stilted, overpolite interaction, with little empathy and much rigidity and eccentricity (Fein et al., 1996).

RATING SCALES OF SEVERITY

The rating scales of severity for autism are: Autism Behavior Checklist (ABC) (Krug, Arick, & Almond, 1980); Autism Diagnostic Interview (Lord, Rutter, & Le Couteur, 1994); Autism Diagnostic Observation Schedule—Generic (ADOS–G) (Lord, Rutter, & Di Lavore, 1996); Childhood Autism Rating Scale (CARS) (Schopler, Reichter, & Renner, 1988); Asperger's—Autism Spectrum Screening Questionnaire (ASSQ) (Ehlers, Gillberg, & Wing, 1999).

PREVALENCE OF AUTISM

The prevalence of autism is traditionally put at around 5–10 per 10,000 (Gillberg, 1998a; Piven, 1997; Waterhouse, Fein, & Modahl, 1996), depending upon criteria and diagnostic conservatism, with a male:female preponderance of around 4:1 (Volkmar, 1996). Indeed, Fombonne (1999) reviewed 23 epidemiological surveys of autism, encompassing 4 million participants, finding a median prevalence of 5 per 10,000, rising to 7 per 10,000 for surveys conducted most recently, with a minimum estimate of 19 per 10,000 for all forms of PDD; intellectual functioning was within the normal range for 20% of cases. However, Bryson (1996) and Gillberg and Wing (1999) believe that the true prevalence of autism is now more like 1 in 1000. It is possible that early studies used strict criteria based on Kanner's descriptions, though there is no evidence of reliable differences between rates found in studies using DSM-III, DSM-III-R, DSM-IV or ICD-10 criteria. Gillberg and Wing (1999) note that small-population studies consistently give high rates, and ask whether rates have apparently increased (at an annual rate of 3.8%!) due to changes in awareness and ascertainment, or whether migration may have played a role. Thus there is evidence of increased rates of autism in the children of parents who had migrated long distances; such translocation may have led to increased risk of new viral infections during pregnancy, because of a lack of maternal immunity to culture-specific infectious agents. There is also the increased risk of having to marry dysfunctional Asperger males because of problems in finding a native partner. It is also possible that rates have generally risen due to increased survival of premature infants. Gillberg and Wing's (1999) figure of 1 in 1000 refers to childhood autism/autistic disorder only, not to autism spectrum disorders such as Asperger's or disintegrative disorder. With Asperger's, a minimum rate of 24–36 per 10,000 children is proposed, and a full prevalence for the entire autism spectrum of disorders of 4–5 per 1000.

There are more first or only born, due perhaps to reproductive stoppage, with parents opting for no more children, and fourth or later born, suggesting a role for obstetric complications, though Cryan, Byrne, O'Donovan, and O'Callaghan (1996) found no differences between individuals with autism and controls in terms of maternal age or parity, birth order, or low birth weight. An apparently higher prevalence in higher socioeconomic groups may merely reflect a greater readiness to present.

COMORBIDITIES AND CAUSATIVE MEDICAL CONDITIONS

There are always problems of definitions in the concept of comorbidity, of causal/correlational relationships, and of categorisation into possible super- or subordinate relationships (Fein et al., 1996). In particular we need to ask if there is a basic core form of autism, with a range of variants; if there is a common aetiology, generating a range of more or less clearly demarcated outcomes, depending on the specific brain regions affected; or whether, instead, autism is the final common pathway for a range of different pathological events (toxic conditions, viral infections, genetically programmed neurodevelopmental deviation).

Apart from Asperger's disorder, autism is often comorbid with Tourette's syndrome, schizophrenia, OCD, ADHD, anxiety, and affective disorder, especially depression and bipolar disorder, substance abuse and alcoholism, in many cases with disturbed serotonin levels (Bolton, Pickles, Murphy, & Rutter, 1998; Pennington & Ozonoff, 1996; Rapin, 1997). Indeed, stereotypic hand clapping or hand movements, rocking, dipping, or swaying of the body, and verbal repetitions are all also commonly found in Tourette's syndrome. Similarly, affective disturbances are common in autism, with tantrums, fearful, frustrated, or socially withdrawn behaviours, and anhedonia. Patients may be unhappy, agitated, hyperactive, hyper-excited, or aggressive in a cyclic fashion (DeLong, 1999). Autism must be differentially diagnosed from its other comorbidities and also from mental retardation, seizure disorder, developmental receptive language disorder, and developmental coordination disorder. Although there exists considerable *symptomatic* overlap between these disorders and autism, there may be much less *genetic* overlap with early-onset (childhood) schizophrenia, or with depression (Wing, 1997; Rapin 1997). Note, however, that according to DeLong (1999) autism is common in families with histories of major depression, bipolar disorder and OCD. Childhood schizophrenia is characterised by hallucinations and delusions, abnormal affect and loose associations, but involves less intellectual impairment than autism (Fein et al., 1996). With developmental receptive language disorder, there is normal interest in interpersonal relationships and in communicating nonverbally.

Seizures are prominent in autism, reaching 25–33% prevalence, especially in the lowest performers, with high-risk periods in infancy and adolescence. Seizure disorders may be a separate medical condition that nevertheless predispose to the development of autism (Fein et al., 1996).

THEORY OF MIND IN AUTISM

Clearly there can be individuals with autism who are relatively outgoing socially, even talkative, and with comparatively few stereotyped mannerisms. What still labels them is a failure of reciprocity in the domain of social interaction, i.e. problems with personal intimacy, mutuality, and shared interests. Such individuals from a very early age are defective in joint attention skills involving pointing and gaze monitoring, the normal precursors to the development (see below) of a theory of mind. By 2½ years of age normal human infants appear able to understand the specific role played by the eyes in deploying attention in others, a capacity that is shared with other primates, notably the chimpanzees. Povinelli and Eddy (1996) systematically explored how the presence of eyes, direct eye contact, and head orientation and movement affected young chimpanzees' choice of two experimenters from whom to request food. They found that the animals could be selectively attracted to other creatures making direct eye contact with them, or that they exhibited postures or movements that indicated directed attention, though perhaps not necessarily appreciating the mentalistic significance of these behaviours.

Pointing with the index finger is universal to all human cultures, and its emergence in infancy has traditionally been linked with the early development of perspective taking, intersubjectivity, and empathy. Chimpanzees do not, however, readily develop a pointing gesture with the index finger, and without tuition rarely point by gesturing with hands or arms. The "fault" may in fact lie with differences in the resting morphology of the index finger in humans and chimpanzees (Povinelli & Davis, 1994). However, gestural communication is important for the great apes in maintaining close-range social interaction with conspecifics (Bradshaw, 1997); although distal pointing may not be a characteristic of apes in their natural habitat, many animals that have had extensive contact with humans do learn to use referential pointing to direct the attention of humans to distal entities and locations. This includes such species as chimpanzees, bonobos, gorillas, and orang-utans (Call & Tomasello, 1994). Training in some kind of communication, or general acculturation, seems to facilitate both production of pointing responses and comprehension of their significance by others. However, Leavens, Hopkins, and Bard (1996) reported on the spontaneous index finger and other referential pointing in three laboratory chimpanzees who had not received language training, The behaviour generally occurred in the presence of a human, referred to objects in the environment, and appeared intentionally communicative. The authors conclude that referential pointing with the index finger is therefore not necessarily species unique to humans, or dependent on linguistic competence or explicit training. Other indications of possession of a theory of mind in the higher primates include throwing of faeces, spitting, and direction of urine (Butovskaya & Kozintsev, 1996), and coaching offspring in how to crack nuts (Boesch, 1991). The former behaviour, when directed at human care-givers, is often accompanied by an expression of *Schadenfreude*—a mixture of malice, slyness, curiosity, and playfulness; it may even indicate a form of primitive humour, a capacity probably lacking in autism. The ability to teach one's young how to crack nuts would also imply the insight that another is ignorant and must acquire knowledge. It is noteworthy that the mother in such situations typically behaves abnormally slowly, and carefully positions and repositions the objects—nut, "anvil"; and stone or branch, "hammer" (Bradshaw, 1997).

Clearly, the preconditions for and precursors of a theory of mind are present in our closest living primate relatives: shared attention by directed gaze, pointing, coaching of infants, and possibly even humour. Our own species *Homo sapiens* has evolved a complex social milieu that depends on the transmission of information via at least three channels (Voeller, 1996):

- Auditory–vocal, via cries, coos, grunts modulated by prosody—a capacity that emerges in the early months of life.
- Joint attention via directed gaze—a capacity that emerges not much later than the first.
- Visual–facial–gestural—a capacity that precedes both phylogenetically (Bradshaw, 1997) and ontogenetically the appearance of language proper.

The above three channels are crucial for the development of social intelligence—a capacity seemingly compromised in autism, and whose nature is of increasing interdisciplinary interest to neuroscientists, evolutionary theorists, primatologists, developmentalists, and psychiatrists (Happé & Frith, 1999). Social intelligence involves the ability, innate and ontogenetically unfolding, or acquired, to attribute mental states (beliefs or desires) to others, and to use these invisible postulates to explain and predict observable behaviour in others. In normal development, according to Happé and Frith (1999):

- By 12 months, infants spontaneously follow eye gaze, and react to others according to their emotional responses.

- By 15 months, they direct others' attention, and establish joint attention.
- By the second year, they engage in pretend play, suggesting that they can consider another's thoughts.
- By the fourth year, they can appreciate that mental states may differ from reality, and that one person may have different beliefs from another.

While this is not the place to debate modularity of cognitive function (Fodor, 1983; see also Bradshaw, 1997), Happé and Frith (1999) see the capacity, lost in autism, to mentalise, or attribute mental states to be ubiquitous and modular, and to underlie communication, cooperation, pedagogy, play-acting and the whole panoply of Machiavellian intelligence of cheating, deception, and outwitting. In individuals with autism there is early evidence of a lack of joint attention, gaze following, and the triadic coordination of attention between infant, another person, and an object or event. Affected individuals may still be able to employ *imperative* pointing, e.g. for personal needs, but not *declarative* pointing for sharing of interests (Charmon, 1998; Dawson, 1996); here the child seeks to share awareness or experience of an object or event by initiating a bid for joint attention, typically via eye contact. The ability to monitor and regulate another's fixations and attentional directions may be particularly important in the social-affective context. Indeed autistic children show reduced affect in jointly viewing objects and sharing attention with others (Charmon, 1998); the superior temporal sulcus is involved in monitoring gaze direction (see Baron-Cohen & Swettenham, 1997), and mesial temporal regions generally in mediating affect, and both regions are probably affected in autism. Some of the most enduring impairments that may be specific to autism do seem to involve attention monitoring and coordination of attention and affect. Thus children with autism are severely impaired in acts of joint attention, such as gaze switching between an adult and a toy, pointing towards toys within reach, and showing toys to others (Charmon, 1998). Attention monitoring may even be impaired during *imperative* acts such as reaching for an inaccessible object, though impairments in basic requesting or imperative gestures are, as we saw, less dramatic or enduring than in the *declarative* context. Individuals with autism are also poor at coordination of gestures with eye contact, and coordination of gaze with affective displays. We should, however, note (see Happé & Frith, 1999) that although there may be a deficit in the ability of such individuals to influence the behaviour of others via *expressive* gestures, they may still be able to do so by *instrumental* acts and, when older, to deliver messages, give honest answers, and engage in stereotypic small talk. They may be unable to engage in lies or deception in competitive tasks, but can often still perform acts of "sabotage".

When older, individuals with autism clearly have difficulty initiating and sustaining a conversation, and engage in monologues or stereotypic sequences of questions and answers, rather than the normal conversational pattern of give-and-take and chit-chat, with eye contact, gesture, and expression (Fein et al., 1996; Minshew, 1997). There is typically a poor grasp of social causes and effects, inadequate judgement or prediction of a partner's reaction or emotional state, poor comprehension of others' social behaviour, awkward or naive responses and so on. Individuals may appear offensive or rude, and as violating social norms and conventions, when really they are simply extremely deficient in social skills. Such difficulties may reflect problems in recognising human features and behaviour, and in the awareness of other people's mental representations. This may particularly involve a lack of an understanding that others have their own perspectives, knowledge, thoughts, feelings, desires, and beliefs, true or false. Thus affected individuals may be unable to intuit or infer what others think or feel (Frith, 1991).

A classic paradigm (Baron-Cohen & Swettenham, 1997) involves a short story with the simplest of plots: one character who was not present when an object was moved, and so did not know it was in a new location. The subject is asked where the character *thinks* the object is. This false belief test assesses the ability to infer a story character's mistaken belief about a situation. Normal 4-year-olds can correctly infer that the character would think that the object was where the character had last left it, rather than where it actually was, while individuals with autism typically say the character would think the object was where it actually *was*. A typical demonstration involves two dolls: In Sally's (but not Anne's) basket there is a marble. Sally is removed and so cannot "see" Anne "move" the marble from Sally's to her own basket. When Sally is returned, the children are asked where she will look for the marble. Unaffected children claim that Sally will look for it where it was before she left, whereas children with autism say she will look for it where it currently is.

While it is tempting to argue that theory-of-mind deficits may underlie poor pretend or symbolic play, joint visual attention, and other social deficits in autism, this may not be true if affected children show symptoms before the normal emergence of theory of mind in normal children (Green, Fein, Joy, & Waterhouse, 1995). Instead, perhaps, a lack of theory of mind in autism could stem from an earlier failure to attend to social cues, a reliance on superficial features or aspects, or a failure to attend to socially relevant or affective cues, emotions, expressions, gestures, or vocalisations in others.

Children with autism also fail to develop a clear understanding of how physical objects differ from *thoughts* about objects, seeming not to understand that seeing leads to knowing. Thus in another demonstration, when shown two dolls, one of which touches a closed box whereas the other looks inside, they cannot say which doll *knows* what is inside the box. As children with Down syndrome are intensely social and seem able to solve theory-of-mind problems, despite severe intellectual deficit, as indeed also can children with Asperger's disorder who are cognitively high functioning but with autistic characteristics, we can neither argue that a theory of mind is just too hard for individuals with autism, nor that it is primary to that disorder, underlying all other symptoms.

Some individuals with autism can pass first-order false-belief tests (inferring what someone else is thinking), but usually not second-order false-belief tests (understanding what one character thinks *another* character thinks), which normal children can usually do by 5–6 years of age. Other related deficits involve reading the facial expressions of emotion; distinguishing between intentional actions by someone, and accidental happenings; deceiving, or understanding that others can deceive; comprehending metaphor, sarcasm, or irony (all intentionally nonliteral statements); and understanding speech pragmatics (Baron-Cohen & Swettenham, 1997). Thus they respond inappropriately and concretely to requests formulated as "can you open the door" by saying "yes"; they are insensitive to speakers' intentions.

A closely associated problem is a delayed or missing interest in or capacity to undertake symbolic or pretend play with dolls or toys. There is a defective comprehension of a toy's symbolic meaning (e.g. a doll as a possible agent of an action maybe involving another doll), and abnormal or inappropriate use of a toy generally; thus a phone may be used instead as a building brick. Toys may be formally or geometrically arranged, with an intense preoccupation with detail or with their parts or with movement, or with their repetitive, stereotypic manipulation (Gillberg & Coleman, 1996; Minshew, 1997). There may be impaired pretend play involving others, with a failure to imitate or interact. Affected children can rarely cope with team sports or complex, imaginative, or cooperative play. Instead, in individuals with high-functioning autism, there is an obsession with games capitalising on visuospatial or rote memory skills, rather than imagination. Often there are unusual attachments to physical objects, with an interest in their nonfunctional aspects, e.g. elementary sensory aspects of taste, feel, or smell.

Neuroimaging studies with theory-of-mind tasks in normal volunteers indicate activity in the right orbitofrontal cortex, left medial frontal cortex, the superior temporal sulcus, and the amygdala (Baron-Cohen & Swettenham, 1997)—all regions that may participate in a neural circuit supporting the processing involved in theory-of-mind activities. The amygdala, hippocampus, and entorhinal cortex are known to be important for social orienting, attention, and empathy (Dawson, 1996), and bilateral amygdalar lesions in primates can cause autistic-like behaviour (Bauman, 1996). Happé and Frith (1999) review evidence for involvement also of regions around the anterior cingulate and medial frontal cortex, and the temporoparietal junction on the right. The anterior cingulate and temporo-parietal junction are known to be involved in monitoring action and biological movement, which implies the concept of *intentionality* in others. Happé and Frith (1999) speculate whether paracingulate regions may be involved in monitoring one's own thoughts, actions, and feelings, and help form connections between reading one's *own* and *others'* minds. Lesion studies have long shown the importance of temporoparietal regions on the right for an understanding of the pragmatics ("intentionality") of speech, metaphor, and humour (Molloy, Brownell, & Gardner, 1990).

What is peculiar about *social* learning, compared to perceptuomotor learning, is that although one can directly observe one's own limbs, *actions* and so on, one cannot directly observe the consequences of one's own *emotional expressions*, except through *other* people's altered behaviour. However, the development of relevant theory-of-mind capacities is likely to occur (whether acquired or unfolding) fairly late, whereas individuals with autism certainly show very early deficits in social behaviour (Rutter, 1999; Voeller, 1996). Does this mean that theory-of-mind deficits, rather than being fundamental to the autistic syndrome, may be secondary to some other more fundamental social or perceptuomotor deficit? Also, how does one link the language deficits observed in autism, and the motor mani-festations and stereotypies, and obsessions, to theory-of-mind (and cog-nitive) deficits?

LANGUAGE AND AUTISM

Parents' concern on initial presentation typically relates to a lack of expressive language (Volkmar, 1996) . (As Lord & Paul, 1997, observe, if the defining feature of autism is deviant social interaction, and the primary function of language is to mediate social interaction, it is hardly surprising if language is deviant.) Lack of fluent speech by 5 years of age is a poor prognosis for the future. Although autism may not be diagnosable before 3 or 4 years, old videos do suggest early problems in communication, such as reduced responsivity to their own names, and delayed or abnormal stages in language acquisition.

About half of affected children never gain useful communication, or may subsequently and regressively lose it. Those that do learn to speak typically exhibit many peculiarities, e.g. echolalia, pronoun reversal, inappropriate cadence or prosody, extreme literalness, inappropriate expression, and deviant or absent gesture as in nodding assent, raising arms to be picked up, etc. Indeed at a very early age there may be failure of simple gestures like pointing, reaching towards an object, pushing away, or shaking the head. There is developmental delay, or loss, of all forms of language, comprehensional or expressive (Fein et al., 1996). Even with the best of outcomes, there are substantial residual deficits at the level of pragmatics, semantics, satire, irony, humour, or innuendo (Minshew, 1997), reminiscent of clinical deficits after right hemisphere lesions (Molloy, Brownell, & Gardner, 1990). Grammar and syntax, and acquisition and use of grapheme–phoneme correspondence rules are less affected (Green et al., 1995), with form better preserved than content. Individuals with autism tend not to use meaning to guide decoding or production, and are likely to use a limited range of morphemes or words repeatedly, with a poor use of available vocabulary. Interactive conversation is grossly deficient.

Lord and Paul (1997) note also that word use is often idiosyncratic, pedantic, concrete, and peculiar. Affected individuals often treat language segments as unanalysed chunks, and merely repeat them echolalically, often in a nonfunctional and self-stimulatory form. There is reduced initiation of spontaneous speech, together with problems in taking turns or following social rules, inappropriate interruptions, the production of noncontingent utterances, and problems generally with social or referential communication. Deictic terms pose special difficulties, with confusion and interchange of personal pronouns ("I", "you"); similarly "this" and "that", "come" and "go" may be used wrongly, suggesting difficulties in understanding another's perspective and a disturbed concept of self. At a suprasegmental level, intonation and stress patterns are odd, with a monotonous, flat, or sing-song manner. There may be similar, if more subtle, anomalies in the use of language in other family members.

Tager-Flusberg (1996) reviews the anomalies of language in autism in the context of theory-of-mind deficits. Noting that computational (syntax and phonology) and semantic aspects are largely preserved, unlike the pragmatics, he sees many language difficulties as stemming from problems in interpreting the actions of others within a mentalistic framework. Infants with autism may gesture or vocalise to express their needs ("protoimperative gestures"), but do not communicate objects of shared interest ("protodeclarative gestures"). Later, they rarely use language to share information with others, or to ask for new information from others. As they may lack an understanding that people know various different things, they fail to use language as a key route to discovering the contents of other individuals' thoughts; they restrict the use of language primarily to instrumental functions and make little conversation, despite maybe a desire to communicate. Such a thwarted desire may explain the tendency to echolalia, repetitiveness, and stereotypies. The reversal of pronouns (I/you) indicates a lack of understanding of others' perspectives, whereas aprosody and lack of gesture even in high-functioning autistics suggest difficulty in conveying emotion.

Autistic difficulties with communication therefore extend also to the nonverbal domain. Thus affected individuals are defective on the recognition of affect; they have great difficulty recognising the facial, gestural, or vocal expressions of the four basic emotions—happy, unhappy, angry and scared (Fein et al., 1996)—out of all proportion to their performance on other natural-world or object tasks.

REPETITIVE BEHAVIOUR IN AUTISM

Repetitive behaviour is a core and defining feature of the condition, though it is of course also found in other developmental, psychiatric, and neurological conditions, such as Tourette's syndrome, OCD, schizophrenia, and Parkinson's disease, and even, in mild form, in many normal healthy children. In autism, however, it is more severe and longer lasting, in both a chronological and a developmental sense, and circumscribed interests are a particular feature of the disorder. Although repetitive behaviour is commonly defined as behaviour with no obvious goal or function, as Turner (1999) observes it is curious that so much research effort has been expended in attempts to explore possible functions of the behaviour pattern.

A child exhibiting repetitive arm flapping, and who spends prolonged periods aligning toys, dislikes changes in routine, and is fascinated with moving objects or components is easily (though not always correctly) diagnosed as autistic, but the concept of repetitive behaviour may be easier to capture than the term is to define. As an umbrella term, repetitive behaviour refers to behaviours that are linked by repetition, rigidity, invariance, and inappropriateness, including, in autism, spontaneous dyskinesias, stereotyped movements, repetitive manipulations of objects, repetitive self-injurious behaviour, specific object attachments, and obsessive desire for sameness, a repetitive use of language, and narrow and circumscribed interests (Turner, 1999). It may be possible to subdivide this list into two levels of behaviour:

- Lower-level behaviours, involving repetition of movement, such as tics, dyskinesias, stereotyped movements, repetitive manipulation of objects, and repetitive forms of self-injurious behaviour.
- Higher-level and more complex behaviours, such as object attachments, insistence on maintenance of sameness, repetitive language, and circumscribed interests.

Various theories have been proposed to account for such repetitive behaviours, whether or not within the context of autism (Turner, 1999). These include a coping mechanism to modulate levels of arousal or of anxiety, an operant behaviour, an inability to inhibit ongoing behaviour, an inability to generate novel forms of behaviour, a consequence of weak "central coherence", and as a symptom of executive dysfunction. Although we shall encounter (below) the last two ideas as possible general explanations, or descriptions, of autism, we might note at this point that not only do the last two seem to fail in the general context, but also none of the above, on their own, seem adequately to account for repetitive behaviour in particular. Indeed, given the evidence, reviewed elsewhere and throughout this book, for a striatal involvement in repetitive behaviour, it seems appropriate to invoke the frontostriatal pathways for a major role in autistic behaviour.

SUBTYPES OF AUTISM

Wing (1997) proposes that autism be subdivided into three subtypes. Members of the *aloof group* present classical symptoms, cutting themselves off from social contact. They become agitated if in close proximity to others, and reject unsolicited physical or social contact, though they may briefly enjoy rough physical play. They may approach others for food or other bodily needs, or occasionally even seek a cuddle, but once satisfied they move abruptly away without a backward glance. Attachment to parents is minimal, and verbal and nonverbal communication is so impaired that they seem deaf, except that they may respond well to sounds that are significant for them. They may remain mute all their lives, or develop echolalia or reversal of pronouns ("you" for "I"). Speech, with idiosyncratic usage, is employed purely to obtain basic needs or to indulge circumscribed interests. Even in infancy they make few demands for social attention; their babble is limited, they do not point, share, or develop joint referencing. Their eye contact is poor, with poverty of expression or of social gestures, and any speech is monotonous or inappropriate. They have difficulty copying another's actions, and have no pretend or symbolic play. Although they may manipulate or dismantle objects, they show no sign of pretending that toys represent real objects; the normal inner world of imagination is entirely lacking. They fill their time with repetitive, stereotyped activities that totally absorb them for long periods, and after many weeks or months are replaced by others. Their stereotypies tend to be extremely simple and self-directed, e.g. finger flicking, arm flapping, or body rocking. Wing notes that some may dextrously spin objects or twirl a piece of string as if transfixed. When older, they may develop more complex repetitive behaviours, collecting certain unusual kinds of objects or organising them into lines or patterns. They insist on lengthy bedtime rituals, and take exactly the same route to school or shops every day, exhibiting tantrums if disturbed. They may ignore personal safety, although nevertheless exhibiting intense fear of harmless objects or colours. Later, these fears may transform into fascinations. They may experience inexplicable mood swings, weeping, or giggling without apparent cause. They may ignore or become distressed or even fascinated by certain sensations, sensory stimuli, qualities, or actions; they may paradoxically cover their eyes on hearing a loud sound, suggesting the possibility of synaesthesia. They may indulge in inappropriate or embarrassing social behaviours. Although their aloofness and indifference may persist lifelong, they may nevertheless develop special skills in drawing, assembling, calculating, or rote memory—the autistic savant syndrome.

Wing's second, *passive* subtype involves individuals who make no spontaneous approaches except for personal needs, but who nevertheless happily accept others' approaches. They can be induced to engage in games, but normally adopt a passive role. They may copy others' actions, though apparently without a full understanding. Although they exhibit echopraxia and echolalia, their speech is better developed than that of the aloof group, but they still fail to engage in interpersonal communication for pleasure. Although they may possess a large vocabulary with good grammar, they tend to be pedantic, like individuals with Asperger's disorder, with a fascination for long words that are nevertheless used repetitively and confined to a narrow range. There is hardly any imaginative play; the activities of others are merely copied without spontaneity or inventiveness. There are fewer stereotyped or odd responses than in the aloof group, with less resistance to interference to routines. They develop circumscribed interests requiring rote memorisation of masses of facts about a chosen subject, though again there is little intuitive understanding. Subtle verbal jokes are not appreciated, while slapstick humour may be enjoyed. They are generally better behaved and of higher ability than the aloof group, and may cope with normal schooling. Wing notes that if poorly uncoordinated, with circumscribed intellectual interests but reasonable cognitive functions, they may fit the criteria for Asperger's disorder.

Wing's third group is the "*active-but-odd*". These individuals may make spontaneous approaches to others, but in a peculiar, naive, and one-sided fashion. They seek to indulge their circumscribed interests by talking at another person, or by asking questions, rather than for the pleasure of reciprocal social interactions. They may be overly persistent, clingy, unwelcome, or boring. Of all three groups they possess the best speech but it is still delayed, abnormal, repetitive, long-winded, and uncolloquial, with repetition of stored phrases, literal usage, and interpretation, and lack of social conventions. Intonation is monotonous or abnormally inflected, with poor breath control, abnormal gestures, and inappropriate eye contact. Play is repetitive or stereotyped and fails to achieve full pretend status. Individuals are typically keen on repetitive computer games; they play with remarkable accuracy but little interest in or comprehension of the games' true meaning.

They may possess a wide range of circumscribed interests—timetables, calendars, race winners, genealogies, etc.—which are pursued relentlessly and exclusively. Motor coordination is often poor, with movements clumsy and puppet-like. Behaviour is socially inappropriate, with temper tantrums and oversensitivity to criticism, and even a tendency to aggression, theft, arson, or other antisocial behaviours.

NEUROPSYCHOLOGICAL PERFORMANCE PROFILE

Most individuals with autism exhibit considerable cognitive impairment, to the extent that the disorder is in some respects a juvenile analogue of the dementia typically associated with ageing. Only 20–25% score within normal or near-normal ranges, one third have no speech, and half have significant behavioural, psychiatric, or medical problems, particularly with respect to aggression, depression, anxiety, epilepsy, and sensory impairment (Bryson, 1996). There are, however, some high-functioning individuals, with intact or superior attentional processes, and relatively normal memory, visuospatial, and even (at perhaps a simple level) language, despite impairments in social behaviour, skilled motor performance, and complex language, reasoning, and memory tasks (DeLong, 1999).

Neurobehavioural theories of autism in the past have variously hypothesised core deficits in sensory or perceptual processes, attention, anterograde memory, auditory information processing, higher-order memory processes, conceptual reasoning ability, or executive function (Minshew, Goldstein, & Siegal, 1997). It is true that some autistic deficits may stem from social or intellectual deprivation secondary to the disorder, and that deficiencies tend to occur when *symbolic* processing is involved. However, there seem to be no gross perceptual deficits (Sigman et al., 1997), despite popular reliance on various remedial fads such as auditory desensitisation, special eyeglasses, vestibular stimulation, skin-brushing to decrease tactile defensiveness etc. (Rapin, 1997). There does seem to be blunting of the experience of pain and pleasure and problems in temporal sequencing. However, the general neuropsychological profile is of a performance IQ that exceeds a verbal IQ, with good performance on Block Design and Object Assembly tests, and on spatial organisation, but with poorer performance on sequencing and abstraction (Sigman et al., 1997). The uneven profile of abilities extends to good rote memory and visuospatial skills, but with problems with abstract comprehension, problem solving, and complex information processing, reasoning, and cognitive flexibility. Thus (and see later) a deficit is apparent in executive functions (working memory, balancing probabilities, holding and shifting set, allocating resources, and attention to competing stimuli) (see, for example, Rapin, 1997). Not surprisingly, on verbal scales individuals with autism do better on Digit Span (which assesses attention and short-term memory) and worse on Comprehension scales (which assess social knowledge). Attentional overselectivity, with an abnormally narrow attentional focus, results in difficulty in shifting attention between modalities, though attention can be sustained, especially if appropriately enforced or if it coincides with an area of specialist interest. Earlier, there was debate as to whether individuals with autism were primarily *hypo-* or *hyper*aroused (and so inclined to gate out all stimuli threatening further arousal) (see, for example, Fein et al., 1996). The debate seems to have been resolved in the direction of a hypersensitivity to novelty, with a resultant narrowing of the attentional focus, and stimulus overselectivity. In this respect there are clear similarities to OCD.

Minshew et al. (1997), in a major study, found that individuals with autism were impaired in skilled motor performance, complex memory, and complex language and reasoning tasks, with intact or superior performance in attention, simple memory, simple language, and visuospatial domains. They conclude in favour of selective impairment in complex, nonvisuo-spatial processing, involving especially the *late* stages of information processing, which, they believe, could even help explain deficits in the social or theory-of-mind realms. They even reject specific problems in set or attention shifting or cognitive flexibility, and, by implication, frontal or executive function.

Executive functions

These functions, ascribed to the basal ganglia and frontal lobes (Pennington & Ozonoff, 1996), involve the ability to maintain appropriate problem-solving set for the attainment of future goals. They require the ability to defer or inhibit responses, a strategic plan of action sequences, and a mental representation of the task. They involve attention, reasoning, problem solving, set maintenance and shifting, interference control, inhibition of competing processes, integration across space and time, planning, working memory, and selection of appropriate responses in the face of competing and contextually inappropriate alternatives. Clearly fluid intelligence is more important in these respects than crystallised. Versions of the Wisconsin Card Sorting Test are frequently used to test executive functions. When sorting cards according, for example, to colour, and the examiner shifts to shape, which the subject must determine from the changed nature of the feedback, "right", or "wrong", prefrontal patients typically exhibit excessive perseveration and the inability to employ feedback. Indeed prefrontal patients may generally exhibit executive deficits in goal-directed behaviour in novel contexts, with competing but erroneous response alternatives. Patients may understand what is required, but fail because of perseveration or impersistence, lack of initiative, or intrusions of task-irrelevant behaviour.

Pennington and Ozonoff (1996), in a meta-analysis of studies of autism, find that individuals with autism are in fact badly affected in executive functions, with problems in cognitive flexibility more than in inhibitory control. They find particular problems with the Wisconsin Card Sorting Test and the Tower of Hanoi task, and argue that affected individuals' difficulties with theory-of-mind tasks stem from their commonalities with executive function tasks. These commonalities involve the ability to disengage from immediate environmental cues to drive behaviour instead via internal rules (a deficit apparent also in Parkinson's disease, another basal ganglia–frontal lobe disorder; see Georgiou et al., 1993), and also the ability to shift between competing alternatives, cognitive sets, or personal attentional perspectives. In fact individuals with autism generally seem to act inappropriately in their environment, fixating on apparently irrelevant stimuli to the exclusion of all else, and perseverating on self-initiated tasks. Perseveration stereotypies, and an insistence on sameness, are reminiscent of the effects of damage to closely associated striatal circuits. However, just as cognitive deficits in autism are probably not just due to language impairment or general retardation, so too an executive system deficit (see Russell, 1998) on its own cannot fully explain the social deficits.

Indeed, if, as we have seen, executive function deficits are also present in other neurodevelopmental disorders, such as Tourette's syndrome and ADHD, we are left with a question of "discriminant validity" (Ozonoff & Jensen, 1999); how can disorders differing in behavioural phenotype share the same cognitive underpinnings? How *useful* are tasks of executive function in these situations? One approach is to *parse* executive functions into specific components, such as planning, flexibility, and inhibition, to see if different disorders demonstrate different executive profiles. Ozonoff and Jensen (1999) found that children with autism had particular problems with flexibility and planning, as evidenced by their performance on the Wisconsin Card Sorting Task and Tower of Hanoi, but (unlike children with ADHD who were unimpaired on these tasks but performed badly on the Stroop) they had few problems of inhibitory control (Stroop).

Central coherence

Individuals with autism are either oblivious to features of their environment, or overfocused on them or overselective in their attention, with a preoccupation upon local detail while missing the more global aspects and interrelationships (Jolliffe & Baron-Cohen, 1999). Thus they may fail to attend to normally salient or meaningful aspects, while focusing on the unusual. They often score highly on the Embedded Figures or Block Design tests, again reflecting a preoccupation with parts over wholes (Baron-Cohen & Swettenham 1997). Nor do they use context to disambiguate the pronunciation of ambiguous words like "tear" ("tear in the eye" vs. "tear in the paper"). Baron-Cohen and Swettenham see this as a deficit in "central coherence"—a failure to integrate information into a broader or more global context. Happé (1999) takes this argument further, claiming that autism may even be seen as a form of preferred cognitive style, rather than as a *deficit*, with consequent assets of a savant nature in mathematics, music, drawing, rote memory, and visuospatial tasks. This cognitive style is biased towards local (rather than global) processing. Normally, we prefer to operate, at least initially, at a global or contextual level, pulling information together to address the overall significance, often at the expense of memory for detail. This "central coherence" is weakened in autism, with processing focused on detail and parts at the expense of the global configuration and contextual meaning. Further support for this idea comes from patients' reduced susceptibility to illusions such as the Titchener Circles (where the presence of surrounding circles normally affects one's ability to judge the size of an inner circle), reduced susceptibility to visually induced apparent motion, local interference in local–global tasks, decreased (compared to normal) performance decrement with inverted (compared to upright) faces, and, as we saw above, unusually good performance on embedded figures (see Figure 8.1). We too (Rinehart et al., in press b) have found that children and adolescents with high-functioning autism and Asperger's disorder, when presented with local and global configurations consisting of congruent and incongruent stimuli (see Figure 8.2), were slower at responding globally when there was local incongruence. Moreover individuals with autism (but not Asperger's disorder) were very slow at shifting attention from a local to a global set (Rinehart et al., in press c). However, it is unlikely that the phenomenon of a deficit in central coherence is central to autism, any more than might be the case with deficits in executive function, or theory of mind.

Memory

In autism, procedural memory typically outperforms declarative, often with good preservation of habit and nonverbal memory. Thus in some respects affected individuals resemble animals with hippocampal lesions—increased general activity, motor stereotypies, reduced environmental exploration and responsivity to novel stimuli when the familiar is present, perseveration and impaired error reduction in learning and memory tasks (Fein et al., 1996). Although one could instead perhaps appeal to frontostriatal deficits, it is clear that autism is not a developmental amnesic syndrome. Indeed exceptional islands of ability ("savant syndrome", hypermnesia) may manifest in rote, verbal, musical, or visuospatial memory, calendrical and mathematical

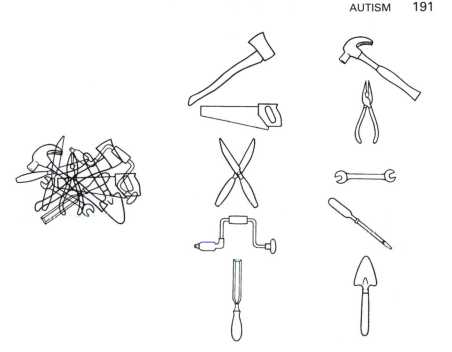

Figure 8.1.   Autistic individuals may be superior at "disembedding" outline drawings of objects when presented in overlapping or overlying format.

calculation and art (Treffert, 1988). Affected individuals may be able to draw a scene with amazing precision after a single brief viewing, play music after a single hearing without a score or knowing musical notation, or read aloud at a very early age (hyperlexia), though typically without compre-hension.

Very superior calendrical, mathematical, or similar performance (e.g. with timetables, athletics records, or horse-race winners) involves a ritual-istic or obsessional preoccupation with a limited aspect of the environment, and a knowledge of rules, regularities, and redundancies that may be tacit, implicit, unformalised, and unconscious. Indeed calendrical calculators are not generally consciously aware of any relevant algorithm, though their need for repetitive behaviours may facilitate the tacit acquisition of requisite skills. Individuals with OCD, Tourette's syndrome, autism, and savant syndrome all share the same repetitive, obsessive stereotyped behaviour. So are such unusual talents the consequence of the overdevelopment of skills due to perseverative attention, some form of hippocampal hyperfunction, or the redirection of cortical association areas to new functions? In the latter context, there are reports (Schlaug, Jäncke, Huang, & Steinmetz, 1995) that the left planum temporale (a structure known to be extremely important in

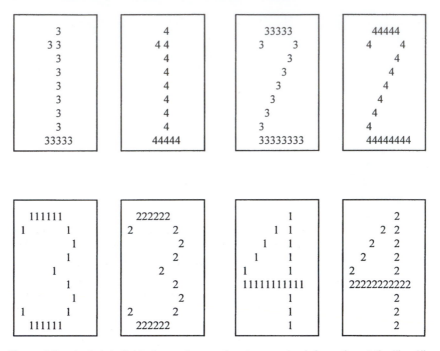

Figure 8.2. Autistic individuals may be superior at processing information at the "local" level (here, the small, constituent numbers) than at the "global" level (the larger figures constituted by the smaller characters).

speech) is enlarged in professional musicians, and especially in those with absolute pitch, though of course we cannot be certain about the direction of any causality. Absolute pitch, while extremely rare in the general population, is relatively common among professional musicians (Sacks, 1995) and among individuals with autism may reach an incidence of 1 in 20; among the savant population, more than one third are musically gifted, and all musical savants seem to have absolute pitch (Rimland & Fein, 1988; Treffert, 1988). We shall return later in this chapter to a more detailed analysis of savant phenomena generally.

NEUROPATHOLOGY AND PATHOPHYSIOLOGY

While there is no specific biological marker for autism, there tends to be an increased incidence of physical anomalies, persistent primitive reflexes, EEG abnormalities, seizures, and neurological soft signs (Volkmar, 1996). As we shall see, abnormalities are sometimes reported in the cerebellum, prefrontal cortex, and in the medial temporal lobe, but perhaps not such as to explain the range of behavioural and neuropsychological abnormalities of the disorder (Piven, 1997). Thus, just as in schizophrenia, no one brain structure can be singled out as defective, suggesting the possibility of a distributed abnormality, maybe at the level of the dendritic architecture. Indeed there is some evidence (see later) of reduced complexity of dendritic branching in the hippocampus and of reduced size of the perikaryon (Fombonne, 1997), increased packing density in the limbic system, and reduced numbers of Purkinje cells in the cerebellum (Courchesne, 1997; Piven, 1997). There is, however, also separate evidence of *enlarged* brain and head size, contrary to what might be expected with retardation. Thus Bailey et al. (1998a) found four of six autistic brains to be megalencephalic, with increased cell numbers (reduced apoptosis? see later) rather than reduced neuronal density. Kemper and Bauman (1998) similarly found increased brain weight in children with autism under 12 years of age, an effect that reversed in adult patients. Filipek (1999) notes that increased head circumference is present in both children and adult patients, the majority exceeding the 50th percentile, a phenomenon that, however, may not be present at birth, perhaps appearing shortly afterwards. Fombonne et al. (1999) found 17% of 126 individuals with autism were *macro*cephalic, especially the *older*, whereas 15% were *micro*cephalic, especially those with other associated medical disorders; there may therefore be a bimodal distribution.

In the hippocampus, subiculum, entorhinal cortex, amygdala, and mammillary bodies there are reports of increased cell density and reduced dendritic arborisation and neuronal size (Kemper & Bauman, 1998); experimental lesions in the limbic circuit in animals lead to impaired social interaction, hyperexploratory behaviour, inability to recognise or remember the significance of examined objects, and altered fear responses—all autistic-like behaviours. In the anterior cingulate there is a less distinct laminar structure. Despite absence of gross brain abnormalities or obvious gliosis, this is all suggestive of a dysgenetic rather than of a destructive process. Haznedar et al. (1997) likewise found that on the right side the anterior cingulate was reduced in volume and less metabolically active in patients. In the cerebellum and inferior olives there are reduced numbers of Purkinje cells, especially in the posterolateral neocerebellar cortex and adjacent archicerebellar cortex (Kemper & Bauman, 1998), perhaps reflecting persistence of a fetal olivary–dentate circuit, which may typically regress after 30 weeks gestation (Rapin, 1999). The cerebellum and prefrontal cortex are of course extensively linked via the fronto-ponto-cerebello-thalamo-cortical loop, such that frontal anomalies would be expected in autism. There are indeed reports (Giedd & Castellanos, 1997), from functional imaging studies, of impaired interactions between frontal and parietal regions, and between frontoparietal regions and the neostriatum and thalamus (Filipek, 1999); these regions are involved in attention—a capacity known to be dysfunctional in autism. There is also evidence of frontal hypoperfusion, especially on the right (Pennington & Ozonoff, 1996), and of abnormal or reduced behavioural or electrical asymmetries (Fein et al., 1996). These observations, together with EEG abnormalities associated with temporal lobe seizures, and reduced P3 amplitudes (the P3 reflects the stage of cognitive information processing; see Burack et al., 1997), all help explain deficits in attention, cognitive skills, and language; they would be compatible with a neurodevelopmental disorder of reduced apoptosis (Minshew, 1997) in the second trimester, as in schizophrenia.

AUTISM AS A NEURODEVELOPMENTAL DISORDER

The medial temporal lobe and limbic anomalies, on the basis of lesion studies in animals, would also help explain certain of the emotional, motivational, and memory findings in autism, the hyperexploratory behaviour, the severely impaired social interactions, the motor stereotypies, the loss of fear of normally aversive stimuli, the withdrawal from previously rewarding social interactions, the compulsive and indiscriminate examination of objects, and the reduced ability to attach meaning to them (Bauman & Kemper, 1995). Lesions of the amygdala in infant monkeys can produce poor social skills *later* in development—a "growing in" to symptoms, as in autism—along with (in conjunction with hippocampal damage) stereotypies, tantrums in novel situations, a lack of eye contact, and cognitive deficit. Indeed, the amygdala is known to be of fundamental importance in the recognition of faces, facial emotions, and affect (LeDoux, 1996).

The general picture therefore is that autism, like schizophrenia, is a neurodevelopmental disorder, maybe of apoptosis rather than of cell migration, though it should be noted that in the fifth week of gestation neurogenesis is under way in the cerebellum, and shortly after in the limbic regions and cortex generally (Courchesne, 1997); this period may represent the window of vulnerability. Regulatory genes guide the formation of brain structures, laying down and pruning by apoptosis, and timing synaptic connectivity especially in regulatory circuits such as the cortico-striato-thalamo-cortical loops.

AUTISM AS A MOVEMENT DISORDER

Although there is as yet comparatively little direct evidence of striatal involvement in autism, though see Siegel et al. (1992), some studies find that parkinsonian characteristics may be present. Thus in addition to obsessiveness, motor stereotypies, and ritualistic compulsive behaviour, the gait may be parkinsonian, with reduced stride length, increased stance time, reduced upper limb movement, markedly flexed elbows, bradykinesia, and postural abnormalities (Damasio & Maurer, 1978). Other possibly parkinsonian features in autism include dystonia of the extremities, involuntary dyskinesia of the mouth and extremities, abnormalities of muscle tone, rigidity, hypertonia, and problems in handling two motor tasks at once. However, Hallett et al. (1993) find gait velocity and step length to be normal in people with autism, and instead argue for a disturbance of the cerebellum. We (Rinehart, Bradshaw, Brereton, & Tonge, in press a) find that individuals with autism and Asperger's disorder, in a simple motor reprogramming task, have atypical movement *preparation*, with an intact ability to *execute* movement.

Leary and Hill (1996) note that studies of autism generally treat possible movement anomalies in autism in the context of a socially interpreted situation or of compromised volition, rather than in terms of a possible underlying akinesia or bradykinesia that might affect spontancity of interactions. Thus rather than addressing possible neurological symptoms, e.g. abnormal posture or tone, or slowness, such terms as "prefers to . . .", "fails to . . .", "unusual interest in . . .", or "lack of spontaneous seeking to share enjoyment" are employed. Movement disturbances (inadequate or excess movements) are present in many syndromes, and may stem from a range of pathologies; they may affect movement dynamics such as starting, executing (speed, control, rate, rhythm, coordination), continuing, stopping, combining, or switching movements. Movements, whether simple or complex, may reflect changes in attention, consciousness, or motivation. Defining movement disturbances as an interference in their regulation or efficiency that cannot be accounted for solely by paralysis or weakness, Leary and Hill (1996) find the following evidence of movement disturbance in autism:

- Apraxia or dyspraxia, in difficulty with motor planning and movement sequencing.
- Clumsiness, problems of gross motor coordination.
- Abnormalities of gait or posture.
- Akinesia, bradykinesia, dyskinesia, hyperkinesia.
- Stereotypies, tics, mannerisms (arm flapping, spinning, rocking).
- Catatonic traits.
- Repetitive movements.
- Abnormal tone.
- Exaggerated quality of movement.
- Choreiform or athetoid movements.

All these phenomena strongly suggest at least some involvement of basal ganglia and frontostriatal mechanisms in autism, though we must not lose sight of the contribution of other brain areas—frontotemporal, parietal, limbic, and cerebellar.

Just as schizophrenia may be apparent in the juvenile years, long before clinical diagnosis, if old home videos are carefully examined, so too autistic disturbances of movement may be detectable by 4–6 months of age, or even at birth (Teitelbaum et al., 1998). In 17 later-diagnosed children with autism, movement disorders varied from child to child: shape of mouth, and in some or all of the milestones of development, such as lying, righting, sitting, crawling, or walking. The authors conclude that movement disturbances are intrinsic to autism, are present at birth, and can be used to diagnose autism in the first few months of life; they also note that such movement disturbances in autistic children typically occur on the *right* side of the body, whereas those reported in schizophrenia in infancy typically occur on the *left* side. Baranek (1999) in a similar retrospective video study on the possible prediction of autism during infancy found a range of subtle symptoms to be present by 9–12 months:

- Poor visual orientation/attention (nonsocial).
- Prompted/delayed response to name.
- Excessive mouthing of objects.
- Social touch aversions.

It would be interesting, and possibly profitable clinically, to determine whether this retrospective video technique, so apparently successful in predicting subsequently developing autism and schizophrenia, can be applied to any of the other frontostriatal neurodevelopmental disorders. Obvious candidates are ADHD, and Tourette's syndrome, though depression and OCD perhaps should not be ignored.

GENETICS OF AUTISM

Although the heritability of autism has been calculated at more than 90%, the mechanism of inheritance is unknown (Folstein, Bisson, Santangelo, & Piven, 1998). Reproductive stoppage is the phenomenon whereby having one such child influences a couple's later reproductive decisions, in the direction of fewer children, thereby biasing the statistics used in calculating family risk (Szatmari et al., 1998). However, as only about 3% of families with autism have more than one affected child, and the recurrence risk for a family to have a second child who meets the criteria for autism is only 6–8% (higher if the proband is female than if male), clinicians did not initially suspect that the condition was inherited (Folstein et al., 1998). Yet this value is between 100 and 200 times the rate expected by chance, given a prevalence of the core autism phenotype of around 4 per 10,000 (though see earlier). Rutter (1999) and Insel et al. (1999) calculate figures of between 60 and 100 times chance baseline.

Twin studies show a 75% or higher concordance rate in monozygotic pairs, with a dizygotic concordance rate less than 20% (Fein et al., 1996; Pennington & Ozonoff, 1996; Piven, 1997). Heritability is therefore high, but clearly some room is left for environmental factors (Rapin, 1999), perhaps an inherited susceptibility to certain deleterious environmental influences, and the numbers militate against the likelihood of finding a single causative gene; conditions inherited in a Mendelian fashion through the action of only one gene usually have a higher recurrence risk for siblings and a higher proportion of concordant dizygotic twins (Folstein et al., 1998). Thus the recurrence risk for recessive disorders both for siblings and for dizygotic twins is 25%, and in dominant conditions it is 50%. Szatmari et al. (1998) reject any simple form of Mendelian transmission (autosomal recessive or dominant, or X-linked recessive); the recurrence risk to relatives is far too low, the gender ratio is inconsistent with autosomal transmission, and evidence of father-to-son transmission is inconsistent with X-linked transmission. They conclude that there is no simple one-to-one correlation between genotype and phenotype, and propose a model of incomplete penetrance with variable expression. Thus family studies reveal that "unaffected" members, especially males (Bailey et al., 1998b) are often characterised by a range of cognitive and social anomalies; these milder subclinical autistic traits include communication, learning and language deficits, delayed speech, mental retardation, lack of empathy, impaired make-believe and social play, conversational impairment, emotional unresponsiveness, obsessive and stereotyped behaviour, mood and bipolar disorder, schizoaffective personality, and tic disorder (Bolton, Pickles, Murphy, & Rutter, 1998). Thus Folstein et al. (1999) found that parents and siblings of autistic probands scored lower on the WAIS-R Full Scale and Performance IQs and on pragmatic language function, and often had a history of language-related difficulties. Family members may appear eccentric, odd, original, rigid, aloof, awkward, hypersensitive to criticism, pedantic, anxious or depressed, with few friends, but with pragmatic language deficits and executive dysfunctions (Bauman & Kemper, 1995)—all perhaps *formes frustes* of autism; they may also display a fascination for fire, explosives, violence and criminality, and a raised tendency, if students, to undertake studies in the physical or computing sciences or engineering, rather than the arts (Baron-Cohen et al., 1998).

The model proposed by Szatmari et al. (1998) thus involves several genes acting independently, conferring susceptibility (to one or more possible environmental factors), and leading to a heterogeneous presentation in a spectrum of related disorders and a range of severity. Indeed there is an excess of other developmental disorders in autistic families (DeLong, 1999; Rapin, 1999; Rutter, 1999), including major depression, bipolar disorder, Tourette's syndrome, schizophrenia, and OCD. Inheritance may therefore be polygenic, and in fact autism has now been linked to anomalies on all but two chromosomes (Gillberg, 1998b), with partial tetrasomy on chromosome 15 looking increasingly likely (International Molecular Genetic Study of Autism Consortium, 1998; Rutter, 1999). Thus DeLong (1999) also concludes that various studies implicate regions on chromosome 15, including a marker in the vicinity of the GABA-A receptor subtype gene, which is also related to uni- and bipolar disorder. The gonosomes and chromosomes 5, 8, 13, 17, and 18 also appear promising candidates in the search for the gene loci of autism.

Although the behavioural phenotype of autistic spectrum disorders clearly can extend, as shown by the family studies, to other PDDs, and the genetic susceptibility would therefore appear to be mediated by more than one locus (International Molecular Genetic Study of Autism Consortium, 1998), affective disorders per se may not constitute part of the autism phenotype. Indeed Bolton et al. (1998) found that autism and affective disorder did not usually co-occur. Thus the characteristics of relatives that were associated with a predisposition to autism-like behaviour (male sex, siblings) differed from those that were associated with a predisposition to affective disorders (female sex, parent). Likewise the proband characteristics that predisposed relatives to autistic-like behaviours differed from those proband characteristics that predisposed relatives to affective disorders. Bolton et al. observe that the fact that both autistic behaviours and affective disorders were familial, while the liabilities to their familiality were not correlated, further supports the view that affective disorders do not con- stitute part of the broader phenotype of autism. Whatever the reason for the finding that there is an increased familial aggregation of affective disorders in the relatives of families with autism, it cannot therefore just be because depression is part of a broader autism phenotype. All this underscores the heterogeneous nature of autism, a final common pathway for various aetiological processes, genetic as well as environmental. The latter may include viral, toxic, and pre- and perinatal problems; thus there is reported to be a high incidence of obstetric problems in autism, including breech delivery, low birthweight, low Apgar score, increased levels of bilirubin, respiratory distress, bleeding in pregnancy, and maternal infection (Fein et al., 1996; Szatmari et al., 1998). Thus season-of-birth effects may operate as in schizophrenia (Bryson, 1996). As Karmiloff-Smith (1998) observes, development involves contributions from both genes and environment, and is not merely the result of predetermined or probabilistic epigenesis. The environment itself plays a role in shaping the developing organism, which in turn can influence its own environment. Thus there is a three-way inter- action between genes, environment, and the developing child, who modifies his/her own environment, and selects from it.

In a recent review, Comi et al. (1999) note that autism shares many characteristics of autoimmune disorders, including a familial predisposition, associated immunological abnormalities, a relationship with viruses, and a boy : girl ratio of 4 or 5 : 1. Autoimmune dysfunction of course involves the complex interaction of genetic (vulnerability) and environmental (trigger) factors. Various immune abnormalities may in fact be evident in autistic children including:

- A lower percentage of helper-induced lymphocytes, and a lower percentage of lymphocytes expressing IL-2 receptors following mitogenic stimulation.
- Various immune imbalances in the numbers and functions of T-cells, activated T-cells, B-cells, complement, and depressed natural killer cell function.
- Antibodies to myelin-based proteins.

There is also an association of autism with the major histocompatibility complex, and an increased frequency of the extended haplotype B44-SC30-DR4 in individuals with autism. Also associated with autism is the null allele of the C4B complement protein gene, and the third hypervariable region (HVR-3) of certain DRBI alleles, both known to be part of the ancestral haplotype B44-SC30–DR4.

Comi et al. (1999) go on to report, in an empirical study, an increased incidence of autoimmune diseases (especially rheumatoid arthritis), and a *decreased* incidence of allergies, in mothers of children with autism. Their procedures eliminated the possibility of hearsay or biased report. Indeed, they reported a *dose* effect on the inherited risk for autism, such that individuals with two or more family members with autoimmune disorders were twice as likely to present with autism; those with at least three family members with autoimmune disease were 5.5 times as likely to have autism, whereas those whose mothers had autoimmune disorders were 8.8 times as likely to be affected.

Such familial clustering is an epidemiological phenomenon, which suggests either inheritance of genetic features, an environmental effect, or both. As Comi et al. (1999) note, genetic predisposition to autoimmune disease is complex and likely to be polygenic. Studies so far have implicated a role for major histocompatibility complex genes, genetically determined complement deficiencies, and genes regulating apoptosis and related cell-signalling pathways. The finding of relationships between familial rheumatoid arthritis and autism squares with the observation that the major histocompatibility complex third hypervariable region sequences 1 and 2 are associated both with autism and rheumatoid arthritis. Although autism is clearly a polygenic disorder, one of the important genes could lie on the X chromosome, thus explaining the 4 : 1 male : female sex ratio; if the effects of this gene were modified in females, this could cause an increased prevalence of autoimmune disease in mothers of autistic probands. The latter may inherit a genetic disposition to autoimmunity, which, in conjunction with appropriate environmental factors, could lead to a period of transient neurological inflammation during an initial period of prenatal development or postnatal apoptosis. Serotonin may even be implicated in this process, given its known impact on both central nervous system development and the autoimmune system.

NEUROCHEMISTRY OF AUTISM

Assays of neurotransmitters and their metabolites have been made of blood and cerebrospinal fluid, in search of possible aberrations of synthesis, metabolism, or receptor function. Serotonin, dopamine, noradrenaline, and the peptides have all been studied (Fein et al., 1996).

Serotonin

Serotonin (5-hydroxytryptamine, 5-HT) is an important regulator and modulator, and is especially significant in the contexts of memory, learning, social processes, sensory and motor function (all of which are compromised in autism), as well as in sleep, mood, temperature, and appetite regulation (Cook & Leventhal, 1996). Indeed individuals with autism may also suffer from sleep and eating disorders and abnormal circadian rhythms. Serotonergic projections from the midbrain raphe nuclei ascend to the entire cortex. Whole blood and plasma levels of serotonin, and its principal metabolite 5-hydroxyindoleacetic acid (5-HIAA) in urine and cerebrospinal fluid, have been studied (for review see Fein et al., 1996). Increased 5-HT levels (hyperserotonaemia) in whole blood, plasma, and platelets in probands and relatives are robust findings, suggesting a marker for genetic liability, though these effects may also occur in other disorders. Platelet effects may reflect systemic 5-HT receptor dysfunction and/or overactive 5-HT synthesis, though the latter hypothesis tends to be discounted. The absence of 5-HT anomalies in the cerebrospinal fluid may suggest that autistic hyperserotonaemia is purely peripheral or an epiphenomenon; however, the clinical efficacy of selective serotonin reuptake inhibitors (SSRIs) such as fenfluramine, with reduction of 5-HT blood levels and behavioural amelioration (improvements in hyperactivity, stereotypies, and inattentiveness, rather than in social or cognitive function) do suggest central nervous system involvement. Similarly the precursor of 5-HT, tryptophan, may worsen the condition, especially the rocking, toe walking, whirling, flapping, pacing, self-hitting, and other motor stereotypies (Cook & Leventhal, 1996).

Moreover 5-HT may be important in developmental neuropathology in the hippocampus, amygdala, and cerebellum—regions associated with autism—and its receptors are expressed in these regions, especially in the fetal brain. Thus 5-HT content, uptake sites, and receptor binding are all higher in the developing brain, and decline before puberty; indeed, in addition to acting as a neurotransmitter, 5-HT plays a major role in corticogenesis, modulating the spread and branching of thalamocortical axons (Chugani et al., 1999; DeLong, 1999). Serotonergic axons have direct inhibitory synapses on to thalamocortical branches during cortical development, which seem to inhibit neurite growth and modulate transmission of action potentials. Moreover a disruption of synaptic connectivity in sensory cortex can result from experimental increase or decrease of brain 5-HT before puberty. Thus 5-HT acts also as a trophic or differentiation factor. Chugani et al. (1999) find that in normal children 5-HT synthesis capacity is more than twice that of adult values until 5 years of age, when it declines towards adult values; in children with autism, it gradually builds up between 2 and 5 years of age to one and a half times normal adult values. Thus normal children undergo a period of high brain 5-HT synthesis during childhood, a developmental process that is disrupted in autism. DeLong (1999) suggests that with 5-HT deficiency there may be excess axonal spreading and neuropil growth (which may explain the brain enlargement reported in autism). There may also be an abnormality in the dentato-thalamo-cortical pathway from the cerebellum (thought also to be implicated in autism) to the cortex, due to excess 5-HT synthesis in the dentate. Thus there is evidence (Kemper & Bauman, 1998) of degenerating dentate neurones in older individuals with autism, and a reduced number of Purkinje cells in the cerebellar cortex.

Finally, animal studies show increased central nervous system levels of 5-HT in autistic-like behaviours, such as a restricted range of activity, an avoidance of novel situations, an inhibited startle reflex, and disrupted attachment behaviour.

Dopamine

Dopamine agonists in animals can also lead to stereotypies, abnormal social relationships, and hyperactivity, whereas neuroleptics such as haloperidol can ameliorate them (Anderson & Hoshino, 1997). Dopamine is important in motor function and cognition, as well as in reward mechanisms, emotion, and selective attention. Fein et al. (1996) review studies of dopamine and its metabolite homovanillic acid (HVA) in plasma, platelets, cerebrospinal fluid, and urine, and note conflicting findings. However, neuroleptics (haloperidol, pimozide) can ameliorate autistic symptoms, such as abnormal speech, social unrelatedness, stereotypies, inattention, and hyperactivity, though at the cost of unwanted parkinsonian dyskinesias, whereas stimulants (dopamine agonists such as amphetamine) exacerbate them. Moreover self-stimulatory behaviour, an absence of interest in conventionally gratifying pursuits, and a resistance to conditioning all implicate mesolimbic and mesocortical dopamine.

Noradrenaline

Noradrenaline is synthesised from dopamine. This catecholamine regulates arousal, attention, activity levels, anxiety, responsivity to stress, memory and learning. Clonidine, an α_2-noradrenergic agonist, may ameliorate autistic symptoms. Central nervous system measurements have been made of noradrenaline's primary metabolite 3-methoxy-4-hydroxyphenylethylene glycol (MHPG), along with plasma, platelet, and urine levels of noradrenaline and MHPG with, according to Fein et al. (1996), inconsistent findings.

Neuropeptides

Neuropeptides such as oxytocin and vasopressin are nine amino acid sequences, synthesised in the hypothalamus, and released to the blood stream from the posterior pituitary (neurohypophysis). These two closely related nonapeptides are involved in reproductive behaviour in ancestral species (Insel et al., 1999); they now act as neurotransmitters, projecting widely in the central nervous system, especially the amygdala and hippocampus. Their receptors are developmentally regulated and more fully expressed in the immature brain; both affect neurodevelopment, especially in the cerebellum—a structure which is being increasingly implicated in autism. In rats, they modulate learning and memory processes, probably via the hippocampus, and seem especially important in the recognition of conspecifics, in social attachments, and in sociosexual behaviour, bonding, affiliation, and grooming. Anomalous levels induce stereotypic behaviours: stretching, repetitive grooming, startle responses, wing flapping in chickens (cf. hand flapping in autism?), and self-directed aggression. Similarly, animals with mutations of either the oxytocin or vasopressin genes exhibit some of the social features of autism. In humans, there is a negative correlation between "grooming" behaviours associated with OCD and vasopressin levels in the cerebrospinal fluid, while plasma concentrations of oxytocin in children with autism are half that of controls; indeed, systematic administration of oxytocin to children with autism increases social interaction (Insel et al., 1999). Abnormal levels of the endogenous opiate endorphin in autism may also account for reduced pain sensitivity and self-injurious behaviour (Fein et al., 1996); the opiate antagonists naloxone and naltrexone reduce self-injurious behaviour and stereotypies, and improve social and communicative behaviour. Conversely, opiate agonists in animals can produce autistic-like behaviour, reductions in affiliative behaviour, distress when infants are separated from their mothers, and increased pain threshold.

TREATMENT

There is no really satisfactory treatment. Neuroleptics are frequently prescribed, with the risk of irreversible tardive dyskinesia, though this problem is minimised with new atypical drugs like clozapine. SSRIs such as fluoxetine, fluvoxamine, sertraline and paroxetine may produce clinical improvement in many but not all cases. Clomipramine, as used in OCD, may improve social relatedness, aggression, and ritualistic behaviour, along with compulsions and adventitious movements; drugs blocking not only the dopamine D2 receptors but also 5-HT_2 receptors, such as risperidone, may be particularly beneficial (Lewis, 1996). Opiate blockers (naltrexone, naloxone) may minimise self-injury, social withdrawal, and stereotypies. Thus autism is probably a spectrum of various disorders and symptoms, and involves various neural systems and neurotransmitters; medication may largely be directed against these various signs and symptoms (anxiety, attention deficits, depression, mania, seizures, obsessionality, ritualism, movement stereotypies, aggression and so on). Training in problem solving and social skills may also be beneficial (Minshew, 1997).

ASPERGER'S DISORDER

Asperger's disorder may or may not be a variant of high-functioning autism (Fein et al., 1996; Pomeroy, 1998; Rapin, 1997). *Autism* was first described by Kanner in 1943, while *Asperger's disorder* was independently described by Asperger in 1944; they were mutually unaware of each other's work, and both used the word "autism" in their descriptions to characterise the solitariness manifested. As currently conceptualised, Asperger's disorder differs from autism in that language and cognitive functions are preserved, though not social interaction. Thus Asperger's disorder is characterised by improved cognitive skills and language, and normal or near normal intelligence, though with a stilted, grandiose, or pedantic style of speaking, often accompanied by inappropriate utterances and flat or exaggerated prosody or gesture. There is a narrow, intense, and obsessive range of often unusual interests or arcane preoccupations (e.g. train schedules, weather forecasting), which are passionately followed for many years and may even form the basis later of a useful career. However, there are usually more or less severe problems with social behaviour, which is at the very least odd and lacking in insight or empathy, with intellectualisation of feelings and an absence of an intuitive understanding of another's viewpoint. Individuals may be able formally to describe others' emotions, but often cannot act on this knowledge, like patients with amygdala damage (LeDoux, 1996). Although they are usually scrupulously law-abiding, they may be sensitive to perceived slights, disruptive, or even antisocial, especially if they think their special interests are at risk.

Patients with Asperger's disorder are often slow to walk, clumsy, and poor at games, often with prominent motor stereotypies, hand flapping, toe walking, whole-body movements and ritualistic, compulsive behaviour, all of which are indicative of developmental motor problems and probable striatal involvement (Ghaziuddin & Butler, 1998); in these respects they do not clearly differentiate from individuals with autism. Although excellent at rote learning, they may be poor at problem solving, abstract thinking, and higher-grade conceptualisation. They may, however, be excellent at puzzles and factual knowledge that relates to their special, obsessional interests. Indeed in a pedantic way they appear to enjoy interacting with adults, especially in their areas of interest. Unlike individuals with autism, they may have poor visuospatial skills, suggesting a possible dysfunction of the right hemisphere, compared to a possible left hemisphere deficit in autism (Ellis & Gunter, 1999). Thus patients are poor at recognising familiar faces, at recognising emotions, at drawing the Rey–Osterreith Complex Figure, at attention to details or focal processing, and in understanding humour, metaphor, the pragmatics of language, and how stories are integrated. Ellis and Gunter (1999) see all this as a "problem of coherence", or the ability to see or understand information within its wider context.

Although they still may have problems in understanding stories of pretence or lies, they are nevertheless better at theory-of-mind tasks (Ziatas, Durkin, & Pratt, 1998). Asperger's disorder tends to present later (around 3 years) than autism, and individuals may also suffer from early depression or bipolar disorder, or outright OCD; there is a 7 or 10 : 1 male : female ratio. Prevalence is around 10–26 per 10,000. Just as with autism, many Asperger's disorder traits are found, perhaps at a subclinical level, in family members (Volkmar, 1996). The DSM-IV criteria are as follows:

- Impaired social interactions: failure to develop appropriate peer relations, and/or a lack of spontaneous seeking to share interests or achievements with others, and/or lack of social or emotional reciprocity.
- Restricted, repetitive, or stereotyped behaviours, interests, or activities, including nonfunctional routines, rituals, and stereotyped and repetitive motor mannerisms; persistent preoccupations with parts of objects.

- Impaired social, occupational etc. functioning.
- No significant general delay in language, cognitive development, age-appropriate self-help skills, adaptive behaviours (except socially), or curiosity about the environment.

Volkmar, Klin, and Pauls (1998) believe that Asperger's disorder lies on a phenomenological continuum with autism; according to them, autism may represent only the most severe phenotype, and the same underlying genetic liability may be expressed, though in milder form, in Asperger's disorder. Family members of children with Asperger's disorder, especially the fathers, often show increased frequency of social deficits, if not a mild version of the actual syndrome. Other psychiatric conditions reported to associate with the disorder include schizophrenia, Tourette's syndrome, OCD, affective disorder, or social disturbance generally.

Kugler (1998) asks how useful it is to differentiate Asperger's disorder from autism. Both are clearly heterogeneous instances of the pervasive developmental disorders, and affect most areas of functioning. Different aetiologies may produce similar symptoms by affecting similar brain systems; conversely, one specific aetiology may have several distinguishable pathologies. Are autism and Asperger's disorder like this, or is the latter merely synonymous with high-functioning autism—autism without the language or cognitive impairment? Clumsiness may seem to characterise Asperger's disorder but not autism; however, motor problems may be noted early in life in the former because affected children are generally so much better at other things than children with autism, whereas the latter are seen to have motor skills as a relative strength, because they are so bad, generally, at most other cognitive tasks. Moreover, language is certainly not unimpaired in Asperger's disorder, given the problems with pragmatics and metaphor. The main differences between Asperger's disorder and high-functioning autism, apart from a relative preservation of language, seem to relate to visuospatial deficits in Asperger's disorder. Kugler (1998) sees individuals with autism as living in a world of their own, as if others do not exist; individuals with Asperger's disorder live in our world in their *own* way. They evade others when necessary and are still socially inept, although they are clearly much better at making friends. They perhaps have more abnormal preoccupations than people with autism, who tend more towards manipulative, visuospatial, or musical skills. Both disorders, however, may have a core deficit of early social cognition, perhaps implicating amygdalar involvement.

Bauman (1996) notes no gross changes in the brains of people with Asperger's disorder, apart perhaps from reduced neuronal cell size and increased packing in the amygdala and entorhinal cortex. The hippocampus, septum, anterior cingulate, and mammillary bodies all appear normal, whereas in the cerebellum there are reduced numbers of Purkinje cells—as in autism. Bauman notes that bilateral amygdalar lesions in primates lead to autistic-like behaviour.

WILLIAMS SYNDROME

Although not classified as a PDD, Williams syndrome is of considerable interest as it bears certain similarities to autism; in other respects, however, it is almost diametrically opposite. It is a rare genetic disorder that carries a distinct profile of medical, psychological, neurophysiological, and neuro-anatomical characteristics (Bellugi, Adolphs, Cassady, & Chiles, 1999). Affected individuals have a distinctive facial appearance, cardiovascular and renal disorders, neurological impairments, and abnormalities in calcium metabolism (Howlin, Davies, & Udwin, 1998). Occurring in approximately 1 in 20,000 live births, it manifests a dysmorphic facies of full cheeks, flared nostrils, wide mouth, full lips, and dental irregularities (Karmiloff-Smith, 1998)—an elfin appearance, which may explain the fairies of folklore. Children are short, very sensitive to noise, and age prematurely with early greying and wrinkles (Lenhoff, Wang, Greenberg, & Bellugi, 1997), due to an inherited mutation in one copy of a gene that confers elasticity to many organs and tissues, including arteries, lungs, gut, and skin. The increased calcium levels in the blood lead to difficulty in feeding, colic, and constipation. There is a hoarse voice and delayed physiological and mental development, often extreme sensitivity to noise, awkwardness, and poor fine motor coordination. Children are also often excessively anxious and distractible, prone to preoccupations and obsessions, eating and sleeping difficulties, and social disinhibition (Lenhoff et al., 1997). The condition results from a microdeletion of one copy of a restricted set of genes on chromosome 7 at q11.23 (Bellugi et al., 1999b; Karmiloff-Smith, 1998), including the genes for elastin, LIM-1 kinase and syntaxin 1a (Bellugi et al., 1999a, b).

Affected individuals have unusually friendly and engaging personalities, may exhibit excessive or even inappropriate sociability with strangers, and may show an unusual positive bias in their social judgements of unfamiliar individuals (Bellugi et al., 1999a, b). Their IQs range between 45 and 87, with a mean of around 50 to 60 (Karmiloff-Smith, 1998). Although they may spontaneously employ surprisingly well-formed sentences and produce highly articulate narratives, their linguistic and social capacities lead to a gross overestimation of their cognitive abilities. In fact 95% have a mild to severe learning disability, with a performance IQ very much lower than their verbal IQ. Indeed there are severe anomalies and deficiencies in their nonlinguistic cognitive functioning (Clahsen & Almazon, 1998). There are extreme deficits in spatial cognition, which co-occur with excellent face processing (Bellugi 1999a, b). As with autism, there is a preoccupation with local at the expense of global processing. They often have extraordinary musical talent, with near-perfect pitch, an uncanny sense of rhythm, and great interest and persistence in musical matters, perhaps reflecting their emotional responsivity (Lenhoff et al., 1997). It is, however, in the realm of language that, relative to their cognitive deficits, their cognitive abilities are perhaps apparently best preserved. They are unusually verbose and highly expressive, and can tell sophisticated stories with a large variety of narrative enrichment devices (Clahsen & Almazon, 1998); they can give accurate and detailed verbal descriptions of objects, although quite unable to construct even the roughest drawing. They can come up with word retrievals of very low frequency items (weasel, newt, salamander, ibex, chihuahua . . .); their syntax may include full passives, embedded relative clauses, conditionals and multiple embedding, although various syntactic, semantic, and pragmatic deficits may nevertheless be apparent (Howlin et al., 1998). According to Lenhoff et al. (1997), they may exhibit excellent phonological working memory and spontaneous control of prosody, pitch, volume, and rhythm to match the emotional tone of the story they are attempting to narrate—again making them seem very much brighter than they really are; however, there may be morphological deficits, involving those facets of grammar that in certain European languages deal with verb conjugation, gender assignment, and pluralisation.

Imaging (and rare autopsy) studies indicate sparing of temporal–limbic regions, primary auditory cortex, and the planum temporale (Lenhoff et al., 1997), all regions known to support the linguistic, musical, and emotional empathy aspects in which such individuals excel. However, electrophysiological studies indicate abnormal (missing or reversed) lateralisation and functional organisation of regions involved in both face and language processing (Bellugi et al., 1999a, b). The palaeocerebellar vermal lobes, occipital, posterior parietal, and possibly amygdalar regions may be relatively (to overall brain size) reduced in area, and the neo-cerebellar lobules increased in area, with evidence of reduced neuronal cell packing density and increased glia. All this is suggestive of neurodevelopmental arrest and even regressive changes. According to Karmiloff-Smith (1998), overall brain size is 80% of normal values, with considerable reduction of total grey matter, abnormal layering, clustering, and size of neurones.

Although the syndrome clearly bears certain similarities to autism, most notably perhaps in terms of local–global functioning, perseverative, and stereotypic behaviours, obsessions, impulsivity, hyperacusis, and anxiety, it is most interesting with respect to sociability, language, and facial functions; here Williams syndrome is in many ways the opposite to autism.

THE SAVANT SYNDROME AND AUTISM

Williams syndrome is one instance of preservation, apparently to high levels, of islands of ability or competence (social and linguistic) in the general context of fairly profound intellectual deficit. In a previous section we have touched upon savant skills; phenomena such as hyperlexia and other forms of abnormally preserved competence or even outstanding abilities are dealt with in detail by, for example, Howe (1999). Moriarty, Ring, and Robertson (1993) noted that the savant syndrome is more common in males and is associated with autism and even Tourette's syndrome; calendrical calculation, or the ability almost instantaneously to provide the day of the week for a date, randomly chosen, far into the future, is a classic instance. Other examples include arithmomania generally, and encyclopaedic knowledge of timetables or of the statistics of race winners, or unusual competence in art or music. Calendrical calculation involves an obsessional preoccupation with a limited section of the environment, and a knowledge of rules, regularities, and redundancies that may be tacit, implicit, unformalised, and unconscious. Thus calendrical calculators seem not to be consciously aware of any algorithm that permits the calculation of calendrical information, although their subjectively experienced need for repetitive behaviours, as in OCD, may facilitate the tacit acquisition of the requisite skills. People with OCD, Tourette's syndrome, autism, and "pure" savant syndrome all share the same stereotyped, repetitive, obsessive behaviour—not perhaps all that different from the dedicated and successful field naturalist or natural scientist. Casey, Gordon, Mannheim, and Rumsey (1993) noted that savants have a deficit in disengaging attention due to deficient attentional orienting processes and overselectivity; they display overly efficient gating of external stimuli, and overfocusing on internal processes.

A classic instance of savant processes in the context of art is provided by Selfe (1977); Nadia, an autistic girl, had little language and severe learning disabilities, in the presence of an amazing and apparently innate capacity to draw horses, other animals, and, latterly, humans. When with special training she acquired language by the age of 9 years, she lost her extraordinary drawing talents, almost as if they occurred at the *expense* of language, as an alternative medium of communication.

The idea that art may indeed be an older alternative (to language) medium of communicating or even of modelling reality is not unattractive. After all, studies of excision of the left hemisphere (hemispherectomy) in infancy, in the presence of otherwise intractable epilepsy, suggest that language is highly "valued", biologically, and may preferentially take over, from the right hemisphere, processing space to the detriment of spatial skills, being maintained in whatever neurological substrate is available

(Baynes, 1990; see also Bradshaw & Mattingley, 1995). At the opposite end of the spectrum, Miller et al. (1998) report the development (unmasking?) of hitherto unsuspected artistic capacities in elderly patients who developed frontotemporal dementia; in these patients with mostly temporal involvement, the dorsolateral prefrontal and parietal cortices were well preserved along with visual skills, whereas language and social capacities (as in autism) were badly affected. One can ask whether degeneration of the anterior temporal (and possibly orbitofrontal) cortex results in reduced inhibition of the more posterior perceptual/"artistic" regions. As Kapur (1996) notes, the results of a lesion in the brain are not just loss of function in a particular topographical or cognitive area, but disinhibitory processes, along with efforts from the rest of the brain to re-establish its maximal potential. Thus paradoxical functional facilitation, via release or absence of inhibitory processes, may account for the savant syndrome in autism and elsewhere.

Snyder and Mitchell (1999) hypothesise that the mental machinery for performing lightning-fast integer arithmetic, lengthy multiplication, division, factorisation, and prime identification, as well as sophisticated artistic capacities, may in fact lie within us all, although it cannot normally be accessed, as we are largely unaware of how our brains process information. They propose that we are highly concept driven—unlike patients with autism—and that this situation allows us to operate automatically; conversely, savants and those with autism may have direct access to "lower" levels of neural information prior to it being integrated into the larger, more "global" picture, while we normally only experience "the whole". Snyder and Mitchell (1999) therefore reject the idea that obsessive focused learning promotes savant skills, or that genius and savants alike have highly developed domain-specific neural structures or innate talent. Indeed, they see savants, and individuals with autism, as having direct or privileged access to the *local* rather than the *global* picture, which may in certain rather artificial or unusual circumstances confer distinct processing advantages. Such a view is clearly congruent with the evidence, discussed earlier, of "local" processing superiorities in autism, and an interest, in close relatives, in the mechanics of computation.

SUMMARY AND CONCLUSIONS

Like schizophrenia, autism was once thought to be due to faulty "refrigerator" parenting, and indeed was only comparatively recently separated from that disorder and recognised as a brain dysfunction. It is now seen as one of the PDDs, which as a group are of interest to educationalists, psychiatrists, neurologists, and developmental psychologists, and are characterised by specific delays in normal developmental processes. Three groups of criteria specifically characterise autism: social impairment (including lack of reciprocity, empathy, and affection, and reduced eye contact); abnormalities or delays in acquisition of language or capacity to communicate; and stereotyped, restricted, or repetitive interests, or unusual attachments to objects or situations. There are also typically anomalies in cognition and attention, and there may be electrophysiological anomalies, a tendency to seizures, hyper- or hyposensitivity to sensory stimulation, and unusual islands of ability or even exceptional talent involving, for example, rote memory, musical, or artistic ability or computational capacities. Various medical conditions may possibly cause, or simulate, autism, together with genetic and a range of possible environmental factors at or before birth. However, none of these conditions may be sufficient, or even necessary, for the disorder to manifest. The disorder is also clearly comorbid with other neurodevelopmental conditions such as schizophrenia, Tourette's syndrome, OCD, ADHD, and depression. Indeed autism is a heterogeneous condition which can manifest in various ways in a range of perhaps only loosely related syndromes and, with a significant familial aggregation in many of the pervasive developmental disorders, risks cross the subtype distinctions.

As with schizophrenia, there may be early preclinical prodromal signs, though clinical manifestation is typically early, around or before 3 years. A major research problem is therefore choice of an appropriate control group, in terms of either chronological or mental age. Prevalence, depending on criteria, may be between 5 and 10 per 10,000 or even as high as 1 in 1000. A form perhaps of juvenile dementia, it is characterised by deficits in problem solving and complex information processing, a failure of central coherence (overfocusing on details at the expense of global interrelationships), hypersensitivity to novelty, a deficit in skilled motor performance, and verbal IQ considerably lower than performance. Language is in fact very significantly affected, often with echolalia, pronoun reversal, an absence of normal prosody and cadence, and extreme literalness. At best, speech is pedantic, concrete, and peculiar.

An important theory of autism is that of a deficit of theory of mind: a failure of social reciprocity, joint attention, eye contact, referential pointing, social intelligence, and the ability to attribute mental states (thoughts, beliefs, desires etc.) to others. In this respect individuals with autism are inevitably deficient in the "Machiavellian intelligence" of the ability to cheat, deceive, outwit, and lie. The False Belief Test assesses an individual's ability to infer a story character's mistaken belief concerning a particular situation; affected individuals may sometimes be able to infer what another is thinking, but not what one character *thinks another* is thinking. Problems, therefore, also extend to the realms of irony, metaphor, sarcasm, and pretend play. However, as affected individuals also show *other* deficits before normal children "unfold" capacities relevant to theory of mind, deficits in the latter domain seem unlikely to be primary to the condition. Nor is it clear exactly how theory-of-mind deficits relate to autistic problems in language, and to stereotypic behaviours.

No specific biological markers indicate the condition, though there may be an increased incidence of neurological soft signs, EEG abnormalities, and seizures. Head size may be increased, with evidence of reduced dendritic branching and increased cell density in the hippocampus and limbic regions. Indeed temporal lobe anomalies may explain hyperexploratory behaviour, motor stereotypies, social withdrawal, and language and communication difficulties. Indeed, amygdalar lesions in infant monkeys can cause the much later development of deficits in social skills. Reduced Purkinje cell numbers have also been reported in the cerebellum. However, overall, there are few gross brain abnormalities, suggestive, as in schizophrenia, of a dysgenetic rather than a destructive process. Again, as with schizophrenia, there may be frontal hypometabolism. At a motor level, parkinsonian gait, dystonia, dyskinesia, and dyspraxia have been noted, along with abnormal tone and choreiform and athetoid movements.

While of unknown mechanism, the disorder is highly heritable, though without any simple Mendelian mode of transmission. "Unaffected" close relatives may be odd, socially inept, or emotionally unresponsive, and may be over-represented in occupations involving computation or detail. Although chromosome 15 may be implicated, there is also evidence for chromosomes 5, 8, 13, 17, 18, and the X gonosome. Indeed, several genes may act independently, conferring a genetic susceptibility to environmental factors, whether viral, toxic, metabolic, obstetric, or (as in schizophrenia) involving season of birth. Moreover, as with Tourette's syndrome, and OCD, and ADHD, various immunological and autoimmune dysfunctions may operate.

The neurochemistry of autism is reminiscent of that of the other neuro-developmental frontostriatal disorders, notably Tourette's syndrome, OCD, ADHD, schizophrenia and depression. Increased 5-HT levels (blood, plasma, and platelets) have been reported in autism, along with abnormalities in 5-HT metabolism; although SSRIs can ameliorate hyperactivity and stereotypies, the 5-HT precursor tryptophan can worsen the condition. 5-HT is an important moderator and regulator in the development of the hippocampus, amygdala, cerebellum, and thalamocortical system, and as a neurotransmitter is important in memory, social, sensory, and motor processes, all of which are compromised in autism. Dopamine agonists can stimulate the development of stereotypies, hyperactivity, and abnormal social relationships in animals, whereas neuroleptics can ameliorate these conditions. The peptides oxytocin and vasopressin, like 5-HT, affect neurodevelopment, and are important in the recognition of conspecifics, social attachments, sociosexual behaviour, and bonding. Anomalous levels may lead to stereotypies, startle responses, and upper limb flapping in birds. Medication, at best palliative, includes SSRIs, drugs that blockade dopamine D2 and $5\text{-}HT_2$ receptors, and opiate blockers.

Asperger's disorder was first described eponymously only a year after Kanner's 1943 account of autism; there is relative preservation of language and cognitive functions, and near-normal intelligence, but not of social functions and interactivity. Behaviour and speech may be inept, stilted, grandiose, and pedantic, with exaggerated prosody, inappropriateness of style and content, narrow obsessionality, and a mien that is odd and lacking in empathy. Affected individuals may be able formally to describe others' emotions, but not to act thereon. They may be clumsy, ritualistic, and compulsive, but (like individuals with autism) excellent at rote learning. Visuospatial processing may typically be poor. Comorbidity with depression and OCD may occur, and debate continues as to whether Asperger's disorder is a unique syndrome in its own right, or is merely a variant of high-functioning autism. The brain is grossly normal, though again, as in autism, there may be a reduction in the number of Purkinje cells in the cerebellum, and increased neuronal packing in the amygdala.

Williams syndrome, not yet classified as a PDD, provides a fascinating counterpoint to autism, with many features in common, and others diametrically opposed. Affected children have a distinct elfin appearance and other body abnormalities, with premature ageing. A mutation on chromosome 7 is responsible. Such children, like those suffering from autism, are very sensitive to noise, anxious, distractible, and poorly coordinated in fine motor skills. They tend also to be preoccupied with local details at the expense of overall global processing, and to be of subnormal intelligence. However, they are very sociable, engaging, and friendly, and aspects of their speech are excellent. Indeed they tend to be verbose and very expressive, and able to tell sophisticated stories, though there may be anomalies of syntax. Very considerable musical talent may be shown, along with an unusual capacity for face recognition. Again, the brain is grossly normal, though there may be subtle cerebellar and amygdalar involvement.

In conclusion, autism may be the paradigm case of a range of pervasive developmental disorders, all of which relate more or less closely to the other frontostriatal neurodevelopmental disorders.

FURTHER READING

Bailey, A., Luthert, P., Dean, A., Harding, B., Janota, I., Montgomery, M., Rutter, M. & Lantos, P. (1998). A clinicopathological study of autism. *Brain*, *121*, 889–905.

Bauman, M.L. (1999). Neuropathology of autism. In A.B. Joseph & R.R. Young (Eds.), *Movement disorders in neurology and neuropsychiatry* (pp. 606–617). Oxford: Blackwell.

Ciaranello, A.L., & Ciaranello, R.D. (1995). The neurobiology of infantile autism. *Annual Review of Neuroscience, 18*, 101–128.

Cohen, D.J., & Volkmar, F.R. (Eds.) (1997). *Handbook of autism and pervasive developmental disorders.* New York: Wiley.

Cook, E.H., & Leventhal, B.L. (1996). The serotonin system in autism. *Current Opinion in Pediatrics, 8*, 348–354.

Courchesne, E. (1997). Brainstem, cerebellar and limbic neuroanatomical abnormalities in autism. *Current Opinion in Neurobiology, 7*, 269–278.

Ellis, H.D., & Gunter, H.L. (1999). Asperger syndrome: A simple matter of white matter. *Trends in Cognitive Science, 3*, 192–200.

Fein, D., Joy, S., Green, L.A., & Waterhouse, L. (1996). Autism and pervasive developmental disorders. In B.S. Fogel, R.B. Schiffer, & S.M. Rao (Eds.), *Neuropsychiatry* (pp. 571–601). Baltimore: Williams & Wilkins.

Filipek, P.A. (1999). Neuroimaging in the developmental disorders: The state of science. *Journal of Child Psychiatry and Psychiatry, 40*, 113–128.

Gillberg, C. (1998). Chromosomal disorders. *Journal of Autism and Developmental Disorders, 28*, 415–425.

Gillberg, C., & Coleman, M. (1996). Autism and mechanical disorders: A review of the literature. *Developmental Medicine and Child Neurology, 38*, 191–202.

Happé, F. (1999). Autism: Cognitive deficit or cognitive style? *Trends in Cognitive Sciences, 3*, 216–222.

Happé, F., & Frith, U. (1999). How the brain reads the mind. *Neuroscience News, 2*, 16–25.

Harris, J.C. (1996). Pervasive developmental disorders. In D.X. Parmelee (Ed.), *Child and adolescent psychiatry: A comprehensive textbook* (pp. 49–67). St Louis: Mosby.

Kemper, T.L., & Bauman, M. (1998). Neuropathology of infantile autism. *Journal of Neuropathology and Experimental Neurology, 57*, 645–652.

Kugler, B. (1998). The differentiation between autism and Asperger syndrome. *Autism, 2*, 11–32.

Minshew, N.J. (1997). Pervasive developmental disorders: Autism and similar disorders. In M.J. Farah (Ed.), *Behavioral neurology and neuropsychology* (pp. 817–825). New York: McGraw Hill.

Rapin, I. (1999). Autism in search of a home in the brain. *Neurology, 52*, 902–904.

Russell, J. (Ed.) (1998). *Autism as an executive disorder.* Oxford: Oxford University Press.

Rutter, M. (1999). The Emmanuel Miller memorial lecture 1998. Autism: Two-way interplay between research and clinical work. *Journal of Child Psychology and Psychiatry, 40*, 169–188.

Schopler, E., Mesibov, G.B., & Kunce, L.J. (Eds.) (1998). *Asperger syndrome or high functioning autism?* New York: Plenum.

Szatmari, P., Jones, M.B., Zwaigenbaum, L., & MacLean, J.E. (1998). Genetics of autism: Overview and new directions. *Journal of Autism and Developmental Disorders, 28*, 351–368.

Volkmar, F.R. (1996). Autism and the pervasive developmental disorders. In M. Lewis (Ed.), *Child and adolescent psychiatry: A comprehensive textbook* (pp. 489–500). Baltimore: Williams & Wilkins.

Volkmar, F.R., Klin, A., & Pauls, D. (1998). Nosological and genetic aspects of Asperger syndrome. *Journal of Autism and Developmental Disorders, 28*, 457–461.

Waterhouse, L., Fein, D., & Modahl, C. (1996). Neurofunctional mechanisms in autism. *Psychological Review, 103*, 457–489.

CHAPTER NINE

Depression

Ὄλβιος δ'οὐδεὶς βροτῶν πάντα χρόνον.
No one can be happy always.

—Bacchylides.

INTRODUCTION

Depression is one of the moods to which we are subject, and mood disorder, which includes also bipolar disorder, considerably exceeds schizophrenia in its frequency and rivals it in its destructive potential; both types of disorder are associated with greatly increased risk of suicide. Like the other neurodevelopmental frontostriatal disorders, it lies on a continuum with normal behaviour, and may be associated with evolutionarily adaptive aspects, in this case in the context of creativity. In this chapter we shall note its recurring characteristics, shared with schizophrenia, its comorbidity with other conditions, its neuropsychological concomitants, and changes, morphometric and functional, that are associated with induced alterations in mood, clinical depression, and bipolar disorder. We shall note the often confusing findings with respect to lateralisation and the absence, so far, of evidence of any particular "Jeremiah gene", despite the high degree of heritability associated with the two major types of mood disorder.

As with all the neurodevelopmental frontostriatal disorders, we shall see that the neurochemical picture is complex, involving as major players the serotonergic, dopaminergic, and noradrenergic systems, along with substance P. We shall address the question of medication and the role of stress and of hippocampal damage in mediating depression, mood, and cognitive change.

PRELIMINARY CONSIDERATIONS

We may distinguish, as a matter of philosophical terminology and definitions (Harris, 1995), between *emotion* (which refers to one's state, with physiological and psychosomatic concomitants of mood), *mood* (a pervasive and sustained emotional or psychological state), *feeling* (the subjective experience or sensation, which like mood may be positive or negative), and *affect* (a complex state of emotional arousal that involves several feelings, which may vary over time, and which is expressed by gesture, tone or facial expression). Emotion and memory are closely interlocked, functionally and anatomically (via the temporolimbic circuits), and emotional arousal may facilitate or suppress memories, which may nevertheless be retained at a tacit, implicit, and relatively inaccessible level. Harris (1995) notes that emotions, which are so characteristically human, may be characterised by type, intensity, and duration, and fall into seven main groups: joy, surprise, fear, sadness, anger, interest, and disgust/contempt. Clearly all involve limbic processes in their experience, frontal mechanisms in their cognitive correlates, and striatal pathways in terms of behavioural release. At a level of pathology, anger (disorder of dyscontrol), fear (anxiety, when prolonged or chronic), and sadness (depression, when prolonged or chronic) are the most prominent, though disgust/contempt features in the obsessions and compulsions, and there is a high degree of mutual comorbidity (which leads to problems of diagnosis) in all the mood disorders (Piccinelli, 1998). However, this is not the place to debate whether, as according to the old James/Lange viewpoint, we perceive the bodily (visceral or autonomic) responses to environmental events as emotion (they are probably too slow and undifferentiated, and emotions persist even with autonomic and visceral disconnection), or whether, as according to the opposite, Cannon, viewpoint, we cry (for example) because we grieve rather than grieving because we cry.

A hint of this debate is seen in *The Anatomy of Melancholy*, written by Sir Robert Burton (1577–1640):

> Some difference I find among writers, about the principle part affected in [melancholy], whether it be the brain, or heart, or some other member. (Cited by Soares & Mann, 1997)

Depression, of course, one of the curses of human existence, has been with us from time immemorial, and has been described at least from the time of the Hippocratic medical writers of ancient Greece (Jackson, 1986). Thus according to Hippocrates, writing around 400 BC, melancholia is a condition associated with an aversion to food, despondency, sleeplessness, irritability, and restlessness; some centuries later Aretaeus of Cappadocia noted the association between melancholia and mania, suggesting that the latter was the end stage of the former. Galen in the second century noted the chronic, recurrent nature of melancholia, and all three ancient authorities, in addition to the above modern-sounding and penetrating observations, saw melancholia as a biological disturbance of the "humors"—"black bile" affecting the brain. In the nineteenth century, two French physicians, Falret and Baillanger, independently saw mania and depression as manifestations of a single illness, *la folie circulaire*, and *la folie à double forme* (Judd & Kunovac, 1997).

DIAGNOSTIC CRITERIA, SIGNS, AND SYMPTOMS

Depression clearly is to be distinguished from dysthymia or "the blues" from which we all suffer, from time to time, and from normal grief or bereavement, which normally last for up to 6 months, with subsequent steady improvement usually without treatment. Clearly of course there is room for some overlap. Thus depression is far more debilitating and dangerous, not least because of its frequent appearance without obvious cause. A feeling of overwhelming sadness combines with other symptoms, including feelings of guilt and worthlessness, difficulty in thinking clearly or remembering, anhedonia, anxiety, lack of energy, trouble with eating and sleeping (though both may sometimes be carried to excess), restlessness (or motor slowing), loss of interest in normal activities, indecisiveness and even suicidal mentation (Nemeroff, 1998).

Unipolar major depression, a chronic lifelong illness that may be aetiologically heterogeneous but clinically appears homogeneous (Judd, 1997), is to be distinguished from depression secondary to medical, drug, or social factors, and is to be seen as occurring in the relative absence of externally precipitating stresses, though in practice it is increasingly accepted that exogenous as well as endogenous factors must also play a role. Thus depression is seen as a consequence of both genetic factors (controlling timed biological events during the life cycle) and often very powerful environmental precipitants (Cicchetti & Toth, 1995). Nevertheless endogenous or melancholic symptoms are emphasised in the diagnosis of major depression, rather than the neurotic or reactive pattern (Goodwin, 1996). Core symptoms are disturbances of mood and affect, and, recently, of cognitive function (Elliott, 1998); the latter is a particular problem with the elderly, where depression must also be distinguished from dementia.

According to DSM-IV diagnostic criteria for depression, five of the following must be met (and see also Fish, 1998):

- Depressed mood of at least 2 weeks' duration.
- Loss of interest or pleasure in all activities.

- Poor appetite or weight loss.
- Insomnia or hyposomnia.
- Psychomotor agitation or retardation.
- Loss of sexual drive.
- Fatigue or loss of energy.
- Feelings of worthlessness, or (maybe delusional) excessive or inappropriate guilt.
- Lack of concentration,
- Recurrent thoughts of death, suicidal ideation or attempt.

Thus major depression is a constellation of signs and symptoms, a syndrome rather than a specific pathological process (Duffy & Coffey, 1997). Its heterogeneity is reflected in the great variability in its age of onset, course, response to treatment, and profile of symptoms (Delgado, 1995), and its neurodevelopmental or traumatic aetiology is evident as a consequence of genetic, environmental, developmental, traumatic, or degenerative factors (Soares & Mann, 1997). Anhedonia, an inability to experience pleasure, however, seems central to the concept, and is present in both unipolar and bipolar (see later) depression; along with amotivation and apathy, it renders positive life events ineffective at altering mood, and curtails usually enjoyable and rewarding activities unless extraordinary effort is expended (Dolan, 1997). Anhedonia is also present in depression secondary to disorders such as Parkinson's disease, and as a consequence of abstinence from cocaine in individuals dependent on the drug, both of which indicate, as discussed below, dysfunction of the mesolimbic dopaminergic system and the mesial prefrontal cortex.

PSYCHOMOTOR ASPECTS

Psychomotor retardation commonly accompanies anhedonia, amotivation and apathy, but may sometimes instead be replaced by intrusive thoughts, anxiety, and psychomotor agitation. Thus Bench et al. (1993) identified three factors in patients' depressive symptoms, and correlated them with regional cerebral blood flow (rCBF):

- A factor with a high loading for anxiety and psychomotor agitation. This factor correlated positively with rCBF in the posterior cingulate and inferior parietal lobule bilaterally. The cingulate cortex of course plays an important role in drive and affect, and interconnects with the higher association cortex.
- A factor with a high loading for psychomotor retardation and depressed mood correlated negatively with rCBF in the dorsolateral

prefrontal cortex and the angular gyrus, on the left. Decreased perfusion of the left dorsolateral prefrontal cortex also occurs with diminished spontaneous speech in aphasia and chronic schizophrenia, the region being important in volitional behaviour and willed, intentional activities, and interconnecting with the cingulate. The angular gyrus, apart from an involvement with reading, plays an important role in visuospatial orientation and attention.

- A factor with a high loading for cognitive performance correlated positively with rCBF in the left anterior medial prefrontal cortex—i.e. decreased rCBF correlated with increasing cognitive impairment.

Psychomotor agitation, a characteristic of melancholic depression, with its intrusive thoughts, may reflect comorbidity of anxiety and OCD. The perhaps more characteristic psychomotor retardation involves a generalised slowing of physical, mental, and emotional reactions; it is similar to the motor slowness (bradykinesia) of Parkinson's disease, and probably involves similar dopaminergic frontostriatal mechanisms, with, in both cases, dorsolateral and medial prefrontal dysfunction resulting in cognitive deficit.

RATING SCALES OF SEVERITY

- *Self-rating scales*: Beck Depression Inventory (Beck et al., 1961); Mood Assessment Scale (Geriatric Depression Scale/AKA) (Yesavage et al., 1983); Zung Self-rating Depression Scale (Zung, 1965).
- *Clinician-rated scales*: Hamilton Rating Scale for Depression (Hamilton, 1960); Montgomery–Esperg Depression Rating Scale (Montgomery & Esberg, 1979); Newcastle Scales (designed to distinguish between endogenous and neurotic depression and to predict response to electroconvulsive therapy) (Carney, Roth, & Garside, 1965).
- *Sign-based scale*: The Core Measure (a rating scale for psychomotor disturbance—intended to identify melancholic from other depressed patients) (Parker, Hickie, & Mason, 1996).

EPISODICITY OF DEPRESSION

Duggan (1997) usefully defines the terms episodicity, remission, recovery, relapse, recurrence, and chronicity in the context of depression. An *episode* of depression is said to occur if symptoms develop for an adequate length of time (at least 2 weeks, according to DSM-IV). *Remission* occurs with spontaneous improvement, or if treatment is initiated and the patient responds; remission can be complete or partial. There is *recovery* if remission is sufficiently long, though that duration is not specified. A *relapse* occurs if there is recurrence within a designated period of remission, and a *recurrence* can occur within a period of recovery. There is said to be *chronicity* if an episode lasts for two or more years. Such considerations indicate a very poor outcome in depression, with only two thirds of those treated *responding* to treatment; 15% fail to *recover* at all and become *chronic*. Among the successful responses, one third will *relapse*, while among those who do recover 75% will have a *recurrence*. Thus, for every 100 depressed patients, 66 will respond and 10–15 will remain chronic; of the 66 responders, 22 will relapse during remission. Of the 44 who recover, 33 will have a recurrence. So only 11 will ever have a single episode.

Despite earlier views, depression can manifest in childhood, though its mean age of onset is between puberty and the mid twenties. It is perhaps commoner in females, who may ruminate more (as in obsessive compulsive disorder [OCD], where there is also a female preponderance), whereas males may tend instead to seek distracting action (Cicchetti & Toth, 1995). With a lifetime risk of between 10% and 20%, depression is our commonest serious mental health problem (Nemeroff, 1998), and is a factor in about one in six new presentations to a general physician (Fish, 1998). Maybe 3–6% develop the chronic disorder dysthymia, and patients commonly experience a variety of depressive subtypes during their courses of illness (Judd, 1997). Sufferers can expect four to six episodes during a lifetime, most resolving within 6–9 months, with maybe 20% persisting for nearly 2 years. As a recurrent illness, the biggest predictive factor for a future episode is a previous one; after a first episode there is a 50% chance of a relapse, a 70% chance after a second, and 90% after a third. Thus it is as if the brain becomes increasingly vulnerable or sensitised after each episode, with a progressively lower threshold, analogous to the kindling phenomenon in epilepsy. The same applies to mania (see below), and in all three cases early medication or management may be vital. During the course of the illness a patient may experience one or more major depressive episodes, dysthmia, recurrent brief depression, and subsyndromal depressive symptoms. Major depressive disorder (MDD, the classical unipolar depressive disorder, characterised by recurrent episodes of continuously depressed mood, insomnia, anhedonia, appetite loss, and psychomotor slowing or agitation) and minor depression (with episodes of around 2 weeks' duration) probably lie on a symptomatic continuum, as expressions of the same disorder, along with dysthymia (dysthymic disorder), a long-standing low-grade depressed mood (Hedaya, 1996). There is, however, long-standing debate as to whether unipolar major depression is a unitary or heterogeneous disorder. Marked psychomotor signs, for example, may be an indicator of a distinct, perhaps more endogenous subtype (melancholia) (Boyce & Hadzi-Pavlovic, 1996).

GENETIC FACTORS

Family, twin, and adoption studies all indicate the role of genetic factors and heritability in affective disorders such as depression. The illness clusters in families, and indeed assortative mating—choosing partners with similar personalities—may accentuate this. The greater the percentage of shared genes, the greater the risk or concordance (Cicchetti & Toth, 1995; Leboyer & Gorwood, 1995). Thus the concordance in monozygotic twins may be as high as 70%, with around 13% in dizygotic twins. A single major locus pattern of inheritance is often favoured, though the findings, including a tendency to transmission via the mother, are not in accord with strict Mendelian principles, and there is no evidence yet for a single "Jeremiah gene". In any case most forms of psychopathology seem to be multi-factorially determined, via several genes operating at different times during the life cycle and in response to various environmental stimulants or triggers. Indeed the scene may be set quite early in development, perhaps with the creation of receptors for certain neurotransmitters that may not operate until much later when the relevant behaviours unfold—as, perhaps, in autism and especially schizophrenia. Indeed the distinction between schizophrenia and schizoaffective disorders is itself blurred in the borderline personality, and schizoaffective disorder, where symptoms of both disorders—schizophrenia and depression—may co-occur. Moreover relatives of schizophrenic patients are at increased risk of depression, and relatives of the depressed may be at increased risk of schizophrenia. Both disorders may in fact be of similar neurodevelopmental origin.

COMORBIDITY

Comorbidity ("any distinct additional clinical entity that has existed or may occur during the clinical course of an index disease"; see, for example, Griez & Overbeek, 1997) is currently a "hot topic" in psychopathological research (Mineka, Watson, & Clark, 1998). There is a major problem, however, in delimiting the concept of a distinct clinical entity, and determining whether a disorder may be a risk factor for, or a complication of, another disorder. There are also problems of multiple comorbidities, and whether their effects may be additive or interactive. There are also different clinical traditions of "lumping" and "splitting", and the problem of severity. Thus the more severe levels of a disorder are likely to have more associated comorbid conditions. Moreover, key symptoms defining theoretically distinct disorders often co-occur; thus difficulty in concentrating occurs in both depression and anxiety, whereas feelings of worthlessness and panic attacks are unique respectively to the former and the latter (Mineka et al., 1998).

There is indeed an ongoing debate as to whether anxiety and depression are separate diagnostic entities, or whether they represent a single underlying dimension of mood disorders. There is certainly extensive comorbidity (around 60% in both directions) over a lifetime, and both are also extensively comorbid with yet other disorders, such as substance abuse, hypochondriasis, somatisation, eating disorders, and conduct and attention deficit disorders (Mineka et al., 1998). Anxiety seems more likely to precede depression than vice versa, and individuals with diagnoses of panic disorder, agoraphobia, and OCD are more likely to experience depression than those with generalised anxiety disorder or phobia. Indeed pure depression is relatively infrequent, and whereas anxiety is characterised more by helplessness, depression is characterised more by hopelessness. Similarly, anxiety is associated more with anticipated threat or danger, whereas depression is often preceded by a major loss event. Other differences reflect the fact that anxiety involves *hyper*arousal, whereas depression involves (largely) *hypo*arousal (apathy, withdrawal, retardation, though there may instead be agitation). Similarly, anxiety involves nervous and muscular tension, tension pain, irritability, restlessness, and delayed sleep, whereas depression involves loss of interest, morning blues, early wakening, inefficient thought, poor concentration, and lack of self-confidence (Piccinelli, 1998). Although it is more likely that anxiety may precede, influence the course of, or even cause depression than vice versa, or that a third factor may cause both (Griez & Overbeek, 1997), when both conditions are comorbid their joint outcomes are likely to be significantly worse. In the past, separate treatments were favoured for anxiety and depression, respectively benzodiazepines and tricyclic antidepressants, but nowadays the anxiolytic and antidepressant properties of selective serotonin reuptake inhibitors (SSRIs) make them favoured medications for both conditions (Piccinelli, 1998).

THE NEUROPSYCHOLOGY OF DEPRESSION: COGNITIVE CORRELATES

The domain of neuropsychology is the study of brain–behaviour relationships, especially cognitive and motor functions and affect, whether for diagnosis, management, treatment, or research. The *emotional*/affective aspect of depression is clearly pre-eminent, as we have seen, perhaps involving orbitofrontal cortex, amygdala, hypothalamus, and limbic regions (see later), and we have already noted the *psychomotor* correlates (retardation or sometimes agitation). In the *cognitive* domain there are consequences in depression for concentration, insight, memory, attentional processes, visuospatial processing, problem solving, abstract reasoning, judgement, and planning (Derix & Jolles, 1997). Difficulties are more apparent with effortful than with automatic processing. Memory and learning deficits may reflect compromise of the hippocampus, which is affected by stress (see later), with impairments of explicit more than of implicit memory, whereas hypometabolism of the anterior cingulate and dorsolateral prefrontal cortex, with consequent impairment of executive functions, may account for many of the other neuropsychological deficits (Elliott, 1998). It is noteworthy that the deficits may not simply be due to poor motivation or inability to sustain effort, as they persist in remission (McAllistair-Williams, Ferrier, & Young, 1998).

Comorbidity of dementia and depression, which may be mutually misdiagnosed, further emphasises the cognitive correlates of depression. Parkinson's disease is associated with depression (in up to 40% of cases), as well as with cognitive impairments and dementia; indeed depression may *predict* the subsequent development of parkinsonian cognitive impairment (Robinson & Travella, 1996), possibly as a consequence of developing Alzheimer-like plaques and tangles, or Lewy bodies, or depletion of cholinergic neurones in the nucleus basalis of Meynert. There is evidence, in sufferers of Parkinson's disease with dementia and depression, of loss of pigmented neurones in the ventral tegmental area; this region contains cell bodies of dopaminergic neurones innervating the prefrontal cortex, nucleus accumbens, and amygdala. Depressed parkinsonian patients show reduced activity in the caudate and inferior frontal cortex, and reduced serum levels of the serotonin (5-HT) metabolite 5-hydroxyindoleacetic acid (5-HIAA), as indeed do depressives generally (Bellivier et al., 1998). Robinson and Travella (1996) speculate whether degeneration of the mesocortical and mesolimbic dopaminergic systems leads to dysfunction of the orbitofrontal cortex, which normally backregulates serotonergic function originating in the raphe nuclei. Indeed serotonergic and noradrenergic agents are more efficacious than dopaminergic medication in parkinsonian depression, with its anxious, sad, pessimistic, irritable ideation, which rarely involves guilt or self-punitive feelings (Duffy & Coffey, 1997). Overall, parkinsonian depression may therefore involve caudate and orbito- and inferofrontal dysfunction, just as in post-stroke depression (see later), whereas the cognitive concomitants may involve dorsolateral and mesial aspects.

NEUROPATHOLOGY AND NEUROIMAGING

Sparing of the more automatic and impairment of the more effortful aspects of processing suggests prefrontal and anterior cingulate involvement in major depression. *Structural* imaging reveals ventricular enlargement (whose degree may correlate with levels of cognitive and psychomotor retardation), with periventricular white matter lesions, reduced striatal volumes, possible cerebellar atrophy and possible frontal and temporal lobe anomalies (D'haenen, 1997; Soares & Mann, 1997), just as in Parkinson's and Huntington's diseases, and depression secondary to stroke. At a *functional* level, early studies generally assessed resting values (during which periods the patient's mental state, e.g. anxious rumination, was not known); they reported hypofrontality, especially of the left dorsolateral prefrontal cortex, and reduced striatal, left temporal (amygdala), and cingulate activity (Elliott, 1998). Increased orbitofrontal perfusion was sometimes noted, perhaps corresponding to inhibitory processes (Delgado, 1995; Rogers, Bradshaw, Pantelis, & Phillips, 1998), though generally there was decreased inferofrontal activity. Indeed while decreased prefrontal activity may well reflect an impoverished mental state, increased activity may instead reflect negative thoughts and ruminations. Later (activation) studies employed various cognitive tasks, for example the Tower of London, with reduced dorsolateral prefrontal and anterior cingulate activation.

Drevets (1998), in a major review of recent activation studies, notes that differences between patients and controls are often small, as are those between patients and those suffering from other illnesses. He notes that differences may reflect either the physiological correlates of depressive emotions and thoughts, or the pathophysiological changes that predispose individuals to, or result from, affective disease. The physiological correlates of depressive symptoms appear as (often reversible) changes in local blood flow and/or metabolism that may normalise with effective treatment, and may to some extent be reproduced in healthy individuals who are subjected to experimentally induced states of anxiety or sadness.

Overall, in individuals in the depressed phase relative to the remitted phase, and in some cases of experimentally induced states of anxiety or sadness in the healthy, the following picture emerges of the more recent activation studies:

- There is reduced activation in the dorsolateral and dorsomedial prefrontal cortex, probably reflecting impaired neuropsychological performance.
- There is increased activation in the medial orbitofrontal cortex, including the posteromedial, lateral orbital, ventrolateral, and orbitofrontal cortices, and the pregenual anterior cingulate; this may reflect the emotional concomitants or experiences, ruminative activity, and attempts at its control.
- There is increased amygdalar activity, as also in sleep, perhaps reflecting a pathology primary to the depressed state as it is one of the strongest and most consistent findings; amygdalar activity may mediate release of corticotropin releasing hormone during stress, and thus act as a link between stress and depression.
- There is reduced activity in the subgenual anterior cingulate, especially on the left, perhaps reflecting reduced drive. It is noteworthy that there is also reduced grey matter volume in this region, which plays an important role in organising emotional responses to complex

personal and social situations (Damasio, 1997). However, rather than there being a reduction in number of neurones, instead the quantity of glial cells appears reduced (Öngur, Drevets, & Price, 1998); glia affects the regulation of extracellular potassium, glucose storage and metabolism, and glutamate uptake, all housekeeping and supportive functions crucial for normal neuronal activity. The subgenual anterior cingulate projects to the rest of association cortex, basal ganglia, periaqueductal grey, amygdala, insula, and hypothalamus; so it is therefore in a good position to be influenced by the images that constitute thought, and to affect activity in neural sectors that control autonomic, endocrine, neurotransmitter, motor, and somatosensory responses, all of which between them constitute emotions, feelings, and mood (Damasio, 1997). Importantly, the region is *activated* during manic phases, and is involved also in the modulation of serotonergic, noradrenergic, and dopaminergic neurotransmission.

Drevets (1998) notes that the ventrolateral, ventromedial (anterior cingulate), and orbital areas of the prefrontal cortex, where blood flow and metabolism are abnormal in the depressed phase, all interconnect extensively with the amygdala, the mediodorsal nucleus of the thalamus, and ventral striatum (ventromedial caudate and nucleus accumbens); all are also involved in other types of emotional behaviour. He suggests that between them they constitute two interconnected circuits:

- A limbic thalamocortical circuit comprising the amygdala, mediodorsal nucleus of the thalamus, and ventral prefrontal cortex.
- A limbo-striato-pallido-thalamic circuit, which now includes the ventral striatum and pallidum.

The amygdala and prefrontal cortex interconnect with each other via excitatory projections, and with the mediodorsal nucleus of the thalamus, so increased metabolic activity here may reflect increased synaptic transmission via the limbic–thalamocortical circuit. Neurosurgery to correct otherwise intractable depression interrupts projections within these circuits, and effective antidepressant treatment reduces activation in the otherwise overactive amygdala, ventral prefrontal cortex, and medial thalamus. Figure 9.1 represents a possible circuit subserving mood.

Blood flow and metabolic changes in depression may reflect a number of independent or interacting phenomena, according to Drevets (1998):

- Pathophysiological changes that predispose individuals to recurrent episodes of abnormal mood.

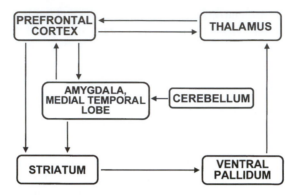

Figure 9.1. A frontostriatal (cortex, striatum, globus pallidus, cortex) circuit for depression, which also includes input from the amygdala and cerebellum.

- The physiological concomitants of the signs and symptoms of depression.
- The physiological correlates of dysfunction at the levels of synaptic connectivity (hyper- or hypoplasia), neurotransmitter synthesis, or receptor sensitivity.
- Compensatory mechanisms invoked to modulate or inhibit pathological processes.
- Areas that have been deactivated during ongoing emotional processing.

Moreover findings will be complicated by the presence, duration, and nature of ongoing medication (antidepressant, antipsychotic or antianxiety), comorbidities (anxiety, obsessive ruminations), hyper- or hyposomnia, psychomotor agitation or slowing, age (with possible additional Parkinson's, Huntington's or Alzheimer's diseases), and whether depression is unipolar or bipolar. Increased metabolism may signify excitatory or inhibitory activity, and reduced metabolism may be partly or wholly a consequence of reduced morphometric volume; if there is less *structure* to support it, *functional* activity may be correspondingly reduced.

MOOD INDUCTION STUDIES

Mood induction studies (via video clips) show that a transient sad state in normal control subjects is associated with *increased* inferomesial prefrontal activation, along with the anterior cingulate and striatum (Duffy & Coffey, 1997; Goodwin, 1996), whereas a transient happy state in such subjects leads to reduced metabolism in temporal, inferoparietal, and prefrontal regions. However, such studies, although possibly reflecting left anterior activation in association with a positive mood, and right anterior activation with a negative mood (see below), may suffer from confounds between mood manipulation and task-related activity. In clinical patients, similarly, we do not know whether reported effects are trait or state dependent. The fact that on treatment or remission there may be increased blood flow in left dorsolateral and mesial prefrontal regions suggests state dependency, though the fact that some studies show incomplete normalisation may indicate that the phenomena are at least partly trait dependent (Elliott, 1998).

BRAIN INJURY AND DEPRESSION

Clearly the whole mood system involves prefrontal, inferior parietal, para-limbic (orbitofrontal, anterior temporal, amygdala, and anterior cingulate), striatal, and associated (pallidal, mediodorsal thalamic) regions (Duffy & Coffey, 1997); each region makes its own specific contributions to the selection, enactment, and ongoing appraisal of goal-related behaviour, with various manifestations of depression following lesions anywhere within this integrated network. Traumatic brain injury results in depression, transient or persistent, in maybe 6% of cases (Robinson & Travella, 1996). The phenomenon is not just reactive to disability, but is probably neurochemical, though prior psychosocial or psychiatric tendencies may be required in addition. Left-sided anterior lesions feature particularly prominently; the closer they are to the frontal pole the more severe the depression. Thus occlusion of the middle cerebral artery is an important aetiological agent. Disruption of amine (noradrenergic or serotonergic, see later) pathways ascending from the brainstem via the median forebrain bundle to the frontal cortex and basal ganglia may be important; indeed animal studies show lateralisation of such systems (Robinson & Travella, 1996). Thus while *left*-sided *anterior* damage is associated in humans with depression and the "catastrophic reaction" (anger, frustration, depression, refusal, shouting, swearing, and other manifestations of pathological emotional incontinence), which may also occur with *right posterior* damage, *right anterior* damage is typically associated with neglect, indifference, euphoria, or even frank mania (Derix & Jolles, 1997; Rogers et al., 1998). (At another level, while left hemisphere pathology may be associated more with disturbed mood, i.e. inner feelings, right hemisphere pathology may instead be more characterised by disturbances of affect, i.e. outward expression.) There are suggestions that while the left hemisphere is dominated by cholinergic and dopaminergic systems, the right, with its emphasis on arousal and novelty, is more largely modulated by serotonergic and noradrenergic neurotransmitter function and pathways (Cicchetti & Toth, 1995). Heller and Nitschke (1997) propose a lateralised two-dimensional model of emotions:

- Valence (pleasant, unpleasant), associated with *anterior* activity, generates greater left than right anterior activation for pleasant experiences, and the opposite for unpleasant.
- Arousal (high, low), associated with *posterior* activity, generates increased right parietotemporal activation with high-arousal experiences, and reduced right parietotemporal activation in low-arousal circumstances.

Thus they argue that depressed patients will exhibit left less than right activation in anterior regions, and reduced right parietotemporal activity, except when there is comorbid anxiety.

In any event, post-stroke depression, with its disruption of orbitobasotemporal and neostriatal circuits, is associated with reduced cerebrospinal levels of metabolites of 5-HT and noradrenaline (Duffy & Coffey, 1997). Since the incidence of stroke increases with age, rising from 10 per 100,000 below age 35, to 6000 per 100,000 after 75, and depression is the commonest emotional disorder associated with cerebrovascular disease (Robinson & Travella, 1996), it is not surprising that post-stroke depression should rival major depression in prevalence. Indeed its phenomenology is almost identical to that of functional or primary mood disorder, except that cognitive and motor slowing may be greater. It persists for at least a year post stroke.

HEMISPHERIC ASYMMETRY AND MOOD IN NORMAL HEALTHY SUBJECTS

The issues largely addressed in this book involve how (disordered) neural activity may relate to (disordered) behaviour. As Canli (1999) notes, the search for an answer lies at the heart of much of neuroscience and psychobiology over recent decades. One approach, using dichotic, divided visual field (tachistoscopic), electrophysiological and, latterly, imaging techniques, has been to investigate functional differentiation between the left and right hemispheres in normal healthy individuals. Laterality differences are thought to reflect brain architecture, revealing differences in hemispheric information processing (Bradshaw, 1989; Bradshaw & Nettleton, 1983). Hemispheric asymmetry has been revealed for a multitude of cognitive and motor functions, including visuospatial and language processes, and handedness. The question of hemispheric asymmetry for emotions ultimately resolves into two major competing models (Canli, 1999):

- *The right hemisphere hypothesis* proposes that the right hemisphere, perhaps analogously to language specialisation by the left, or due to its greater role in arousal and attention, is more strongly involved than the left in all aspects of emotionality, including the perception and expression of both positive and negative emotions.

- *The valence hypothesis* proposes that the right hemisphere largely mediates negative emotions, and the left, positive emotions; a modification is the approach–withdrawal (rather than positive–negative valence) dimension, according to which approach-related behaviour or emotions may be lateralised towards the left hemisphere, and withdrawal-related activity toward the right.

Canli (1999) notes the confusion in the research literature stemming from two sources:

- The task and measurement parameters, including for example speed or accuracy indices with (visually or dichotically) lateralised stimuli, activation levels (electrophysiological or metabolic), facial expressions, or rated emotional feelings on exposure to "appropriate" (as judged subjectively by the experimenters) stimuli.
- The interpretation of the term "laterality" in the context of either an interhemispheric or an intrahemispheric approach; the former addresses such questions as "Does the right hemisphere activate more strongly than the left to negative stimuli?", whereas the latter addresses such questions as "Does the right hemisphere respond more strongly to negative than to positive stimuli?", and "Does the left hemisphere respond more strongly to positive than to negative stimuli?"

Functional imaging studies investigating the neural basis of emotional processes have investigated a range of experiences (e.g. fear, pain, sadness, happiness, and general negative or positive affect), using a range of induction techniques (e.g. aversive conditioning, mood induction via emotional memories, imagery, visual stimuli, exogenous substances) and employing manipulation checks in the form of self-report or physiological measures other than brain activation.

According to Canli's (1999) analysis, *fear* would be expected to be lateralised towards the right hemisphere, but few studies have been confirmatory. *Sadness* and *disgust* should be lateralised towards the right, and *happiness* towards the left; again, findings are remarkably inconsistent, as is the case with studies manipulating general negative or positive affect. Canli discusses possible reasons for these failures, but in the end one is left wondering how genuine or deep are the emotions evoked in or reported by the participants.

NEUROCHEMISTRY OF DEPRESSION

Depression, of whatever aetiology, clearly involves dysfunction of cortical, subcortical, and multiple neurotransmitter systems. Since rapidly increasing or decreasing concentrations of catecholamines or indoleamines do not of themselves always greatly improve or worsen *clinical* depression, the condition is unlikely to be due to a simple change in any one neurotransmitter system. It is in any case a heterogeneous disorder with, probably, multiple biological subtypes (Delgado, 1995). However, as we have seen, common regions of the brain, or at least networks modulated by various neurotransmitter systems, may be dysfunctional regardless of underlying aetiology. Patients with different symptom profiles may have lesions in different sections of the circuit or circuits, leading to subtle differences in symptom profile, whereas overall dysfunction of the system will account for any similarities. Thus rather than just invoking disturbance of monoamine systems per se, we should look also to the brain networks modulated by them, especially the frontostriatal and the temporolimbic. Indeed while low levels of 5-HT, noradrenaline, and dopamine may be associated with depression, artificially lowering or increasing their levels in *normal* individuals has remarkably little effect on mood (Duman, Heninger, & Nestler, 1997; Nemeroff, 1998). Antidepressant medication may work by facilitating transmission, over time, of specific monoamines (whether catecholamine, like noradrenaline, or indoleamine, like 5-HT) via changes in receptor sensitivity, rather than by altering levels of neurotransmitter availability; this is the case even though there is some evidence of deficiencies of noradrenaline or 5-HT in urine, blood, or cerebrospinal fluid of depressives, and, as we saw, in post-stroke depression there may be decreased metabolite levels of noradrenaline and 5-HT.

Serotonin

Serotonergic fibres arising in the raphe nuclei project widely to the frontal cortex, limbic system, basal ganglia, and hypothalamus. The system, the largest cohesive neurotransmitter system in the brain (Delgado, 1995; Staley, Malison, & Innis, 1998), is therefore significant in affecting immune function, movement, learning, mood, sleep, circadian rhythms, food intake, and sexual activity—all functions affected in depression (Smith & Cowen, 1997). Projections to postsynaptic 5-HT_{1A} receptors in the hippocampus are particularly important in maintaining adaptive behaviour in the face of aversive stimuli. System failure can thus result in helplessness, depression, and cognitive dysfunction. Conversely, antidepressant treatment enhances 5-HT_{1A} receptor function and improves resilience, coping, and cognitive function. Because 5-HT is a precursor of melatonin, itself a regulator of many neuroendocrine functions, and because with age the pineal produces less melatonin, we may also expect to find age-related mood changes (Conwell & Henderson, 1996). We might also note that serum cholesterol levels may be reduced in suicides and conduct-disordered individuals (Conwell & Henderson, 1996), and that there is an ongoing debate as to whether cholesterol-lowering drugs (which alter 5-HT metabolism) may increase depression.

Nemeroff (1998) reviews the evidence for a role for 5-HT in depression: its concentration, or that of its major metabolite 5-HIAA, is reduced in the cerebrospinal fluid of drug-free patients; there is reduced uptake of 5-HT and fewer transporter binding sites in the brain and in the blood platelets of patients; there is increased density of 5-HT receptor binding sites in the brain and platelets of patients; there is a reduced plasma concentration of the 5-HT precursor tryptophan in drug-free patients; there is a blunted neuroendocrine response to fenfluramine and other serotonergic provocative challenges in patients; there is altered regional glucose utilisation in the central nervous system in response to fenfluramine; SSRIs are highly efficacious in treatment, and they lose this efficacy after tryptophan depletion. To this list, Staley, Malison, and Innis (1998) add that pharmacological agents facilitating serotonergic neurotransmission may mildly elevate mood in the healthy (though Knutson et al., 1998, found only a reduction in hostility and negative affect, with no change in indices of positive affect). They also note that there is a whole range of 5-HT receptor subtypes that are distinguished by differences in molecular structure, anatomical localisation, mechanisms of signal transduction, and pharmacological responses to 5-HT receptor agonists and antagonists. Dysregulation of transmission at the level of the regulatory autoreceptor or the postsynaptic receptor may stem from a range of such abnormalities, and alterations in synthesis, storage, release, reuptake, or metabolism may affect serotonergic neurotransmission. 5-HT is also a powerful vasoconstrictor, so local or global blood flow can easily be modulated. In remitted patients who underwent tryptophan depletion, metabolism reduced in the dorsolateral prefrontal cortex, orbitofrontal cortex, and thalamus—regions critically implicated in depression—and correlated with symptom onset. Symptoms and metabolic abnormalities reversed with antidepressant treatment, suggesting prefrontal changes index *state* rather than *trait* markers of depression.

Findings, however, with respect to serotonergic function in depression are far from consistent (Mann, 1998; Smith & Cowen, 1997). Blood platelets may indeed be used as a model of neuronal 5-HT uptake, as the 5-HT transporter responsible for the uptake of the transmitter into blood platelets is similar to that on 5-HT neurones; in drug-free depressives, the uptake of 5-HT into platelets is usually decreased, with a compensatory increase in the number of receptors in platelets and central nervous system. It is, however, possible that this situation holds more true of suicide victims or individuals with high aggression levels. Similarly, findings of reduced levels of the 5-HT metabolite 5-HIAA are inconsistent, and again may relate more to suicide victims and to individuals with high levels of aggression (Conwell & Henderson, 1996; Nemeroff, 1998; Smith & Cowen, 1997). Decreased numbers of hippocampal postsynaptic 5-HT$_{1A}$ receptors in depression may stem from increased cortisol secretion associated with stress (see later). Conversely, antidepressants may work by enhancing serotonergic transmission in the hippocampus and limbic system (McAllister-Williams et al., 1998); indeed depletion of brain 5-HT by reducing the availability of its precursor tryptophan, in normal healthy individuals, can lead to mild impairment in the retrieval of learned material. However, as we saw, similar manipulations have little effect on mood, except in those already vulnerable (from personal or family history) to depression, and if the latter are *already* depressed, there is little *further* worsening of mood (McAllister-Williams et al., 1998; Smith & Cowen, 1997). Thus 5-HT levels may not relate in any simple way to severity of depression; brain levels may therefore be more important in triggering and maintaining depression than in determining its severity, and depression may be less a function of reduced 5-HT levels and more a function of altered postsynaptic neuronal activity (Staley et al., 1998).

Dopamine

5-HT also modulates the levels of the other catecholamines: dopamine and noradrenaline. Cell bodies of the dopaminergic system originate in the ventral mesencephalon and project throughout the central nervous system, almost parallel to the serotonergic system (by which they are modulated), to the nigrostriatal (motor), mesocortical, and mesolimbic systems (Anand & Charney, 1997; Delgado, 1995). They thus form part of an integrated reward system mediating hedonia, motivation, behavioural reinforcement, goal-directed behaviour, and psychomotor activity. Clearly, hypofunction can result in anhedonia, loss of motivation, and depression, whereas hyperfunction can result in excitability and mania. However, dopamine-enhancing agents (e.g. dopamine agonists like bromocriptine) are only weakly efficacious as antidepressants.

Two subtypes of dopamine receptors have been identified (Anand & Charney, 1997)—D1 and D2—with opposing functions. D3 (a subtype of D2) and D5 (a subtype of D1) receptors are present in abundance in limbic regions, whereas D4 (a subtype of D2) receptors are present in high numbers in the frontal cortex, midbrain, amygdala, and medulla, and at lower levels in the basal ganglia. (They are implicated in the action of clozapine, which reverses both the positive and negative symptoms of schizophrenia, with minimal parkinsonian or extrapyramidal effects.) D1 receptor agonists may reduce the reinforcement of reward-seeking behaviour, whereas D2 receptor agonists may have the opposite effect. Thus anhedonia in depression may be due to increased D1 receptor activity, and/or decreased activity of D2 receptor sites. Anand and Charney (1997) therefore suggest that antidepressants may increase the sensitisation of D2/D3 receptors in the mesocortical and mesolimbic systems. (They may of course also affect other neurotransmitter systems.) As D1 receptor agonists reduce reward-seeking behaviour, depression may again be due to increased sensitivity of D1 receptors. A correlate of depression, psychomotor retardation, may also be associated with increased numbers of D2 receptors in the basal ganglia; indeed decreased cerebrospinal fluid levels of homovanillic acid (HVA), a major dopamine metabolite, correlate better with psychomotor retardation than with mood. (However, there are better correlations between cerebrospinal fluid levels of homovanillic acid and mood in *bipolar* disorder; indeed dopamine-enhancing agents like amphetamine and bromocriptine are more efficacious modulators of mood in bipolar disorder than in major depression.) Again, however, it must be emphasised that 5-HT, dopamine, and noradrenaline all interact, even though the dopaminergic system might be the final common pathway in aspects of medication (Duffy & Coffey, 1997). Thus electrical or glutamatergic stimulation of the medial prefrontal cortex, or chronic antidepressant medication, results in dopaminergic activity in the nucleus accumbens in the limbic striatum.

Noradrenaline

The major noradrenergic nucleus is the locus coeruleus in the dorsal pons. Cell bodies project widely, modulating their targets like the serotonergic neurones (Anand & Charney, 1997; Delgado, 1995). Some neurones may even release noradrenaline like a hormone. The locus coeruleus is very sensitive both to external environmental stimuli and to changes in the body's internal homeostasis. It is involved in conditional behaviour, memory consolidation, selective attention, and responses to novelty. It also regulates the fight or flight response, arousal, and the sympathetic nervous system. Consequently the noradrenergic system is involved in a range of psychiatric disorders, including addiction withdrawal, anxiety, and depression, and interacts with the serotonergic, dopaminergic, GABAergic, glutamatergic, and the opioid systems. The stress hormone corticotropin releasing hormone influences the firing rate of the locus coeruleus. As with the dopaminergic cells of the substantia nigra, cells from the locus coeruleus are progressively lost with ageing, the amount of loss correlating roughly with depressed mood. The evidence is inconclusive that depressives have altered noradrenaline levels, though Conwell and Henderson (1996) note a possible inverse correlation between cerebrospinal fluid levels of the metabolite

3-methoxy-4-hydroxyphenylethylene glycol (MHPG), and suicidal intent in depressives, arsonists, and violent offenders; depressives may nevertheless have raised β-adrenergic receptor density (Nemeroff, 1998) and altered growth hormone responses to noradrenergic probes like clonidine. More-over noradrenergic reuptake inhibitors like reboxetine may increase levels of noradrenaline in the synapses, and improve mood. Thus noradrenaline may at least play a modulatory role in the pathophysiology of depression (Delgado, 1995).

Other neurotransmitters

Acetylcholine was the first neurotransmitter to be identified; it is involved in the parasympathetic nervous system, the regulation of voluntary movement, memory, and cognition. There are multiple subtypes of muscarinic cholin-ergic receptors. Excess cholinergic activity is associated with mania and depression; anticholinergics can cause dementing symptoms and euphoria, but not as strongly as the noradrenergic and dopaminergic releasers cocaine and amphetamine (Delgado, 1995).

Other systems possibly involved in depression include the opiate system and the neuropeptides (Conwell & Henderson, 1996). Concentrations of β-endorphin may be reduced (on the left) in frontal, temporal, and caudate regions of depressives, whereas in similar regions concentrations of neuro-peptide Y (which coexists with the monoamines and with the inhibitory neurotransmitter GABA) may be lowered in suicides. Kramer et al. (1998) note that substance P (a small protein involved in pain pathways) is the most abundant neurokinin in the mammalian central nervous system, with a receptor that is highly expressed in brain regions critical for the regulation of affective behaviour and neurochemical responses to stress. This distri-bution provides multiple opportunities for interaction between substance P and the convergent noradrenergic and serotonergic pathways through which established antidepressant drugs act. Thus substance P antagonists may have clinical utility; indeed Kramer et al. (1998) in a trial found robust antidepressant effects with the substance P antagonist MK-869. Nor did substance P antagonists appear to interact with monoamine systems in a manner seen with established antidepressant drugs.

Depression is clearly a heterogeneous condition resulting from dysfunc-tion of several neurotransmitter systems, and all antidepressants seem to have different effects upon the serotonergic and noradrenergic systems, though the dopaminergic system may well act in some way as a final common path. Depletion of 5-HT or noradrenaline rarely leads to depressive symp-toms in normals, or even to a deepening of mood in the already depressed, but patients experiencing remission on either SSRIs or noradrenaline-selective reuptake inhibitors are vulnerable to relapse on depletion of the corresponding monoamine. Thus although 5-HT and noradrenaline are somehow involved in the maintenance of an antidepressive response, they cannot alone explain either the mechanism of action of antidepressants or the full pathophysiology of depression (Duman et al., 1997). Similarly, several weeks are normally required for antidepressants to work, even though monoamine levels increase rapidly. (A somewhat similar situation obtains with the neuroleptic treatment of schizophrenia.) Thus there must be additional factors operating to cause depression initially, and to explain the efficacy of treatment. Re-regulation of receptor sensitivity may be one such mechanism.

MEDICATION

Although the aetiology of major depression may be heterogeneous, the brain systems involved in determining specific symptoms (the emotions, cognitions, and somatic responses) are likely to be similar across patients (Delgado, 1995). Most antidepressant drugs work in a similar fashion for everyone, so they probably affect the various brain regions involved in all patients. Most effective antidepressants potently affect monoamine transmission, as well as working on milder mood disorders such as anxiety, panic, OCD, and eating disorders. Rather than simply increasing concentrations of catecholamines or indoleamine, which as we saw do not always correlate well with mood, antidepressants (including electroconvulsive therapy) may increase receptor sensitivity; thus the often-delayed therapeutic effects of treatment may relate to similar time-dependent alterations in receptor sensitivity, just as with schizophrenia—and more than one neurotransmitter system is likely to be involved (Nestler, 1998). Indeed it is far too simplistic to invoke one neurotransmitter for each disorder—noradrenaline for depression, 5-HT for anxiety, dopamine for schizophrenia, and acetylcholine for dementia. Just as multiple neurotransmitter systems are likely to be involved in the disorder, so too most drugs may affect a relatively broad spectrum of systems.

The older antidepressants, the monoamine oxidase inhibitors (MAOIs), e.g. phenelzine and moclobemide, worked by stopping the destruction of monoamines in the synapse; the newer tricyclic antidepressants (TCAs), e.g. amitriptyline, clomipramine, and desipramine, probably operated by inhibiting the reuptake of monoamines, especially noradrenaline and 5-HT, though at the cost of serious side effects probably involving α-adrenergic blocking (Hale, 1997). As noradrenaline is the transmitter most clearly associated with motivation, antidepressants with a particular affinity for that system are especially indicated for depression where psychomotor retardation is prominent (Fish, 1998). Dopaminergic antidepressants also appear to be more effective than those with minimal dopaminergic action (such as the SSRIs) in treating melancholic depression (Mann & Kapur, 1995; Clerc, Ruimy, & Verdeau-Pailles, 1994). 5-HT is the transmitter most closely associated with anxiety and repetitive, ruminatory, or compulsive behaviour, so SSRIs are indicated for anxiety states that include panic or OCD in the disease spectrum. The MAOIs and new reversible inhibitors of monoamine oxidase (RIMAs) enhance the availability of 5-HT; they are efficacious where other antidepressants have failed, and may be particularly indicated for phobias, hypochondriasis, and somatic symptoms. The older TCAs, which nevertheless sensitise postsynaptic neurones to the effects of 5-HT, may have unacceptable side effects on cholinergic receptors. Thus all antidepressants differentially affect the serotonergic system, the SSRIs blocking the presynaptic reuptake transporters by desensitising the presynaptic, inhibitory autoreceptors (Delgado, 1995). The SSRIs include fluoxetine, fluvoxamine, paroxetine, and sertraline. All differ in potency of reuptake inhibition, but without clear relationship to clinical effectiveness (Hale, 1997). Their side effects include the "serotonergic syndrome", analogous to the anticholinergic syndrome of the TCAs. Thus patients may complain of nausea, insomnia, nervousness, agitation, extrapyramidal effects, headaches, and sexual dysfunction, due in part to the direct effect of 5-HT on unprotected, postsynaptic, 5-HT_2 (brain) and 5-HT_3 (gut) receptors (Fish, 1998).

While selective serotonergic and noradrenergic medications are efficacious, they may take, as we saw, some time to work, even though their antidepressant effects may be rapidly reversed by depleting the neurotransmitter that is the target of the particular antidepressant (Mann, 1998). Also, the more impaired the neuroendocrine response to a medication, the poorer the antidepressant effect. Thus reuptake inhibitors may depend upon a certain minimum level of activity or neurotransmitter release in the relevant monoamine system, so as to increase neurotransmission and thereby have an antidepressant effect. Similarly, in Parkinson's disease, dopaminergic medication only continues to be effective in the continuing presence of an at least partially functioning system.

Finally, it should be noted that, according to Anand and Charney (1997), postsynaptic β-adrenergic receptor downregulation, followed by downregulation of α_2-adrenergic receptors, seems to be the most consistent effect of most antidepressant agents including electroconvulsive therapy.

ELECTROCONVULSIVE THERAPY

Electroconvulsive therapy (ECT) has for some time proved efficacious for the severely ill who fail to respond to other treatments, for a range of disorders including mania, depression, psychosis, abnormal motor activity (catatonia, parkinsonism, stupor), and even for impaired cognition (dementia) (see, for example, Fink, 1997). Indeed, according to Frank (1978), in the first century AD electric eels were placed on the heads of Roman patients to alleviate headaches. It is not clear why it is so effective against so many different disorders; does this suggest the existence of a single underlying psychosis, or does the procedure affect different brain regions according to the patient's disorder? Nor indeed is it known how it works, though stimulation of the centrencephalic regions (hypothalamus and pituitary) seems essential for efficacy. There may be beneficial release of hypothalamic peptides (including prolactin), adrenocorticotrophic hormone (ACTH), neurophysins, endorphins, or thyroid releasing hormone (TRH), all of which circulate in the blood and cerebrospinal fluid. It is possible that ECT somehow stimulates and resets the whole system (Fink, 1997). It is noteworthy that seizures need not be generated electrically for clinical efficacy, as the drugs pentylenetetrazole (Metrazole) and flurothyl (Indoklon) also work. Although modern unilateral procedures are no longer accompanied, as before, by intense fear, bone fractures, cognitive impairment, prolonged seizures, or cardiovascular or pulmonary complications, there is nevertheless a high relapse rate, with occasional persistent changes in memory and cognition.

Recently, transcranial magnetic stimulation (TMS) has also been used, a little like ECT, to ameliorate the symptoms of depression (George et al., 1997; Grunhaus, Dannon, & Schreiber, 1998; Reid, Shajahan, Glabus, & Ebmeier, 1998). So far, its effects appear beneficial, at least as good as ECT, with few side effects. It is applied to prefrontal regions, though it is still unclear whether fast or slow stimulation, to left or right side, is the more beneficial, nor are the exact mechanisms clear.

In Parkinson's disease, deep-brain stimulation is increasingly being used to help alleviate motor (and cognitive) symptoms. Agid's group has also reported, with bilateral stimulation of the subthalamic nucleus or internal globus pallidus, a mild but significant improvement in mood (Ardouin et al., 1999). However, the same group also notes the occurrence of transient acute depression with high-frequency deep-brain stimulation (Bejjani et al., 1999). Such findings underline the complex nature of frontostriatal mediation of mood.

SUICIDE

Suicide may be regarded as the ultimate complication of depression. The word itself first appears in the seventeenth century, although its Latin etymology (self-killing) is clearly much older, as indeed is the practice, which has been condemned by many religions, though accepted by the Graeco-Romans (Conwell & Henderson, 1996). Three levels have been classified: committers (highest in the elderly), attempters (highest in the young), and those with suicidal ideation (between 50% and 80% of the population at some time). About 12 per 100,000 suicide annually, with a 4 : 1 male : female ratio, and about 500 per 100,000 attempt it annually, mostly female. Of attempters, two thirds go no further. All these figures (from Conwell & Henderson, 1996) are probably considerably under-reported. Suicide rates increase during times of economic depression (when it is "every man for himself"), and decrease during war (when "we must all pull together"). Firearms are the means of choice for men, poisoning for women. Incidence is lower in the married, and higher in the unemployed or those exposed to stressful life events. There is a strong familial (and presumably genetic) component, as shown by twin and adoptive studies, and as we have already seen disorders of the neurotransmitters serotonin, GABA, dopamine, noradrenaline, and maybe acetylcholine seem to be involved.

BIPOLAR DISORDER

Bipolar disorder involves episodes of elevated (mania) and lowered (depressed) mood, with disturbances of sleep, appetite, energy, concentration, sexual activity, and self-esteem (Freimer & Reus, 1993). Cyclothymia involves a milder presentation of an otherwise similar disorder. Patients vary enormously in the number, frequency, severity, and regularity of episodes, the ratio of manic to depressive events, and their response to treatment. A genetic component is indicated by family, adoption, and twin studies; however, as Mendlewicz (1994) observes, more than one gene is likely to be involved, and because of variability in age of onset relatives of probands may be wrongly diagnosed as unaffected at time of study, only later becoming ill. Leonhard (1957) was the first to distinguish between unipolar depression and bipolar disorder, though the distinction is clearly supported by genetic, biochemical, and pharmacological distinctions (Judd & Kunovac, 1997).

Jamison (1993) traces the early history of the concept, and its relation to artistic creativity. Indeed she notes (MacKinnon, Jamison, & DePaulo, 1997) that while the classical Greeks were aware of such a relationship, Kraepelin in 1921 was the first to describe manic depressive illness: "As a rule the disease runs its course in isolated attacks . . . manic states with the essential morbid symptoms of flight of ideas, exalted mood and pressure of activity, and melancholia or depressive states with sad, anxious moodiness, and also sluggishness of thought and action." The term manic depressive illness is not now used clinically as a diagnostic category, but denotes a phenotype that includes the modern diagnosis bipolar disorder type I and other disorders of mood instability. However, MacKinnon et al. (1997) believe that manic depressive illness better captures the phenotype. There is much dispute about its boundaries and presentation; within manic depressive illness, bipolar disorder type II should probably also be included, where depression occurs with less severe mania (hypomania).

The manic phase is characterised by behavioural disturbances of such severity as to signify loss of contact with reality and the need for treatment. There is reduced need for sleep, rapid thought and speech, hyperactivity, agitation, euphoric or irritable mood, paranoia, impulsiveness, delusions of grandeur, a propensity to engage in potentially destructive activities like promiscuous sex, spending sprees, reckless driving, and grossly impaired judgement (Hedaya, 1996; Nemeroff, 1998). The depressed phase closely resembles that of major depression. The disorder occurs in 1–1½% of the population, equally distributed across the sexes unlike the female preponderance in major depression, with a peak onset in adolescence and the early twenties (though usually with earlier prodromal signs); it is therefore like schizophrenia, with which as a possible neurodevelopmental disorder it has other resemblances. It leads to severe social, interpersonal, and occupational impairment, with a suicide rate of 15–20%, along with associated comorbidities of alcoholism and substance abuse (60%), and anxiety and panic disorder (20%). However, many sufferers ascribe their depression to ill fortune, and enjoy their hypomanias as relief from gloom and lethargy, deriving much creative energy and religious meaning from transient states of exaltation and despair (MacKinnon et al., 1997). Apart from suicide the disorder is not usually fatal; it has an intermittent course, is treatable, even preventable, and may even benefit the individual or society. Thus evidence that early treatment (as in depression, see earlier) improves the eventual outcome shows that prophylaxis is important. Lithium as a mood stabiliser has long been the mainstay, in this regard, of preventative treatment, along with the anticonvulsants carbamazepine and valproic acid.

Bipolar disorder, while rare, can occur in children when it is enormously disabling; major symptoms overlap with those of attention deficit hyperactivity disorder (ADHD). Children with bipolar disorder often do not present with the classic adult picture, but instead exhibit a more chronic, irritable, dysphoric course characterised by impulsivity, hyperactivity, and inattention. Normally, however, onset occurs in adolescence or the early twenties, with the first manic episode usually preceded by multiple episodes of depression. Once the bipolar course is established, each manic episode is usually followed by depression.

Nongenetic factors (marital status, health and stability of the rest of the family, birth order, and availability of substances of abuse) are clearly important, and sufferers should avoid stressful jobs and sleep deprivation. However, there is a strong familial component, possibly even more so than in major depression, with risk increasing in proportion to shared genetic endowment. Monozygotic concordance may be higher than 70%, with dizygotic concordance ranging to 30%. As yet there is no single Mendelian mode of transmission evident, though according to MacKinnon et al. (1997) single major locus models are favoured over multifactorial. However, two or more genes could act together, with one perhaps leading to benign mood cycling (cyclothymia), the presence of the other being necessary for psychosis. To date, chromosomes 11, 18 and 21, with a gene somewhere on the X chromosome, have been implicated (McInnes et al., 1998; Nemeroff, 1998), though the findings are controversial or unconfirmed. An environmental cofactor could explain possible incomplete penetrance. There is some evidence of the genetic phenomenon of anticipation, as in Huntington's disease, which perhaps accounts for differences in severity within a family. The phenomenon of imprinting, moreover, would explain the gender imbalance in the transmission of manic depressive illness, which is more likely to be passed on from the mother. There is as yet no evidence of linkage to receptors for dopamine, GABA, noradrenaline, 5-HT, or the glucocorticoid hormones. However, Bellivier et al. (1998) note that the tryptophan hydroxylase gene, coding for the rate-limiting enzyme of 5-HT biosynthesis, may be a susceptibility factor for manic depressive illness.

Drevets (1999b) notes that dopaminergic projections from the ventral tegmental area and substantia nigra into the ventral striatum and medial prefrontal cortex may be important in bipolar disorder. Thus manic symptoms decrease with dopamine receptor antagonists or dopamine synthesis inhibitors, whereas dopamine receptor agonists can precipitate symptoms in vulnerable patients. Drevets (1999b) also notes that in the depressed phase there is decreased metabolism in the anterior cingulate, and increased metabolism during the manic phase; this region receives massive dopaminergic and serotonergic innervation. Moreover, lesions to the amygdala, ventral prefrontal cortex, and striatum can lead to manic and disinhibited behaviour, and failure to comprehend the adverse consequences of inappropriate social behaviour.

Ghaemi, Boiman and Goodwin (1999) review the kindling paradigm, as originally invoked as a model for understanding seizure disorders, in the context of the episodic nature of bipolar disorder. Thus intermittent subthreshold electrical or chemical stimuli can produce increasingly strong neuronal depolarisation (sensitisation), with temporal properties similar to the episodic behaviour disturbances of bipolar disorder. Symptoms may commence with psychosocial stressors, and recur at ever lower thresholds, suggesting the need for early, aggressive, prophylactic intervention, as later episodes may be less responsive; this may be even more true with the young, as younger animals are more sensitive to kindling than older animals, and at lower intensities.

According to Ghaemi et al. (1999), second-messenger systems may be involved in kindling and sensitisation to recurrent episodes of depression. They transmit information from the synapse to the cell nucleus, generating longer-acting and longer-lasting changes, similar to the effects of anti-depressant medication upon symptomatology. G-proteins may be central to the mechanism, interacting with "traditional" dopaminergic, noradrenergic, and serotonergic modulatory systems. The beneficial moderating or damp-ening effect of lithium may work by inhibiting stimulatory G-proteins (and thus suppressing an excessively excited system), and inhibiting inhibitory G-proteins (and thereby activating an underactive pathway). (Lithium, a small molecule closely related to sodium and potassium, was discovered quite by accident 50 years ago to have a tranquillising effect.) Other possibly relevant second-messenger systems include phosphatidylinositol, protein kinase C, and intracellular calcium. Ultimately, all such changes in second-messenger systems will result in changes in gene expression. Consequently, life events may trigger neurotransmitter changes, and lead via a cascade of second-messenger effects to an "experiential change in gene expression"—a model clearly relevant to other neurodevelopmental frontostriatal disorders such as schizophrenia, where environmental triggers or experiences may trigger disease processes in the genetically susceptible.

CREATIVITY AND PSYCHOPATHOLOGY

During a manic phase, unusual levels of energy may be available, and although this may sometimes be coupled with corresponding achievements (Jamison, 1993) it is also true that the period may be characterised by excess and disaster. The other side of the picture, however—the extent of psycho-pathology in people of creativity and genius—is less well understood. According to Seneca 2000 years ago, *nullum magnum ingenium sine mixtura dementiae fuit*, "there never has been a great mind without some madness" or, loosely, genius is akin to madness. But how do we define, and identify, *magnum ingenium*—genius or talent? While productivity (number of publi-cations, pictures, novels, sculptures, inventions . . .) can clearly be quantified, judgements of quality may depend upon peer review, the winning of extremely prestigious awards (Nobel Prizes, fellowships of exclusive societies etc.), or inclusion in biographical dictionaries of notables (*Who's Who* etc.). Marzullo (1996) employed biographical sources (e.g. Marquis' *Who's Who in America, The Dictionary of Literary Biography, The Macmillan Encyclopedia of Music and Musicians*, and other similar compendia) in his study of notable individuals, scientists, artists, musicians etc. with respect to season of birth. The context of his research was the finding that schizophrenia is largely caused by genetic factors, but is also associated with a preponderance of springtime births, and of reduced (but not falling) reproductive rates. He notes that the phenomenon of a "heterozygote advantage" might operate, whereby the reproductive *disadvantage* experienced by those who inherit a full dose of a disease-causing gene (or genes) is offset by a reproductive *advantage* experienced by relatives of the proband. Such relatives, having inherited a less-than-critical dose of these gene(s), are themselves largely symptom free, and as in the case of creativity may in fact benefit. (Marzullo even noted a bias in the season of birth of various categories of genius, which, however, was often out of phase with the seasonal bias of schizophrenic births.)

Post (1994) sought to determine the prevalence of various psychopathologies in outstandingly creative individuals from the fields of science, thought, politics, and art. The membership of six series of scientists and inventors, thinkers and scholars, statesmen and national leaders, painters and sculptors, composers, and novelists and playwrights was determined from biographies; extracted data were transformed into diagnoses in accordance with DSM-III-R criteria. Post found that all excelled not only by virtue of their abilities and originality, but also through their drive, perseverance, industry, and meticulousness. With a few exceptions, these men were emotionally warm, with a gift for friendship and sociability. Most had unusual personality characteristics, and minor neurotic abnormalities were somewhat more common than in the general population. Severe personality deviations were unduly frequent only in the case of visual artists and writers. Functional psychoses were largely restricted to the affective varieties; only depression and alcoholism were more prevalent than expected in some professional categories, though strikingly so in writers. Thus, while seasonality of birth may be biased in very high achievers, just as (but not necessarily in phase) with schizophrenia, it may not be schizophrenia but depression (or bipolar disorder) that is overrepresented in certain creative individuals. Jamison (1993) reported on the frequency of psychiatric treatments received by a series of 47 living prize-winning British poets, playwrights, novelists, biographers, and artists. Treated affective illnesses were found in 63% of playwrights and in 15% of novelists. Unlike the poets, her prose writers had not received treatment for manic conditions, but many reported periods of elation coinciding with high creativity.

Jamison (1993) notes that, as occasionally an exhilarating and powerfully creative force but more often destructive, mania can drive creativity, and depression destroy the creator. Both are in different ways life threatening, although yet also conferring great creative advantages. Cure the condition and you lose the gift, so not surprisingly patients may eschew medication. Although lithium may stabilise the condition and the mood swings it is at a cost. Given to normal, healthy individuals, lithium reduces social involvement and activity; mood and initiative are lowered and boredom increases, with emotional dampening, mental slowing, and impairments of concentration, long-term memory, semantic retrieval, and information processing. Psychomotor retardation may also manifest.

Environmental factors, again as in schizophrenia, may interact with an inherited, genetic predisposition. Thus there are reports of obstetric complications, an excess of winter births, and exposure of the mother to influenza A virus during the second trimester of pregnancy. In both neurodevelopmental disorders, therefore, adverse fetal or perinatal events may alter brain development in the genetically vulnerable (Nasrallah, 1996). Indeed neuroimaging reveals similar anomalies in both disorders: ventricular enlargement that is nonprogressive (without further atrophy or gliosis), widening of cortical sulci and fissures, cerebellar atrophy, reduced cerebral volume, a hypoplastic hippocampus, parahippocampal gyrus and superior temporal gyrus, abnormal caudate volumes, and frontal lobe pathology (Nasrallah, 1996).

Mania after stroke is rare, occurring most often after right-sided lesions of the orbitofrontal cortex, or the basal and polar areas of the temporal lobe or head of the caudate (Robinson & Travella, 1996). Lesions leading to secondary mania may do so via *distant* effects upon the right basotemporal cortex (diaschisis). Again, however, pre-existing psychiatric or psychosocial dysfunction may be necessary. Mania after traumatic brain injury is commoner than after stroke, and again may involve anterior temporal lesions. However, *bipolar* disorder after stroke or traumatic brain injury seems to occur mostly after right-sided damage to the head of the caudate, or the thalamus. Robinson and Travella (1996) hypothesise that as the orbitofrontal cortex exerts tonic inhibition over the amygdala via the uncinate fasciculus and basotemporal cortex, lesions in the latter location will disinhibit the amygdala. The latter structure, in the limbic portion of the temporal lobe, is of course important in instinctive emotional responses. Connected to the amygdala, moreover, is the anterior cingulate; in the manic phase of bipolar disorder increased glucose metabolism has been reported in the anterior cingulate, with decreased activity during the depressed phase (Dolan, 1997). Mania may be ameliorated by dopamine synthesis inhibitors, whereas it is precipitated by dopamine receptor agonists (Dolan, 1997).

Bipolar disorder (manic depressive illness) highlights the ethical problem posed by genetic tests. They measure only the potential for a disease, and we all of us carry potentially fatal recessive genes. Indeed manic depressive illness can even convey advantages (as might the gene for Tourette's syndrome in terms of movement control when in low penetrance); thus many artists, scientists, business, religious, and social leaders may attribute their success to their disorder (MacKinnon et al., 1997), as there are greatly increased rates of manic depressive illness in renowned members of such creative groups. Creativity, high energy states, intense emotionality, and risk taking are under certain circumstances socially advantageous. It is possible that a balanced polymorphism in this regard has long benefited both individual and society.

STRESS

A variety of stressors (restraint, psychosocial stimuli or events, chronic anxiety, glucocorticoid treatment, ischaemia, hypoglycaemia) can decrease the expression of brain-derived neurotrophic factor and lead to atrophy of populations of stress-vulnerable hippocampal neurones, especially CA3 pyramidal cells (Duman et al., 1997). The result can be decreased hippocampal volume, depression, cognitive impairment, or even dementia (McAllister-Williams et al., 1998). Depression likewise, and in turn, is associated with a decreased ability of the hippocampus to regulate the hypothalamic–pituitary–adrenal (HPA) axis, which controls our generalised stress responses (see Nestler, 1998). Thus with depression there is increased amygdalar activation and increased secretion of corticotropin releasing factor, and loss of the normal diurnal variation of plasma cortisol (produced by the adrenal cortex), with resultant day-long hypercortisolaemia. This leads to increased volume of the adrenal cortex and pituitary, an overactive HPA axis, and lack of dexamethasone suppression of cortisol secretion. Thus it was initially thought that raised cortisol could be used to diagnose and index depression via the dexamethasone test. This tests for whether there is normal control of levels of cortisol with dexamethasone, a substance resembling cortisol. With healthy individuals, 1 mg of dexamethasone injected at 11 p.m. causes the system to respond as if there had been an increase in the level of cortisol, and next day there is a measured decrease in steroid cortisol production—a decrease that is not observed in most depressed individuals (Hedaya, 1996); the situation may normalise with effective treatment of psychological symptoms, via hippocampal serotonergic systems. However, the procedure is criticised by Robinson and Travella (1996) on the grounds of unreliability; indeed, while a considerable number of the depressed fail to show this suppression, it may instead also occur, for example, in those who are physically unwell or stressed, or who have recently lost weight. Other pharmacological challenges for the diagnosis of depression include a blunted thyrotrophin response to infusion of thyrotropin releasing hormone (Conwell & Henderson, 1996), hyposecretion of growth hormone in response to the challenge of insulin-induced hypoglycaemia, and hypersecretion of prolactin in response to L-5-hydroxytryptophan, which increases 5-HT turnover (Cicchetti & Toth, 1995). The growth hormone response to desipramine may be a sensitive marker of post-stroke depression.

Thus there is a two-way interaction between these systems and the corticosteroid mechanisms of the HPA axis, with abnormalities in either limb leading to depression and neuropsychological/cognitive impairment. Indeed healthy individuals given corticosteroids exhibit decrements in learning and declarative memory—both mediated by the hippocampus— just like the depressed (McAllister-Williams et al., 1998).

Duman and Charney (1999) review the evidence for a stress-related decrease in neuronal and glial density in the prefrontal cortex and hippocampus of major depressives at post-mortem. They note that cortical cell layers affected in these anatomical studies have extensive interconnections with other cortical and subcortical regions, and receive much input from dopaminergic and serotonergic neurotransmitter systems; this may explain many of the affective, cognitive, and psychomotor symptoms of depression. Although the direction of causality (reduced regional cell density, and depression) is not necessarily certain, increased glucocorticoid production, through stress, is likely to cause the cell loss and atrophy. Duman and Charney (1999) note that 5-HT stimulates production of new hippocampal granule cell neurones, possibly through 5-HT_{1A} receptors, and that chronic stress downregulates hippocampal 5-HT_{1A} receptors, with resultant reduction in hippocampal cell numbers. Although stress also decreases the expression of brain-derived neurotrophic factor in the hippocampus, antidepressants, perhaps through their serotonergic effects, increase the expression of neurotrophic factor.

Depression is associated with a range of related (psycho)somatic disorders (Hedaya, 1996), including bowel dysregulation (irritable bowel syndrome), peripheral pain regulation (chronic pain syndrome), feeding disorders (anorexia and bulimia nervosa), respiratory disorders (asthma), vascular disorders (migraine, hyper- and hypotension, and see later), and altered immune function (allergy). Thus there is an interaction between the central nervous system and the immune system, with the former responding to histamine from the latter, and the latter responding to 5-HT from the former, and both acting upon the HPA axis. Indeed an immune inflammatory response may participate in the pathophysiology of major depression (Maes, 1997), via suppression (immunosuppression) of cell-mediated immunity; this may lead to a reduced antigen-induced lymphoproliferative response and delayed-type hypersensitivity skin responses to standard antigens. Thus psychological stressors (anxiety, examinations, loneliness, bereavement, unemployment) can reduce immune responsiveness via increased activity of the HPA axis, and increased cortisol and catecholamine levels; they can likewise increase levels of depression and temporarily (or, if prolonged, maybe permanently via hippocampal damage) reduce cognitive function.

Depressed individuals are also more susceptible to vascular disease (Nemeroff, 1998); their blood platelets are especially sensitive to activation signals issued by the serotonergic system, which amplifies blood platelet reactivity. Moreover the platelets of such individuals bear decreased numbers of 5-HT reuptake transporters. Thus their platelets are less able to take up 5-HT from the environment and so reduce their exposure to platelet activation signals.

Sheline (1998) notes that late-onset depression may be precipitated by damage to the same brain structures that are probably involved in the more classical early-onset depression: frontal cortex, hippocampus, caudate, thalamus, and basal ganglia. Late-onset depression is typically associated with an increased number of white matter hyperintensities, which probably represent small, silent infarcts due perhaps to cerebrovascular disease. Thus the depressed with an increased number of white matter hyperintensities have an increased prevalence of risk factors for cerebrovascular disease, e.g. hypertension, diabetes, coronary artery disease, and smoking. Sheline also notes that, at all ages, loss of hippocampal volume correlates with the number of recurrent depressive episodes. The causative mechanism could be repeated episodes of hypercortisolaemia, from dysregulation of the HPA axis, itself a consequence of chronic corticosteroid exposure or stress alone, increasing neuronal vulnerability to glutamate toxicity. Glial cells sequester glutamate, maintain metabolic and ionic homeostasis, and produce trophic factors. Their loss would therefore increase neuronal vulnerability to neurotoxic damage. There is indeed evidence of loss of glial cells in the orbital and medial prefrontal cortex, indicative of glutamate neurotoxicity in the limbo-cortico-striato-pallido-thalamo-cortical circuit. Depression may of course also exert its neurotoxic effect through elevations of cortico-tropin releasing hormone.

SUMMARY AND CONCLUSIONS

Although there are subtle distinctions (temporal, subjective) between emotion, mood, feeling, and affect, the emotions (joy, surprise, interest, disgust/contempt, and especially fear, anger, and sadness/depression) are all characterised by type, intensity, and duration; they are all limbic in their experiential aspects, frontal with respect to their cognitive correlates, and striatal in their behavioural release or inhibition. Although unipolar major depression, affecting perhaps over 10% of the population, is to be distinguished from normal day-to-day "blues", nevertheless as with all the neurodevelopmental frontostriatal disorders there is a continuum between "normality" (i.e. personality characteristics and momentary mood) and clinical depression. The latter, perhaps of heterogeneous aetiology, though clinically fairly homogeneous, is a lifelong illness, a constellation of signs and symptoms, a syndrome, maybe, rather than a specific pathological process. Anhedonia, along with apathy and amotivation, may be central to the disorder, which is episodic (maybe five or six episodes in a typical lifetime) in its presentation, followed by remissions (rather than recovery), with recurrences (rather than relapses). Indeed diagnostically there must be several recurrent episodes, each of which tends to occur with a lower precipitating threshold, suggestive of a "kindling" effect as in epilepsy.

Although usually of onset in young adulthood, it can occur in childhood, and is commoner in females. Although it is highly heritable, it may be that, as with the other neurodevelopmental frontostriatal disorders, a vulnerability is inherited to environmental factors; in any event, the condition is multifactorial and probably polygenic, and no single "Jeremiah gene" has as yet been identified. The condition is highly comorbid with anxiety, panic disorder, agoraphobia, OCD, mania and possibly schizophrenia. However, the anxious tend to experience *hyper*arousal, whereas the depressed tend to experience *hypo*arousal. Nevertheless this distinction may merely parallel the motor correlates of psychomotor agitation and psychomotor retardation. Although the former may relate to anxiety, the latter manifestation of depression is reminiscent of dopaminergic dysfunction and Parkinson's disease.

Neuropsychologically, apart from the motor correlates, there are typically problems with concentration, insight, memory, attention, reasoning, problem solving, planning, and judgement—the classical dysexecutive syndrome of the dorsolateral prefrontal cortex and anterior cingulate. Effortful rather than automatic processing is affected, and explicit rather than implicit memory. Hippocampal involvement may explain memory problems, which may merge with apparent dementia of the sort seen in Parkinson's disease; again, dopaminergic involvement (and prefrontal circuits) also seem to be involved.

Imaging studies may indicate ventricular enlargement, as in Alzheimer's and Huntington's diseases, and schizophrenia, together with periventricular white matter lesions, decreased striatal volume, frontal and temporal anomalies, and possible cerebellar atrophy.

Functionally, there is decreased anterior cingulate metabolism (especially in the subgenual region, with decreased numbers of glial cells), and hypometabolism of the left dorsolateral prefrontal cortex, left temporal regions, and striatum. Increased orbitofrontal activity (reversible with treatment) may correspond to inhibitory processes and rumination. Recent activation studies indicate increased amygdalar activity, correlating with stress and reversible with treatment. It is not clear whether the activation changes of depression predispose individuals to such moods, or are correlates, consequences, or compensatory mechanisms for the disorder. Medication of course also affects activity, and reduced activation may merely be due to volumetric reductions.

Mood induction studies in normal healthy individuals offer contradictory findings, as indeed so also do the clinical, lesion, and laterality studies. If any conclusions can be drawn, during periods of natural or induced lowered mood there is reduced activation in the dorsolateral and dorsomedial prefrontal cortex, perhaps reflecting impaired cognitive processes, and increased activation in the medial and lateral orbitofrontal cortex, maybe reflecting emotional and ruminative activity. There is also increased amygdalar activity possibly reflecting aspects of stress, and reduced activity in the subgenual anterior cingulate, especially on the left, along with reduced glial cell numbers, indicative of reduced drive. This region is instead activated during manic phases. The frontostriatal circuits thus link with the amygdala in the experience of mood. With respect to lateralisation, it is unclear whether the right hemisphere is simply more emotional than the left, or whether it is involved with negative emotions, and the left with positive. Indeed lesion studies suggest an additional anterior–posterior distinction: left anterior damage may be associated with depression, right anterior damage with indifference, euphoria or neglect, and right posterior damage with anger and frustration.

No less complex is the interaction between neurotransmitters and with the various brain regions. Moreover artificially raising or lowering neurotransmitter levels has surprisingly little effect upon normal, healthy individuals, though it can considerably accentuate mood in clinical patients. The serotonergic system is the largest cohesive neurotransmitter system in the brain, and is important in neurogenesis, mood, immune function, movement, learning, sleep, and circadian rhythms. 5-HT is a precursor of the rhythm modulator, melatonin; the latter decreases with age, in proportion to lowered mood. Lowered serum cholesterol is associated with lowered 5-HT metabolism and lowered mood. Dysregulation of 5-HT activity seems central to depression, though there are many inconsistencies and 5-HT levels do not relate in any simple way to severity of depression; postsynaptic neuronal activity in the limbic system may be the more important variable, along with stress as a mediating factor. 5-HT also modulates levels of the other neurotransmitters: dopamine and noradrenaline.

The dopaminergic system closely parallels the serotonergic and provides an integrated reward system, mediating hedonia, motivation, reinforcement, and psychomotor activity. *Hypo*dopaminergia is associated with anhedonia and *hyper*dopaminergia with mania, but dopamine agonists are poor antidepressants. Nevertheless, anhedonia and depression may stem from increased D1 receptor activity and/or reduced D2 receptor activity, with antidepressants sensitising D2/D3 receptors in the mesocortical and mesolimbic systems; psychomotor retardation may be due to increased numbers of D2 receptors in the basal ganglia. The dopamine system may be the final common pathway for the interacting dopaminergic, serotonergic and noradrenergic systems. The latter system is of course involved in a range of psychiatric disorders, including addiction, withdrawal, anxiety, and depression, and its activity is influenced by levels of stress. Cells from the system are progressively lost with ageing, in proportion to lowered mood; the depressed may also have altered noradrenergic activity.

Substance P is involved in the experience of pain, and its receptor is highly expressed in regions critical for regulating affective behaviour and responsivity to stress; there is an interaction with the dopaminergic and serotonergic systems. Substance P antagonists may be successful antidepressants. Antidepressants, including ECT and the recently developed procedure of TMS, may increase receptor sensitivity via multiple interacting systems. The MAOIs act by halting destruction of monoamines in the synapse; TCAs inhibit their reuptake. In both cases the serotonergic system is especially affected, and the SSRIs block the presynaptic reuptake of that neurotransmitter by desensitising the presynaptic, inhibitory autoreceptors. Similar mechanisms may explain why most forms of intervention take time to work. Depression is thus a heterogeneous disorder due to dysfunction involving multiple transmitter systems. Transmitter depletion may not necessarily result in depression but may increase vulnerability.

Bipolar disorder involves episodes of raised (manic) and lowered (depressed) mood. There is considerable variability in the number, frequency, severity, and regularity of the cycles. In the manic phase there is loss of contact with reality, hyperactivity, agitation, euphoria, paranoia, irritability, impulsiveness, and delusions of grandeur. Over 1% of the population may be affected, equally distributed across the sexes, unlike the female preponderance in unipolar major depression. The condition is familial, though no gene has as yet been identified, and again stress can precipitate an attack. So too do dopamine agonists, whereas the condition is ameliorated by dopamine antagonists. During the manic phase activity increases in the anterior cingulate and decreases during the depressed phase. Lesions of the amygdala, striatum, and ventral prefrontal cortex can result in manic disinhibited behaviour. As with unipolar disorder, there seems to be a kindling or sensitisation effect, perhaps involving second messengers and G-proteins, which may interact with "traditional" dopaminergic, noradrenergic, and serotonergic modulatory systems. Lithium may dampen mood swings by inhibiting stimulatory and inhibitory G-protein activity.

Creativity, especially in poetry, the novel, and in the visual arts, has been associated with mood disorder, especially bipolar. Although difficult to assess objectively, it nevertheless also seems associated with seasonality of birth (as with schizophrenia, which too manifests somewhat similar patterns of morphometric imaging to bipolar disorder). Mania may in fact be a powerful creative force, with perhaps disinhibition of the amygdala (which connects to the anterior cingulate, a source of "drive") a major factor.

Stress is an important intervening variable in mood disorder. It is associated with reduced expression of brain-derived neurotrophic factor, which leads in turn to hippocampal atrophy, depression, and dementia. The hippocampus is also then less able to back-regulate the stress-mediating HPA axis, leading to a vicious circle of hypercortisolaemia, and reductions in neuronal and glial density in the prefrontal cortex, particularly in the dopaminergic and serotonergic systems; thus cognitive changes associated with stress may be explained. Various pharmacological challenges have been proposed for the diagnosis of stress-induced depression; all, however, have proved controversial. Stress leads to altered immune function and psychosomatic disorders; interactions between the central nervous system and the immune system, via stress, are now emerging, with hypercortiso-laemia and increased neuronal vulnerability to glutamate toxicity acting as intermediaries. Conversely, 5-HT stimulates production of new granule cell neurones in the hippocampus, an effect that is reduced with stress.

FURTHER READING

Canli, T. (1999). Hemispheric asymmetry in the experience of emotion: A perspective from functional imaging. *The Neuroscientist, 5,* 201–207.

Dolan, R.J. (1997). Mood disorders and abnormal cingulate cortex. *Trends in Cognitive Sciences, 1,* 283–286.

Drevets, W.C. (1998). Functional neuroimaging studies of depression: The anatomy of melancholia. *Annual Review of Medicine, 49,* 341–361.

Drevets, W.C. (1999). Mania. In M.J. Zigmond, F.E. Bloom, S.C. Landis, J.L. Roberts, & L.R. Squire (Eds.), *Fundamental neuroscience* (pp. 1254–1255). San Diego: Academic Press.

Duffy, J.D., & Coffey, C.E. (1997). The neurobiology of depression. In M.R. Trimble & J.L. Cummings (Eds.), *Contemporary Behavioral Neurology* (pp. 275–288). New York: Butterworth-Heinemann.

Duman, R.S., & Charney, D.S. (1999). Cell atrophy and loss in major depression. *Biological Psychiatry, 45,* 1083–1084.

Elliott, R. (1998). The neuropsychological profile in unipolar depression. *Trends in Cognitive Sciences, 2,* 447–454.

Ghaemi, S.N., Boiman, E.E., & Goodwin, F.K. (1999). Kindling and second messengers: An approach to the neurobiology of recurrence in bipolar disorder. *Biological Psychiatry, 45,* 137–144.

Goldberg, J.F., & Harrow, M. (Eds.) (1998). *Bipolar disorders: Clinical course and outcome.* Washington, DC: American Psychiatric Press.

Goodnick, P.J. (Ed.) (1998). *Mania: Clinical and research perspectives.* Washington, DC: American Psychiatric Press.

Goodwin, G.M. (1996). Functional imaging, affective disorder and dementia. *British Medical Bulletin, 52,* 495–512.

Honig, A., & Van Praag, H.M. (Eds.) (1997). *Depression: Neurobiological, psychopathological and therapeutic advances.* New York: Wiley.

Jamison, K.R. (1993). *Touched by fire: Manic-depressive illness and the artistic temperament.* New York: Free Press.

Jamison, K.R. (1995). Manic-depressive illness and creativity. *Scientific American,* February, 46–51.

Joseph, A.B. (1999). Disorders of mood and movement: An overview. In A.B. Joseph & R.R. Young (Eds.), *Movement disorders in neurology and neuropsychiatry* (pp. 299–303). Oxford: Blackwell.

Kessler, R.C. (1997). The effects of stressful life events on depression. *Annual Review of Psychology, 48,* 191–214.

MacKinnon, D.F., Jamison, K.R., & DePaulo, J.R. (1997). Genetics of manic depressive illness. *Annual Review of Neuroscience, 20*, 355–373.

McAllister-Williams, R.H., Ferrier, I.N., & Young, A.H. (1998). Mood and neuropsychological function in depression: The role of corticosteroids and serotonin. *Psychological Medicine, 28*, 573–584.

Mineka, S., Watson, D., & Clark, L.A. (1998). Comorbidity of anxiety and unipolar mood disorders. *Annual Review of Psychology, 49*, 377–412.

Nemeroff, C.B. (1998). Psychopharmacology of affective disorders in the 21st Century. *Biological Psychiatry, 44*, 514–525.

Robinson, R.G., & Travella, J.I. (1996). Neuropsychiatry of mood disorders. In B.S. Fogel, R.B. Schiffer, & S.M. Rao (Eds.), *Neuropsychiatry* (pp. 287–305). Baltimore: Williams & Wilkins.

Rogers, M.A., Bradshaw, J.L., Pantelis, C.K., & Phillips, J.G. (1998). Fronto-striatal deficits in unipolar major depression. *Brain Research Bulletin, 47*, 297–310.

Soares, J.C., & Mann, J.J. (1997). The anatomy of mood disorders: Review of structural neuroimaging studies. *Biological Psychiatry, 41*, 86–106.

Staley, J.K., Malison, R.T., & Innis, R.B. (1998). Imaging of the serotonergic system: Interactions of neuroanatomical and functional abnormalities of depression. *Biological Psychiatry, 44*, 534–549.

Wolpert, L. (1999). *Malignant sadness: The anatomy of depression.* London: Faber & Faber.

CHAPTER TEN

An interpretation

Καὶ ἀρχὴ καὶ τέλος νοῦς.
Mind is the beginning and the end.
—*Ethica Nichomachea* VI, 11, 6, Aristotle

The decade of the brain has coincided with a new rapprochement between neurology and psychiatry, and the emergence of neuropsychology as both a research and a clinical discipline. Neuroimaging, moreover, has provided a new window on the interface between brain and mind, whether in sickness or in health—and indeed the latter distinction, in the context of neuropsychiatry, should itself be seen as involving a continuum, rather than a dichotomy, a continuum that reflects fundamental dimensions of personality. Thus those cognitive and behavioural aspects of interest to the neuropsychiatrist necessarily involve circuitry, the frontostriatal system, which underlies our very personal identities, as frugal, exploratory, rash, paranoid, depressive, hyperactive, obsessive, profane, salacious, or restrained. Indeed our highly evolved frontal regions, as the seat of our personalities, may underlie the very essence of our humanity. The *dorsolateral prefrontal cortex*, with associated frontostriatal circuitry, may be concerned with the highest cognitive or executive functions, including the setting of global plans, strategies, and schemata, the capacity to operate via self-direction or without external guidance, the organisation of new behaviours, cognitive flexibility, the maintenance or shifting of set and attention, and general problem solving and judgement. The *lateral orbitofrontal cortex* and associated circuitry may be involved with self-monitoring and the inhibition of inappropriate behaviours. The *anterior cingulate* and associated circuitry may mediate intentionality, the initiation of action, and focused attention.

The release of actual responses may be achieved via the premotor areas: the *lateral premotor area*, which may be more responsive to the occurrence of external events in the sequential release of response elements; and the mesially located *supplementary motor area* which, with its striato-pallido-thalamic input from the basal ganglia, may more reflect internally driven aspects of volition and will.

These frontostriatal circuits enable us to decide what to do, and when and how to achieve it, with additional bias from limbic mechanisms. Modulatory neurotransmitters, notably dopamine, noradrenaline, and serotonin, along with acetylcholine, the neuropeptides, GABA, glutamate, and substance P (though this list is very far from exhaustive), help to "drive" the system. Crucial to the process may be the roles of the cerebellum, whose manifold functions are yet to be fully understood, and of the basal ganglia. Both "extrapyramidal" structures form cortico-thalamo-cortical re-entrant loops, and play roles in selecting, inhibiting, releasing, filtering, modulating, and automating behaviours. We have a clearer picture of the physiology and function of the basal ganglia, through which pass parallel segregated loops from and back to the major frontal regions just described. These loops, between striatum and globus pallidus, each consist of a direct (facilitatory) and indirect (inhibitory) pathway, under overall dopaminergic control. Normally their respective influences are maintained in a balanced equilibrium for the release of wanted and inhibition of unwanted action patterns. Frontostriatal disorders may thus result in release of unwanted behaviours, thoughts, or feelings, or retardation of appropriate behaviours, thoughts, or feelings. Another, possibly related, role of the basal ganglia may be to automatically link together ("bind" or "chunk") thought or action sequences without conscious feedback, control or supervision, a process that may break down in the disorganised thought of schizophrenia.

In this, final, chapter, I shall briefly review the six neurodevelopmental disorders from a frontostriatal perspective, before trying to determine their commonalities and differences. In particular, I shall revisit the issues of inhibition or disinhibitory release; the distinction between compulsivity and impulsivity; the fluctuating or episodic course of many of the disorders; the concept of a developmental delay or arrest; the idea that the disorders may be continuously distributed with respect to each other, and to normality, on various continua; the differential contributions of structural pathology versus neurochemical imbalance; the possibly adaptive nature of "subclinical" levels of the "disorder" in close relatives; the very concepts, in consequence, of disorder and diagnosis, state and trait markers, and comorbidity; the likely need for both an underlying (genetic) predisposition, and triggering environmental factors or contingencies. Other, recurring, incidental issues to be noted are the heterogeneous nature of the disorders, the frequent occurrence of anomalies of lateralisation, and sex differences.

Tourette's syndrome is a classic frontostriatal disorder of release or disinhibition, with its motor or vocal tics, and unwanted echo- and "copro-" phenomena—phenomena that lie in the murky borderlands between voluntary and involuntary, and whose nature may be influenced by environmental, cultural, and social factors. Although their eventual release may be inevitable, it nevertheless may be briefly postponed, as indeed is also the case with many of the unwanted behaviours of the other frontostriatal disorders: the compulsions of obsessive compulsive disorder (OCD), the unruliness of attention deficit hyperactivity disorder (ADHD), the extravagant claims of the bipolar patient in the manic phase, and the paranoia of the patient with schizophrenia. Like these other unwanted behaviours, moreover, the symptoms of Tourette's syndrome may fluctuate in time, place, and content, and may be partially disguisable under the cloak of other ongoing activities. Like, too, the obsessions of OCD, many of the behaviours associated with ADHD, and certain aspects of autism, the clinical features of Tourette's syndrome seem often to reflect a developmental delay or arrest, with the affected individuals impelled to behave in what is no longer an age-appropriate fashion.

Obsessive compulsive disorder, like Tourette's syndrome, presents with the appearance of "possession" or invasion by unwanted forces, and many of its symptoms seem almost to be extended versions of that latter syndrome. Sufferers know the irrationality of their obsessive thoughts and compulsive behaviours, but are driven to indulge them. To quantify for diagnosis, behaviours must be inappropriate, intense, and lengthy enough to cause distress, but not intrinsically gratifying, and should be accompanied by preservation of insight concerning the situation's intrinsic futility—an insight that is typically absent from similar behaviour in schizophrenia. Similarly, there is an element of single-minded overfocused attention in OCD that is absent from Tourette's syndrome, ADHD, and schizophrenia, but which may reappear in the stereotypies of autism and the ruminations of depression. Many of the preoccupations of this disorder relate to those of normal childhood: hoarding, dirt, bodily functions, symmetry, and rituals. Although the condition is clearly heritable, perhaps in the form of a predisposition or vulnerability, environmental factors may also play a role; indeed childhood streptococcal infection, as with Tourette's syndrome and possibly ADHD, may trigger antineuronal antibodies that target the striatum.

Attention deficit hyperactivity disorder, unlike many if not most of the other frontostriatal disorders, is an externalising disorder that affects others far more than the individual concerned. However, as with Tourette's syndrome and OCD, symptomatology has to be beyond what might otherwise be expected of a child of that chronological age. Thus nearly all children below a certain age may tend to be inattentive, hyperactive, and impulsive. The borderline therefore between normality and pathology is particularly indistinct in this disorder, leading to possible over- (or even under-) diagnosis to a considerable degree. Impulsivity may be the most significant or disruptive symptom: an inability to delay responses or gratification, impetuosity, and a low tolerance of frustration. Hyperactivity may be absent in a variant that is perhaps more common in girls, and which is less likely to be associated with aggressive dyscontrol, conduct disorder, or oppositional defiant syndrome. Novelty seeking, impulsivity, exploratory behaviour, and excitability may be "normal" extensions along a personality continuum which, like the disorder itself, may be associated with reduced sensitivity of the dopamine D4 receptor. However, as with the other frontostriatal disorders, other modulatory neurotransmitters are almost certainly also involved. Nevertheless in certain aspects the disorder clearly contrasts with the overfocused aspect of OCD.

Schizophrenia is regarded as our most disabling adult neuropsychiatric disorder, whereas autism is considered to be our most disabling neuropsychiatric condition of childhood. Both may also possess possible degenerative characteristics, perhaps only in certain instances, and both share with adult neurodegenerative disorders, such as Alzheimer's and Huntington's diseases, a dementing character. Both may also manifest very early preclinical signs sometimes evident in old home movies. Schizophrenia typically manifests later than the other neurodevelopmental disorders—in young adulthood, in fact—with the possible exception of depression. Moreover it possesses a positive and negative symptomatology that shares certain characteristics with that of depression, more particularly perhaps bipolar disorder. Complex and more intractable than the other disorders, it affects the whole spectrum of behaviour, including emotional reactivity, interpersonal relationships, perceptual and thought processes, and motivation. It develops gradually with incomplete remissions and prolonged impairment. Positive symptoms include delusions, hallucinations, and disorganisation of thought, speech, and behaviour; negative symptoms—the more difficult to treat, though some progress is being made with newer, atypical antipsychotics—include flattening of affect, anhedonia, alogia, avolition, and poverty of action. In addition to the frontostriatal system, wider temporolimbic involvement is certain, though many of the symptoms mirror the effects of discretely localised frontal lesions, and abnormal *interactivity* between the two regions may characterise the disorder. A failure of reality monitoring, misattribution, or an inability to differentiate between one's own and other people's beliefs and actions may underlie delusional behaviour, which, like the inappropriate profanities of Tourette's syndrome, are partly determined by social context. More perhaps than in all the other five frontostriatal disorders, though to some extent present in autism and depression, structural pathologies, in addition to neurochemical imbalances, may play a role. Cerebellar maldevelopment, as in autism, may be significant in this context. In cognition, nearly all aspects are affected. Perhaps more clearly than in any of the other disorders, anomalies of neurodevelopment at a critical stage in the second trimester of pregnancy have been implicated. These may account for dysmorphies of face and minor dermatoglyphic anomalies, though there is ongoing debate as to whether there is thereafter a static neuropathy, or also continuing neurodegeneration without gliosis. If maldevelopment, and/or abnormal pruning or apoptosis is responsible, why are clinical signs so slow to appear? Do the requisite structures, and behaviours, have first to mature? The genetics of schizophrenia are no clearer than in any of the other disorders, though an inherited vulnerability along with an interaction with environmental factors seems more evident than in the other disorders. Although disorders of both 5-HT and dopamine regulation have been proposed, again a complex interaction seems likely that also involves glutamate and nitric oxide. Both frontal hypodopaminergia and temporo-limbic hyperdopaminergia may occur. Both 5-HT and glutamate, moreover, may play an early role in the developing architecture of the central nervous system, although glutamate, and the basal ganglia, may be involved in "binding", of which schizophrenia may be deemed a disorder.

Autism, like schizophrenia, was once thought to be due to faulty parenting. It is characterised by social impairment (lack of reciprocity, empathy, and affection, and reduced eye contact), abnormalities or delays in acquisition of language or capacity to communicate, and stereotyped, restricted, or repetitive interests or unusual attachments to objects or situations. Cognition and attention are also usually severely affected; there may be a tendency to seizures, with hyper- or hyposensitivity to sensory stimulation, and there may be unusual islands of ability or even talent. Of all the disorders, clinical manifestation occurs earliest, around 3 years of age. Although various medical conditions may possibly cause, or simulate, autism, none may be sufficient or even necessary for its manifestation, though the condition, like the other disorders, is highly heritable. Like schizophrenia, seasonality-of-birth effects suggest additional environmental (maternal infection) factors, although as with Tourette's syndrome and OCD, immunological dysfunctions may play a role. A deficit in theory-of-mind "Machiavellian intelligence" is suggested by performance in the False Belief Test, but may not be primary to the condition; nor, probably, is a deficit in executive function or a failure of central coherence (overfocusing on details at the expense of global interrelationships). As with schizophrenia and, after that disorder, more clearly than in any of the others, there is evidence of structural changes macro- and microscopically in the central nervous system, and of cerebellar dysfunction. Again as with schizophrenia, there are pronounced parkinsonian features and indications of dopaminergic and serotonergic involvement. However, like OCD, the neuropeptides also seem to play a role, and may be responsible for certain stereotypic aspects. Asperger's disorder shares with autism a severe degree of social impairment, though there is relative preservation of language and cognitive function; in Williams syndrome social function and aspects of language are extremely well preserved or even exaggerated, whereas there may be other deficits characteristic of autism.

Unipolar major depression is the commonest neuropsychiatric disorder and, like schizophrenia, the most likely to end in suicide. It is to be distinguished from the normal "blues" and from bipolar disorder in the (hypo)manic phase. Anhedonia, apathy, and amotivation may be central to the disorder, which, like schizophrenia in many instances, is episodic, with about five or six major events in a typical lifetime. Each episode seems to lower the threshold for the next; the same may possibly occur with schizophrenia and both disorders typically onset in young adulthood, though again in both disorders there may be instances of childhood or maturity onset. No single "Jeremiah gene" has been isolated, and a polygenic inheritance of vulnerability to environmental precipitants again seems likely. Motor correlates include either psychomotor agitation or retardation of a parkinsonian nature. There are also typically problems with concentration, attention, insight, memory, problem solving, planning and judgement, i.e. executive processes involving effortful processing. Ventricular enlargement may occur, as in Alzheimer's and Huntington's diseases and schizophrenia, and depression shares with schizophrenia and autism evidence of structural changes. These occur in addition to "merely" functional anomalies (increased orbitofrontal activity, as in OCD, perhaps reflecting obsessive ruminations). Structural changes may stem from the action of stress-related hormones upon frontal and limbic–hippocampal regions. A complex interaction between 5-HT (and cholesterol), dopamine, noradrenaline, and substance P seems implicated in depression, and most effective antidepressants target more than one transmitter system. The manic phase of bipolar disorder shares clear commonalities with some of the positive symptoms of schizophrenia, and both disorders may be associated with aspects of increased creativity or lateral thinking.

In the neurodevelopmental disorders there are few biological markers for diagnosis, which must usually be made on the basis of history and behaviour. Thus we often cannot say categorically that someone has a certain disorder when, as here, that disorder involves a continuous distribution with the normal healthy state. This is particularly apposite if we view the manifestations of such disorders as merely interruptions or delays in a normal, ongoing, ontogenetic or neurodevelopmental process. Indeed the disorders themselves tend to be almost arbitrary (though specified for a particular purpose or context) constellations of signs and symptoms that distribute continuously with normal behaviour. Differences in such diagnostic criteria account largely for apparent differences in prevalences between different countries. Diagnoses themselves are concepts that evolve over time, whose usefulness is judged by their ability to inform concerning relevant patho-physiology, treatment, and possible prevention or diagnosis.

One of the aims of biological psychiatry is to identify possibly useful markers of the various disorders. Such markers may reflect either the current state of an illness, which therefore may be active or in remission phase, or of the trait of a predisposition toward that illness. State markers, which may or may not be genetic, should revert to normal on recovery or remission, and so presumably relate somehow to current symptomatology, rather than to the basic aetiology. Trait markers, however, must somehow relate to the underlying biological substrates, persisting whatever the patient's current state of health, and perhaps even being found in "unaffected" relatives. They are therefore stable characteristics that constantly deviate from normal levels, independently of any remissions or medication, being present even when the individual is asymptomatic. Consequently, when cognitive or behaviour therapy leads to a resolution, temporary or permanent, of the symptoms of, for example, depression or OCD, and at the same time normalises previously aberrant patterns of functional imaging, the latter patterns should be seen as state rather than trait markers; they should also be seen as exercising any causality at a level that at most is proximal to the symptoms, rather than initial or fundamental to the disorder. Their diagnostic certainty should therefore be regarded as questionable; they may *aid* diagnosis, but should not perhaps be regarded as in any way definitive.

Comorbidity—the additional presence of a distinct clinical entity before or during the course of an index disease—is an important if vexatious issue in psychopathy. It is not always clear whether, or how, two (or more) clinical entities can be separated, e.g. anxiety and depression. Thus while there is presumption of two or more simultaneous, independent diseases, it may in fact be the case that the patient is suffering from a single underlying condition that displays features of two arbitrarily defined and differentiated disorders. Alternatively, there may be an associated *predisposition* to the two disorders; or one disorder, such as ADHD, may be a risk factor for another, such as conduct disorder, unless one argues that they both represent some single or common underlying dimension. Similarly, depression may be viewed as a complication of OCD, rather than as a distinct condition. Thus there are different clinical traditions of "lumping" and "splitting"; this is particularly difficult when key symptoms defining theoretically distinct disorders co-occur, as with problems in concentration with both anxiety and depression, and with the paranoia of schizophrenia and the manic phase of bipolar disorder. Furthermore greater severity in the presentation of a disorder is likely to be associated with more concomitant comorbid conditions.

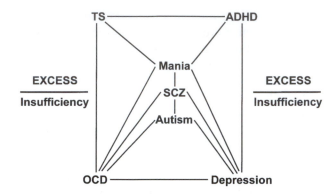

Figure 10.1. Comorbidities, commonalities, and links between the frontostriatal disorders: TS, Tourette's syndrome; ADHD, attention deficit hyperactivity disorder; OCD, obsessive compulsive disorder; SCZ, schizophrenia.

In practice, comorbidity affords additional problems, as often the comorbid condition, e.g. ADHD, is more distressing or disruptive than the index condition, typically Tourette's syndrome. Moreover, the two disorders may exercise interactive or synergistic effects, and appropriate medications for one condition may be inappropriate for the other. Thus dopamine agonists, while ameliorating the affects of ADHD, may exacerbate the tics of comorbid Tourette's syndrome. Similarly, selective serotonin reuptake inhibitors may ameliorate OCD, while again worsening tics.

There are clear overlaps, if not frank comorbidities, between Tourette's syndrome and OCD, ADHD, and mania; there are similar links involving ADHD, with mania and depression; mania with OCD, depression, and schizophrenia; depression with schizophrenia, autism, and OCD; and schizophrenia with autism and OCD. Figure 10.1 represents a possible pattern of such associative relationships.Which disorder manifests may depend upon how the frontostriatal system happens to be compromised, as a result of inherited genetic predispositions and environmental contingency.

Ultimately, it must be remembered that signs and symptoms are behaviour patterns that, from a particular medical, social, or even historical viewpoint, are judged as somehow deviant, excessive, or deficient, and a disorder is an "arbitrary" constellation of such symptoms, or at least a grouping that has been judged as clinically or practically useful in a given context. In the extreme instance, such as the frontostriatal *neurodegenerative* disorder, Huntington's disease, we see a behaviour pattern that involves the mutation and autosomal-dominant transmission of a single gene. However, it must be remembered that all characteristics, whether behavioural or not, originally involved mutations that proved more or less adaptive to a particular environment. Some mutations merely prove less maladaptive than others, or even positively advantageous. However, the frontostriatal *neurodevelopmental* disorders are likely to be polygenic in inheritance, and are certainly far less uniform and consistent in their presentation than Huntington's disease, with its remorseless inevitability of progression. It is here that the boundaries between disorder and "normality", and between the disorders themselves, are inevitably blurred.

The six neurodevelopmental disorders of the frontostriatal system discussed in this book have clear commonalities with the later-developing neurodegenerative disorders of that system—Parkinson's and Huntington's diseases—and some similarities with the more pervasive disorder of ageing: Alzheimer's disease. While both Huntington's disease (neurodegenerative) and Tourette's syndrome (neurodevelopmental) are prototypical disorders of hyperkinesia, Parkinson's disease (neurodegenerative) and certain aspects of melancholic depression (neurodevelopmental) typify hypokinesia. (ADHD is more a disorder of disinhibition or impulse dyscontrol.) Hyperkinesia (pure, tremorous, dystonic, dyskinetic, athetotic, choreic, myoclonic, or involving tics) is clearly more complex than hypokinesia, which may range through akinesia, bradykinesia, hypometria, and catatonia. Even the neurodevelopmental/neurodegenerative distinction may not be absolute, as degenerative processes may be apparent in schizophrenia and autism, and possibly in certain forms of depression, though probably not in Tourette's syndrome, OCD, or ADHD. Nevertheless, neurochemical dysregulation rather than structural alterations tend to characterise the neurodevelopmental disorders, though again degenerative structural changes may be apparent in schizophrenia and depression. That said, all the disorders are open to behavioural, genetic, epidemiological, clinical, molecular, and neuroimaging study.

In the broadest sense, the neurodevelopmental disorders, in addition to the six that involve the frontostriatal system to some considerable extent, and with which this book is concerned, include also mental retardation and specific disorders of speech, arithmetic, and motor ability. All are associated with abnormal brain morphology of some kind, deficits or alterations in neural migration, microgyria, lissencephaly, microcephaly, or hydrocephaly, abnormalities of apoptotic pruning, altered asymmetries (structural, functional, or behavioural), and specific histological or biochemical abnormalities. All involve some form of developmental delay or halt at a particular stage or milestone, though the consequences thereof may not manifest until considerably later, when appropriate structures or behaviours have "unfolded". Indeed it may be for this reason that the various disorders seem to occur at different developmental stages, though, again, careful retrospective analysis of preclinical information (e.g. old home movies) may reveal precursor phenomena back almost to infancy. In any case, there are typically delays in emotional, cognitive, or motor functioning, with disturbances of behaviour, posture, or movement. These deficits are not generally progressive, and at various levels (neurodevelopment, especially of the cerebellum, and in terms of neurotransmitter function and behaviour) seem to involve serotonin. All the disorders dealt with in this book are limbic in their experiential aspects, frontal with respect to their cognitive characteristics, and striatal in terms of behavioural release or inhibition. Nevertheless they differ in the degree to which they share these cognitive, affective, and motor aspects, in that some are more motor, some are more affective, and some are more cognitive in their predominant symptomatology. Thus they exhibit various "mixes" of these cognitive, affective, or motor aspects:

- Tourette's syndrome—mostly motor and affective.
- OCD—mostly affective, with some cognitive aspects.
- ADHD—mostly cognitive and motor, though often with strong affective aspects.
- Schizophrenia—mostly affective and cognitive, though often with considerable motor involvement.
- Autism—mostly cognitive and affective.
- Depression—mostly affective, though with some cognitive and motor involvement.

Thus each disorder involves a range of structural and neurochemical substrates:

- Different parts, and combinations of parts, of the various frontostriatal circuits.
- Different mixes of direct (facilitatory) and indirect (inhibitory) pathways.
- Different mixes of the major neuromodulatory neurotransmitters, neuropeptides, sex steroids etc. (with the latter partly accounting for the often marked sex differences in prevalence and severity).
- Different *additional* regions, e.g. cerebellum, parietal, and temporal lobes.

Ultimately, all of the above, but especially perhaps the frontostriatal system, may determine which disorders present, and how, and the very bases of our normal, healthy personalities. Thus the disorders lie on continua, both with respect to each other, and to the normal healthy state; they are in effect *spectrum* disorders. They are therefore all highly comorbid, perhaps even with common heritability factors; the presence of one disorder within the family may increase the risk levels for another.

As disorders of developmental delay, or even arrest, their symptomatology by definition has to be beyond what might be expected of the behaviour of normal children of that particular developmental age. Thus most normal children at some point in their development may be expected to exhibit behaviour patterns otherwise characteristic of the various disorders: copro- or echophenomena (if not outright tics), obsessions, rituals, stereotypies, "bizarre" beliefs, impulsive or disorganised behaviour, and so on. There is therefore in each disorder a continuum with normal, healthy behaviour, not only in terms of persistence of apparently juvenile behaviour patterns, but also in terms of what normal healthy adults may themselves do on occasion. This continuum may perhaps be clearest with mood disorder (we are all sometimes depressed), impulse dyscontrol, and the obsessive compulsive *personality*, somewhat less obvious with schizophreniform paranoia and autistic "oddness", and perhaps least with the tics of Tourette's syndrome; after all, tics are either present or absent. Nevertheless, we are all subject to the "infectiousness" of a yawn, and have our own personal rituals if not stereotypies. Thus there are in fact personality versions (schizoid, pessimistic, obsessive compulsive, unruly, salacious, autistic–odd) of all the disorders except perhaps for Tourette's syndrome; even there, perhaps, we see the exuberant, iconoclastic, unseemly individual in society. Similarly, many of the disorders shade off, spectrum-wise, into other, related conditions (e.g. autism–Asperger's, OCD–kleptomania, ADHD–conduct disorder, and so on). In some ways the disorders, in mild presentation, should perhaps be seen rather as personality biases. Indeed, our personalities themselves may be characterised by our positions on a prefrontal vectorial system whose extensions end in what we arbitrarily choose to call pathology. We are all subject to depression, paranoid jealousy, or suspicion, urges to commit the socially unacceptable, to tread on the cracks in the pavement or to avoid them, to throw caution to the winds—or dedicate our lives obsessively to the pursuit of an arcane line of knowledge. We are sociable or otherwise, outgoing or introverted—and while these *traits* may be fairly consistent at a personal or even family level, from time to time our moods or medications may change our momentary *states* of mind. It is tempting to link *traits* to fairly permanent *structural* configurations of the frontostriatal system, and *states* to more variable neurochemical balances, but this may be oversimplification.

Many of these disorders possess a long folk-history, especially of bewitchment or possession for aspects of Tourette's syndrome, OCD and schizophrenia. Depressive states were noted by the classical authors 2000 years ago or more; ADHD in the premodern era may simply have been unremarkable, but the apparent absence of any account reminiscent of autism is perhaps of note. They are all of course very heterogeneous in presentation, if not also in aetiology, and of widely differing baseline frequencies. Nowadays, depression and ADHD are clearly the most prevalent, and autism the least, with the other three disorders occupying the middle ground. In earlier societies the *criteria* for diagnosis, had they existed, would probably have been different from nowadays; it is possible also that had *today's* criteria been applied the prevalence figures and relative frequencies might also have differed. Certainly cultural determinants of the expression of unacceptable words or actions ("coprophenomena") might have been different in Tourette's syndrome, as might have been the obsessions and compulsions of OCD and the delusional beliefs of schizophrenia. The unruly behaviour of ADHD would probably have befitted a young warrior, and depression might prove to be largely a luxury of leisure.

Environmental events of course are also important in the short term in determining disordered behaviour. Thus "capture" by external objects can cause parkinsonian freezing, or release bizarre behaviours in Tourette's syndrome, OCD, schizophrenia, and autism. Some of these behaviours can be voluntarily suppressed for brief intervals, or camouflaged within other ongoing behaviours, or blocked by *gestes antagonistes*, leading to questions about anosognosia and levels of insight. Such insight is likely to be least evident in autism and schizophrenia, and greatest in Tourette's syndrome, OCD, and (at least in the older person) ADHD. The behaviours, moreover, are more likely to manifest during periods of high or low arousal, and least likely when arousal levels are intermediate, or the environment is challenging or interesting.

In many of the disorders, as with Parkinson's and Huntington's diseases—the archetypal neurodegenerative disorders—we can identify both positive and negative signs and symptoms. These are particularly clear in schizophrenia, autism, and depression (psychomotor agitation or retardation), and less clear in OCD. Perhaps only positive symptoms are evident in Tourette's syndrome and ADHD, and negative in attention deficit disorder (without hyperactivity). In all the disorders these symptoms may fluctuate in form and time, and many, but not all, of the disorders display an episodicity in their manifestation. Thus episodicity characterises Tourette's syndrome, schizophrenia, and especially depression, and to some extent OCD, but not ADHD or autism; however, episode durations and remission intervals vary between disorders, being longest for schizophrenia and depression. Remission, partial or complete, may be spontaneous or, more commonly, with treatment. After a sufficiently long period of remission, shorter perhaps with Tourette's syndrome than schizophrenia or depression, recovery may be said to have occurred, though clearly such a judgement must always remain to some extent provisional. A relapse will be deemed to occur with recurrence within a designated period of remission, whereas the disorder will be said to have recurred with reappearance after the patient is thought to have recovered. Again, these periods and judgements are necessarily somewhat arbitrary, with critical intervals reflecting the generally longer "cycle times" of depression, followed by schizophrenia.

Episodicity, when it occurs, may also be accompanied by a "kindling" effect, with provocation thresholds being lowered for each subsequent attack. We see this phenomenon in depression, mania (bipolar disorder), and schizophrenia. The initial episode of a disorder may be gradual and subtle, as with Tourette's syndrome, OCD, and schizophrenia, or rather more abrupt, as in depression and possibly autism; with ADHD there may merely be an inappropriate continuation of what in previous developmental terms would have been viewed as normal behaviour. Of course Tourette's syndrome, ADHD and autism are essentially disorders of childhood initiation, unlike schizophrenia, OCD and depression, which typically manifest at or after puberty; however, childhood versions of all three are in fact reported, and late-onset schizophrenia and OCD (but never autism) are not unknown. Nevertheless, in the latter instances, a neurological cause should probably be suspected, especially with behaviour reminiscent of Tourette's syndrome or ADHD. At the other extreme, there is little evidence that people ever really "grow out" of Tourette's syndrome, autism, or ADHD.

The hyper-/hypokinetic *motor* distinction is useful within and between the disorders: within, where both motor states may manifest at some point (schizophrenia, autism, depression); and between, with Tourette's syndrome, mania, and ADHD being essentially hyperkinetic, and attention deficit disorder being essentially hypokinetic. Old home videos may demonstrate precursors of such disordered movements in the preclinical phase with autism and schizophrenia, and it would be interesting to apply the technique to the other disorders. Anhedonia, the correlate of *mood* disorder, is evident in depression, autism, schizophrenia, and possibly ADHD, while all six disorders demonstrate to varying extents *cognitive* deficits, especially in terms of the dysexecutive syndrome of the dorsolateral prefrontal cortex, and where processing is effortful or controlled, rather than automatic. Thus executive difficulties (set, attention, strategy, problem solving, reasoning, working memory, cognitive flexibility, interference control etc.) are of low discriminant value. Similarly, perseveration may commonly manifest in one form or another in all the neurodevelopmental frontostriatal disorders. Anomalies of lateralisation (structural, functional, or behavioural) are also all-pervasive within the *neurodevelopmental* but *not* the *neurodegenerative* disorders, and may in fact act as markers, though they are unlikely to be of aetiological significance. The fact that medication not only controls the clinical manifestations of the disorder, but also often "corrects" the anomalous lateralisation, suggests that the *expression* of many asymmetries has at least partly a neurochemical basis, which may modulate any underlying *structural* asymmetries.

A useful distinction might be *"compulsivity"* (as in OCD, Tourette's syndrome, autism, and aspects of schizophrenia and depression) and *impulsivity*, as in Tourette's syndrome (again), ADHD, and bipolar disorder. The dopamine D2 A1 allele may have increased frequency in both compulsive and impulsive disorders, and disorders of addiction and substance abuse. A disordered belief system is evident in schizophrenia, bipolar disorder (manic phase), and OCD, whereas a disorder of self-individuation is apparent in schizophrenia (failure of reality monitoring) and autism (failure of theory of mind) where, as a result, social dysfunction is a major problem.

Brain injury or medical conditions can lead to, or simulate, Tourette's syndrome, OCD, ADHD, depression, bipolar disorder (manic phase), autism and many of the features of schizophrenia; overt neuropathology may be evident in autism, schizophrenia, and depression. It would therefore be nice if we could offer a neat neuropathological model of the frontostriatal system for each disorder. At this stage it is just not possible; indeed, as noted in Chapter 3, the current "consensus" model of Parkinson's disease, Huntington's disease, and normality, in terms of the direct and indirect pathways, is at best an approximation or guide, as the effects of surgery are not fully compatible with all aspects of the model. However, it is offered in this book, along with the action of the various frontostriatal circuits, as an interpretive aid; even the "five circuits" account may prove in the end to be an approximation. Nevertheless, as noted above, most of the disorders do have their neurological counterparts, with lesions to known areas. The following major relationships (hyper- or hypoactivation) are tentatively offered:

- Dorsolateral prefrontal cortex involvement—all six disorders to varying degrees.
- Anterior cingulate involvement—all disorders (perhaps helping determine positive or negative symptomatology) except possibly autism.
- Lateral orbitofrontal cortex—all disorders, perhaps normally in opposition to the anterior cingulate, except maybe in OCD, where both regions may be active.
- Cerebellum—schizophrenia and autism.

Autosomal dominant transmission with many interacting genes, and high but incomplete penetrance and variable expression, seems best to *describe* the genetics of most of the disorders. Many chromosomes have been implicated, with many failures to confirm, and an inherited vulnerability, in the presence of environmental risk factors, for a range of possible expressions or disorders, seems likely. Thus the risk levels for all disorders seem to cross the boundaries between them; for example, autism in the family may increase the risk that someone else develops OCD. Environmental risk factors include adverse pre- and perinatal events, maternal infections in mid gestation, streptococcal infections in childhood with associated immune dysfunctions (Tourette's syndrome, autism, ADHD, and OCD), but *not* faulty or "refrigerator" parenting (autism and schizophrenia)! Early "education" of the immune system by controlled exposure to pathogens is increasingly being suggested, by medical authorities generally, not only to aid acquisition of early natural immunity, but also to reduce the incidence of immune dysfunction diseases like the allergies; one wonders whether children's natural fascination with "coprophenomena" is an evolutionary-adaptive aspect of this situation.

Maternal stress during pregnancy is another, possibly underrated, environmental factor. Such stress can affect neurotransmitter levels in the blood, and the development of receptors and structure generally in the developing fetus. The dopaminergic and serotonergic systems may be particularly important in this context.

A neurodevelopmental account, therefore, of these frontostriatal disorders might, as we saw earlier, invoke the turning on or off of normal copies of vulnerability genes at specific developmental points, with input from environmental factors. Abnormal copies may alter this development by changing the timing or expression of gene products in response to environmental influences; alternatively they may alter brain development with excess expression or abnormal persistence of normal developmental characteristics, or may selectively inhibit or disinhibit certain frontostriatal circuits, either the two (anterior cingulate and lateral orbitofrontal cortex) that are naturally in opposition, or the two striatopallidal pathways, direct and indirect, which serve to release or inhibit behaviours.

At a neurochemical level, it is noteworthy that drug intoxication can simulate or lead to behaviours associated with schizophrenia, depression, and ADHD, though not perhaps Tourette's syndrome, autism, or OCD. We have already noted that dopaminergic and serotonergic dysfunction plays a role in all the disorders. Noradrenergic disorder is most clearly evident in depression and schizophrenia, though it may also be relevant in autism and ADHD. Cholinergic involvement (nicotinic) is evident in Huntington's disease, schizophrenia, ADHD, Tourette's syndrome, and depression, often with self-medication via smoking. Nicotine may promote the presynaptic release of acetylcholine, and potentiate the action of dopamine D2 antagonists. The neuropeptide and opiate systems may also be involved in OCD, autism, and depression. Sex differences in prevalence and onset age indicate a modulatory role from the gonadal steroid hormones.

An increasingly important concept in modern medical theory is that a disorder may persist in the genome because, with heterozygous representation or low penetrance, it may prove adaptive or protective against worse contingencies. Thus people with the sickle-cell gene may be protected against malaria. Similarly, the gene or genes for the frontostriatal neuro-developmental disorders may provide clinically "unaffected" close relatives with certain advantages. In this book we have seen that *autism* is associated, in relatives, with increased representation of the careers of engineering, physics, mathematics and accounting, and affected individuals may be superior at processing fine detail. *Tourette's syndrome* patients, and their relatives, may excel at jazz improvisation, gymnastics, dance, and games, and may even be more force-efficient in certain tasks demanding fine motor control. *Depression* is associated with literary creativity, especially in bipolar disorder. *Schizophrenia* may be associated with lateral associations and thinking, and the cunning, paranoid aloofness of the Odyssean personality. *Attention deficit hyperactivity disorder* is perfect for the explorer or hunter who must be hyperactive, impulsive, risk taking and ready for the unexpected. *Obsessive compulsive disorder*, conversely, with its concentration on hygiene, safety, checking, hoarding, and ordering, may characterise aspects of the personality of the scientist, physician, or homemaker.

Indeed, adaptiveness is always relative to the current ecology or society. In many native societies, people exhibiting aspects of what from *our* perspective we label as schizophrenia, ADHD or Tourette's syndrome may have been unremarkable as shamans, hunters, or song-and-dance men or women. Humans are, in evolutionary terms, the ultimate generalists. Our success in this respect lies in the maintenance, in our genome, of genes that code for what, in this book, and from the standpoint of present society, we have chosen to label as the neurodevelopmental frontostriatal disorders. In another age their number and representation might change. Πάντων χρημάτων μέτρον 'ο 'άνθρωπος: Man is the measure of all things. Protagoras (c. 481–411 BC).

References

AACAP Official Action (1998). Practice parameters for the assessment and treatment of children and adolescents with obsessive compulsive disorder. *Journal of the American Academy of Child and Adolescent Psychiatry, 37* (Suppl. 10), 27S–45S.

Achenbach, T.M. (1986). *Manual for the child behavior checklist direct observation form.* Burlington, VT: University of Vermont.

Adler, L.A., Freedman, R., Ross, R.G., Olincy, A., & Waldo, M.C. (1999). Elementary phenotypes in the neurobiological and genetic study of schizophrenia. *Biological Psychiatry, 46,* 8–18.

Adler, L.A., Olincy, A., Waldo, M., Harris, J.G., Griffith, J., Stevens, K., Flach, K., Nagamoto, H., Bickford, P., Leonard, S., & Freedman, R. (1998). Schizophrenia, sensory gating, and nicotinic receptors. *Schizophrenia Bulletin, 24,* 189–202.

Adolphs, R., Tranel, D., Bechara, A., Damasio, H., & Damasio, A.R. (1996). Neuro-psychological approaches to reasoning and decision making. In A.R. Damasio, H. Damasio, & Y. Christen (Eds.), *Neurobiology of decision making* (pp. 157–170). New York: Springer.

Alexander, G.E. (1997). Anatomy of the basal ganglia and related motor structures. In R.L. Watts & W.C. Koller (Eds.), *Movement disorders: Neurologic principles and practice* (pp. 73–83). New York: McGraw-Hill.

Alsobrook, J.P., & Pauls, D.L. (1998). The genetics of obsessive compulsive disorder. In M.A. Jenike, L. Baer, & W.E. Minichiello (Eds.), *Obsessive compulsive disorders: Practical management* (pp. 276–288). St Louis: Mosby.

Altemus, M. (1995). Neuroendocrinology of obsessive compulsive disorder. In J. Panksepp (Ed.), *Advances in biological psychiatry* (Vol. 1, pp. 215–233). London: JAI Press.

Anand, A., & Charney, D.S. (1997). Catecholamines in depression. In A. Honig & H.M. Van Praag (Eds.), *Depression: Neurobiological, psychopathological and therapeutic advances* (pp. 147–178). New York: Wiley.

Anderson, G.M., & Cohen, D.J. (1996). Neurobiology of neuropsychiatric disorders. In M. Lewis (Ed.), *Child and adolescent psychiatry: A comprehensive textbook* (2nd ed., pp. 30–38). Baltimore: Williams & Wilkins.

Anderson, G.M., & Hoshino, M.L. (1997). Neurochemical studies of autism. In D.J. Cohen & F.R. Volkmar (Eds.), *Handbook of autism and pervasive developmental disorders* (pp. 325–343). New York: Wiley.

Anderson, G.M., Leckman, J.F., & Cohen, D.J. (1999). Neurochemical and neuropeptide systems. In J.F. Leckman & D.J. Cohen (Eds.), *Tourette's syndrome: Tics, obsessions, compulsions* (pp. 261–281). New York: Wiley.

Anderson, S.W., Bechara, A., Damasio, H., Tranel, D., & Damasio, A.R. (1999). Impairment of social and moral behaviour related to early damage in human prefrontal cortex. *Nature Neuroscience, 2*, 1032–1037.

Andreasen, N.C. (1984). *Scale for the assessment of positive symptoms (SAPS)*. Iowa City: University of Iowa.

Andreasen, N.C. (1989). Scale for the assessment of negative symptoms (SANS). *British Journal of Psychology, 155* (Suppl. 7), 53–58.

Andreasen, N.C. (1997). Linking mind and brain in the study of mental illnesses: A project for a scientific psychopathology. *Science, 275*, 1586–1593.

Andreasen, N.C., Paradiso, S., & O'Leary, D.S. (1998). "Cognitive dysmetria" as an integrative theory of schizophrenia: A dysfunction in cortical–subcortical–cerebellar circuitry. *Schizophrenia Bulletin, 24*, 203–218.

Ardouin, C., Pillon, B., Peiffer, E., Bejjani, B.P., Limousin, P., Damier, P., Arnulf, I., Benabid, A.L., Agid, Y., and Pollak, P. (1999). Bilateral subthalamic or pallidal stimulation for Parkinson's disease affects neither memory nor executive functions: A consecutive series of 62 patients. *Annals of Neurology, 46*, 217–223.

Arnold, S.E. (1999). Cognition and neuropathology in schizophrenia. *Acta Psychiatrica Scandinavica, 99* (Suppl. 395), 41–50.

Arzimanoglou, A.A. (1998). Gilles de la Tourette syndrome. *Journal of Neurology, 245*, 761–765.

Asperger, H. (1944). Die autistichen Psychopathen im Kindersalter. *Archiv für Psychiatrie und Nervenkrankheiten, 117*, 76–136.

Awh, E., & Gehring, W.J. (1999). The anterior cingulate cortex lends a hand in response selection. *Nature Neuroscience, 2*, 853–854.

Baddeley, A.D. (1996). Cognition, neurology, psychiatry: Golden triangle or Bermuda triangle? *Cognitive Neuropsychiatry, 1*, 185–189.

Bailey, A., Luthert, P., Dean, A., Harding, B., Janota, I., Montgomery, M., Rutter, M., & Lantos, P. (1998a). A clinicopathological study of autism. *Brain, 121*, 889–905.

Bailey, A., Palferman, S., Heavey, L., & Le Couteur, A. (1998b). Autism: The phenotype in relatives. *Journal of Autism and Developmental Disorders, 28*, 369–392.

Baranek, G.T. (1999). Autism during infancy: A retrospective video analysis of sensory–motor and social behaviors at 9–12 months of age. *Journal of Autism and Developmental Disorders, 29*, 213–223.

Barkley, R.A. (1990). *Attention deficit hyperactivity disorder: A handbook for diagnosis and treatment*. New York: Guilford Press.

Barkley, R.A. (1997). Behavioral inhibition, sustained attention, and executive functions: Constructing a unifying theory of ADHD. *Psychological Bulletin, 121*, 65–94.

Barkley, R.A. (1998). Attention-deficit hyperactivity disorder. *Scientific American*, September, 44–49.

Barnett, P., Maruff, P., Purcell, R., Wainwright, K., Kyrios, M., Bremer, W., & Pantelis, C. (1999). Impairment of olfactory identification in obsessive compulsive disorder. *Psychological Medicine, 29*, 1227–1233.

Baron-Cohen, S., & Swettenham, J. (1997). Theory of mind in autism: Its relationship to executive function and central coherence. In D.J. Cohen & F.R. Volkmar (Eds.), *Handbook of autism and pervasive developmental disorders* (pp. 880–889). New York: Wiley.

Baron-Cohen, S., Bolton, P., Wheelwright, S., Scahill, V.L.S., Mead, G., & Smith, A. (1998). Does autism occur more often in families of physicists, engineers and mathematicians? *Autism, 2*, 296–301.

Barondes, S.H. (1999). An agenda for psychiatric genetics. *Archives of General Psychiatry, 56*, 549–552.

Barondes, S.H., Alberts, B.M., Andreasen, N.C., Bargmann, C., Benes, F., Goldman-Rakic, P., Gottesman, I., Heinemann, S.F., Jones, E.G., Kirschner, M., Lewis, D. et al. (1997). Workshop on schizophrenia. *Proceedings of the National Academy of Sciences of the USA, 94*, 1612–1614.

Bassett, A.S., & Honer, W.G. (1994). Evidence for anticipation in schizophrenia. *American Journal of Human Genetics, 54*, 864–870.

Bauman, M.L. (1996). Brief report: Neuroanatomic observations of the brain in pervasive developmental disorders. *Journal of Autism and Developmental Disorders, 26*, 199–203.

Bauman, M.L., & Kemper, T.L. (1994). *Neurobiology of autism*. Baltimore: Johns Hopkins University Press.

Bauman, M.L., & Kemper, T.L. (1995). Neuroanatomical observations of the brain in autism. In L. Panksepp (Ed.), *Advances in biological psychiatry* (Vol. 1, pp. 1–26). London: JAI Press.

Baumgardner, T.L., Singer, H.S., Denckla, M.B., Rubin, M.A., Abrams, M.T., Colli, M.J., & Reiss, A.L. (1996). Corpus callosum morphology in children with Tourette syndrome and attention deficit hyperactivity disorder. *Neurology, 47*, 477–482.

Bax, M. (1999). Specific learning disorders/neurodevelopmental disorders. *Developmental Medicine & Child Neurology, 41*, 147.

Baynes, K. (1990). Language and reading in the right hemisphere: Highways or byways of the brain. *Journal of Cognitive Neuroscience, 2*, 159–179.

Bechara, A., Damasio, H., Tranel, D., & Damasio, A.R. (1997). Deciding advantageously before knowing the advantageous strategy. *Science, 275*, 1293–1296.

Beck, A.T., Ward, C., Mendelson, M., Mock, J., & Erbaugh, J. (1961). An inventory for measuring depression. *Archives of General Psychiatry, 4*, 53–63.

Bejjani, B.P., Damier, P., Arnulf, I., Thivard, L., Bonnet, A.M., Dormont, D., Cornu, P., Pidoux, B., Samson, Y., and Agid, Y. (1999). Transient acute depression induced by high-frequency deep-brain stimulation. *New England Journal of Medicine, 340*, 1476–1480.

Bellgrove, M.A., Bradshaw, J.L., Velakoulis, D., Pantelis, C., & Johnson, K.A. (2000). Bimanual coordination in schizophrenia. Manuscript submitted for publication.

Bellivier, F., Leboyer, M., Courtet, P., Buresi, C., Beaufils, B., Samolyk, D., Allilaire, J.-F., Feingold, J., Mallet, J., & Malafosse, A. (1998). Association between the tryptophan hydroxylase gene and manic-depressive illness. *Archives of General Psychiatry, 55*, 33–37.

Bellugi, U., Adolphs, R., Cassady, C., & Chiles, M. (1999a). Towards the neural basis for hypersociability in a genetic syndrome. *Neuroreport, 10*, 1653–1657.

Bellugi, U., Lichtenberger, L., Mills, D., & Galaburda, A. (1999b). Bridging cognition, the brain and molecular genetics: Evidence for Williams syndrome. *Trends in Neuroscience, 22*, 197–207.

Ben-Artsy, A., Glicksohn, J., Soroker, N., Margalit, M., & Myslobodsky, M. (1996). An assessment of hemineglect in children with attention-deficit hyperactivity disorder. *Developmental Neuropsychology, 12*, 271–281.

Bench, C.J., Friston, K.J., Brown, R.G., Frackowiak, R.S.J., & Dolan, R.J. (1993). Regional cerebral blood flow in depression measured by positron emission tomography: The relationship with clinical dimensions. *Psychological Medicine, 23*, 579–590.

Berardelli, A., Hallett, M., Rothwell, J.C., & Marsden, C.D. (1996). Single joint rapid arm movements in normal subjects and in patients with motor disorders. *Brain, 119*, 661–674.

Blanes, T., & McGuire, P. (1997). Heterogeneity within obsessive compulsive disorder: Evidence for primary and neurodevelopmental subtypes. In M.S. Keshaven & R.M. Murray (Eds.), *Neurodevelopment and adult psychopathology* (pp. 206–214). Cambridge, UK: Cambridge University Press.

Blum, K., Cull, J.G., Braverman, E.R., & Comings, D.E. (1996). Reward deficiency syndrome. *American Scientist, 84* (March/April), 132–145.

Boesch, C. (1991). Teaching among wild chimpanzees. *Animal Behaviour, 41*, 530–532.

Boliek, C.A., & Obrzut, J.E. (1997). Neuropsychological aspects of attention deficit/ hyperactivity disorder. In C.R. Reynolds & E. Fletcher-Janzen (Eds.), *Handbook of clinical child neuropsychology* (2nd ed., pp. 619–633). New York: Plenum Press.

Bolton, P.F., Pickles, A., Murphy, M., & Rutter, M. (1998). Autism, affective and other psychiatric disorders: Patterns of familial aggregation. *Psychological Medicine, 28*, 385–395.

Boyce, P., & Hadzi-Pavlovic, D. (1996). Issues in classification: I. Some historical aspects. In G. Parker & D. Hadzi-Pavlovic (Eds.), *Melancholia: A disorder of movement and mood* (pp. 9–19). Cambridge, UK: Cambridge University Press.

Bradshaw, J.L. (1989). *Hemispheric specialization and psychological function.* New York: Wiley.

Bradshaw, J.L. (1997). *Human evolution: A neuropsychological perspective.* Hove, UK: Psychology Press.

Bradshaw, J.L. (1998). Schizophrenia as failure of hemispheric dominance for language: Commentary on Crow. *Trends in Neurosciences, 21*, 145–146.

Bradshaw, J.L., & Mattingley, J.B. (1995). *Clinical neuropsychology: Behavioural and brain science.* San Diego: Academic Press.

Bradshaw, J.L., & Nettleton, N.C. (1981). The nature of hemispheric specialization in man. *Behavioral and Brain Sciences, 4*, 51–63.

Bradshaw, J.L., & Nettleton, N.C. (1983). *Human cerebral asymmetry.* Englewood Cliffs, NJ: Prentice-Hall.

Brooks, D.J. (1996). Basal ganglia function during normal and parkinsonian movement. PET activation studies. In L. Battistin, G. Scarlato, T. Caraceni, & S. Ruggieri (Eds.), *Advances in Neurology* (Vol. 69, pp. 433–441). Philadelphia: Lippincott-Raven.

Brown, P., & Marsden, C.D. (1998). What do the basal ganglia do? *The Lancet, 351*, 1801–1804.

Bryson, S.E. (1996). Brief report: Epidemiology of autism. *Journal of Autism and Developmental Disorders, 26*, 165–167.

Buchanan, R.W., & Carpenter, W.T. (1997). Neuroanatomies of schizophrenia. *Schizophrenia Bulletin, 23*, 367–372.

Buchanan, R.W., Buckley, P.F., Tamminga, C.A., & Schulze, S.C. (1998). Schizophrenia research: A biennium of progress. Proceedings from the sixth international congress on schizophrenia research. Colorado Springs, CO, 12–16 April, 1997. *Schizophrenia Bulletin, 24*, 501–518.

Bucher, S.F., Seelos, K.C., Oertel, W.H., Reiser, M., & Trenkwalder, C. (1997). Cerebral generators involved in the pathogenesis of restless legs syndrome. *Annals of Neurology, 41*, 639–645.

Buchsbaum, M.S., & Hazlett, E.A. (1998). Positron emission tomography studies of abnormal glucose metabolism in schizophrenia. *Schizophrenia Bulletin, 24*, 343–364.

Buchsbaum, M.S., Hazlett, E.A., Haznedar, M.M., Spiegel-Cohen, J., & Wei, T.C. (1999). Visualizing fronto-striatal circuitry and neuroleptic effects in schizophrenia. *Acta Psychiatrica Scandinavica, 99* (Suppl. 395), 129–137.

Buckley, P.F. (1998). The clinical stigmata of aberrant neurodevelopment in schizophrenia. *Journal of Nervous and Mental Disease, 186*, 79–86.

Burack, J.A., Enns, J.T., Stauder, J.E.A., Mottron, L., & Randolph, B. (1997). Attention and autism: Behavioral and electrophysiological evidence. In D.J. Cohen & F.R. Volkmar (Eds.), *Handbook of autism and pervasive developmental disorders* (pp. 226–242). New York: Wiley.

Butovskaya, M.L., & Kozintsev, A.G. (1996). A neglected form of quasi-aggression in apes: Possible relevance for the origins of humor. *Current Anthropology*, *37*, 716–717.

Byne, W., & Davis, K.L. (1999). The role of prefrontal cortex in the dopaminergic dysregulation of schizophrenia. *Biological Psychiatry*, *45*, 657–659.

Byrne, M., Hodges, A., Grant, E., Owens, D.C., & Johnstone, E.C. (1999). Neuropsychological assessment of young people at high genetic risk for developing schizophrenia compared with controls. *Psychological Medicine*, *29*, 1161–1173.

Call, J., & Tomasello, M. (1994). Production and comprehension of referential pointing by orangutans (*Pongo pygmaeus*). *Journal of Comparative Psychology*, *108*, 307–317.

Canli, T. (1999). Hemispheric asymmetry in the experience of emotion: A perspective from functional imaging. *The Neuroscientist*, *5*, 201–207.

Carney, M.W.P., Roth, M., & Garside, R.F. (1965). The diagnosis of depressive syndromes and the prediction of ECT response. *British Journal of Psychiatry*, *111*, 659–674.

Carpenter, W.T., & Buchanan, R.W. (1994). Schizophrenia. *New England Journal of Medicine*, *330*, 681–689.

Carter, A.S., Pauls, D.L., & Leckman, J.F. (1995). The development of obsessionality: Continuities and discontinuities. In D. Cicchetti & D.J. Cohen (Eds.), *Developmental psychopathology: Risk disorder and adaptation* (Vol. 2, pp. 609–632). New York: Wiley.

Carter, C.S., Krener, P., Chaderjian, M., Northcutt, C., & Wolfe, V. (1995). Asymmetrical visual-spatial performance in attention deficit hyperactivity disorder: Evidence for a right hemisphere deficit. *Biological Psychiatry*, *37*, 789–797.

Casey, B.J., Gordon, C.T., Mannheim, G.B., & Rumsey, J.M. (1993). Dysfunctional attention in autistic savants. *Journal of Clinical and Experimental Neuropsychology*, *15*, 933–946.

Casey, B.J., Trainor, R.J., Orendi, J.L., Schubert, A.B., Nystrom, L.E., Giedd, J.N., Castellanos, X., Haxby, J.V., Noll, D.C., Cohen, J.D., Forman, S.D., Dahl, R.E., & Rapoport, J.L. (1997). A developmental functional MRI study of prefrontal activation during performance of a go–no–go task. *Journal of Cognitive Neuroscience*, *9*, 835–847.

Castellanos, F.X., Giedd, J.N., Marsh, W.L., & Hamburger, S.D. (1996). Quantitative brain magnetic resonance imaging in attention deficit hyperactivity disorder. *Archives of General Psychiatry*, *53*, 607–616.

Ceballos-Baumann, A.O., & Brooks, D.J. (1997). Basal ganglia function and dysfunction revealed by PET activation studies. In J.A. Obeso, M.R. DeLong, & C.D. Marsden (Eds.), *The basal ganglia and new surgical approaches for Parkinson's disease: Advances in neurology* (Vol. 74, pp. 127–139). Philadelphia: Lippincott-Raven.

Changeux, J.-P., & Dehaene, S. (1996). Neuronal models of cognitive functions associated with the prefrontal cortex. In A.R. Damasio, H. Damasio, & Y. Christen (Eds.), *Neurobiology of decision-making* (pp. 125–140). New York: Springer.

Charlton, B.G., & McClelland, H.A. (1999). Theory of mind and the delusional disorders. *Journal of Nervous and Mental Disease*, *187*, 380–383.

Charmon, T. (1998). Specifying the nature and course of the joint attention impairment in autism in the preschool years. *Autism*, *2*, 61–79.

Chokroverty, S., & Jankovic, J. (1999). Restless legs syndrome: A disease in search of identity. *Neurology*, *52*, 907–910.

Chugani, D.C., Muzik, O., Behen, M., Rothermel, R., Janisse, J.J., Lee, J., & Chugani, M.D. (1999). Developmental changes in brain serotonin synthesis capacity in autistic and nonautistic children. *Annals of Neurology*, *45*, 287–295.

Ciaranello, A.L., & Ciaranello, R.D. (1995). The neurobiology of infantile autism. *Annual Review of Neuroscience, 18*, 101–128.

Cicchetti, D., & Toth, S.L. (1995). Developmental psychopathology and disorders of affect. In D. Cicchetti & D.J. Cohen (Eds.), *Developmental psychopathology: Risk, disorder, and adaptation* (Vol. 2, pp. 369–420). New York: Wiley.

Clahsen, H., & Almazon, M. (1998). Syntax and morphology in Williams syndrome. *Cognition, 68*, 167–198.

Clerc, G.E., Ruimy, P., & Verdeau-Pailles, J. (1994). A double-blind comparison of venlafaxine and fluoxetine in patients hospitalised for major depression and melancholia. *International Clinical Psychopharmacology, 9*, 139–143.

Cloninger, C.R. (1997). Multilocus genetics of schizophrenia. *Current Opinion in Psychiatry, 10*, 5–10.

Cohen, D.J., Stein, D.J., & Hollander, E. (1997). The neuropsychiatry of obsessive compulsive disorder. In E. Hollander & D.J. Stein (Eds.), *Obsessive compulsive disorders: Diagnosis, etiology, treatment* (pp. 75–80). New York: Marcel Dekker.

Cohen, R.A., Kaplan, R.F., Moser, D.J., Jenkins, M.A., & Wilkinson, H. (1999). Impairments of attention after cingulotomy. *Neurology, 53*, 819–824.

Comi, A.M., Zimmerman, A.W., Frye, V.H., Law, P.A., & Peeden, J.N. (1999). Familial clustering of autoimmune disorders and evaluation of medical risk factors in autism. *Journal of Child Neurology, 14*, 388–394.

Comings, D.E. (1990). *Tourette syndrome and human behavior*. Duarte, CA: Hope Press.

Comings, D.E. (1995). Dopamine D2 receptor and Tourette's syndrome. *Archives of Neurology, 52*, 441–442.

Conwell, Y., & Henderson, R.E. (1996). Neuropsychiatry of suicide. In B.S. Fogel, R.B. Schiffer, & S.M. Rao (Eds.), *Neuropsychiatry* (pp. 485–522). Baltimore: Williams & Wilkins.

Cook, E.H., & Leventhal, B.L. (1996). The serotonin system in autism. *Current Opinion in Pediatrics, 8*, 348–354.

Cornish, K.M., Munir, F., & Cross, G. (1998). The nature of the spatial deficit in young females with fragile X syndrome: A neuropsychological and molecular perspective. *Neuropsychologia, 36*, 1239–1246.

Courchesne, E. (1997). Brainstem, cerebellar and limbic neuroanatomical abnormalities in autism. *Current Opinion in Neurobiology, 7*, 269–278.

Crider, A. (1997). Perseveration in schizophrenia. *Schizophrenia Bulletin, 23*, 63–74.

Crow, T.J. (1980). Molecular pathology of schizophrenia: More than one disease process? *British Medical Journal, 280*, 66–68.

Cryan, E., Byrne, M., O'Donovan, A., & O'Callaghan, E. (1996). Brief report: A case-control study of obstetric complications and later autistic disorder. *Journal of Autism and Developmental Disorders, 26*, 453–462.

Cummings, J.L. (1993). Frontal-subcortical circuits and human behavior. *Archives of Neurology, 50*, 873–879.

Cunnington, R., Bradshaw, J.L., & Iansek, R. (1996). The role of the supplementary motor area in the control of voluntary movement. *Human Movement Science, 15*, 627–647.

Cunnington, R., Iansek, R., & Bradshaw, J.L. (1999a). Movement-related potentials in Parkinson's disease: External cues and attentional strategies. *Movement Disorders, 14*, 63–68.

Cunnington, R., Iansek, R., & Bradshaw, J.L. (1999b). Relationships between movement initiation times and movement-related cortical potentials in Parkinson's disease. *Human Movement Science, 18*, 443–459.

Cunnington, R., Iansek, R., Bradshaw, J.L., & Phillips, J.G. (1995). Movement-related potentials in Parkinson's disease: Presence and predictability of temporal and spatial cues. *Brain, 118*, 935–950.

Cunnington, R., Iansek, R., Bradshaw, J.L., & Phillips, J.G. (1996). Movement related potentials associated with movement preparation and motor imagery. *Experimental Brain Research, 111*, 429–436.

Cunnington, R., Iansek, R., Johnson, K.A., & Bradshaw, J.L. (1997). Movement-related potentials in Parkinson's disease: Motor imagery and movement preparation. *Brain, 120*, 1339–1353.

Curtis, C.E., Iacono, W.G., & Beiser, M. (1999). Relationship between nailfold plexus visibility and clinical, neuropsychological and brain structural measures in schizophrenia. *Biological Psychiatry, 46*, 102–109.

Damasio, A.R. (1994). *Descartes' error*. New York: Grosset/Putnam.

Damasio, A.R. (1997). Toward a neuropathology of emotion and mood. *Nature, 386*, 769–770.

Damasio, A.R., & Maurer, R.G. (1978). A neurological model for childhood autism. *Neurology, 35*, 777–786.

Damasio, H. (1996). Human neuroanatomy relevant to decision-making. In A.R. Damasio, H. Damasio, & Y. Christen (Eds.), *Neurobiology of decision-making* (pp. 1–12). Berlin: Springer.

David, A.S. (1999). Auditory hallucinations: Phenomenology, neuropsychology and neuroimaging update. *Acta Psychiatrica Scandinavica, 99* (Suppl. 395), 95–104.

Dawson, G. (1996). Brief report: Neuropsychology of autism: A report on the state of the science. *Journal of Autism and Developmental Disorders, 26*, 179–185.

Deecke, L., & Lang, W. (1996). Generation of movement-related potentials and fields in the supplementary sensorimotor area and the primary motor area. In H.O. Lüders (Ed.), *Advances in neurology: Supplementary sensorimotor area* (Vol. 70, pp. 127–146). Philadelphia: Lippincott-Raven.

Degrandpre, R.J. (1999). Just cause. *The Sciences*, March /April, 14–18.

Delgado, P.L. (1995). Neurobiological basis of depression. In J. Panksepp (Ed.), *Advances in biological psychiatry* (Vol. 1, pp. 161–214). London: JAI Press.

DeLisi, L.E. (1999). A critical overview of recent investigations into the genetics of schizophrenia. *Current Opinion in Psychiatry, 12*, 29–39.

DeLong, G.R. (1999). Autism. *Neurology, 52*, 911–916.

Department of Health, Education and Welfare (1974). *Abnormal involuntary movement scale*. Washington, DC: Alcohol, Drug Abuse and Mental Health Administration.

Derix, M.M.A., & Jolles, J. (1997). Neuropsychological abnormalities in depression: Relation between brain and behavior. In A. Honig & H.M. Van Praag (Eds.), *Depression: Neurobiological, psychopathological and therapeutic advances* (pp. 109–128). New York: Wiley.

D'haenen, H.A.H. (1997). Brain imaging in depression. In A. Honig & H.M. Van Praag (Eds.), *Depression: Neurobiological, psychopathological and therapeutic advances* (pp. 225–234). New York: Wiley.

Diamond, J., & Mattsson, Å. (1996). Attention-deficit/hyperactivity disorder. In D.X. Parmelee (Ed.), *Child and adolescent psychiatry: A comprehensive textbook* (pp. 69–81). St Louis: Mosby.

Dolan, R.J. (1997). Mood disorders and abnormal cingulate cortex. *Trends in Cognitive Sciences, 1*, 283–286.

Dolan, R.J. (1999). On the neurology of morals. *Nature Neuroscience, 2*, 927–929.

Dolan, R.J., Fletcher, P.C., McKennan, P., Friston, K.J., & Frith, C.D. (1999). Abnormal neural integration relating to cognition in schizophrenia. *Acta Psychiatrica Scandinavica, 99* (Suppl. 395), 58–67.

Downing, M.E., Phillips, J.G., Bradshaw, J.L., Vaddadi, K.S., & Pantelis, C. (1998a). Cue-dependent right hemineglect in schizophrenia: A kinematic analysis. *Journal of Neurology, Neurosurgery and Psychiatry, 65,* 454–459.

Downing, M.E., Phillips, J.G., Bradshaw, J.L., Vaddadi, K.S., & Pantelis, C. (1998b). Response programming in patients with schizophrenia: A kinematic analysis. *Neuropsychologia, 36,* 603–610.

Drevets, W.C. (1998). Functional neuroimaging studies of depression: The anatomy of melancholia. *Annual Review of Medicine, 49,* 341–361.

Drevets, W.C. (1999a). Obsessive compulsive disorder (Box 34.4) in J.W. Mink's chapter: The basal ganglia. In M.J. Zigmond, F.E. Bloom, S.C. Landis, J.L. Roberts, & L.R. Squire (Eds.), *Fundamental neuroscience* (pp. 963). San Diego: Academic Press.

Drevets, W.C. (1999b). Mania. In M.J. Zigmond, F.E. Bloom, S.C. Landis, J.L. Roberts, & L.R. Squire (Eds.), *Fundamental neuroscience* (pp. 1254–1255). San Diego: Academic Press.

du Feu, M., & McKenna, P.J. (1999). Prelingually profoundly deaf schizophrenic patients who hear voices: A phenomenological analysis. *Acta Psychiatrica Scandinavica, 99,* 453–459.

Duffy, J.D., & Campbell, J.J. (1994). The regional prefrontal syndromes: A theoretical and clinical overview. *Journal of Neuropsychiatry, 6,* 379–387.

Duffy, J.D., & Coffey, C.E. (1997). The neurobiology of depression. In M.R. Trimble & J.L. Cummings (Eds.), *Contemporary behavioral neurology* (pp. 275–288). New York: Butterworth-Heinemann.

Duggan, C.F. (1997). Course and outcome of depression. In A. Honig & H.M. Van Praag (Eds.), *Depression: Neurobiological, psychopathological and therapeutic advances* (pp. 31–40). New York: Wiley.

Duman, R.S., & Charney, D.S. (1999). Cell atrophy and loss in major depression. *Biological Psychiatry, 45,* 1083–1084.

Duman, R.S., Heninger, G.R., & Nestler, E.J. (1997). A molecular and cellular theory of depression. *Archives of General Psychiatry, 54,* 597–606.

Duncan, G.E., Sheitman, B.B., & Lieberman, J.A. (1999). An integrated view of pathophysiological models of schizophrenia. *Brain Research Review, 29,* 250–264.

Dykens, E.M., & Volkmar, F.R. (1997). Medical conditions associated with schizophrenia. In D.J. Cohen & F.R. Volkmar (Eds.), *Handbook of autism and pervasive developmental disorders* (pp. 388–407). New York: Wiley.

Eapen, V., & Robertson, M.M. (1996). Gilles de la Tourette syndrome and attention deficit hyperactivity disorder. *Neurology, 9,* 192–196.

Egan, M.F., & Weinberger, D.R. (1997). Neurobiology of schizophrenia. *Current Opinion in Neurobiology, 7,* 701–707.

Ehlers, S., Gillberg, C., & Wing, L. (1999). A screening questionnaire for Asperger syndrome and other high-functioning autism spectrum disorders in school age children. *Journal of Autism and Developmental Disorders, 29,* 129–142.

Eidelberg, D., Moeller, J.R., Antonini, A., Kazamuta, K., Dhawan, V., Budman, C., & Feigin, A. (1997). The metabolic anatomy of Tourette's syndrome. *Neurology, 48,* 927–934.

Elliott, R. (1998). The neuropsychological profile in unipolar depression. *Trends in Cognitive Sciences, 2,* 447–454.

Ellis, H.D., & Gunter, H.L. (1999). Asperger syndrome: A simple matter of white matter. *Trends in Cognitive Science, 3,* 192–200.

Epstein, J.N., Conners, C.K., Swanson, J.M., Erhardt, D., & March, J.S. (1997). Asymmetrical hemispheric control of visual-spatial attention in adults with attention deficit hyperactivity disorder. *Neuropsychology, 11,* 467–473.

Evans, D.W., Gray, F.L., & Leckman, J.F. (1999). The rituals, fears and phobias of young children: Insights from development, psychopathology and neurobiology. *Child Psychiatry and Human Development, 29,* 261–277.

Faraone, S.V., & Biederman, J. (1998). Neurobiology of attention-deficit hyperactivity disorder. *Biological Psychiatry*, *44*, 951–958.

Fein, D., Joy, S., Green, L.A., & Waterhouse, L. (1996). Autism and pervasive developmental disorders. In B.S. Fogel, R.B. Schiffer, & S.M. Rao (Eds.), *Neuropsychiatry* (pp. 571–601). Baltimore: Williams & Wilkins.

Feinstein, C., & Reiss, A.L. (1998). Autism: The point of view from fragile X studies. *Journal of Autism and Developmental Disorders*, *28*, 393–396.

Filipek, P.A. (1999). Neuroimaging in the developmental disorders: The state of science. *Journal of Child Psychiatry and Psychiatry*, *40*, 113–128.

Finger, S. (1994). *Origins of neuroscience: A history of explorations into brain function.* Oxford: Oxford University Press.

Fink, M. (1997). Electroconvulsive therapy in affective disorders: Efficacy and mode of action. In A. Honig & H.M. Van Praag (Eds.), *Depression: Neurobiological, psychopathological and therapeutic advances* (pp. 397–412). New York: Wiley.

Fish, D. (1998). New choices in treating depression. *The Practitioner*, *242*, 24–32.

Fisher, B.C. (1998). *Attention deficit misdiagnosis.* Boca Raton, FL: CRC Press.

Fletcher, P. (1998). The missing link: A failure of fronto-hippocampal integration in schizophrenia. *Nature Neuroscience*, *1*, 266–267.

Fodor, J.A. (1983). *The modularity of the mind: An essay on faculty psychology.* Cambridge, MA: MIT Press.

Folstein, S.E., Bisson, E., Santangelo, S.L., & Piven, J. (1998). Finding specific genes that cause autism: A combination of approaches will be needed to maximize power. *Journal of Autism and Developmental Disorders*, *28*, 439–446.

Folstein, S.E., Santangelo, S.L., Gilman, S.E., Iven, J., Landa, R., Lainhart, J., Hein, J., & Wzorek, M. (1999). Predictors of cognitive-test patterns in autism families. *Journal of Child Psychology and Psychiatry*, *40*, 1117–1128.

Fombonne, E. (1997). Autism: Recent research findings. *Current Opinion in Psychiatry*, *10*, 373–377.

Fombonne, E. (1999). The epidemiology of autism: A review. *Psychological Medicine*, *29*, 769–786.

Fombonne, E., Rogé, B., Claverie, J.S.C., & Frémolle, J. (1999). Microcephaly and macrocephaly. *Journal of Autism and Developmental Disorders*, *29*, 113–117.

Foti, D.J., & Cummings, J.L. (1997). Neurobehavioral aspects of movement disorders. In R.L. Watts & W.C. Koller (Eds.), *Movement disorders: Neurologic principles and practice* (pp. 15–30). New York: McGraw-Hill.

Foulds, J. (1999). The relationship between tobacco and mental disorders. *Current Opinion in Psychiatry*, *12*, 303–306.

Frank, L.R. (1978). *The history of shock treatment.* San Francisco: Frank Leary.

Freimer, N.B., & Reus, V.I. (1993). The genetics of bipolar disorder and schizophrenia. In R.N. Rosenberg, S.B. Prusiner, S. DiMauro, R.L. Barchi, & L.M. Kunkel (Eds.), *The molecular and genetic basis of neurological disease* (pp. 951–963). Boston: Butterworth-Heinemann.

Friedman, J.I., Temporini, H., & Davis, K.L. (1999). Pharmacologic strategies for augmenting cognitive performance in schizophrenia. *Biological Psychiatry*, *45*, 1–16.

Friston, K.J. (1999). Schizophrenia and the disconnection hypothesis. *Acta Psychiatrica Scandinavica*, *99* (Suppl. 395), 68–79.

Frith, C.D. (1992). *The cognitive neuropsychology of schizophrenia.* Hove, UK: Lawrence Erlbaum Associates Ltd.

Frith, U. (1991). *Autism and Asperger syndrome.* Cambridge, UK: Cambridge University Press.

Fuster, J.M. (1999). Synopsis of function and dysfunction of the frontal lobe. *Acta Psychiatrica Scandinavica*, *99*, 51–57.

Garavan, H., Ross, T.J., & Stein, E.A. (1999). Right hemispheric dominance of inhibitory control: An event-related functional MRI study. *Proceedings of the National Academy of Sciences of the USA, 96,* 8301–8306.

Geddes, J.R., Verdoux, H., Takei, N., Lawrie, S.M., Bovet, P., Eagles, J.M., Heun, R., McCreadie, R.G., McNeil, T.F., O'Callaghan, E., Stober, G., Willinger, U., & Murray, R.M. (1999). Schizophrenia and complications of pregnancy and labor: An individual patient data meta-analysis. *Schizophrenia Bulletin, 25,* 413–423.

Geller, D.A. (1998). Juvenile obsessive compulsive disorder. In M.A. Jenike, L. Baer, & W.E. Minichiello (Eds.), *Obsessive compulsive disorders: Practical management* (pp. 44–64). St Louis: Mosby.

Gené-Cos, N., Ring, H.A., Pottinger, R.C., & Barrett, G. (1999). Possible roles for mismatch negativity in neuropsychiatry. *Neuropsychiatry, Neuropsychology, and Behavioral Neurology, 12,* 17–22.

George, M.S., Wasserman, E.M., Kimbrell, T.A., Little, J.T., Williams, W.E., Danielson, A.L., Greenburg, B.D., Hallett, M., & Post, R.M. (1997). Mood improvement following daily left prefrontal repetitive transcranial magnetic stimulation in patients with depression. *American Journal of Psychiatry, 154,* 1752–1756.

Georgiou, N., Iansek, R., Bradshaw, J.L., Phillips, J.G., Mattingley, J.B., & Bradshaw, J.A. (1993). An evaluation of the role of internal cues in the pathogenesis of Parkinsonian hypokinesia. *Brain, 116,* 1575–1587.

Georgiou, N., Bradshaw, J.L., Phillips, J.G., Bradshaw, J.A., & Chiu, E. (1995). The Simon effect and attention deficits in Gilles de la Tourette syndrome and Huntington's disease. *Brain, 118,* 1305–1318.

Ghaemi, S.N., Boiman, E.E., & Goodwin, F.K. (1999). Kindling and second messengers: An approach to the neurobiology of recurrence in bipolar disorder. *Biological Psychiatry, 45,* 137–144.

Ghaziuddin, M., & Butler, E. (1998). Clumsiness in autism and Asperger syndrome: A further report. *Journal of Intellectual Disability Research, 42,* 43–48.

Giedd, J.N., & Castellanos, F.X. (1997). Developmental disorders. In K.R.R. Krishnan & P.M. Doraiswamy (Eds.), *Brain imaging in clinical psychiatry* (pp. 121–137). New York: Marcel Dekker.

Gillberg, C. (1998a). Neuropsychiatric disorders. *Current Opinion in Neurology, 11,* 109–114.

Gillberg, C. (1998b). Chromosomal disorders. *Journal of Autism and Developmental Disorders, 28,* 415–425.

Gillberg, C., & Coleman, M. (1996). Autism and mechanical disorders: A review of the literature. *Developmental Medicine and Child Neurology, 38,* 191–202.

Gillberg, C., & Wing, L. (1999). Autism: Not an extremely rare disorder. *Acta Psychiatrica Scandinavica, 1999,* 399–406.

Gilles de la Tourette, G. (1884). Jumping, lahat, myriachit. *Archives de Neurologie, 8,* 68–84.

Glenthøj, B.Y., & Hemmingsen, R. (1999). Transmitter dysfunction during the process of schizophrenia. *Acta Psychiatrica Scandinavica, 99* (Suppl. 395), 105–112.

Golden, G.S. (1995). Attention deficit disorder. In M.M. Robertson & V. Eapen (Eds.), *Movement and allied disorders* (pp. 57–67). New York: Wiley.

Goldman-Rakic, P.S. (1994). Working memory dysfunction in schizophrenia. *Journal of Neuropsychiatry and Clinical Neurosciences, 6,* 348–357.

Goldman-Rakic, P.S., & Selemon, L.D. (1997). Functional and anatomical aspects of prefrontal pathology in schizophrenia. *Schizophrenia Bulletin, 23,* 437–458.

Gooding, D.C., & Iacono, W.G. (1995). Schizophrenia through the lens of a developmental psychopathology perspective. In D. Cicchetti & D.J. Cohen (Eds.), *Developmental psychology: Risk, disorder, adaptation* (Vol. 2, pp. 535–580). New York: Wiley.

Goodman, W.K., & Price, L.H. (1992). Assessment of severity and change in obsessive compulsive disorder. *Psychiatric Clinics of North America, 15*, 861–869.

Goodman, W.K., & Price, L.H. (1998). Rating scales for obsessive-compulsive disorder. In M.A. Jenike, L. Baer, & W.E. Minichiello (Eds.), *Obsessive compulsive disorders: Theory and management* (2nd ed., pp. 97–120). Littleton, MA: Year Book Medical Publishers.

Goodwin, G.M. (1996). Functional imaging, affective disorder and dementia. *British Medical Bulletin, 52*, 495–512.

Gourovitch, M.C., & Goldberg, T.E. (1996). Cognitive deficits in schizophrenia: Attention, executive functions, memory and language processing. In C. Pantelis, H.E. Nelson, & T.R.E. Barnes (Eds.), *Schizophrenia: A neuropsychological perspective* (pp. 71–86). New York: Wiley.

Graybiel, A.M. (1997). The basal ganglia and cognitive pattern generators. *Schizophrenia Bulletin, 23*, 459–469.

Graybiel, A.M. (1998). The basal ganglia and chunking of action repertoires. *Neurobiology of Learning and Memory, 70*, 119–136.

Green, L., Fein, D., Joy, S., & Waterhouse, L. (1995). Cognitive functioning in autism: An overview. In E. Schopler & G.B. Mesibov (Eds.), *Learning and cognition in autism* (pp. 13–31). New York: Plenum Press.

Griez, E., & Overbeek, T. (1997). Comorbidity of depression and anxiety. In A. Honig & H.M. Van Praag (Eds.), *Depression: Neurobiological, psychopathological and therapeutic advances* (pp. 41–58). New York: Wiley.

Groenewegen, H.J., Wright, C.I., & Beijer, A.V. (1996). The nucleus accumbens. In G. Holstege, R. Bandler, & C.B. Saper (Eds.), *The emotional motor system* (pp. 485–512). New York: Elsevier.

Grunhaus, L., Dannon, P., & Schreiber, S. (1998). Effects of transcranial magnetic stimulation on severe depression: Similarities with electroconvulsive therapy. *Biological Psychiatry, 43*, 76S.

Gualtieri, C.T. (1995). The contributions of the frontal lobes to a theory of psychopathology. In J.J. Ratey (Ed.), *Neuropsychiatry of personality disorders* (pp. 149–171). Oxford: Blackwell Science.

Gur, R.E., & Pearlson, G.D. (1993). Neuroimaging in schizophrenia research. *Schizophrenia Bulletin, 19*, 337–353.

Hale, A.S. (1997). The treatment of depression: The reuptake inhibitors. In A. Honig & H.M. Van Praag (Eds.), *Depression: Neurobiological, psychopathological and therapeutic advances* (pp. 365–384). New York: Wiley.

Hallett, M., Lebiedowska, M., Thomas, S.L., Stanhope, S.J., Denckla, M.B., & Rumsey, J. (1993). Locomotion of autistic adults. *Archives of Neurology, 50*, 1304–1308.

Hamilton, M. (1960). A rating scale for depression. *Journal of Neurology, Neurosurgery and Psychiatry, 23*, 56–62.

Happé, F. (1999). Autism: Cognitive deficit or cognitive style? *Trends in Cognitive Sciences, 3*, 216–222.

Happé, F., & Frith, U. (1999). How the brain reads the mind. *Neuroscience News, 2*, 16–25.

Harcherik, D.F., Leckman, J.F., Detlor, J., & Cohen, D.J. (1984). A new instrument for clinical studies of Tourette's syndrome. *Journal of the American Academy of Child Psychiatry, 23*, 153–160.

Harris, J.C. (1995). *Developmental neuropsychiatry*. Oxford: Oxford University Press.

Harris, J.C. (1996). Pervasive developmental disorders. In D.X. Parmelee (Ed.), *Child and adolescent psychiatry: A comprehensive textbook* (pp. 49–67). St Louis: Mosby.

Harrison, P.J. (1999). The neuropathology of schizophrenia: A critical review of the data and their interpretation. *Brain, 122*, 593–624.

Harvey, C.A., Curson, D.A., Pantelis, C., Taylor, J., & Barnes, T.R.E. (1996). Four behavioural syndromes of schizophrenia. *British Journal of Psychiatry*, *168*, 562–570.

Hayes, A.E., Davidson, M.C., Keele, S.W., & Rafal, R.D. (1998). Toward a functional analysis of the basal ganglia. *Journal of Cognitive Neuroscience*, *10*, 178–198.

Hazeltine, E., Grafton, S.T., & Ivry, R. (1997). Attention and stimulus characteristics determine the locus of motor-sequence encoding: A PET study. *Brain*, *120*, 123–140.

Haznedar, M.M., Buchsbaum, M.S., Metzger, M., Solmando, A., Spiegel-Cohen, J., & Hollander, E. (1997). Anterior cingulate gyrus volume and glucose metabolism in autistic disorder. *American Journal of Psychiatry*, *154*, 1047–1050.

Heckers, S., Rauch, S.L., Goff, D., Savage, C.R., Schachter, D.L., Fischman, A.J., & Alpert, N.M. (1998). Impaired recruitment of the hippocampus during conscious recollection in schizophrenia. *Nature Neuroscience*, *1*, 318–323.

Hedaya, R.J. (1996). *Understanding biological psychiatry*. New York: W.W. Norton.

Heinrichs, R.W., & Zakzanis, K.K. (1998). Neurocognitive deficit in schizophrenia: A quantitative review of the evidence. *Schizophrenia Bulletin*, *12*, 426–445.

Heller, W., & Nitschke, J.B. (1997). Regional brain activity in emotion: A framework for understanding cognition in depression. *Cognition and Emotion*, *11*, 637–661.

Hodgson, R.J., & Rachman, S. (1977). Obsessional compulsive complaints. *Behavioral Research and Therapy*, *15*, 389–395.

Hollander, E., & Stein, D.J. (Eds.) (1997). *Obsessive compulsive disorders: Diagnosis, etiology, treatment*. New York: Marcel Dekker.

Howe, M.J.A. (1999). *The psychology of high abilities*. London: Macmillan.

Howlin, P., Davies, M., & Udwin, O. (1998). Cognitive functioning in adults in Williams syndrome. *Journal of Child Psychology and Psychiatry*, *39*, 183–189.

Hyde, T.M., Stacey, M.E., Coppola, R., Handel, S.F., Rickler, K.C., & Weinberger, D.R. (1995). Cerebral morphometric abnormalities in Tourette's syndrome: A quantitative magnetic resonance imaging study of monozygotic twins. *Neurology*, *45*, 1176–1182.

Iansek, R., Bradshaw, J.L., Phillips, J.G., Cunnington, R., & Morris, M. (1995). Interaction of the basal ganglia and supplementary motor area in the elaboration of movement. In D. Glencross & J. Piek (Eds.), *Motor control and sensorimotor integration* (pp. 37–59). Amsterdam: Elsevier.

Insel, T.R., O'Brien, D.J., & Leckman, J.F. (1999). Oxytocin, vasopressin, and autism: Is there a connection? *Biological Psychiatry*, *45*, 145–155.

International Molecular Genetic Study of Autism Consortium (1998). A full genome screen for autism with evidence for linkage to a region on chromosome 7q. *Human Molecular Genetics*, *7*, 571–578.

Jackson, S. (1986). *Melancholia and depression: From hippocratic times to modern times*. New Haven, CT: Yale University Press.

Jahanshahi, M., & Frith, C.D. (1998). Willed action and its impairments. *Cognitive Neuropsychology*, *15*, 483–533.

Jamison, K.R. (1993). *Touched by fire: Manic-depressive illness and the artistic temperament*. New York: Free Press.

Javitt, D.C. (1997). Psychophysiology of schizophrenia. *Current Opinion in Psychiatry*, *10*, 11–15.

Jenike, M.A. (1998). Drug treatment of obsessive compulsive disorders. In M.A. Jenike, L. Baer, & W.E. Minichiello (Eds.), *Obsessive compulsive disorders: Practical management* (pp. 469–532). St Louis: Mosby.

Jenike, M.A., & Wilhelm, S. (1998). Illnesses related to obsessive compulsive disorder: Introduction. In M.A. Jenike, L. Baer, & W.E. Minichiello (Eds.), *Obsessive compulsive disorders: Practical management* (pp. 121–142). St Louis: Mosby.

Jenike, M.A., Baer, L., & Minichiello, W.E. (1998). An overview of obsessive compulsive disorder. In M.A. Jenike, L. Baer, & W.E. Minichiello (Eds.), *Obsessive compulsive disorders: Practical management* (pp. 3–11). St Louis: Mosby.

Jensen, P.S., Martin, D., & Cantwell, D.P. (1997a). Comorbidity in ADHD: Implications for research, practice and DSM-V. *Journal of the American Academy of Child and Adolescent Psychiatry, 36*, 1065–1079.

Jensen, P.S., Mrazek, M.D., Knapp, P.K., Steinberg, L., Pfeffer, C., Schowalter, J., & Shapiro, T. (1997b). Evolution and revolution in child psychiatry: ADHD as a disorder of adaptation. *Journal of the American Academy of Child and Adolescent Psychiatry, 36*, 1672–1679.

Jeste, D.V., Galasko, D., Corey-Bloom, J., Walens, S., & Granholm, E. (1996). Neuropsychiatric aspects of the schizophrenias. In B.S. Fogel, R.B. Schiffer, & S.M. Rao (Eds.), *Neuropsychiatry* (pp. 325–342). Baltimore: Williams & Wilkins.

Johns, C., & McGuire, P.K. (1999). Verbal self monitoring and auditory hallucination in schizophrenia. *The Lancet, 353*, 469–470.

Jolliffe, T., & Baron-Cohen, S. (1999). A test of coherence theory: linguistic processing in high-functioning adults with autism or Asperger syndrome: Is local coherence impaired? *Cognition, 71*, 149–185.

Jones, E.G. (1997). Cortical development and thalamic pathology in schizophrenia. *Schizophrenia Bulletin, 23*, 483–501.

Jonkman, L.M., Kemner, C., Verbaten, M.N., Koelega, H.S., Camfferman, G., Gaag, R.-J., Buitelaar, J.K., & van Engeland, H. (1997). Event-related potentials and performance of attention-deficit hyperactivity disorder: Children and normal controls in auditory and visual selective attention. *Biological Psychiatry, 41*, 595–611.

Judd, L.L. (1997). The clinical course of unipolar major depressive disorders. *Archives of General Psychiatry, 54*, 989–990.

Judd, L.L., & Kunovac, J.L. (1997). Diagnosis and classification of depression. In A. Honig & H.M. Van Praag (Eds.), *Depression: Neurobiological, psychopathological and therapeutic advances* (pp. 3–16). New York: Wiley.

Juncos, J., & Freeman, A. (1997). Pathophysiology and differentiated diagnosis of tics. In R.L. Watts & W.C. Koller (Eds.), *Movement disorders* (pp. 561–568). New York: McGraw-Hill.

Kado, S., & Takagi, R. (1996). Biological aspects. In S. Sandberg (Ed.), *Hyperactivity disorders of childhood* (pp. 246–279). Cambridge, UK: Cambridge University Press.

Kakei, S., Hoffman, D.S., & Strick, P.L. (1999). Muscle and movement representations in the primary motor cortex. *Science, 285*, 2136–2139.

Kanner, L. (1943). Autistic disturbances of affective contact. *Nervous Child, 2*, 217–250.

Kapur, N. (1996). Paradoxical functional facilitation in brain-behaviour research: A critical review. *Brain, 119*, 1775–1790.

Karmiloff-Smith, A. (1998). Development itself is not the key to understanding developmental disorders. *Trends in Cognitive Sciences, 2*, 389–398.

Karp, B.I., Porter, S., Toro, C., & Hallett, M. (1996). Simple motor tics may be preceded by a premotor potential. *Journal of Neurology, Neurosurgery and Psychiatry, 61*, 103–106.

Katsetos, C.D., Hyde, T.M., & Herman, M.M. (1997). Neuropathology of the cerebellum in schizophrenia—An update: 1996 and future directions. *Biological Psychiatry, 42*, 213–224.

Kay, S.R., Fiszbein, A., & Opler, L.A. (1987). The positive and negative syndrome scale (PANSS) for schizophrenia. *Schizophrenia Bulletin, 13*, 261–276.

Keefe, R.S.E., Silva, S.G., Perkins, D.O., & Lieberman, J.A. (1999). The effects of atypical antipsychotic drugs on neurocognitive impairment in schizophrenia: A review and meta-analysis. *Schizophrenia Bulletin, 25*, 201–222.

Kemper, T.L., & Bauman, M. (1998). Neuropathology of infantile autism. *Journal of Neuropathology and Experimental Neurology, 57*, 645–652.

King, R.A., Leckman, J.F., Scahill, L., & Cohen, D.J. (1999). Obsessive compulsive disorder, anxiety, depression. In J.F. Leckman & D.J. Cohen (Eds.), *Tourette's syndrome: Tics, obsessions, compulsions* (pp. 43–62). New York: Wiley.

King, R.A., & Scahill, L. (1995). Obsessive compulsive disorder in children and adolescents. In M.M. Robertson & V. Eapen (Eds.), *Movement and allied disorders* (pp. 43–56). New York: Wiley.

Knoll, J.L., Garver, D.L., Ramberg, J.E., Kingsbury, S.J., Croissant, D., & McDermott, B. (1998). Heterogeneity of the psychoses: Is there a neurodegenerative psychosis? *Schizophrenia Bulletin, 24,* 365–379.

Knutson, B.K., Wolkowitz, O.M., Cole, S.W., Chan, T., Moore, E.A., Johnson, R.C., Terpstra, J., Turner, R.A., & Reus, V.I. (1998). Selective alteration of personality and social behavior by serotonergic intervention. *American Journal of Psychiatry, 155,* 373–379.

Koziol, L.F. (1994a). Obsessive compulsive disorder and related spectrum disturbances. In L.F. Koziol & C.E. Stout (Eds.), *The neuropsychology of mental disorders: A practical guide* (pp. 106–128). Springfield, IL: C.C. Thomas.

Koziol, L.F. (1994b). Attention deficit disorder, frontal lobe syndromes, and related psychiatric disturbances. In L.F. Koziol & C.E. Stout (Eds.), *The neuropsychology of mental disorders* (pp. 52–79). Springfield, IL: C.C. Thomas.

Kramer, M.S., Cutler, N., Feighner, J., Shrivastava, R., Carman, J., Sramek, J.J., Reines, S.A., Liu, G., Snavely, D., Wyatt-Knowles, E. et al. (1998). Distinct mechanism for antidepressant activity by blockade of central subcutaneous substance P receptors. *Science, 281,* 1640–1645.

Krug, D.A., Arick, J., & Almond, P. (1980). Behavior checklist for identifying severely handicapped individuals with high levels of autistic behavior. *Journal of Child Psychology and Psychiatry, 21,* 221–229.

Kugler, B. (1998). The differentiation between autism and Asperger syndrome. *Autism, 2,* 11–32.

Kurlan, R. (1994). Hypothesis II: Tourette's syndrome is part of a clinical spectrum that includes normal brain development. *Archives of Neurology, 51,* 1145–1150.

Kurlan, R. (1998). Tourette's syndrome and "PANDAS": Will the relation bear out? *Neurology, 50,* 1530–1534.

Kutchins, H., & Kirk, S.A. (1997). *Making us crazy: DSM: The psychiatric bible and the creation of mental disorders.* New York: Free Press.

LaHoste, G.J., Swanson, J.M., Wigal, S.B., Glabe, C., Wigal, T., King, N., & Kennedy, J.L. (1996). Dopamine D4 receptor gene polymorphism is associated with attention deficit hyperactivity disorder. *Molecular Psychiatry, 1,* 121–124.

Lawrie, S.M., Whalley, H., Kestelman, J.N., Abukmeil, S.S., Byrne, M., Hodges, A., Rimmington, J.E., Best, J., Owens, D., & Johnstone, E. (1999). Magnetic resonance imaging of brain in people at high risk of developing schizophrenia. *The Lancet, 353,* 30–33.

Leary, M.R., & Hill, D.A. (1996). Moving on: Autism and movement disturbance. *Mental Retardation, 34,* 39–53.

Leavens, D.A., Hopkins, W.D., & Bard, K.A. (1996). Indexical and referential pointing in chimpanzees (*Pan troglodytes*). *Journal of Comparative Psychology, 110,* 346–353.

Leboyer, M., & Gorwood, P. (1995). Genetics of affective disorders and schizophrenia. In J. Panksepp (Ed.), *Advances in biological psychiatry* (Vol. 1, pp. 27–65). London: JAI Press.

Leckman, J.F., & Cohen, D.J. (1996). Tic disorders. In M. Lewis (Ed.), *Child and adolescent psychiatry: A comprehensive textbook* (2nd ed., pp. 622–629). Baltimore: Williams & Wilkins.

Leckman, J.F., & Cohen, D.J. (1999a). Beyond the diagnosis: Darwinian perspectives on pathways to successful adaptation. In J.F. Leckman & D.J. Cohen (Eds.), *Tourette's syndrome: Tics, obsessions, compulsions* (pp. 140–151). New York: Wiley.

Leckman, J.F., & Cohen, D.J. (1999b). Evolving models of pathogenesis. In J.F. Leckman &

D.J. Cohen (Eds.), *Tourette's syndrome: Tics, obsessions, compulsions* (pp. 155–175). New York: Wiley.

Leckman, J.F., Peterson, B.S., Anderson, G.M., Arnsten, A.M.F.T., Pauls, D.L., & Cohen, D.J. (1997). Pathogenesis of Tourette's syndrome. *Journal of Child Psychology and Psychiatry, 38*, 119–142.

Leckman, J.F., King, R.A., & Cohen, D.J. (1999). Tics and tic disorders. In J.F. Leckman & D.J. Cohen (Eds.), *Tourette's syndrome: Tics, obsessions, compulsions* (pp. 23–42). New York: Wiley.

LeDoux, J. (1996). *The emotional brain*. New York: Simon & Schuster.

Lees, A.J., & Tolosa, E. (1993). Tics. In J. Jankovic & E. Tolosa (Eds.), *Parkinson's disease and movement disorders* (2nd ed., pp. 329–336.). Baltimore: Williams & Wilkins.

Lenhoff, H.M., Wang, P.P., Greenberg, F., & Bellugi, U. (1997). Williams syndrome and the brain. *Scientific American*, December, 42–47.

Leonhard, K. (1957, translated 1979). *The classification of endogenous psychoses*. New York: Wiley.

Lewis, M.H. (1996). Brief report: Psychopharmacology of autism spectrum disorders. *Journal of Autism and Developmental Disorders, 26*, 230 235.

Lichter, D.G., Jackson, L.A., & Schachter, M. (1995). Clinical evidence of genomic imprinting in Tourette's syndrome. *Neurology*, 924–928.

Lieberman, J.A., Mailman, R.B., Duncan, G., Sikich, L., Chakos, M., Nichols, D.E., & Kraus, J.E. (1998). Serotonergic basis of antipsychotic drug effects in schizophrenia. *Biological Psychiatry, 44*, 1099–1117.

Lohr, J.B., & Wisniewski, A.A. (1987). *Movement disorders: A neuropsychiatric approach*. New York: Guilford Press.

Lord, C., & Paul, R. (1997). Language and communication in autism. In D.J. Cohen & F.R. Volkmar (Eds.), *Handbook of autism and pervasive developmental disorders* (2nd ed., pp. 195–218). New York: Wiley.

Lord, C., Rutter, M., & Le Couteur, A. (1994). Autism diagnostic interview—revised: A revised version of a diagnostic interview for caregivers of individuals with possible developmental diosrders. *Journal of Autism & Developmental Disorders, 24*, 659–685.

Lord, C., Rutter, M., & Di Lavore, P. (1996). *Autism diagnostic observation schedule—generic (ADOS-G)*. Chicago: University of Chicago.

Luppino, G., Matelli, M., Camarda, R., & Rizzolatti, G. (1993). Corticocortical connections of area F-3 (SMA-proper) and area F6 (pre-SMA) in the macaque monkey. *Journal of Comparative Neurology, 338*, 114–140.

MacKinnon, D.F., Jamison, K.R., & DePaulo, J.R. (1997). Genetics of manic depressive illness. *Annual Review of Neuroscience, 20*, 355–373.

Madsen, A.L., Karle, A., Rubin, P., Cortsen, M., Andersen, H.S., & Hemmingsen, R. (1999). Progressive atrophy of the frontal lobes in first-episode schizophrenia: Interaction with clinical course and neuroleptic treatment. *Acta Psychiatrica Scandinavica, 100*, 367–374.

Maes, M. (1997). The immune pathophysiology of major depression. In A. Honig & H.M. Van Praag (Eds.), *Depression: Neurobiological, psychopathological and therapeutic advances* (pp. 197–216). New Work: Wiley.

Maier, W., & Schwab, S. (1998). Molecular genetics of schizophrenia. *Current Opinion in Psychiatry, 11*, 19–25.

Malla, A.K., Norman, R.M.G., Aguilar, O., Carnahan, H., & Cortese, L. (1995). Relationship between movement planning and psychopathology profiles in schizophrenia. *British Journal of Psychiatry, 167*, 211–215.

Manly, T., Robertson, I.H., & Verity, C. (1997). Developmental unilateral visual neglect: A single case study. *Neurocase, 3*, 19–29.

Mann, J.J. (1998). The role of in vivo neurotransmitter system imaging studies in understanding major depression. *Biological Psychiatry*, *44*, 1077.

Mann, J.J., & Kapur, S. (1995). A dopaminergic hypothesis of major depression. *Clinical Neuropharmacology*, *18* (Suppl. 1), S57–S65.

Marazziti, D., Akiskal, S., Ross, A., & Cassano, G.B. (1999). Alteration of the platelet serotonin transporter in romantic love. *Psychological Medicine*, *29*, 741–746.

Marsden, C.D., Deecke, L., Freund, H.J., Hallett, M., Passingham, R.E., Shibasaki, H., Tanji, J., & Wiesendanger, M. (1996). The functions of the supplementary motor area. *Advances in Neurology*, *70*, 477–487.

Martin, P., & Albers, M. (1995). Cerebellum and schizophrenia: A selective review. *Schizophrenia Bulletin*, *21*, 241–250.

Maruff, P., & Currie, J. (1996). Neuropsychology of visual attentional deficits in schizophrenia. In C. Pantelis, H.E. Nelson, & T.R.E. Barnes (Eds.), *Schizophrenia: A neuropsychological perspective* (pp. 87–105). New York: Wiley.

Marzullo, G. (1996). *Month of birth, creativity and the two classes of men*. New York: Per Aspera Books.

Mataro, M., Garcia-Sanchez, C., Junque, C., Estévez-González, A., & Pujol, J. (1997). Magnetic resonance imaging measurement of the caudate nucleus in adolescents with attention deficit hyperactivity disorder, and its relationship with neuropsychological behavioral methods. *Archives of Neurology*, *54*, 963–968.

McAllister-Williams, R.H., Ferrier, I.N., & Young, A.H. (1998). Mood and neuropsychological function in depression: The role of corticosteroids and serotonin. *Psychological Medicine*, *28*, 573–584.

McCarney, S.B. (1995). *The attention deficit disorders evaluation scale*. Columbia: Hawthorne Eductional Services.

McEvoy, J.P., Freudenreich, O., & Wilson, W.H. (1999). Smoking and therapeutic response to clozapine in patients with schizophrenia. *Biological Psychiatry*, *46*, 125–129.

McInnes, L.A., Reus, V.I., & Freimer, N.B. (1998). Mapping genes for psychiatric disorders and behavioral traits. *Current Opinion in Genetics & Development*, *8*, 287–292.

McPhillips, M.A., & Barnes, R.E. (1997). Negative symptoms. *Current Opinion in Psychiatry*, *10*, 30–35.

Mega, M.S., & Cummings, J.L. (1994). Frontal-subcortical circuits and neuropsychiatric disorders. *Journal of Neuropsychiatry and Clinical Neurosciences*, *6*, 358–370.

Meltzer, H.Y., & McGurk, S.R. (1999). The effects of clozapine, risperidone, and olanzapine on cognitive function in schizophrenia. *Schizophrenia Bulletin*, *25*, 233–255.

Mendez, M.F., Van Gorp, W., & Cummings, J.L. (1995). Neuropsychiatry, neuropsychology, and behavioral neurology: A critical comparison. *Neuropsychiatry, Neuropsychology, and Behavioral Neurology*, *8*, 297–302.

Mendlewicz, J. (1994). The search for a manic-depressive gene: From classical to molecular genetics. In F. Bloom (Ed.), *Progress in brain research* (Vol. 100, pp. 255–259). Amsterdam: Elsevier.

Merzenich, M. (1998). Long-term change of mind. *Science*, *282*, 1062–1063.

Middleton, F.A., & Strick, P.L. (1997). New concepts about the organization of basal ganglia output. In J.A. Obeso, M.R. DeLong, C. Ohye, & C.D. Marsden (Eds.), *The basal ganglia and new surgical approaches for Parkinson's disease: Advances in neurology* (Vol. 74, pp. 57–68). Philadelphia: Lippincott-Raven.

Miller, B.L., Cummings, J., Mishkin, F., Boone, K., Prince, F., Ponton, M., & Cotman, C. (1998). Emergence of artistic talent in frontotemporal dementia. *Neurology*, *51*, 978–982.

Mineka, S., Watson, D., & Clark, L.A. (1998). Comorbidity of anxiety and unipolar mood disorders. *Annual Review of Psychology*, *49*, 377–412.

Mink, J.W. (1998). Basal ganglia. In M.J. Zigmond, F.E. Bloom, S.C. Landis, J.L. Roberts, & L.R. Squire (Eds.), *Fundamental neuroscience* (pp. 951–971). San Diego: Academic Press.

Minshew, N.J. (1997). Pervasive developmental disorders: Autism and similar disorders. In M.J. Farah (Ed.), *Behavioral neurology and neuropsychology* (pp. 817–825). New York: McGraw-Hill.

Minshew, N.J., Goldstein, G., & Siegal, D.J. (1997). Neuropsychologic functioning in autism: Profile of a complex information processing disorder. *Journal of the International Neuropsychological Society, 3,* 303–316.

Moffit, T.E. (1993). The neuropsychology of conduct disorder. *Development and Psychopathology, 5,* 135–151.

Moldin, S.O., & Gottesman, I.I. (1997). At issue: Genes, experience, and chance in schizophrenia—positioning for the 21st century. *Schizophrenia Bulletin, 23,* 547–561.

Molloy, R., Brownell, H.H., & Gardner, H. (1990). Discourse comprehension by right hemisphere stroke patients: Deficits of prediction and revision. In Y. Joanette & H.H. Brownell (Eds.), *Discourse ability and brain damage: Theoretical and empirical perspectives* (pp. 113–130). New York: Springer.

Montgomery, S., & Esberg, M. (1979). A new depression scale designed to be sensitive to change. *British Journal of Psychiatry, 134,* 382–389.

Moore, H., West, A.R., & Grace, A.A. (1999). The regulation of forebrain dopamine transmission: Relevance to the pathophysiology and psychopathology of schizophrenia. *Biological Psychiatry, 46,* 40–55.

Moriarty, J., Ring, H.A., & Robertson, M.M. (1993). An idiot savant calendrical calculator with Gilles de la Tourette syndrome: Implications for an understanding of the savant syndrome. *Psychological Medicine, 23,* 1019–1021.

Mortenson, D.D., Pedersen, C.B., Westergaard, T., Wohlfahrt, J., Ewald, H., Mars, O., Andersen, P., & Melbye, M. (1999). Effects of family history and place and season of birth on the risk of schizophrenia. *New England Journal of Medicine, 340,* 603–608.

Narita, A.S., Shawkat, F.S., Lask, B., Taylor, D.S.I., & Harris, C.M. (1997). Eye movement abnormalities in a case of Tourette syndrome. *Developmental Medicine & Child Neurology, 39,* 270–273.

Nasrallah, H.A. (1996). Neurodevelopmental models of affective disorder. In B.S. Fogel, R.B. Schiffer, & S.M. Rao (Eds.), *Neuropsychiatry* (pp. 198–203). Baltimore: Williams & Wilkins.

Nemeroff, C.B. (1998). Psychopharmacology of affective disorders in the 21st century. *Biological Psychiatry, 44,* 514–525.

Nestler, E.J. (1998). Antidepressant treatments in the 21st century. *Biological Psychiatry, 44,* 526–533.

Nestor, P.G., & O'Donnell, B.F. (1998). The mind adrift: Attentional dysregulation in schizophrenia. In R. Parasuraman (Ed.), *The attentive brain* (pp. 528–547). Cambridge, MA: MIT Press.

Niehaus, D.J.H., & Stein, D.J. (1997). Obsessive-compulsive disorder: Diagnosis and assessment. In E. Hollander & D.J. Stein (Eds.), *Obsessive compulsive disorders: Diagnosis, etiology, treatment* (pp. 1–22). New York: Marcel Dekker.

Nigg, J.T., Swanson, J.M., & Hinshaw, S.P. (1997). Covert visual spatial attention in boys with attention deficit hyperactivity disorder: laterality effects, methylphenidate response and results for parents. *Neuropsychologia, 35,* 165–176.

Nopoulos, P.C., Ceilley, J.W., Gailis, E.A., & Andreasen, N. C. (1999). An magnetic resonance imaging study of cerebellar vermis morphology in patients with schizophrenia: Evidence in support of the cognitive dysmetria concept. *Biological Psychiatry, 46,* 703–711.

Obeso, J.A., Rodriguez, M.C., & DeLong, M.R. (1997). Basal ganglia pathophysiology: A critical review. In J.A. Obeso, M.R. DeLong, C. Ohye, & C.D. Marsden (Eds.), *The basal ganglia and new surgical approaches for Parkinson's disease* (Vol. 74, pp. 3–18). Philadelphia: Lippincott-Raven.

Öngur, D., Drevets, W.C., & Price, J.L. (1998). Glial reduction in the subgenual prefrontal cortex in mood disorders. *Proceedings of the National Academy of Sciences of the USA, 95*, 13290–13295.

Ozonoff, S., & Jensen, J. (1999). Brief report: Specific executive function profiles in three neurodevelopmental disorders. *Journal of Autism and Developmental Disorders, 29*, 171–177.

Palumbo, D., Maughan, A., & Kurlan, R. (1997). Hypothesis III: Tourette syndrome is only one of several causes of a developmental basal ganglia syndrome. *Archives of Neurology, 54*, 475–483.

Pantelis, C., & Brewer, W. (1996). Neurocognitive and neurobehavioural patterns and the syndromes of schizophrenia: Role of frontal-subcortical networks. In C. Pantelis, H.E. Nelson, & T.R.E. Barnes (Eds.), *Schizophrenia: A neuropsychological perspective* (pp. 317–343). New York: Wiley.

Parent, A., & Cicchetti, F. (1998). The current model of basal ganglia organization under scrutiny. *Movement Disorders, 13*, 199–202.

Parker, G., Hickie, I., & Mason, C. (1996). Validity of the CORE III: Outcome and treatment prediction. In G. Parker & D. Hadzi-Pavlovic (Eds.), *Melancholia: A disorder of movement and mood* (pp. 82–129). Cambridge, UK: Cambridge University Press.

Parkin, R. (1997). Obsessive compulsive disorder in adults. *International Review of Psychiatry, 9*, 73–81.

Parry-Jones, B. (1992). A bulimic ruminator? The case of Dr Samuel Johnson. *Psychological Medicine, 22*, 851–862.

Pato, M.T., Eisen, J.L., & Pato, C.N. (1994). Rating scales for obsessive compulsive disorder. In E. Hollander, J. Zohar, D. Marazzati, & B. Olivier (Eds.), *Current insights in obsessive compulsive disorder* (pp. 77–91). New York: Wiley.

Pauls, D.L., Alsobrook, J.F., Gelerntner, J., & Leckman, J.F. (1999). Genetic vulnerability. In J.F. Leckman & D.J. Cohen (Eds.), *Tourette's syndrome: Tics, obsessions, compulsions* (pp. 194–211). New York: Wiley.

Paus, T., Koski, L., Caramanos, Z., & Westbury, C. (1998). Regional differences in the effects of task difficulty and motor output on blood flow response in the human anterior cingulate cortex: A review of 107 PET activation studies. *Neuroreport, 9*, R37–R47.

Pearlson, G.D., & Pulver, A.E. (1994). Sex, schizophrenia and the cerebral cortex. In R. Ancill (Ed.), *Schizophrenia: Exploring the spectrum of psychosis* (pp. 345–361). New York: Wiley.

Pennington, B.F., & Ozonoff, S. (1996). Executive functions and developmental psychopathology. *Journal of Child Psychology and Psychiatry, 37*, 51–87.

Peterson, B.S., Leckman, J.F., & Cohen, D.J. (1995). Tourette's syndrome: A genetically predisposed and an environmentally specified developmental psychopathology. In D. Cicchetti & D. Cohen (Eds.), *Developmental psychopatholgy: Risk disorder and adaptation* (Vol. 2, pp. 213–242). New York: Wiley.

Peterson, B.S., Riddle, M.A., Cohen, D.J., Katz, L.D., Smith, J.C., Hardin, N.T., & Leckman, J.F. (1993). Reduced basal ganglia volumes in Tourette's syndrome using 3-dimensional reconstruction techniques from magnetic resonance images. *Neurology, 43*, 941–949.

Peterson, B.S., Leckman, J.F., Arnsten, A., Anderson, G.M., Staib, L.H., Gore, J.C., Bronen, R.A., Malison, R., Scahill, L., & Cohen, D.S. (1999a). Neuroanatomical circuitry. In J.F. Leckman & D.J. Cohen (Eds.), *Tourette's syndrome: Tics, obsessions, compulsions* (pp. 230–259). New York: Wiley.

Peterson, B.S., Leckman, J.F., Lombroso, P., Zhang, H., Lynch, K., Carter, A.S., Pauls, D.L., & Cohen, D.J. (1999b). Environmental risk and protective factors. In J.F. Leckman & D.J.

Cohen (Eds.), *Tourette's syndrome: Tics, obsessions, compulsions* (pp. 213–229). New York: Wiley.

Piacentini, J., & Graae, F. (1997). Childhood obsessive compulsive disorder. In E. Hollander & D.J. Stein (Eds.), *Obsessive compulsive disorders: Diagnosis, etiology, treatment* (pp. 23–46). New York: Marcel Dekker.

Piccinelli, M. (1998). Comorbidity of depression and generalized anxiety: Is there any distinct boundary? *Current Opinion in Psychiatry, 11*, 57–60.

Piven, J. (1997). The biological basis of autism. *Current Opinion in Neurobiology, 7*, 708–712.

Plenz, D., & Kital, S. (1999). A basal ganglia pacemaker formed by the subthalamic nucleus and external globus pallidus. *Nature, 400*, 677–682.

Plomin, R., Owen, M.J., & McGuffin, P. (1994). The genetic basis of complex human behaviors. *Science, 264*, 1733–1739.

Pomeroy, J.C. (1998). Subtyping pervasive development disorder: Issues of validity and implications for child psychiatric diagnosis. In E. Schopler, G. Mesibov, & C.J. Kunce (Eds.), *Asperger syndrome and high functioning autism*. New York: Plenum.

Posner, M.I., Early, T.S., Reiman, E., Pardo, P.J., & Dhawan, M. (1988). Asymmetries in hemispheric control of attention in schizophrenia. *Archives of General Psychiatry, 45*, 814–821.

Posner, M.I., & Raichle, M.E. (1994). *Images of mind*. New York: Scientific American Library.

Post, F. (1994). Creativity and psychopathology: A study of 291 world-famous men. *British Journal of Psychiatry, 165*, 22–34.

Povinelli, D.J., & Davis, D.R. (1994). Differences between chimpanzees (*Pan troglodytes*) and humans (*Homo sapiens*) in the resting state of the index finger: Implications for pointing. *Journal of Comparative Psychology, 108*, 134–139.

Povinelli, D.J., & Eddy, T.J. (1996). Factors influencing young chimpanzees' (*Pan troglodytes*) recognition of attention. *Journal of Comparative Psychology, 110*, 336–345.

Purcell, R., Maruff, P., Kyrios, M., & Pantelis, C. (1998). Cognitive deficits in obsessive compulsive disorder on tests of frontal-striatal function. *Biological Psychiatry, 43*, 349–357.

Quay, H.C. (1997). Inhibition and attention deficit hyperactivity disorder. *Journal of Abnormal Child Psychology, 25*, 7–13.

Raedler, T.J., Knable, M.B., & Weinberger, D.R. (1998). Schizophrenia as a developmental disorder of the cerebral cortex. *Current Opinion in Psychiatry, 8*, 157–161.

Raichle, M.E. (1998). The neural correlates of consciousness: An analysis of cognitive skill learning. *Philosophical Transactions of the Royal Society of London B, 353*, 1889–1901.

Rapin, I. (1997). Classification and causal issues in autism. In D.J. Cohen & F.R. Volkmar (Eds.), *Handbook of autism and pervasive developmental disorders* (pp. 847–860). New York: Wiley.

Rapin, I. (1999). Autism in search of a home in the brain. *Neurology, 52*, 902–904.

Rapoport, J.L., Giedd, J.N., Blumenthal, J., Hamburger, S., Jeffries, N., Fernandez, T., Nicolson, R., Bedwell, J., Lenane, M., Zijdenbos, A., Paus, T., & Evans, A. (1999). Progressive cortical change during adolescence in childhood-onset schizophrenia. *Archives of General Psychiatry, 56*, 649–654.

Ratey, J.R., Middeldorp-Crispijn, C.W., & Leveroni, C.L. (1995). Influence of attention problems on the development of personality. In J.J. Ratey (Ed.), *Neuropsychiatry of personality disorders* (pp. 79–119). Oxford: Blackwell Science.

Rauch, S.L., & Baxter, L.R. (1998). Neuroimaging in obsessive compulsive disorder and related disorders. In M.A. Jenike, L. Baer, & W.E. Minichiello (Eds.), *Obsessive compulsive disorders: Practical management* (pp. 289–317). St Louis: Mosby.

Rauch, S.L., Whalen, P.J., Dougherty, D., & Jenike, M.A. (1998). Neurobiologic models of obsessive compulsive disorder. In M.A. Jenike, L. Baer, & W.E. Minichiello (Eds.), *Obsessive compulsive disorders: Practical management* (pp. 222–253). St Louis: Mosby.

Reid, P.D., Shajahan, P.M., Glabus, M.F., & Ebmeier, K.P. (1998). Transcranial magnetic stimulation in depression. *British Journal of Psychiatry*, *173*, 449–452.

Rimland, B., & Fein, D. (1988). Special talents of autistic savants. In L.K. Obler & D. Fein (Eds.), *The exceptional brain* (pp. 474–492). New York: Guilford.

Rinehart, N.J., Bradshaw, J.L., Brereton, A.V., & Tonge, B.J. (in press a). Anomalies in movement preparation in autism and Asperger's disorder. *Journal of Autism and Developmental Disorders.*

Rinehart, N.J., Bradshaw, J.L., Moss, S.A., Brereton, A.V., & Tonge, B.J. (in press b). A typical interference of local detail on global processing in high functioning autism and Asperger's disorder. *Journal of Child Psychology and Psychiatry.*

Rinehart, N.J., Bradshaw, J.L., Moss, S.A., Brereton, A.V., & Tonge, B.J. (in press c). A deficit in shifting attention which is present in high functioning autism but not Asperger's disorder. *Autism: An International Journal of Research and Practice.*

Rison, R.A. (1998). Schizophrenia and N-methyl-D-aspartate receptors: Evolutionary adaptations from malfunctioning molecules? *Neuropsychiatry, Neuropsychology and Behavioral Neurology*, *11*, 236–240.

Robertson, M.M., & Eapen, V. (1995). Gilles de la Tourette syndrome. In M.M. Robertson & V. Eapen (Eds.), *Movement and allied disorders* (pp. 1–29). New York: Wiley.

Robertson, M.M., & Yakeley, J. (1996). Gilles de la Tourette syndrome and obsessive-compulsive disorder. In B.S. Fogel, R.B. Schiffer, & S.M. Rao (Eds.), *Neuropsychiatry* (pp. 827–870). Baltimore: Williams & Wilkins.

Robinson, R.G., & Travella, J.I. (1996). Neuropsychiatry of mood disorders. In B.S. Fogel, R.B. Schiffer, & S.M. Rao (Eds.), *Neuropsychiatry* (pp. 287–305). Baltimore: Williams & Wilkins.

Rogers, M.A., Bradshaw, J.L., Pantelis, C.K., & Phillips, J.G. (1998). Fronto-striatal deficits in unipolar major depression. *Brain Research Bulletin*, *47*, 297–310.

Rosenberg, D.R., & Keshavan, M.S. (1998). Toward a neurodevelopmental model of obsessive compulsive disorder. *Biological Psychiatry*, *43*, 623–640.

Rosenberg, D.R., Averbach, D.H., O'Hearn, K.M., Seymour, A.B., Birmaher, B., & Sweeney, J.A. (1997). Oculomotor response inhibition abnormalities in pediatric obsessive compulsive disorder. *Archives of General Psychiatry*, *54*, 831–838.

Rossell, S.L., & David, A.S. (1997). The neuropsychology of schizophrenia: recent trends. *Current Opinion in Psychiatry*, *10*, 26–29.

Roth, B.L., Willins, D.L., Kristiansen, K., & Kroeze, W.K. (1999). Activation is hallucinogenic and antagonism is therapeutic: Role of $5-HT_{2A}$ receptors in atypical antipsychotic drug actions. *The Neuroscientist*, *5*, 254–262.

Rund, B.R. (1998). A review of longitudinal studies of cognitive functions in schizophrenia patients. *Schizophrenia Bulletin*, *24*, 425–435.

Russell, J. (Ed.). (1998). *Autism as an executive disorder.* Oxford: Oxford University Press.

Rutter, M. (1999). The Emmanuel Miller memorial lecture 1998. Autism: Two-way interplay between research and clinical work. *Journal of Child Psychology and Psychiatry*, *40*, 169–188.

Rutter, M., Bailey, A., Simonoff, E., & Pickles, A. (1997). Genetic influences of autism. In D.J. Cohen & F.R. Volkmar (Eds.), *Handbook of autism and pervasive developmental disorders* (pp. 370–387). New York: Wiley.

Sachdev, P. (1999). Attention deficit hyperactivity disorder in adults. *Psychological Medicine*, *29*, 507–514.

Sacks, O. (1992). Tourette's syndrome and creativity: Exploiting the ticcy witticisms and witty ticcicisms. *British Medical Journal*, *305*, 1515–1516.

Sacks, O. (1995). Musical ability. *Science*, *268*, 621.

Sagvolden, T., & Sergeant, J.A. (1998). Attention deficit/hyperactivity disorder: From brain dysfunctions to behavior. *Behavioural Brain Research, 94*, 1–10.

Saunders, R.C., Kolachana, B.S., Bachevalier, J., & Weinberger, D.R. (1998). Neonatal lesions of the medial temporal lobe disrupt prefrontal cortical regulation of striatal dopamine. *Nature, 393*, 169–172.

Savage, C.R. (1998). Neuropsychology of obsessive compulsive disorder: Research findings and treatment implications. In M.A. Jenike, L. Baer, & W.E. Minichiello (Eds.), *Obsessive compulsive disorders: Practical management* (pp. 254–275). St Louis: Mosby.

Schlaug, G., Jäncke, L., Huang, Y., & Steinmetz, H. (1995). In vivo evidence of structural brain asymmetry in musicians. *Science, 267*, 699–701.

Schnider, A., & Ptak, R. (1999). Spontaneous confabulators fail to suppress currently irrelevant memory traces. *Nature Neuroscience, 2*, 677–682.

Schopler, E., Reichter, R.J., & Renner, A. (1988). *The childhood autism rating scale (CARS)*. Los Angeles: Western Psychological Services.

Schultz, R.T., Carter, A.S., Scahill, L., & Leckman, J. (1999). Neuropsychological findings. In J.F. Leckman & D.J. Cohen (Eds.), *Tourette's syndrome: Tics, obsessions, compulsions* (pp. 80–103). New York: Wiley.

Schultz, S.K., & Andreasen, N.C. (1999). Schizophrenia. *The Lancet, 353*, 1425–1430.

Schwartz, B.D., Maron, B.A., Evans, W.J., & Winstead, D.K. (1999). High velocity transient visual processing deficits diminish ability of patients with schizophrenia to recognize objects. *Neuropsychiatry, Neuropsychology and Behavioral Neurology, 12*, 170–177.

Selemon, L.D., & Goldman-Rakic, P.S. (1999). The reduced neuropil hypothesis: A circuit based model of schizophrenia. *Biological Psychiatry, 45*, 17–25.

Selfe, L. (1977). *Nadia: A case of extraordinary drawing ability in an autistic child*. New York: Academic Press.

Serretti, A., Macciardi, F., Catalano, M., Bellodi, L., & Smeraldi, E. (1999). Genetic variants of dopamine receptor D4 and psychopathology. *Schizophrenia Bulletin, 25*, 609–618.

Sheline, Y.I. (1998). Neuroanatomical changes associated with unipolar major depression. *The Neuroscientist, 4*, 331–334.

Sheppard, D.M., Bradshaw, J.L., Mattingley, J.B., & Lee, P.L. (1999a). Effects of stimulant medication on the lateralisation of line bisection judgements of ADHD children. *Journal of Neurology, Neurosurgery and Psychiatry, 66*, 57–63.

Sheppard, D.M., Bradshaw, J.L., Purcell, R., & Pantelis, C. (1999b). Tourette's and comorbid syndromes: Obsessive compulsive and attention deficit hyperactivity disorder. A common aetiology? *Clinical Psychology Review, 19*, 531–552.

Sherman, D.K., Iacono, W.G., & McGue, M.K. (1997). Attention deficit hyperactivity disorder dimensions: A twin study of inattention and impulsivity–hyperactivity. *Journal of the American Academy of Child and Adolescent Psychiatry, 36*, 745–753.

Shytle, R.D., Silver, A.A., Newman, M.B., & Sanberg, P.R. (in press). Nicotinic therapeutics for Tourette's syndrome and other neuropsychiatric disorders. In D.F. Emerich, R.L. Dean, & P.R. Sanberg (Eds.), *Innovative animal models of central nervous system diseases: From molecule to therapy*. Totowa, NJ: Humana Press.

Shytle, R.D., Silver, A.A., & Sanberg, P.R. (1996). Clinical assessment of Tourette's syndrome. In P.R. Sanberg, K.P. Ossenkopp, & M. Kavaliers (Eds.), *Motor activity and movement disorders* (pp. 343–360). Totowa, NJ: Humana Press.

Siegel, B.V., Asarnow, R., Cale, J.D., Abel, L., Ho, A., Lott, I., & Buchsbaum, M.S. (1992). Regional cerebral glucose metabolism in adults with a history of childhood autism. *Journal of Neuropsychiatry and Clinical Neuroscience, 4*, 406–414.

Sigman, M., Dissanayake, C., Arbelle, S., & Ruskin, E. (1997). Cognition and emotion in children and adolescents with autism. In D.J. Cohen & F.R. Volkmar (Eds.), *Handbook of autism and pervasive developmental disorders* (pp. 248–269). New York: Wiley.

Singer, H.S., Reiss, A.L., Brown, J.E., Aylward, E.H., Shih, B., Chee, E., Harris, E.L., Reader, M.J., Chase, G.A., Bryan, R.N., & Denckla, M.B. (1993). Volumetric MRI changes in basal ganglia of children with Tourette's syndrome. *Neurology, 43*, 950–956.

Smalley, S.L. (1998). Autism and tuberous sclerosis. *Journal of Autism and Developmental Disorders, 28*, 407–414.

Smith, K.A., & Cowen, P.J. (1997). Serotonin and depression. In A. Honig & H.M. Van Praag (Eds.), *Depression: Neurobiological, psychopathological and therapeutic advances* (pp. 129–146). New York: Wiley.

Snowdon, J. (1980). Comparison of written and postbox forms of the Leyton obsessional inventory. *Psychological Medicine, 10*, 165–170.

Snyder, A.W., & Mitchell, D.J. (1999). Is integer arithmetic fundamental to mental processing? The mind's secret arithmetic. *Proceedings of the Royal Society of London B, 266*, 587–592.

Soares, J.C., & Mann, J.J. (1997). The anatomy of mood disorders: Review of structural neuroimaging studies. *Biological Psychiatry, 41*, 86–106.

Spitzer, M. (1997). A cognitive neuroscience view of schizophrenic thought disorder. *Schizophrenia Bulletin, 23*, 29–50.

Staley, J.K., Malison, R.T., & Innis, R.B. (1998). Imaging of the serotonergic system: Interactions of neuroanatomical and functional abnormalities of depression. *Biological Psychiatry, 44*, 534–549.

Starr, A., & Sporty, L.D. (1994). Similar disorders viewed with different perspectives. *Archives of Neurology, 51*, 977–980.

Stein, J., & Richardson, A. (1999). Cognitive disorders: A question of misattribution. *Current Biology, 9*, R374–R376.

Stevens, J.R. (1997). Anatomy of schizophrenia revisited. *Schizophrenia Bulletin, 23*, 373–383.

Strandburg, R.J., Marsh, J.T., Brown, W.S., Asarnow, R.F., Higa, J., Harper, R., & Guthrie, D. (1996). Continuous-processing: Related event-related potentials in children with attention deficit hyperactivity disorder. *Biological Psychiatry, 40*, 964–980.

Straube, A., Mennicken, J.-B., Riedel, M., Eggert, T., & Muller, N. (1997). Saccades in Gilles de la Tourette syndrome. *Movement Disorders, 12*, 536–546.

Stuss, D.T., Alexander, M.P., & Benson, D.F. (1997). Frontal lobe functions. In M.R. Trimble & J.L. Cummings (Eds.), *Contemporary behavioral neurology* (pp. 169–186). New York: Butterworth-Heinemann.

Surguladze, S.A., & David, A.S. (1998). Cognitive neuropsychiatry and schizophrenia. *Current Opinion in Psychiatry, 11*, 39–44.

Swanson, J.M. (1997). Hyperkinetic disorders and attention deficit hyperactivity disorders. *Current Opinion in Psychiatry, 10*, 300–305.

Swanson, J., Castellanos, F.X., Murias, M., LaHoste, G., & Kennedy, J. (1998a). Cognitive neuroscience of attention deficit hyperactivity disorder and hyperkinetic disorder. *Current Opinion in Neurobiology, 8*, 263–271.

Swanson, J., Posner, M.I., Cantwell, D., Wigal, S., Crinella, F., Filipek, P., Emerson, J., Tucker, D., & Nalcioglu, O. (1998b). Attention-deficit/hyperactivity disorder: Symptom domains, cognitive processes, and neural networks. In R. Parasuraman (Ed.), *The attentive brain* (pp. 445–459). Cambridge, MA: MIT Press.

Szatmari, P., Jones, M.B., Zwaigenbaum, L., & MacLean, J.E. (1998). Genetics of autism: Overview and new directions. *Journal of Autism and Developmental Disorders, 28*, 351–368.

Tager-Flusberg, H. (1996). Brief report: Current theory and research on language and communication in autism. *Journal of Autism and Developmental Disorders, 26*, 169–172.

Tamminga, C.A. (1998). Serotonin and schizophrenia. *Biological Psychiatry, 44*, 1079–1080.

Tannock, R. (1998). Attention deficit hyperactivity disorder: Advances in cognitive, neurobiological, and genetic research. *Journal of Child Psychology and Psychiatry, 39*, 65–99.

Tarsy, D. (1992). Restless legs syndrome. In A.B. Joseph & R.R. Young (Eds.), *Movement disorders in neurology and neuropsychiatry* (pp. 397–400). Oxford: Blackwell Scientific.

Taylor, E. (1998). Clinical foundations of hyperactivity research. *Behavioural Brain Research, 94,* 11–24.

Teeter, P.A., & Semrud-Clikeman, M. (1995). Integrating neurobiological, psychosocial, and behavioral paradigms: A transactional model for the study of ADHD. *Archives of Clinical Neuropsychology, 10,* 433–461.

Teitelbaum, P., Teitelbaum, O., Nye, J., Fryman, J., & Maurer, R. G. (1998). Movement analysis in infancy may be useful for early diagnosis of autism. *Proceedings of the National Academy of Sciences of the USA, 95,* 13982–13987.

Towbin, K.E., & Riddle, M.A. (1996). Obsessive compulsive disorder. In M. Lewis (Ed.), *Child and adolescent psychiatry: A comprehensive textbook* (pp. 684–693). Baltimore: Williams & Wilkins.

Towbin, K.E., Peterson, B.G., Cohen, D.J., & Leckman, J.F. (1999). Differential diagnosis. In J.F. Leckman & D.J. Cohen (Eds.), *Tourette's syndrome: Tics, obsessions, compulsions* (pp. 118–139). New York: Wiley.

Travis, M.J., & Kerwin, R. (1997). Neuroimaging. *Current Opinion in Psychiatry, 10,* 16–25.

Treffert, D.A. (1988). The idiot savant: A review of the syndrome. *American Journal of Psychiatry, 145,* 563–572.

Tsuang, M.T., & Faraone, S.V. (1999). The concept of target functions in schizophrenia research. *Acta Psychiatrica Scandinavica, 99* (Suppl. 395), 2–11.

Turken, A.U., & Swick, D. (1999). Response selection in the human anterior cingulate cortex. *Nature Neuroscience, 2,* 920–924.

Turner, M. (1999). Annotation: repetitive behavior in autism: A review of psychological research. *Journal of Child Psychology and Psychiatry, 40,* 839–849.

Van der Meere, J. (1996). The role of attention. In S. Sandberg (Ed.), *Hyperactivity disorders of childhood* (pp. 111–148). Cambridge, UK: Cambridge University Press.

Voeller, K.K.S. (1996). Brief report: Developmental neurobiological aspects of autism. *Journal of Autism and Developmental Disorders, 26,* 189–193.

Voeller, K.K., & Heilman, K.M. (1988). Attention deficit hyperactivity disorder in children: A neglect syndrome. *Neurology, 38,* 806–808.

Vogel, G. (1997). Scientists probe decisions behind decision-making. *Science, 275,* 1269.

Vogeley, K., & Falkai, P. (1999). Brain imaging in schizophrenia. *Current Opinion in Psychiatry, 12,* 41–46.

Volkmar, F.R. (1996). Autism and the pervasive developmental disorders. In M. Lewis (Ed.), *Child and adolescent psychiatry: A comprehensive textbook* (pp. 489–500). Baltimore: Williams & Wilkins.

Volkmar, F.R., Klin, A., & Pauls, D. (1998). Nosological and genetic aspects of Asperger syndrome. *Journal of Autism and Developmental Disorders, 28,* 457–461.

Waddington, J.L., Lane, A., Larkin, C., & O'Callaghan, E. (1999). The neurodevelopmental basis of schizophrenia: Clinical clues from cerebro-craniofacial dysmorphogenesis, and the roots of a lifetime trajectory of disease. *Biological Psychiatry, 46,* 31–39.

Walkup, J.F., Scahill, L.D., & Riddle, M.A. (1995). Disruptive behavior, hyperactivity and learning disabilities in children with Tourette's syndrome. In W.J. Weiner & A.E. Lang (Eds.), *Behavioral neurology of movement disorders: Advances in neurology* (pp. 259–272). New York: Raven Press.

Waterhouse, L., Fein, D., & Modahl, C. (1996). Neurofunctional mechanisms in autism. *Psychological Review, 103,* 457–489.

Weinberger, D.R. (1999). Cell biology of the hippocampal formation in schizophrenia. *Biological Psychiatry, 45,* 395–402.

Weiner, J.D. (1997). The connections of the primate subthalamic nucleus: Indirect pathways and the open-interconnected scheme of basal ganglia–thalamocortical circuitry. *Brain Research Reviews, 23,* 62–78.

Weiss, G. (1996). Attention deficit hyperactivity disorder. In M. Lewis (Ed.), *Child and adolescent psychiatry: A comprehensive textbook* (pp. 544–563). Baltimore: Williams & Wilkins.

Wichmann, T., & DeLong, M.R. (1997). Physiology of the basal ganglia and pathophysiology of movement disorders of basal ganglia origin. In R.L. Watts & W. Koller (Eds.), *Movement disorders: Neurologic principles and practice* (pp. 87–96). New York: McGraw-Hill.

Wichmann, T., & Delong, M.R. (1999). Oscillations in the basal ganglia. *Nature, 400,* 621–622.

Wilson, K.D. (1998). Issues concerning the cognitive neuroscience of obsessive compulsive disorder. *Psychonomic Bulletin and Review, 5,* 161–172.

Wing, L. (1997). Syndromes of autism and atypical development. In D.J. Cohen & F.R. Volkmar (Eds.), *Handbook of autism and pervasive developmental disorders* (pp. 148–165). New York: Wiley.

Wise, R.A. (1996). Neurobiology of addiction. *Current Opinion in Neurobiology, 6,* 242–251.

Wolf, S.S., Jones, D.W., Knable, M.B., Gorey, J.G., Lee, K.S., Hyde, T.M., Coppola, R., & Weinberger, D.R. (1996). Tourette syndrome: Prediction of phenotypic variation in monozygotic twins by caudate nucleus D2 receptor binding. *Science, 273,* 1225–1227.

Wolpert, D.M., Miall, R.C., & Kawato, M. (1998). Internal models in the cerebellum. *Trends in the Cognitive Sciences, 2,* 338–347.

Yazgan, M.Y., Peterson, B., Wexler, B.E., & Leckman, J.F. (1995). Behavioral laterality in individuals with Gilles de la Tourette syndrome and basal ganglia alterations. *Biological Psychiatry, 38,* 386–390.

Yesavage, J.A., Brink, T.L., Rose, T.L., Lum, O., Huang, V., Adey, M.B., & Leirer, V.O. (1983). Development and validation of a geriatric depression rating scale: A preliminary report. *Journal of Psychiatric Research, 17,* 37–49.

Young, A.B., & Penney, J.B. (1998). Biochemical and functional organization of the basal ganglia. In J. Jankovic & E. Tolosa (Eds.), *Parkinson's disease and movement disorders* (pp. 1–13). Baltimore: Williams & Wilkins.

Zald, D.H., & Kim, S.W. (1996). Anatomy and function of the orbitofrontal cortex II: Function and relevance to obsessive compulsive disorder. *Journal of Neuropsychiatry and Clinical Neurosciences, 8,* 249–261.

Zametkin, A.J. (1995). Attention deficit hyperactivity disorder: Born to be hyperactive? *Journal of the American Medical Association, 273,* 1871–1874.

Zametkin, A.J., & Ernst, M. (1999). Problems in the management of attention-deficit-hyperactivity disorder. *New England Journal of Medicine, 340,* 40–46.

Ziatas, K., Durkin, K., & Pratt, C. (1998). Belief term development in children with autism, Asperger's syndrome, specific language impairment, and normal development: Links to theory of mind development. *Journal of Child Psychology and Psychiatry, 39,* 755–763.

Zipursky, R.B., & Kapur, S. (1998). New insights into schizophrenia from neuroimaging. *Current Opinion in Psychiatry, 11,* 33–37.

Ziv, I., & Melamed, E. (1998). Role of apoptosis in the pathogenesis of Parkinson's disease: A novel therapeutic opportunity? *Movement Disorders, 13,* 865–870.

Zohar, A., Apter, A., King, R., Pauls, D., Leckman, J., & Cohen, D. (1999). Epidemiological studies. In J.F. Leckman & D.J. Cohen (Eds.), *Tourette's syndrome: Tics, obsessions, compulsions* (pp. 177–193). New York: Wiley.

Zung, W. (1965). A self-rating depression scale. *Archives of General Psychiatry, 12,* 63–70.

Author index

Subject index